Re-imagining Rwanda

Conflict, Survival and Disinformation in the Late Twentieth Century

The tragic conflict in Rwanda and the Great Lakes in 1994 to 1996 attracted the horrified attention of the world's media. Journalists, diplomats and aid workers struggled to find a way to make sense of the bloodshed. Johan Pottier's troubling study shows that the post-genocide regime in Rwanda was able to impose a simple yet persuasive account of Central Africa's crises upon international commentators new to the region, and he explains the ideological underpinnings of this official narrative. He also provides a sobering analysis of the way in which this simple, persuasive, but fatally misleading analysis of the situation on the ground led to policy errors that exacerbated the original crisis. Professor Pottier has extensive field experience in the region, from before and after the genocide.

JOHAN POTTIER is Professor of Social Anthropology at the School of Oriental and African Studies, University of London. His previous publications include 'Anthropology of Food: The Social Dynamics of Food Security' (1999) and 'Migrants No More: Settlement and Survival in Mambwe Villages, Zambia' (1988).

A list of books in this series can be found at the end of this volume.

Re-imagining Rwanda

*Conflict, Survival and Disinformation
in the Late Twentieth Century*

Johan Pottier

School of Oriental and African Studies, University of London

PUBLISHED BY THE PRESS SYNDICATE OF THE UNIVERSITY OF CAMBRIDGE
The Pitt Building, Trumpington Street, Cambridge, United Kingdom

CAMBRIDGE UNIVERSITY PRESS
The Edinburgh Building, Cambridge CB2 2RU, UK
40 West 20th Street, New York, NY 10011-4211, USA
477 Williamstown Road, Port Melbourne, VIC 3207, Australia
Ruiz de Alarcón 13, 28014 Madrid, Spain
Dock House, The Waterfront, Cape Town 8001, South Africa

http://www.cambridge.org

First published 2002

Printed in the United Kingdom at the University Press, Cambridge

Typeface Times 10/12 pt.   *System* LaTeX 2_ε [TB]

A catalogue record for this book is available from the British Library

ISBN 0 521 81366 2 hardback
ISBN 0 521 52873 9 paperback
African edition ISBN 0 521 53308 2

Dedicated with affection

to 'auntie' Adelina Goddyn –
who taught me kinship knows no bounds

and in memory of Béatrice Chika –
whose children became my own

Our knowledge base of Rwanda and the Great Lakes is low ... We, therefore, need to be realistic and use the coming years to build a firmer political, economic and social knowledge base which we can use to judge the effectiveness and progress of our partnership.

Department For International Development, UK, September 1999

Contents

List of maps   *page* x
Acknowledgements   xi
List of abbreviations   xiii

    Introduction: information and disinformation in times of conflict   1

1 Build-up to war and genocide: 9
    society and economy in Rwanda and eastern Zaire

2 Mind the gap: 53
    how the international press reported on society,
    politics and history

3 For beginners, by beginners: 109
    knowledge construction under the Rwandese Patriotic Front

4 Labelling refugees: 130
    international aid and the discourse of genocide

5 Masterclass in surreal diplomacy: 151
    understanding the culture of 'political correctness'

6 Land and social development: 179
    challenges, proposals and their imagery

    Conclusion: representation and destiny   202

Appendix: Summary of key dates and events   208
Notes   211
Bibliography   233
Index   248

Maps

1   Rwanda   *page* xv
2   Great Lakes region   xvi
3   Rwanda: refugees and displaced populations, 31 March 1995   xvii

Acknowledgements

The past decade has been a time of grief, hope, reflection, research and information sharing on the subject of Rwanda. Never before have I met so many with whom so much needed to be mulled over and shared as a matter of urgency. While all remain in my thoughts, I thank in particular the many people in Rwanda who facilitated my visits following the war and genocide: the Rwanda-based staff of Save The Children (UK), especially Maureen Rogers and Gay Harper; the members of Team III of the Joint Evaluation of Humanitarian Assistance to Rwanda, expertly led by John Borton (Overseas Development Institute, London); and Bert Poelman, my brother-in-law, who supplied valuable media clips in the early days of the tragedy. I must also acknowledge the excellent service of the United Nation's IRIN Humanitarian Information Unit, which provides daily updates on the Great Lakes region, and that of the Library and Documentation Service of ABOS/AGCD, Belgium's development administration, which issues a weekly press review.

Writing this book has been time-consuming. I have incurred debts to my family, for allowing me the time and space to work in; to the Leverhulme Trust for funding the sabbatical year (1997–98) without which this book could not have been written; and to the colleagues and friends who have given so generously of their precious spare time to comment on draft chapters. For their invaluable insights and support, I give warm thanks to James Fairhead, Lindsey Hilsum, Augustin Nkundabashaka, Nigel Eltringham and the anonymous readers for Cambridge University Press.

Appreciation is extended to the many seminar organisers and participants who over the past few years have invited me to speak at their venues, particularly at the universities of Oxford (Queen Elizabeth House), Leeds (African Studies Unit), Edinburgh (Centre of African Studies), Manchester, London (Institute of Commonwealth Studies, London School of Economics, School of Oriental and African Studies (Student Union, Anthropology Department), East Anglia (School of Development Studies), Sussex (Institute of Development Studies), Free University of Brussels (African Studies Centre), Louvain-La-Neuve, Roskilde (Centre for Development Studies), Copenhagen (Anthropology Department), Helsinki and Wageningen. Sincere thanks also go to the organisers and participants of recent international workshops organised by the Nordic African Institute and by the Universities of Bologna and Naples in collaboration with the Feltrinelli Foundation (Milan). While these stimulating exchanges have hugely enriched my own thinking on Rwanda and the Great Lakes, it remains true that any book examining conflict will reflect the inescapable dilemma that one side's 'impartiality' is another side's 'partiality'. Bound by this inevitable predicament, I nonetheless accept that I and I alone remain responsible for the synthesis and views expressed in this book.

A most special thank you, of the kind that defies words, is due to my 'new children' Rukia and Hadija, both survivors of the 1994 genocide, who joined the family after the death of *Maman Béatrice*. They have added a new dimension to what it means to share, to persevere and to seek understanding. Heartfelt thanks are due also to Agnès, Fifi, Sam and Tim for enduring my nomadic writing habit of always moving through the house in search of sunlight or a quiet corner.

Johan Pottier

Abbreviations

ADFL	Alliance of the Democratic Forces for the Liberation of Congo-Zaire
AEF	African Education Fund
CDR	Coalition pour la Défense de la République / extremist offshoot of MRND(D), Rwanda
CIA	Central Intelligence Agency, USA
CNS	Conférence Nationale Souveraine, Zaire
DFID	Department For International Development, UK (formerly ODA)
DPKO	Department of Peace-Keeping Operations, UN
DRC	Democratic Republic of the Congo, formerly Zaire
FAO	Food and Agriculture Organisation, UN
FAR	Forces Armées Rwandaises / Rwandan Armed Forces
FAZ	Forces Armées Zairoises / Zairean Armed Forces
FIDH	Fédération Internationale des Droits de l'Homme / International Federation of Human Rights
GOR	Government of Rwanda
GTZ	Gesellschaft für Technische Zusammenarbeit (Society for Technical Cooperation), Germany
HRFOR	Human Rights Field Operation in Rwanda, UN
ICRC	International Committee of the Red Cross
IDP	Internally Displaced Person
IFRC	International Federation of the Red Cross
IMF	International Monetary Fund
IRC	International Rescue Committee
IRIN	Integrated Regional Information Network, UN, Department of Humanitarian Affairs
IWACU	Centre de Formation et de Recherche Cooperatives, Rwanda
MDR	Mouvement Démocratique Républicain / Democratic Republican Movement, Rwanda
MINIREISO	Ministry of Rehabilitation and Social Reintegration, Rwanda

MINITERE   Ministry of Lands, Human Resettlement and
                Environmental Protection, Rwanda
MINITRAP   Ministry of Public Works, Rwanda
MPR   Mouvement Populaire pour la Révolution, Zaire
MRND(D)   Mouvement Révolutionnaire National pour le
                Développement (1991–94); also Mouvement Républicain
                National pour la Démocratie et le Développement / National
                Revolutionary Movement for Development, Rwanda
MSF   Médecins Sans Frontières / Doctors Without Borders
NPA   Norwegian People's Aid
ODA   Overseas Development Administration, UK (now DFID)
PL   Parti Libéral / Liberal Party, Rwanda
PRP   Parti de la Révolution Populaire, Zaire
PSD   Parti Sociale Démocrate / Social Democratic Party, Rwanda
RPA   Rwandese Patriotic Army / Armée Patriotique Rwandaise
                (APR)
RPF   Rwandese Patriotic Front / Front Patriotique Rwandais
                (FPR)
SCF(UK)   Save The Children Fund, United Kingdom
UNAMIR   United Nations Assistance Mission to Rwanda
UNDP   United Nations Development Programme
UNHCR   United Nations High Commissioner for Refugees
UNICEF   United Nations Children's Fund
UNREO   United Nations Rwanda Emergency Office
WB   The World Bank
WFP   World Food Programme, United Nations

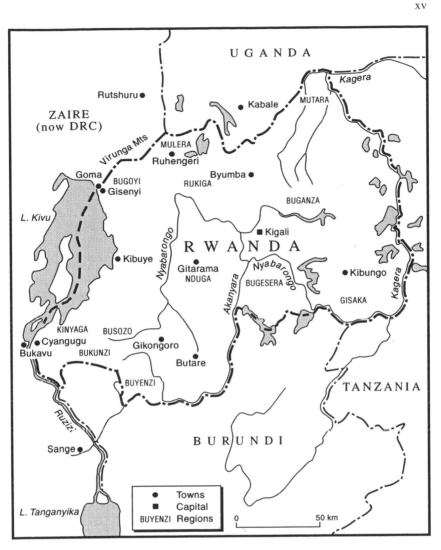

1 Rwanda

2 Great Lakes region

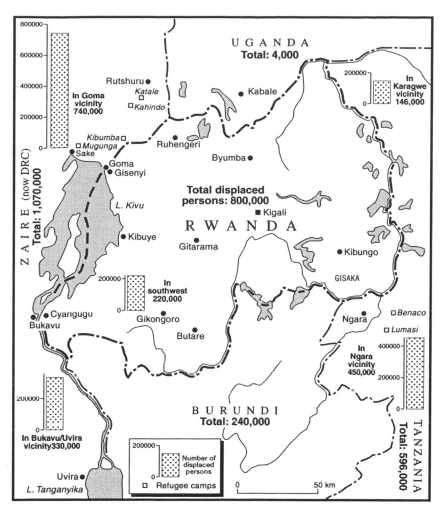

3   Rwanda: refugees and displaced populations, 31 March 1995

Introduction: information and disinformation in times of conflict

Once the chief vehicle for disseminating knowledge about Central Africa, the academic monograph has lost out against journalistic accounts and the 'grey literature' of aid agencies. The monograph was pronounced dead at a mid-1990s conference on *The Fate of Information in the Disaster Zone*.[1] While there are good reasons for accepting this verdict, I also note that it was made before Rwanda got 'involved' in Zaire in late 1996, that is, before journalists and aid workers realised, and admitted, that all had not been what it seemed. Today, the international community understands better that information and disinformation merge in times of conflict, and that confusion, often spread deliberately, is the inevitable outcome.

It is with processes of fusion and confusion that this book is concerned. I wish to demonstrate that there still is a place for the academic monograph in conflict situations, that there still is a need for scholarly analysis and reflexivity. The growing attraction of media- and aid-driven accounts notwithstanding attractive because of their presumed immediate practical value – the writings of journalists and aid workers must not be taken at face value. They must, instead, be seen for what they are: products regularly conditioned by scant background information, tight deadlines, the demand for simplified commentary, and sometimes powerful manipulations. These conditions make it imperative that the quality of instant, 'real time' information be scrutinised. Quality control may mean checking for accuracy, or weighing claims about the present against recorded history, or supplying context. Mostly all three services are needed. This is what the present monograph aims to do with reference to the crisis in Rwanda and eastern Zaire. Monographs are not themselves immune from bias, of course not, yet it surely is time to apply to popular information outlets the standard of rigorous self-questioning to which the social sciences have become accustomed. Of the many truth claims that have emerged regarding Central Africa, we must ask: what claims are made? how do we know? why should we think the way we do?

The challenge is to understand and reflect on how contemporary knowledge is produced. A hard-hitting photograph may be worth a thousand words, as is sometimes said, but one thousand words may not be enough to convey

1

the photograph's full context. Moreover, even where it is clear to all that a photograph has a story to tell, we still need to ask, '*whose story*' does it tell? Niranjan Karnik's critique of disaster photography in the Great Lakes poses this question and concludes that disaster photography forms a specific type of Orientalist discourse in which suffering is universalised to suit the needs of both news and humanitarian agencies (Karnik 1998: 36). The photographer's input mostly goes undetected. Instantly readable, visually and conceptually, disaster images appeal to a vast humanitarian 'industry' and public who believe they tell a full and objective story. That images may obscure more than they reveal is not often considered; there may be a reason for this. In the Rwandan context, by portraying Rwandans as helpless victims in need, the West can cast itself in the role of altruistic saviour; a saviour stripped of ambiguity. What this portrayal obscures, though, is the full text, the context. The disaster photographs do not inform on how a Rwandan refugee crisis went virtually unreported for thirty years, how the 1994 genocide in Rwanda related to the 1972 genocide in Burundi and to fears of a repeat genocide in 1993, how the coffee crash of 1989 created massive despair among poor farmers, how the World Bank/International Monetary Fund (IMF) failed to bail Rwanda out (whereas Mexico and South Korea fared much better when their economies crashed), how the Tutsi-dominated Rwandese Patriotic Front (RPF) invaded Rwanda in 1990, how the 'international community' imposed multi-partyism in the mistaken belief that this meant democracy, how the UN succumbed to indifference when failing to intervene in Kigali in April 1994, how Rwanda's 1994 genocide was callously planned.

Context was equally lacking when Laurent Kabila triumphed in Kinshasa. Holding the moral highground as the champion of 'the Banyamulenge', an ethnic group threatened with extermination, being hailed by Nelson Mandela, having reached Kinshasa with the military help of Rwanda and Uganda, Kabila was regarded by powerful, mostly anglophone diplomats, and by many in the media and aid world, though by no means all, as Central Africa's new saviour. The pictures carried little text: Kabila arrived on the scene ready-made, the reincarnation of many promises (Newbury 1997). Once again, the world was not entitled to context. Not entitled to know, for instance, that Paul Kagame, Rwanda's military leader and vice-president (now president), had masterminded the so-called Banyamulenge rebellion, and that he had yielded to Museveni's insistence on Kabila becoming the rebellion's figurehead. Such information remained outside 'the frame' until 9 July 1997, when, in *The Washington Post*, Kagame revealed his position and role. Kabila's military force, moreover, was presented as strongly united, and the world, the anglophone world especially, seemed happy that this should be so. Awkward questions were not often asked, nor did members of the 'international community' consult the academic literature. Instead, it was Kigali's representation of events and conditions in eastern

Zaire which became authoritative. Few challenged the Kigali narrative and accompanying discourse, there seemed to be no need. And so, two years on, the world learned to its surprise and dismay that Kabila's campaign had failed, that the war needed to be relaunched – this time *against* Kabila. That famous photo opportunity when Mandela had raised Kabila's arm in victory had needed a larger frame, more context. The world had failed to appreciate that Kabila was 'a person as well as an image' (Newbury, 'Guerillas in the Mist', e-mail circular, 25 April 1997). The problem, David Newbury reflected, was

that outsiders often imagine Kabila through some simple formula or 'outside' analogy – through some mechanism . . . that they can relate to and understand. The problem is that these intellectual mechanisms often are more closely tied to the person proposing them than to the events on the ground. (Newbury, 25 April 1997)

The images that appealed, in other words, were *imaginings the world wanted to see* and the 'morally pure' post-genocide regime in Kigali wanted to promote. These imaginings evoked Kabila the Pan-Africanist; Kabila the local freedom fighter; Kabila the 'anti-Mobutu'; Kabila a reincarnated Lumumba; Kabila a Museveni for Zaire. To those unfamiliar with Zairean politics, the imagery was so persuasive it made scrutinising 'Kabila' akin to moral crime. The imagery, though, as Newbury had warned, would turn out to be less than illuminating, saying indeed more about the world of the proposers than about the politics of the Great Lakes. Kabila was not a new Museveni (for unlike Museveni, he had not gained the respect and loyalty of the people in eastern Zaire, his home base); Kabila was not a reincarnated Lumumba (for unlike Lumumba, he never formulated policies for the people of Zaire); he may have been an 'anti-Mobutu', but so were millions of other Zaireans. Among them,

the women who refused to pay illegal taxes at market, and those who refused the inflated and meaningless high-denomination bills, and those who demonstrated in the streets, or who stayed at home on *journées mortes*, and those who sang the caricatures of the *grosses légumes* in Kinshasa, as well as those who overtly addressed political issues. (Newbury, 25 April 1997)[2]

Recontextualisation, bringing these ordinary citizens back into the frame, permitted a new way of viewing the situation. As Newbury notes,

if the ADFL has found power in the streets and taken it up, it is because the people put it there. It was popular struggle, popular resistance, and the use of many hidden transcripts over 32 years that emptied Mobutu's regime of legitimacy, it was the people, who in many small but meaningful actions, divested the regime of any meaningful authority, and ultimately of power. (Newbury, 25 April 1997)

Tragically, popular struggle remained outside the broad picture which media and aid workers conjured up, nor was attention paid to the many Zaireans who actively opposed Kabila. The media had eyes and ears only for those who could be seen to be fighting, 'really' fighting, with sophisticated weapons and, sometimes, a sprinkle of magic. In short, during the Banyamulenge uprising in eastern Zaire, the world was told to accept *a particular version* of events; a version dressed up globally as 'the African way' of seeing and resolving things, a version promoted by the powerful New Pan-African lobby group and unequivocally adopted by its chief Western allies, the Clinton administration and British Government. That this authoritative version amounted to a particular, contestable view of society and history was not considered; that there were struggles within the struggle to oust Mobutu, struggles rooted in the modern history of eastern Zaire, was of no interest either. It was only later that the world asked questions about context, that journalists with authority queried the standard representation of Zaire's 'problem' and 'internal solution'. Suddenly, the familiar representation showed up as flawed. In May 1997, journalist Lindsey Hilsum reflected: 'In Central Africa we have a sense of knowing what is going on: aid agencies and reporters are on the ground and pictures are on the television screen. But it is misleading.'[3] More context, better context, would have made the images and messages less misleading.

In this book I am concerned with the process of recontextualisation. First and foremost, I aim to reflect on how 'Rwanda' and 'eastern Zaire' came to be re-imagined in 1994–96 through a synchronised production of knowledge, i.e. a process, pervasive even though not always consciously pursued, by which 'instant' journalists, diplomats, aid workers and academics accepted, formulated and spread images of Rwanda that chimed well with the RPF-led regime, now in power in Kigali. Wanting to put the record straight once and for all, the regime befriended international opinion makers who were cowed into believing some easy-to-grasp narratives regarding Central Africa's crises and solutions; narratives so seductively simple that no one new to the region thought of asking about their ideological underpinnings. Within the international community, these narratives were embraced, actively constructed, sometimes elaborated on, and spread. Most striking about these narratives was that they had little historical depth. By recontextualising the narratives the international community lived by in 1994–96, I hope to bring some insight into the process of knowledge construction. This insight should matter not just to those whose task it is to reflect on Central Africa's diverse reality, but to everyone committed to building a better Rwanda: re-building Rwanda cannot be done by the uninformed who believe in simple explanations.

A reflexive approach to understanding recent events in Rwanda and the Great Lakes requires a critical look at the origins, power and pervasiveness of the grand narratives that have come to dominate and shape Western perceptions of, and attitudes towards, the region. Part of the challenge here is to be critical of the persistent claims to objective knowledge, to be critical of social categories that group large entities or experiences. Social scientists now routinely question

claims to objective knowledge ('objective' therefore appearing in inverted
commas), they increasingly expose such claims as ahistorical and homogenising. Presumed objective accounts of 'other cultures', it has been clear for a
while, lack timeframes and pay insufficient attention to internal heterogeneity.

But the debate has progressed further. Grounding one's analysis is not just
a question of accessing a plurality of local voices, the critic must also ask
whether anyone, outsiders especially, can have the right to speak for someone
else. Within social anthropology, my discipline, the emerging consensus is
that anthropological (and all outsider) representations are embedded in power
relations between North and South. The implication is that researchers should
relinquish the right to 'speak for' other groups, that is groups whose points of
view the anthropologist has learned to share (Cornwall and Lindisfarne 1994:
43–5). In line with this position, I do not claim to have the right to speak
on behalf of 'the people of Rwanda', an excessively homogenising label anyway,
but I do claim the right to speak *to* members of the 'international community'
since they need to take responsibility for the representations they accept, bring
into the world or help sustain.

To Edward Said we owe the wisdom that untinged, objective writing is an impossibility. Said, however, also reassured international observer-commentators
that they can be better aware of the circumstances of their actuality, and hence
less influenced by it (Said 1993: 136–7). In the context of research in Central
Africa, Said's optimism has been shared by V. Y. Mudimbe, who announced,
already in the early 1980s, that official orthodoxies inherited from the colonial
period were being challenged both by African scholars and by a new generation
of Westerners. This new generation, Mudimbe wrote, included Jean-Pierre
Chrétien, Bogumil Jewsiewicki and Jean-Claude Willame, researchers who
were

more conscious of the objective limitations that their own subjectivity and regional socio-
historic determinations impose[d] on their dealings with African matters. . . . [They knew
an end had to come to] the dialogue with 'big brothers' [which had] been from the
beginning ambiguous, made up of mutual understanding and rejection, collaboration
and suspicion. (Mudimbe 1985: 206)

In collaborating with African scholars, this new generation was expected to
boost the quest for 'new alternatives, regional compatibilities and, above all,
the possibility of a new economy between power and knowledge' (Mudimbe
1985: 209). Mudimbe's optimism, formulated specifically within a debate on
African gnosis and philosophy, spoke of the necessity of new epistemological
arrangements that would herald the cultural renaissance of African nations.

But what does the possibility of a new economy between power and knowledge mean in terms of the positioning of contemporary African scholars *vis-à-vis*
political processes *within* Africa and the world at large? Should we, outsiders,

not ask of these scholars the very same questions that Mudimbe and Said have asked of Western scholars and their representations? Should academic 'outsiders' not ask how the agendas and findings of African scholarly research are conditioned internally? And ask, too: which systems of knowledge are emerging, which failing, and why? Who speaks for whom, and why? The inquiry into cultural hegemony must not be confined to the question of how constructs of 'the Other' result from power relations embedded in the colonial past, for intellectual hegemony exists not only between regions and cultures, but also within them. The renaissance Mudimbe announced is a process just begun. A process, moreover, which can easily be derailed by dominant interest groups from within the formerly colonised regions and states, groups which may well themselves make use of the (old) Western paradigms. (Old paradigm: 'Reality is what I say it is. Because I say so.') If the economically and politically dominant 'West' enjoyed the prerogative that it could construct reality under colonialism, and claim objectivity for its constructions, then why should we not expect to see the ascendancy of post-colonial elites that occupy the same privileged niche because they too claim to be rational in their epistemology?

The danger that certain post-colonial representations gain currency and legitimacy simply because they have replaced those of the erstwhile coloniser, must not be dismissed lightly. Moreover, as recent research on the construction of policy discourse in colonial Zambia, then Northern Rhodesia, has shown, it would be wrong to pretend that colonial constructs were ever free of local inputs. This was particularly so where 'indirect rule' became the norm. In *Cutting Down Trees*, Moore and Vaughan (1994) demonstrate for Zambia's Northern Province that the construction of a policy discourse on rural development, a discourse anchored in the presumed non-sustainability of agricultural and moral systems, had arisen with the active participation of the Bemba political elite. Colonial administrators, agricultural scientists and anthropologists, missionaries and Bemba chiefs had all worked together to produce the discourse that spoke of a spiralling decline, ecologically and socially. The local political elite took an active part in constructing 'the Other', Bemba-ness in this case, because it too, like the European coloniser, aspired to be in control.[4]

Concentrating on Rwanda during the 1994–96 crisis, this book examines the manner in which members of the 'international community' have engaged with the politics and culture of the Great Lakes region. What images have they accepted and spread regarding the nature of Rwandan society? What have they said about Rwandan history? How has the refugee crisis been portrayed, and what has the impact been on the outcome of that crisis? How does the international community understand Rwanda's post-war economy? How were the Kivu 'crisis' and its 'local solution' (October 1996 onwards) presented to the world?

In answering these questions, I shall focus on how key actors in the drama – national and international leaders, foreign diplomats, humanitarians, journalists, aid workers and academics – have accessed information, processed information, spread information. And sometimes disinformation. Thus we learn how imaginings about Rwanda were created and spread through the media (revealing partiality and/or ignorance); created and spread, too, in diplomatic circles (by diplomats who 'needed' to simplify); in the camps for internally displaced people and refugees (by humanitarians with routine approaches to crisis management); through statements by Rwanda's new leaders; through academic avenues (by instant experts with limited knowledge of Rwandan society, history and politics); through development activities organised around rehabilitation and reconstruction (by technocrats whose familiarity with the region is mostly non-existent). In one way or other, all have contributed significant words and actions towards a systematic re-imagining of Rwanda.

Most crucially, and providing the *raison d'être* for the structure of this book, the various imaginings have cross-fertilised one another to produce a remarkable degree of 'politically correct' consistency around the concept of social identity. Where people 'come from' and where they are 'going', so to speak, has been an essential preoccupation of all who have sought to understand, analyse and comment on Rwanda. In this respect, media and diplomatic imaginings of the place and its people reveal considerable affinity with the thinking behind current policies for land reform, with the way humanitarians engaged with the Rwandan refugee crisis, and with the way academics unfamiliar with Rwanda before the genocide have sought to comprehend what went wrong. From a scholarly point of view, the critical issue is how this global, interconnected search for understanding and consistency has dealt with the problem of context. As the chapters in this book reveal, the search has resulted in a conspicuous hesitancy to consider detailed contexts; analysts and commentators have opted for 'easy handles' on some very complex issues.

At the heart of this hesitancy lies a mixture of institutional incapacity or demand (e.g. media reportings need to be crisp; humanitarian work cannot afford to be 'philosophical') and moral sympathy with the people of Rwanda who emerged from the terrible tragedy of 1994. There were perfectly good reasons for this moral sympathy: besides the scale of the tragedy and its suffering, there was the undeniable fact that the crisis had been planned with massive intellectual complicity within Rwanda and an ultra-extreme national media in which 'Hutu Power' academics played a key role (see Chrétien 1995). The five years leading up to the genocide had seen a considerable radicalisation in local academic and political reflections on Rwanda; a pro-Hutu radicalisation which, after the genocide, would be construed as merely the continuation of three decades of post-independence research. Against this background of radicalisation, international caution in accepting academic reflection on 'the problem' of Rwanda was not only to be expected, it was also perfectly correct. The international response, broadly speaking, was to accept a clean slate position on Rwanda and to give legitimate voice to the RPF, which had halted the genocide. Accepting the proverbial clean slate, Rwanda's new leaders and many in the international community then returned to a model of Rwandan society and history popularised in the 1950s.

The present book maintains that post-independence research on Rwanda must not now be labelled 'all bad' and swept under the carpet, that there is in fact much of continued value if analysts and commentators wish to move towards a better informed understanding of the transformations on which Rwanda has embarked. There is a need, in other words, to 'recontextualise' the rather simplifying imaginings which international opinion has not only absorbed but also actively helped to generate, reinforce and spread.

1   Build-up to war and genocide: society and economy in Rwanda and eastern Zaire

The eruption of conflict and civil war in the 1990s, in both Rwanda and eastern Zaire, had its origin in modern struggles for power and wealth. The world, however, easily overlooked this modern origin, since the confrontations it witnessed appeared to have taken on strongly ethnicised, seemingly 'tribal' overtones and justification. The Rwandan 1994 genocide in particular, more than the fighting in eastern Zaire (1996 onwards), was for too long and at too great a cost portrayed by the media as rooted in tribalism. Rwanda's bloodbath was not tribal. Rather it was a distinctly modern tragedy, a degenerated class conflict minutely prepared and callously executed. Most of the world failed to see it that way, and continued to think of the conflict – this after all was Africa – in terms of 'centuries-old tribal warfare'.

The power of shamelessly twisted ethnic argument for the sake of class privilege was demonstrated most shockingly in the blatant imaginings about history that galvanised Rwanda's 'Hutu Power' extremists. These extremists killed Rwanda's Tutsi and sent their bodies 'back to Ethiopia' via the Nyabarongo and Akagera rivers. The imagined origin of 'the Tutsi', along with their (poorly understood) migrations and conquest of Rwanda, were evoked by power-crazed Hutu politicians to instil 'ethnic hatred' in the very people they themselves oppressed: the victims of class oppression were spurred on to kill a minority group which the oppressors had labelled 'the real enemy'. Some 800,000 Tutsi and moderate Hutu who declared their sympathy with the Rwandese Patriotic Front (RPF) were slaughtered in a matter of three months. Today, those who govern post-genocide Rwanda also imagine the past in order to make sense of the present, but they do so in different, more subtle ways. Post-genocide leaders regard Rwanda's pre-colonial past as something of a golden era, a state of social harmony later corrupted by Europeans. Vital to the justification of minority rule, their message is delivered in a well-rehearsed manner and style, marked sometimes by omission (of well-established counter-evidence) and sometimes by disregard for context. Complexity and context are continuously screened out of contemporary representations of 'the Old Rwanda', as could be seen, for instance, in official testimonies just prior to Zaire's civil war (detailed in Chapter 5). Against available empirical evidence, the Rwandan government's representation of the historically evolved border separating the two countries evoked a late nineteenth-century situation in which Rwanda and eastern Zaire had been linked in political harmony.

Distortion, or the screening out of complexity and context, are techniques that work best in situations where confusion – about people's past, their identities, their rights – has been institutionalised and built into the fabric of everyday life. In situations of acute poverty, and both Rwanda and Zaire hit extreme levels of poverty in the late 1980s, institutionalised confusion becomes a weapon that power-hungry politicians wield to significant personal advantage and with deadly accuracy. In the early 1990s Zaire's Kivu province exemplified this power of confusion. On the brink of so-called 'ethnic' war, Kivu had an extraordinarily complex array of contradictory viewpoints on people and their entitlements. Not only did two quite different systems of land ownership and land access co-exist, but they co-existed in the midst of a bewildering range of 'conflicting laws and legal interpretations concerning land rights' (Fairhead 1997: 58). Claims to land depended on whether the claimant was considered 'autochthonous' or 'foreign', the latter being a rapidly expanding category. By the early 1990s, a sizeable proportion of Kivu's Kinyarwanda-speaking population, or Banyarwanda, had questionable identity and rights. The growth of this institutionalised confusion over land rights, combined with the 1981 withdrawal of citizenship for people of Rwandan origin, made it easy for so-called autochthones to recoup, often by violent means, the ancestral lands they had previously lost or claimed they had lost.

In the late 1980s and early 1990s, Rwanda, too, was hit by institutionalised confusion. Its land shortages and disputes derived more from straightforward population pressure than from a complex political economy comparable to that of Kivu, yet here as well the laws regarding land were remarkably open to interpretation. As the country descended into economic chaos, the list of social categories barred from access to land was known to be growing rapidly. Like in Kivu, this generalised confusion played into the hands of the wealthy, who, when the crisis deepened, expertly reframed the nature of the crisis – from class struggle to ethnic struggle – in order to buy the loyalty of the oppressed. In combination, acute poverty, externally induced economic malaise and the ruthlessness of embattled politicians gave rise to a restless, deadly social layer of desperately poor, easy-to-manipulate young thugs.

Reframing the nature of economic hardship and class struggle means 'remembering' the past: who's who? where do my neighbours come from? who are they, really? what rights do they have, really? and are they not cultivating land my ancestors once owned? These questions are not unique to the conflict in Central Africa, but they are at the core of that continuous reinterpretation of reality which sustains the potential for conflict. As a result, this chapter is not just an overview of the local scene and its complexities, but also an overview of how key aspects of the past – people's migrations, their identities, their entitlements – have recently come to assume new meanings. It is not the complexities *per se* that demand our attention, but the fact that they are easily reinterpreted for political gain.

The 'international community', we also need to recognise, engages actively with these 'local' discourses of identity, legitimacy and entitlement. Most crucially, international actors share with local stakeholders a propensity for simplistic visions, for decontextualised, standardised accounts of what is going on. The task in this chapter, then, is to provide and explore empirical evidence through which de-contextualised representations can be detected and queried. We begin with a look at what scholarly research over the past forty years, but especially in the 1960s and 1970s, has taught us about migration, arrangements for settlement, and the making of social identities in Rwanda and eastern Zaire.

Migration and social identity in Rwanda and eastern Congo-Zaire

Throughout the first half of the twentieth century, Rwanda's population was sparse and geographically mobile. Persistent drought and other calamity, including political upheaval, often resulted in people moving on a more or less permanent basis. Thus the famine called *Rwakayihura* (1928–29), which left 30,000 dead, caused some 100,000 people – or nearly 7 percent of Rwanda's then total population – to move to Uganda and the Belgian Congo (Cornet 1996: 10, 39). Another well-remembered famine, *Ruzagajura* (1943), also caused many Rwandans to move into Congo, where they settled in Bwisha, an area the kingdom of Rwanda had annexed around 1800 before losing it to Congo when Europe imposed its artificial borders (Fairhead 1989b). Many poor agriculturalists coped with *Ruzagajura* by moving away and joining better-off relatives elsewhere (Reisdorff 1952).

Migration was a common response also in the event of political strife. The political migrations significant to the present study include the exodus of Tutsi cattle keepers from western Rwanda into South Kivu when the Rwandan king Kigeri Rwabugiri expanded his administration in the nineteenth century, and the forced migration of some 150,000 Rwandan Tutsi who fled their country as independence approached (1959–61). The first migration, discussed in detail later, included the forebears of the group that in 1995–96 would be introduced to the world as 'the Banyamulenge'. Equally significant, in view of later developments, was the assisted migration of Rwandans to eastern Congo under Belgian rule, especially between 1937 and 1955, and the more recent internal distress migrations by communities and individuals facing acute land shortages. These latter migrations include both the relocation of numerous Hutu from Rwanda's densely populated north-west to Bugesera in the east, where their arrival and hunger for land led to the massacre of Tutsi in 1992, and the migration in the early 1980s of Kivu-based Banyarwanda from Masisi to Walikale, where a good decade later many would be murdered by Nyanga militias in (once again) clashes over land.

Where land is scarce, claims are frequently contested on the basis of perceived social status. And perceptions of status change when circumstances change. The upshot is that certain communities or individuals may suddenly *be remembered* to have immigrant status, and thus be undeserving of land rights and citizenship. It is a fine line which divides history's 'true reality' from the way this reality is remembered; fact and fantasy easily become one.

Given the central importance of how the past is remembered, it is useful at the start of this study to take a look at some documented evidence regarding the chief migrations, their implications for identity formation, and their significance for the making and unmaking of political alliances.

Early migrations into Rwanda and the 1959 exodus of Rwandan Tutsi

One popular thesis about Rwanda's pre-colonial past holds that its three ethnic groups – Twa (0.5 per cent), Hutu (87 per cent) and Tutsi (12.5 per cent) – arrived in Rwanda during different historical periods (Sirven 1975: 56–7). It seems certain that Twa arrived first, followed by Hutu, who cut large tracts of forest and confined Twa to whatever forest remained. Then came the Tutsi pastoralists. Related to the Hima people, one-time rulers of the Ugandan kingdoms of Bunyoro and Buha, the Tutsi arrived in successive waves, possibly from about the fifteenth century. In simplified pro-Tutsi terms, received wisdom claims that Hutu agriculturalists admired the Tutsi cattle so much that they readily accepted to be part of the well-organised Tutsi polity. The southwardly migrating Tutsi adopted the Hutu language and a good deal of Hutu culture before installing their own hegemony through the *nyiginya* dynasty, to which King Rwabugiri belonged. An extension of this narrative, popularised since Rwanda's 1994 genocide, stresses that the term ethnicity is inappropriate to Rwanda, that the country's inhabitants are all people of Rwanda (this is reviewed in Chapter 3). The concept of ethnic difference, the same narrative claims, was introduced after the European colonists invented the term.

While academics must always scrutinise received knowledge about the past, a point I shall return to in the conclusion of this book, it is equally imperative that they acknowledge that a good deal of empirical research on Rwanda's past has taken place, not just during the colonial period but also in the decades following independence in 1962. What then have we learned about this past? For the period up to 1860, it is correct to say that historians know next to nothing about how the terms 'Twa', 'Hutu' and 'Tutsi' were used in social discourse; whether these terms denoted social or physical classifications, for instance, is simply unclear. From about 1860, however, when Rwabugiri expanded the sphere of domination and influence of the Tutsi royal court, the situation becomes clearer. As research has revealed, Rwabugiri began, or consolidated, a process of ethnic polarisation.[1] In the areas he brought under his control, Rwabugiri introduced a number of institutions, most notably *ubuhake* cattle clientship and a labour prestation called *uburetwa*, institutions which came to signify the loss of local political autonomy (Newbury 1988: 82). *Uburetwa*, the hated *corvée* labour service through which populations regained access to the lands they had lost to Rwabugiri, was the central institution; it was restricted to Hutu. Tutsi commoners, while also heavily exploited by the ruling central court and its aristocracy (Newbury 1978: 21, 1988: 13; Vidal 1969: 399; Chrétien 1985: 150), enjoyed freedom from *uburetwa* (Czekanowski 1917: 270–1; Jefremovas 1991a: 68; Newbury 1988: 140; Reyntjens 1985: 133–4; Rwabukumba and Mundagizi 1974: 22). The labour due under *uburetwa* was originally set at one day out of five, but it was raised by the chiefs to two or even three days out of six once the Belgian administration was in place (Lemarchand 1970: 122). In contrast, the labour service for Tutsi consisted merely of seasonal maintenance work on the reed enclosures surrounding chiefly residences (Newbury 1988: 140). Also exempt from *uburetwa* were Hutu selected to enter into cattle *ubuhake*, but all poor Hutu were bound by it. The number of Hutu allowed into the 'cattle contract', however, was never more than a small percentage of the population, whether in south central Rwanda, where the central court was established, or in Kinyaga, south-western Rwanda, which Rwabugiri came to rule (Newbury 1981: 144, referring to Saucier 1974: 73–88). Even though many Hutu in Kinyaga owned cattle, relatively few had acquired their cattle through *ubuhake* (Newbury 1981: 139).

Uburetwa undermined the livelihood security of Hutu commoners and made survival more difficult. By the late nineteenth century, as Claudine Vidal argues for parts of south-central Rwanda, also known as Nduga, as much as half the Hutu peasantry was forced to sell its labour regularly. Among the poorest, both men and women would sell their labour, even though the more common pattern was for a man to sell his labour and for a woman to work her husband's land (Vidal 1974: 58–64). Vidal's informants may have exaggerated the size of this much-oppressed class of peasants, as Iliffe contends on the basis of Czekanowski's ethnographic research in 1907–8 (Iliffe 1987: 61–2), yet Iliffe accepts that the Polish ethnographer Czekanowski had been 'quick to see that the Tutsi ruled Rwanda as a conquered territory in which *ubuletwa* was the core of subjection' (Iliffe 1987: 62).[2] It was through *uburetwa* that social relations took on a strong ethnic character before the European colonists arrived.

For the south-western region of Kinyaga, where she researched, Catharine Newbury explains that ethnicity was not a principal organising factor before 1860, and that social mobility was common. Before Rwabugiri's administration 'made the labels of "Hutu" and "Tuutsi" meaningful and necessary in Kinyaga, social identification belonged principally to the unit that performed corporate political functions – in this case, the lineage or neighborhood residential group' (Newbury 1988: 11). At this time, a fluid situation marked by social mobility prevailed. Newbury summarises:

Social relations between land patrons and their clients were characterized by strong affective ties; outsiders who received land on the *ubukonde* domain enjoyed the position of a 'relative of inferior rank.' Even this subordinate status could disappear over time, as land clients often forged close links to the donor lineage through neighborhood friendships, or marriage alliance. The descendants of those who married into the lineage would sometimes come to be recognized members of the donor kin group. (Newbury 1988: 79)

The *ubukonde* domain, denoting a plot cut from forest and collectively owned, is a concept policy makers in Rwanda have recently re-examined and re-presented. The theme will be taken up in Chapter 6.

With the arrival of Rwabugiri and his administrators, Newbury notes that

classification into the category of Hutu or Tuutsi tended to become rigidified. *Lineages that were wealthy in cattle and had links to powerful chiefs were regarded as Tuutsi; lineages lacking these characteristics were relegated to non-Tuutsi status.* During the period of Tuutsi rule, later overlaid by European rule, the advantages of being Tuutsi and the disadvantages of being Hutu increased enormously. (Newbury 1988: 11; emphasis added)

This passage is fundamental: *wealth, not race*, was the basis of the ethnic distinction between Hutu and Tutsi. Importantly, however, the number of cattle-owning lineages at that time was not very large (see Chapter 3).

Despite the harsh conditions Rwabugiri imposed, it seems right to suggest that some kind of harmonious co-existence had evolved by the turn of the century, since the districts subjected to central rule were headed by two officials – one Hutu, one Tutsi – who worked independently of one another. The Hutu land chief acted as arbitrator in land disputes and organised agricultural tribute (*ikoro*) and dues in labour (*uburetwa*), while the Tutsi cattle chief was responsible for collecting taxes on cattle (Kagame 1972; Lemarchand 1968). To these two chiefs a third one, the army chief, must be added; he, too, was appointed by the king (*mwami*). In certain ways, the land chief and cattle chief engaged in continuous reciprocal surveillance, a pastime from which the *mwami* and the Hutu masses derived some benefit. Tutsi cattle chiefs needed to listen to the complaints put forward by their Hutu colleagues in order to safeguard or extend their own powers (Reyntjens 1985: 113–15). When the Belgian administration abolished this tripartite structure in 1926, wrongly assuming this would better the lot of the Hutu masses, the latter ceased to be politically represented. It was one of many colonial interventions that sharply accentuated, indeed racialised, the Hutu–Tutsi ethnic division. But it was Rwabugiri, and not the Europeans, who crafted ethnic labels on the basis of cattle ownership; a point Alexis Kagame, the central court's renowned historian, once made himself when discussing the tripartite surveillance system. In this system, Kagame wrote, the Hutu land chief (*umutware ubutaka*) had authority over subjects who did not possess any cattle (Kagame 1972: 184–5).

The Belgian colonists also amplified, one might say created, Rwanda's regional north–south divide, another strong identity marker, when they aided the central court in its campaign to subjugate those areas still outside its influence, especially the north-west and the Hutu kingdoms of Bukunzi and Busozo (see Map 1). These regions did not come under rule by the central region until the 1920s, when Belgium intervened militarily to impose 'double colonialism' (Reyntjens 1985: 176–7).[3] Belgium supported the Tutsi royal court right up to the eve of independence. Although the colonial power destroyed the mythico-religious underpinnings of divine kingship over a period of several decades, a quasi-secularisation process ending with Rwanda's 'consecration to Christ the King' in 1947, Belgium continued to politically support the Rwandan Tutsi aristocracy.[4] Only in the late 1950s did the Belgian administration bow to international pressure by the UN and switch sides, abruptly, to support the Hutu social revolution.

When violence erupted in 1959, many Rwandan Tutsi fled to Uganda, where they were welcomed because of their historical connection with the Bahima royal family. These long-standing ties had been reinforced in the nineteenth century when 'Rwanda extended its nominal hegemony to Bufumbira', which lies in present-day Kigezi district (Otunnu 1999a: 6). The relationship meant that the Tutsi and Bahima royal families were always ready to help each other when trouble struck (Byaruga 1989: 150). The arrival of Rwandan refugees, mostly Tutsi, which continued for a number of years, would inevitably impact on Bufumbira, where conditions resembled those left behind in Rwanda. Foster Byaruga (1989) details the scene:

there are two ethnic groups: the Bahima and the Bairu. The Bahima were the traditional rulers while the Bairu were the serfs, like the Bahutu in Rwanda. Traditionally, though now disappearing, there have been conflicts between the ruling Bahima and the ruled Bairu. So whereas the Bahima were willing to let the Batutsi come in, the Bairu saw them as invaders who had to be fought and thrown out. The Batutsi were coming in to join hands with the Bahima to take away the little land belonging to Bairu. (Byaruga 1989: 150)

Since the refugees arrived at a time when the power struggles between Bahima and Bairu had intensified, serious political impact seemed unavoidable (Otunnu 1999a: 13). To add to the complexity and potential for future conflict over resources, some 200,000 economic refugees, mostly Hutu, had arrived in south Uganda during the colonial period after fleeing Belgium's regime of state-conscripted labour and fierce taxation (Otunnu 1999a: 5). As in eastern Congo-Zaire, colonialism created a complex 'ethnic' map.

The free and easy movement of people across the Rwanda–Uganda border continued until the early 1960s, when exiled Tutsi launched incursions into Rwanda hoping to retake the country (Otunnu 1999a: 7). On realising that the incursions heightened political tensions in Rwanda, which in turn increased the likelihood of new retaliation against Tutsi and thus further exodus, the Ugandan authorities decided to patrol the Rwanda–Uganda border more effectively.

Migrations from Rwanda into South Kivu

Migrations from Rwanda into South Kivu also continued in an open-ended fashion until 1959–61. And here too, as with Uganda, border crossings had a long history.

One early migration, particularly well remembered and meaningful today, occurred in the second half of the nineteenth century, possibly earlier, when a great number of people from Rwanda, nearly all Tutsi, arrived in eastern Congo. The bulk of these immigrants, as their descendants recalled in the early 1970s, had fled Rwanda because of King Rwabugiri's administrative/military campaign and the heavy taxation system (Depelchin 1974: 68; also Newbury 1988: 48–9). Following their arrival in Congo, the king of the Bafulero, also known as Fulero or Furiiru, gave the Tutsi immigrants grazing land in exchange for an animal tribute (Depelchin 1974: 70). They settled between Mulenge and the upper Sange river (1974: 65–6) and stopped paying tribute to Rwanda's central court (see Map 2). Situated at an altitude of some 1,800 meters, Mulenge became the immigrants' quasi-capital, while the migrants began to be referred to as 'Banya-Mulenge' (1974: 70). The integration, though, was not unproblematic. From about 1924, when the extortionist demands of the then *mwami* Mokogabwe decimated their herds, many Banyamulenge fanned out to Mulenge's south and west. Some families moved 'as far as Itombwe where they found vast stretches of flat and excellent grazing land, and also the long-sought after isolation from other ethnic groups as well as from the colonizers' law. Paradoxically, however, the movement away from the Furiiru capital [Lemera] increased the Tutsi's reliance on the Furiiru for food' (Depelchin 1974: 71–2). This reliance produced a situation in which Bafulero cultivators would regularly take surplus food to 'Banya-Mulenge' in the hope of receiving cattle, a vital ingredient in Fulero bridewealth (1974: 75).

After Mokogabwe's death in 1930, many Tutsi returned to Mulenge to enjoy renewed wealth because of their highly mobile, instantly transformable cattle. But they faced an obstacle that with the years would grow in significance: the land was not theirs (1974: 75). Banyamulenge never secured their own modern administration (*collectivité*), which perpetuated their political vulnerability. In South Kivu, where the administrative map coincides roughly with an ethnic map drawn up under colonialism, Banyamulenge were the only group not to secure their own administration (Reyntjens and Marysse 1996: 15).

This state of affairs, in which substantial wealth and political insecurity existed side by side, turned disastrous during the 1964–65 rebellion in eastern Congo, when Banyamulenge once again lost a great deal of their herds (Depelchin 1974: 80). The rebellion had been launched, alongside other rebellions in Kwilu, Kisangani, Maniema and northern Katanga, because of people's frustration over the country's deteriorating political and economic situation. The fruits of independence were not being shared out. Also known as the 'Muleliste' rebellion, after Pierre Mulele who directed the insurrection in Kwilu province, the uprising brought latent ethnic antagonisms to the fore. Drawn mainly from Bafulero, Bavira and Babembe groups, the rebels in eastern Congo indiscriminately killed wealthy people, both within their own groups and among those whose ancestors had come from Rwanda and Burundi. Wealth meant cattle, stores and trucks (1974: 56). Facing an increasing problem over access to land, Bafulero, as the region's first inhabitants, or 'autochthones', now strongly resented the presence of immigrants from Rwanda and Burundi, and became vocal about what they perceived to be their indigenous rights.

So drastic was the decimation of Tutsi herds that it forced some Tutsi out of cattle keeping and into the market for casual agricultural labour. The transition caused severe distress, since Tutsi regarded tilling the soil to be well beneath their dignity (1974: 81–2). As casual labourers to wealthy Bafulero, poor Banyamulenge were still a statistical rarity by the early 1970s, even though other Tutsi from Mulenge were now also experiencing reduced prosperity. Their economic decline was caused once again by circumstances they did not control. Depelchin explains that 'Furiiru were no longer eager to carry food to the Tutsi. They had realized that the same quantity of food sold on the market could buy [not just one] but two or more cows. The Furiiru felt they were being cheated' (Depelchin 1974: 76–7). But Banyamulenge, too, felt cheated. After losing so many cattle during the rebellion, they simply could not afford to sell at low prices. As a result, their 'bitterness and resentment against those who initiated the 1964 rebellion', blamed mostly on Bafulero, continued (Depelchin 1974: 82).

This suffering made Banyamulenge side with President Mobutu's national army, which, in 1966, crushed the rebellion. Mobutu's army also had the backing of mercenaries and other local groups opposed to Bafulero and

Babembe, notably Bashi from Kabare. Still, it was the contribution of the Banyamulenge which would live on in people's memory. At the time of the 1996 'Banyamulenge' uprising, Jean-Claude Willame wrote that 'in South Kivu, people readily recall that during the 1960s the Banyamulenge helped the national army with its bloody repression of the local insurrections. So, too, in Maniema [capital: Kindu], where entire villages still accuse one another of having taken part in repressive raids.'[5] The passage is of interest as it reminds us that past events are often recalled in different, sometimes opposed ways. Where autochthones remember the ferocity of Banyamulenge during the repression, Banyamulenge recall the persistent insecurity which resulted from the rebellion itself. As this rebellion had threatened the economic and cultural survival of the Banyamulenge community, a group politically unrecognised, its members had had little choice but to side with those who tried to crush it.

The end of the rebellion sent leaders into exile, but only temporarily. When they returned to relaunch the maquis, a lasting rift occurred between Gaston Soumialot, who had led the rebellion in eastern Congo, and Laurent Désiré Kabila, who had served as a second-rank commander. Their differences came into the open in 1967 when Kabila re-entered Fizi to set up his own base at Kibamba, 'where he was welcomed by the population of the *collectivité* of Lulenge' (Cosma 1997: 15). From here, Kabila pursued his utopic socialist dream and on 24 December 1967 launched the Parti de la Révolution Populaire (PRP). Kabila's followers, however, were mainly Babembe from the administrative *secteurs* of Lulenge, Ngandja and Itombwe (Cosma 1997: 43).[6] A mere footnote at the time, but phenomenally important three decades later and not understood by the international community, these Babembe resented their Banyamulenge neighbours. By November 1996, the world had forgotten how Banyamulenge had suffered in the rebellion before taking Mobutu's side. A lasting alliance between Banyamulenge and Kabila? – not very likely.

Ethnic prejudice by Babembe against their Tutsi neighbours, now increasingly calling themselves Banyamulenge, was rampant by the late 1980s. Wilungula Cosma, who originates from eastern Zaire, observed after his field research:

Babembe consider Tutsi to be good-for-nothings, incapables, lacking in physical strength, uncircumcised, an inferior people who drink milk all day and bemoan not their dead but their cattle. For their part, Tutsi regard Babembe as trouble makers, barbaric, haughty, good only for heavy [agricultural] labour in exchange for a calf close to death. (Cosma 1997: 24, referring to Kimona Kicha 1982)

While some Banyamulenge and Banyarwanda elites may have benefited from helping Mobutu to crush the rebellion, the major weakness of Banyamulenge, their not having their own land and administration, their own *collectivité*, continued. This vulnerability was revealed starkly in July 1987 when 'Rwandan' residents in South Kivu boycotted the elections, angry that their candidates had been left off the ballot papers. The boycott, moreover, reminded the residents of South Kivu how the results of a previous election had been annulled after a 'Rwandan' candidate was elected. The power and influence of 'the Rwandans' was increasingly feared by the autochthonous population, whose politicians became adept at exploiting this sentiment.

Fear of Banyarwanda, some sources suggest, was not unfounded. Although the majority of Banyamulenge had suffered during the rebellion, their assistance to Mobutu had brought significant economic advantages to some. Besides being empowered to levy taxes in local markets, some Banyamulenge authorities allegedly gained a superior ability to access land.

According to B. Muchukiwa [n.d.], the economic power of Banyamulenge increased notably: the old 'volontaires' recruited by the Congolese army to track down [Muleliste] rebels 'now have a real stronghold over the [autochthonous] populations; they begin to acquire tracts of land and collect tributes and taxes in a number of markets in Itombwe'. (Willame 1997: 83)

This portrayal may well offer another glimpse of how history is selectively reworked and re-presented. While certain Banyamulenge benefited from their opposition to the Muleliste rebellion, as Muchukiwa asserts, the majority had remained poor and economically vulnerable, as Depelchin's research (1974) has shown so very clearly (also Vlassenroot 2000). The vulnerability of the Banyamulenge majority would come into focus again when over a million Rwandan Hutu refugees fled to Kivu in 1994.

Migrations from Rwanda into North Kivu

Before the planned migrations got under way in 1937, some Rwandans, Hutu and Tutsi, had already migrated into North Kivu, possibly from about the seventeenth century. Following his research in Bwisha, North Kivu, James Fairhead gave this account of the early migrations:

Bwisha was relatively independent of Rwandan rule until the mid-nineteenth century. During the seventeenth and eighteenth century there was a gradual influx of a few Batutsi pastoralists into highland Bwisha, who came searching for good pasture which was available in the harvested fields and recently abandoned fallows of Bwisha. Like other outsiders, the Batutsi initially recognized the legitimacy of the Bahutu Chiefs, who maintained their political independence from the pastoralists. (Fairhead 1989b: 5)

With time, and under conditions of increasing population density, Banyarwanda in Bwisha would become part of a complex ethnic mosaic, which also comprised Banande, some Batwa (Bwisha's presumed first inhabitants), Bakiga and Bafumbira from Kigezi in Uganda (Pottier and Fairhead 1991: 441).

Banyarwanda arrived in high numbers during colonialism, when Belgium ran its programme for planned in-migration. Running parallel to the steady flow of spontaneous migrants who fled drought and famine, assisted migrants were picked by the colonial administration to work the plantations or to decongest Rwanda of excess cattle (Fairhead 1990; Newbury 1988). The planned insertion of Banyarwanda into North Kivu had two peak waves – from 1937 to 1945 (25,000 arrivals), and from 1949 to 1955 (60,000 arrivals).[7] A great many immigrants in the 1930s settled in Rutshuru, but the bulk, arriving later, moved to sparsely populated Masisi, Bwito and Lubero.

The assisted migrations caused heavy pressure on land, grazing land especially, so much so that local Hunde chiefs regularly complained that there was 'too great a proportion of Batutsi among the immigrants' (Reyntjens and Marysse 1996: 14). Also of long-term significance, Belgium pursued its own brand of apartheid by having separate settlements for Banyarwanda and 'autochthones', with Hutu chiefs being appointed for the areas where assisted migrants had settled. The supreme appointment was that of Hutu chief Ndeze II who, except for some five years around independence, ruled Bwisha from 1920 until 1980 (Fairhead 1990: 84–6). This strategy of appointing Hutu chiefs was aimed at creating a contrast with Ruanda-Urundi, where Tutsi administrators were in control (Tshibanda Mbwabwe wa Tshibanda 1976: 224; Willame 1997: 42), but resulted in the marginalisation of educated Hunde, Nyanga, Nande and other autochthones. By raising 'ethnic' consciousness, the strategy backfired after independence.

Identity, land and the politics of entitlement

Despite regular out-migrations before and during European colonialism, Rwanda's history of land occupation became a catalogue of dwindling entitlements due to population pressure. Throughout the twentieth century, family farms in Rwanda decreased, a process accompanied by deepening poverty. By the middle of the twentieth century, 'the typical [Rwandan] peasant family lived on a hill which supported between 110 and 120 inhabitants per km^2; in 1970, that same family [had] to make a living on a hill which support[ed] between 280 and 290 people per km^2' (Prioul 1976: 74). The impact on food production was profound: compared with the average family of a generation ago, households now harvested half the customary amounts of sorghum, beans and bananas (Meschi 1974: 49). Official efforts to intensify agriculture notwithstanding, the downward trend continued and the statistics turned alarming. From two million inhabitants in 1940, the population in 1991 had reached 7.15 million (Waller 1993: 47). 'If it increases at 3.1 per cent each year,' David Waller concluded, 'the population of Rwanda will have reached 10 million by 2002 AD' (1993: 47). The national average of people per square kilometer of arable land had already shot up to 422, with one northern commune reaching 820 (1993: 18). This occurred in the early 1990s, and there was virtually no more arable land to be claimed. On top of this, elites close to President Habyarimana were buying up land sold because of poverty, especially in the north-west from where they originated. Rooted in the growing disparity between rich and poor, the boom of this illegal land market was accompanied by a discourse of social exclusion (detailed in Chapter 6).

In earlier decades, the government of Rwanda (GOR) had 'sought development' through reliance on donor assistance, which often meant pursuing a project-based strategy aimed to raise off-farm incomes (Godding 1987; Nkundabashaka and Voss 1987). Such projects, however, were rarely friendly to the environment, hardly ever self-financing and did not really boost incomes (Pottier 1993). Resource-poor farmers reacted in three ways: by allocating the maximum possible amount of land to the cultivation of cash crops (mainly bananas and coffee); by cultivating marshlands (*marais*), which were state-owned;[8] and by maximising income through seasonal wage labour. As households often needed to pursue all three strategies simultaneously, calamity struck when the international coffee price plunged by over 50 per cent in 1989. This lethal blow to Rwanda's economy came when the International Coffee Agreement reached a deadlock because of 'political pressures from Washington on behalf of the large US coffee traders' (Chossudovsky 1997: 111). With 60 per cent of Rwanda's smallholders growing coffee, the collapse demonstrated that Rwanda was now firmly in the grip of forces it did not control (Waller 1993: 60). The collapse sentenced many poor to unprecedented levels of despair, making them vulnerable to manipulation by politicians in search of extreme solutions to their country's (and their own) growing insecurity.

The year 1989 was calamitous also in other ways. Throughout the 1980s the government of Rwanda (GOR) had rescued poor smallholders by building upon the National Food Strategies concept which the European Community had introduced (CEC 1982). Accepting that food security depended more on distribution and exchange than actual availability, the Rwandan government had agreed to set up the Office pour la Promotion, la Vente et l'Importation des Produits Agricoles (OPROVIA), which would protect farmgate prices for two staple crops: beans and sorghum. OPROVIA bought post-harvest surpluses at prices well above those in the deflating 'free market' and sold stocks below 'free market' prices when smallholders could not afford to pay more. OPROVIA's commitment to price stabilisation was courageous, but, lacking financial muscle, the policy could not be sustained without strong government backing.

Following the very poor harvests of 1988, a disaster coinciding with the influx of refugees from Burundi and an official ban on food imports, the Rwandan government failed to underwrite OPROVIA's debts. In April 1989, the Ministry of Agriculture, Livestock and Forestry admitted that government had let OPROVIA down: 'The Rwandan Government still needs to reimburse OPROVIA the promised 28.000.000 RwF it lost in 1988 after selling at artificially low prices the sorghum it had bought too dearly in 1986' (République Rwandaise 1989: 4).[9] At about the same time, possibly earlier, government also dropped its support to the Cooperative Movement, which had become a hotbed for social contestation and change (Pottier 1989b). Smallholders loathed the lack of public support, particularly in south Rwanda where suspicion towards the ruling north grew day by day.

The question 'Who rules Rwanda?' became pertinent when Habyarimana, under pressure from the European Economic Community (EEC), agreed upon a Structural Adjustment Programme with the World Bank/IMF in the wake of the crash in coffee incomes (Newbury 1998: 89). This happened just three months before the RPF invaded in October 1990 (Kamukama 1997: 52; Prunier 1995: 160). Following the invasion, as the different sides struggled for supremacy, it became alarmingly clear that multi-partyism did not mean democracy and that much of Rwanda's sovereignty was now 'invested in the Paris Club of creditor nations, in the European Community, and in the World Bank' (Waller 1993: 27). Rwanda had been sold.

Politicians faithful to Habyarimana began to organise in an informal structure called 'Hutu Power', itself something of a club (Prunier 1995: 188); they reacted to the selling of Rwanda by redefining the enemy within: the class antagonism and the threat of militancy which they themselves faced were converted into 'ethnic hatred' and a readiness to kill the 'real' – now ethnicised – enemy. The tactic was tried out in March 1992 in Bugesera, where landless Hutu from the north-west had resettled. Competing for land with Bugesera's Tutsi, themselves resettlers from the 1950s, and 'encouraged' by the exceedingly explicit, 'Hutu Power' threats that Tutsi needed to be sent back to their (imagined) homeland in Ethiopia, the northern Hutu migrants took out their anger on Tutsi and members of opposition parties, killing at least 300 Tutsi (Africa Watch 1992; Reyntjens 1994: 308). The most explicit threat had come from Léon Mugesera, vice-president of the country's formerly sole political party, Mouvement Révolutionnaire National pour le Développement (MRND), who in November 1992 incited the Hutu majority to eliminate all Tutsi and everyone opposed to Habyarimana. '"Your country is Ethiopia," Mugesera told Tutsi, "and we shall soon send you back via the Nyabarongo [river] on an express journey. There you are. And I repeat, we are quickly getting organised to begin this work"' (original quotation in Reyntjens 1994: 119). The Bugesera massacres, and later massacres in Gisenyi prefecture (1992–93), resulted in an inquiry mandated by the International Federation of Human Rights (FIDH), Africa Watch, the Union africaine des droits de l'homme et des peuples and the Montreal-based Centre international des droits de la personne et du développement démocratique. The inquiry exposed many human rights violations and warned that the rising tide of political extremism could easily develop into unprecedented chaos and violence (FIDH *et al.* 1993).

By now Rwanda was a country at war with the RPF, which had invaded from Uganda. The timing of this invasion, some sources allege, was linked to the so-called 'old caseload' refugees from 1959 overstaying their welcome.

Rwanda's Tutsi ('59-ers') in Uganda

The arrival in Uganda of the Rwandan refugees from 1959–61, especially of Tutsi cattle keepers, made a dramatic political and environmental impact as the country passed through successive political regimes (Byaruga 1989; Otunnu 1999a). With time, the refugees' meddling in politics, their high-profile military engagements and privileged status as refugees resulted in a gradual swell of anti-Tutsi sentiment, also dubbed 'hospitality fatigue' (Otunnu 1999a: 10).[10] There had been early warnings that the Rwandan Tutsi refugees might overstay their welcome, as when Prime Minister Milton Obote told them in the 1960s to stop using Uganda as a base for attacking their home country (Lemarchand 1970: 208–9).

Anti-Tutsi sentiment escalated under Obote's first government, which emphasised Ugandanisation, while life under President Amin brought no improvements either. When the Amin era ended with the return of Obote, the armed faction of the Rwandan Tutsi refugees chose to join opposition leader Yoweri Museveni, who was of Hima origin and thus 'related' to the Rwandan Tutsi. Joining Museveni's bush war against Obote intensified the persecution of ordinary Tutsi refugees, especially at the hands of Obote's Uganda People's Congress (UPC) party. The snowball effect was immediate and brutal. A series of ambushes by Tutsi soldiers, in which unarmed Ugandan civilians were killed,

induced the [Obote] regime and UPC functionaries to target Rwandese refugees in the army and elsewhere for reprisals. The more [Museveni's] Popular Resistance Army (PRA, later the National Resistance Army – NRA) intensified its armed struggle, the more the regime and the UPC functionaries terrorized Rwandese refugees. The more the refugees were persecuted, the more they fled and joined the NRA. The more they joined the NRA, the more their increased presence in the NRA tended to confirm the claim that the NRA was a Tutsi organization. (Otunnu 1999a: 17)

This strong Rwandan Tutsi support for Museveni's war set the scene for official condemnations and sanctions, which culminated in the massacre and eviction of many Rwandan refugees in the early 1980s. When tens of thousands were forcefully repatriated to Rwanda, the Habyarimana regime reacted nervously and confined the repatriates to isolated, heavily guarded camps (Otunnu 1999a: 20–2).

Following Museveni's military victory in 1986, greatly assisted by high-ranking Rwandan refugee officers, Fred Rwigyema and Paul Kagame among them, Uganda's new president continued to make use of the 'warrior refugees' in counter-insurgencies in Acholi, Teso, West Nile and other unsettled regions. The partnership meant that a Rwanda Patriotic Army (RPA), with the Rwanda Patriotic Front (RPF) as its political wing, could develop and prepare for an invasion of Rwanda more or less undetected. Many factors influenced the invasion and its timing, not in the least Museveni's wish to see the powerful and all too visible Rwandan military 'removed' from Uganda (Otunnu 1999b: 38). When, on 1 October 1990, this wish turned into reality, the invasion intensified anti-Rwandan sentiment inside Uganda. It was now official: the Rwandan refugee guests, and their warriors, had overstayed their welcome (see Otunnu 1999b for a comprehensive overview).

Eastern Congo-Zaire

Two episodes in the history of eastern Congo-Zaire – colonisation by the Rwandan state from about the mid-nineteenth century, and the arrival of successive waves of Rwandan migrants under Belgian rule – impacted seriously on land rights. Regarding the first episode, Fairhead (1989b) has argued that while there is uncertainty over 'how and when the Batutsi came to rule over Bwisha', it is much better established that there have been different times and forms of rule. This diversity, as we shall see in Chapter 5, was negated by Rwanda's post-genocide leaders when they explained their moral assistance to Banyamulenge in terms of a 'Greater Rwanda' polity. For Bwisha, Fairhead highlights the diverse, historically evolved interactions with central Rwanda, noting first that

[i]t is important to distinguish between . . . (a) conquering, (b) rule through delegates, and (c) economic exploitation of the region through systematic taxation. Although Bwisha seems to have been 'conquered' more than 500 years ago, it was ruled by delegates from the Rwandan royal court only from the late eighteenth century, and was systematically taxed only from the mid-nineteenth century. (Fairhead 1989b: 3)

'Conquering' refers to periodic incursions by Rwandan monarchs that did not alter the system of rule by traditional ('autochthonous') chiefs, called Bahinza. In the late eighteenth century, rule by Rwanda became more direct and delegates were sent from the central court to rule over annexed territory. These delegates displaced the Bahinza chiefs in an administrative overhaul completed under King Rwabugiri (1853–95), who imposed heavy taxes and enforced labour, *uburetwa*. Rwanda's rule over its out-reaches, however, was 'continually disputed by the inhabitants, and the *mwami* could not always find delegates brave enough to accept the posting'. This resulted in a diversity of structured engagements:

In certain areas, the Monarchy was more powerful than in others. Jomba, which was quite heavily inhabited by the Batutsi, was the province most under the control of Rwanda, and was ruled by imposed Batutsi delegates of the king, who ousted the Bahinza. In Gisigari, where Batutsi did not live until 1910, less control could be exerted by Rwanda, and the indigenous Bahinza maintained their positions as Chiefs there, although they still depended for their power on the Rwandan *mwami*. In the sparsely populated and heavily forested principalities of Bukoma, Binza, Bwito and Masisi, Rwandan influence was less strong still, but nevertheless local leaders were obliged to pay tax to the Royal court to maintain their positions, and prevent invasion. (Fairhead 1989b: 3)

As a similar array of arrangements existed elsewhere in the region; for instance, in Bunande and Bushi, we may conclude that the varied quality of local administrative links with Rwanda's royal court marked the whole length of the Congo–Rwanda border.

Fixing territories and the international border was an act of colonial intervention. In Bwisha in 1910, 'the existing Provinces which were ruled by the Rwandan *mwami* through his mandates were officially recognized as "autonomous Chiefdoms", [while] the provincial Chiefs, who were the delegates of the Rwandan *mwami*, were given the power to continue to rule along traditional lines, as long as "public order" was not disturbed' (Fairhead 1989b: 4). In 1918, Belgium also intervened to radically alter the administration of eastern Congo, which it did by creating a ruthless 'traditional' structure capable of extorting labour at very low rates of pay. Belgium's policy succeeded throughout Kivu: 'In Uvira, Bunande, Bushi, Bwisha, and Fizi, local Chiefs who were more or less powerful in their domains were reinforced by colonial authority, and made vastly more powerful. This policy (not tradition) is responsible for the creation of powerful Bami [kings] throughout the region' (Fairhead 1989b: 4). Under this regime of invented tradition, some of the new powerful kings were able to sell not only the land of their own people, but also land previously under the jurisdiction of chiefs whom the Belgian authorities did not favour. Thus Ndeze II, who came to control all of Bwisha following his elevation to *mwami* in 1929, saw fit to colonise Bwito. He ousted Bwito's Bahunde chiefs and installed his own Bahutu delegates. To protect Bwisha and destroy his enemies in Bwito, Ndeze II asserted vacancy and sold large areas of Bwito for personal gain (Fairhead 1989b: 8). The situation which resulted is best described as institutional confusion.

Despite 'fixing' the Congo–Rwanda border, the Belgian authorities encouraged further population movement into Kivu to meet the need for plantation workers and administrators. To obtain land for the migrants, whose move to North Kivu they had authorised, the Belgian authorities made autochthonous chiefs sign lease agreements in return for financial compensation (Pabanel 1991: 33). This kind of expropriation was not too problematic in the less densely populated areas, including Masisi, but it was more difficult in Rutshuru, where the older plantations were located. Here, there was 'confusion of land rights between plantations and the new immigrants' (Fairhead 1989b: 12); a confusion aggravated by the influx of Bwisha highlanders who were seeking to be relocated.

The high number of immigrants, combined with the extensive need for pasture, meant that the potential for future contestations over land rights was now in place. The crisis would have its first climax in the deregulatory aftermath of Congo's independence, when autochthones voted with their feet and entered the Banyarwanda settlements to reclaim their 'inheritance'. Throughout Kivu, those who considered themselves to be the rightful inheritors of land began to (re?)claim what they considered to be inalienable, ancestral land (Fairhead 1989b: 15). The outcome was that the Rwandan immigrants and their descendants, who believed they had been allocated land on an inheritable basis, came to be 'redefined as "impostors" who had no long-term rights' (Fairhead 1989b: 15–16). Banyarwanda migrants thus became targets for confrontation because of their 'foreignness', a problem some Banyarwanda managed to overcome through a strategy of dispersal (Willame 1997: 44). Difficulties notwithstanding, many Banyarwanda, often from Rutshuru and linked to Ndeze II, would rise to prominence in commerce and politics.

The Banyarwanda sense of vulnerability was increased in 1959–61 when Tutsi refugees from Rwanda entered Kivu. Following an initial spell in UNHCR camps in Masisi, Walikale and Kalehe, these refugees progressively integrated themselves into existing communities, while a good number also joined the 'Muleliste' rebellion in Uvira-Fizi (Young 1970: 996). More Tutsi refugees followed after Rwanda's pogroms of 1963–64, prompted by the failed invasion of Bugesera by armed Tutsi exiles from Burundi. At this point, demographic pressure and Banyarwanda affluence combined to set off eastern Zaire's first 'nationality crisis'. Until 1964, Banyarwanda had had voting rights in the République Démocratique du Congo, then a young state; nationality had not been an issue. But land scarcity and the migrants' economic success turned 'nationality' into an issue for public debate and scape-goating. The more Banyarwanda and autochthonous elites jostled for political power, the more strongly the theme of 'the foreigner' – and that of ethnicity – emerged in political discourse. Banyarwanda in Kivu now stood accused of having massively infiltrated the host nation.

The 1964 Constitution did not help Banyarwanda. It granted Congolese nationality only to those residents 'with an ancestor who [was] or had been a member of a tribe or part of a tribe established within the Congolese territory before 18 October 1908' (cited in Willame 1997: 46). The majority of Banyarwanda were excluded. One direct consequence of the new law, and highly significant in the rise of 'ethnic consciousness', was that Masisi's Hutu administrators, appointed under colonial rule, were replaced by autochthones, mostly Hunde. This loss of power for Banyarwanda resulted in a loss of property: houses, shops, cattle, plantations were all (re?)claimed by autochthones. When Banyarwanda fought back to regain their civil and political rights, their resolve made them liable to the accusation they were 'Muleliste' guerillas. While unfounded in the vast majority of cases, the accusation led to scores of Banyarwanda – Hutu and Tutsi – being tortured, expelled or killed.

In the long run, however, President Mobutu had a strategic plan for eastern Congo-Zaire from which many Banyarwanda would benefit. This plan encouraged the political ascendancy of leaders whose ethnic groups could not possibly threaten central government, either because they were numerically insignificant on the national scale or because they had an ambiguous status. Fulfilling both these conditions, Banyarwanda became ideal candidates for political promotion. The most successful of these was Barthélémy Bisengimana, who in 1969 came to direct the Bureau of the Presidency of the Republic, a post he held for eight years. Bisengimana became 'the godfather' of all Banyarwanda, but 'especially of Tutsi who legally or illegally [had] come to live in Zaire' (Willame 1997: 53). His main achievement was to make the Political Bureau of the MPR, Zaire's then sole political party, adopt a law in 1972 through which everyone of Rwandan or Burundian origin established in Kivu before 1 January 1950, and who had lived there uninterruptedly, was entitled to citizenship. This new law did not solve the problem of the Tutsi '59-ers', nor indeed that of the assisted migrants who had arrived between 1950 and 1955, but their presence in Zaire ceased to be a point of public debate.[11] The new legislation, however, harmed the interests of North Kivu's autochthonous groups, especially Nyanga and Hunde, who overnight had been turned into minority groups.

Bisengimana's influence with Mobutu enabled the increasingly prosperous Banyarwanda not only to retake the lands lost in 1964, but also to acquire important new lands. Protected *and zaïrois*, the Banyarwanda elite bought into an economy where new riches awaited. In this, they were greatly helped by the land law passed in 1973, known as the Bakajika law, which legalised private ownership.[12] At this point, Zaire had already launched its 'authenticity' campaign, through which many foreigners, non-Africans mainly, had had their properties confiscated by the state and transferred to 'authentic' Zaireans. Riding on the crest of authenticity, the Banyarwanda elite acquired up to 90 per cent of the European plantations in Masisi and Rutshuru (see Mafikiri Tsongo 1996).

Certain 'autochthonous' chiefs also took advantage of the new law and sold for personal gain lands that had always been managed under 'customary law'. Their greed, often resulting in landlessness for autochthones, widened the scope for contestation and violence. It was thus that many Banyarwanda Hutu lost the valuable arable land they had cultivated for decades (Reyntjens and Marysse 1996: 50, referring to Bucyalimwe Mararo 1996). Dispossessed, they resettled in Walikale where many, once also robbed of their nationality (1981), would later be murdered by Nyanga militias.

For Banyarwanda, the golden age lasted until 'godfather' Bisengimana lost his political position and influence, and dispossessed Hunde and Nyanga fought to recoup the properties lost since 1972 (Willame 1997: 55). Bisengimana's dismissal coincided with the discourse of authenticity moving up a gear: the 'ex-Rwandans' once again turned 'Rwandans'. The discourse drove a first wedge into the Banyarwanda community: 'Hutu' began to take their distance from 'Tutsi', declaring they themselves were Hutu *and zaïrois*. But autochthones were not persuaded. Fearing that the (perceived) process of colonisation by Banyarwanda had already gone too far, autochthones did not generally buy the Hutu declaration and pressured central government to annul the 1972 law. The annulment, which came in 1981, hit Banyarwanda hard: a census was announced; they needed to apply for naturalisation. The wider significance of 1981, however, was the context in which it was passed: with elections looming, heightened political struggle easily turned into scapegoating against 'foreigners'.

Crucially, the 1981 annulment sapped the ability of Banyarwanda to exercise political authority on two fronts: within the region *vis-à-vis* autochthones, and internally in terms of lineage and community organisation. The latter decline, the end point of a process already begun in colonial days (Fairhead 1990; Pottier and Fairhead 1991), would make it harder for Banyarwanda to successfully defend their land claims. Without strong lineage heads, Banyarwanda found it difficult to make convincing representations in court (Willame 1997: 60), which meant that autochthonous leaders could now re-assert themselves as the true guardians of the land. Control over land became fully ethnicised and exceedingly aggressive.

Ten years after losing the battle for citizenship, the crisis deepened for Banyarwanda, both Hutu and Tutsi, when the 1992 National Conference (Conférence nationale souveraine, or CNS) excluded their representatives. To some degree, the exclusion reflected the past pro-Mobutu stance of elite Banyarwanda (autochthones were now exceedingly anti-Mobutu), but it was also a backlash for the strong support and sympathy Banyarwanda Tutsi had shown for the cause of the Rwandese Patriotic Front (RPF) in October 1990. Such sympathy and support were understood to mean that Banyarwanda – all Banyarwanda, but Tutsi more than Hutu – identified with Rwanda and should therefore be denied Zairean citizenship indefinitely. Just before the 1992 National Conference, North Kivu's deputy governor expressed the sentiment when declaring:

'Rwanda will have to accept the return of its emigrants instead of letting them roam around the world like Palestinians. History has shown that the Tutsi, ever-eager for power, have long been destabilisers. By all possible means they try to subvert established authority. . . . The population of the zone of Walikale has elected me to prevent that the zone be invaded by Tutsi. . . '. (quoted in Vlassenroot 1997: 53)

Banyarwanda Hutu reacted in self-defence to their exclusion from the National Conference, and reconfirmed strongly and openly that they were Zairean. Taking their distance from 'the Tutsi', militant Hutu prepared for confrontation: initially with Banyarwanda Tutsi in Bwito in 1992, then with autochthonous leaders through a campaign of civil disobedience led by the Mutuelle agricole des Virunga (MAGRIVI). The conflict escalated. Between February and December 1992, several Banyarwanda were assassinated in Masisi and hundreds of cattle culled. Acts of revenge against Hunde were also reported (Willame 1997: 65).

Not only Banyarwanda, but the rural poor everywhere had seen their vulnerability increase in the 1970s and 1980s. Once a food exporter, Kivu was now plagued by sometimes severe deficits. The contradiction indicated that food security was 'not just about aggregate food supply, but about access to that supply' (Fairhead 1989a: 3). Unlike in the middle of the nineteenth century, when food and livelihood security was achieved through spreading one's 'community' far and wide, and through belonging to large groups that spread risk, security by the late 1980s had become a lot harder to achieve (Fairhead 1989a: 4). There were signs that 'certain regions in Kivu [were] becoming less able to support the destitute' (Fairhead 1989a: 17), which gave ruthlessness and militancy a better chance. As often happens under such circumstances, politicians expertly converted economic and class struggle into a manifestation of seemingly ancient 'ethnic hatred'.

In Kivu, 'ethnic' tensions went out of control in early 1993, when all so-called non-local *gendarmes* in Walikale and Masisi were replaced by Nande, Hunde and Nyanga *gendarmes*. These autochthonous groups, mostly through their Mayi-Mayi and Bangilima militias,[13] began to ethnically cleanse Masisi of its Banyarwanda. Directed by politicians, both local and from outside Kivu, the 'cleansing' at times looked like 'a "plan" for the systematic elimination of Banyarwanda' (Willame 1997: 65). Banyarwanda, Hutu and Tutsi, were massacred in Walikale market and in several churches. So, too, in Masisi, where Banyarwanda retaliated. Casualties were high on both sides, as was the number of Internally Displaced People (IDPs) that resulted from the fighting. The NGOs and security services in North Kivu attested 'that the number of autochthones who died or disappeared (966) [was] not that much below that of the "immigrants" (1,238), whereas the number of displaced [was] fairly even for the two communities (59,000 autochthonous Hunde and Nyanga, 72,000 among the Banyarwanda)' (Willame 1997: 66).

These figures were later revised upwards. In 1994, USAID suggested that over 6,000 people had lost their lives (USAID 1994: 54), Oxfam put the loss at around 10,000 (Mackintosh 1996: 46), while one Médecins Sans Frontières (MSF) worker stationed in Kivu since 1992 spoke of 60,000 dead.[14] Unicef/Oxfam also raised the number of internally displaced to 350,000, *of which roughly 100,000 had yet to return to Masisi when the Rwandan Hutu refugees started spilling across the border in July 1994* (see Simmance, Page and Guindo 1996: 15). This observation is important. The displaced, predominantly Banyarwanda Hutu, would become political allies to the Rwandan Hutu refugees who sought to resettle in Masisi. Equally important, in the early 1990s, and despite growing tensions between Banyarwanda Hutu and Tutsi, Banyarwanda continued to be singled out and persecuted as one group. For North Kivu, *and before the 1994 refugee crisis*, it would be incorrect to isolate 'the Tutsi' as a target for persecution by autochthonous groups. They *were* targeted, but as Banyarwanda.

Throughout these turbulent times, South Kivu remained relatively calm. This situation would change dramatically when over one million Rwandan Hutu refugees – driven out of Rwanda by the architects of a genocide that killed three-quarters of a million Tutsi and tens of thousands of Hutu moderates – arrived in eastern Zaire.

Genocide in Rwanda: identity, death and international indifference

As with the crisis in North Kivu, the Rwanda genocide grew out of an explosive struggle for resources which embattled politicians *ethnicised* to their advantage, if only fleetingly. A crisis rooted in class and regional interests was turned into a conflict for which an ethnic minority, 'the Tutsi', was held responsible.

While most in the 'international community' initially failed to understand the genocide's multiple causes, some knowledgeable academics showed and shared their insights. Informed scholars like Catharine and David Newbury, for instance, addressed media workers right from the onset of the crisis to emphasise that the early killings were 'not a case of instantaneous chaos, an "orgy" of ethnic violence throughout the country, as many early [press] reports implied'.[15] Carried out principally by Habyarimana's presidential guard, the early killings eliminated Rwandans outspoken on human rights and prominent in multipartyism. The guard also killed Prime Minister Agathe Uwilingiyimana, one of Africa's first female heads of government. Her assassination, too, was planned. As Alison Des Forges, a historian of Rwanda turned human rights activist, explained to the press, the prime minister had been killed as part of a wider plan for systematic elimination:

Soldiers [of the presidential guard] . . . did not hesitate to kill the United Nations guards who were protecting her. Her summary execution was anything but a random killing, outburst of anarchy or an instance of 'tribal conflict'. Uwilingiyimana was Hutu, one of the majority group, as were the soldiers who killed her.[16]

Preparations for genocide, invariably dressed up as self-defence against the Rwandese Patriotic Front, an organisation ethnicised as 'the Tutsi invader', had started some two years before the actual slaughter when every *nyumba kumi* (ten houses) – every cell, the smallest administrative unit – received a gun from the national army. The availability of about 150,000 guns meant that the state authorities could mobilise every prefecture, commune, sector and *nyumba kumi* in a matter of hours.[17] The national army, the *Forces Armées Rwandaises* (FAR), also trained death squads whose recruits came mainly from among the landless and unemployed youth. These deadly militias were known as *interahamwe*, those who stand together. Almost exclusively Hutu, the *interahamwe* militias were part of a masterplan for the extermination of Habyarimana's political opponents and all Tutsi; a plan already in existence in 1993 and exposed by the Commission internationale d'enquête sur les violations des droits de l'homme au Rwanda, an inquiry led by the International Federation of Human Rights. Jean Carbonare, commission member, later said not to have been surprised by the violence that erupted on 6 April 1994,[18] the day Habyarimana's plane was shot down and the president killed. Also killed were Burundi's newly elected President Cyprien Ntaryamira, several senior members of Habyarimana's staff and three French crew.

When the genocidal machine unleashed its fury, it would still be some time before the interplay of the tragedy's multiple causes became clear to media workers (see Chapter 2), with some notable exceptions granted. Tragically, as surveys of the reporting have shown (Hilsum 1995a; Johansson 1995; Livingston and Eachus 1995), there was

relatively little change . . . in the media coverage [in Britain, France and the US] after 6 April compared to the paucity before. There was a blip with the shooting down of the plane and the reporting on the slaughters – generally portrayed as ancient tribal feuds – but with the withdrawal of foreign personnel [from Rwanda] there was a precipitous drop in coverage. When the genocide was accelerating, the Western press virtually ceased to report on Rwanda. The lack of coverage cannot be blamed simply on the relative disinterest in Rwanda. The real danger, the genuine confusion on the ground, the restricted mobility of reporters, and the inability to fly out photos or videos were major handicaps. In addition, American employers had ordered their reporters out for reasons of safety, and possibly also because of cost. But some stayed and accurately reported events, demonstrating all the more the failure of those who did neither. (Joint Evaluation 1996a: 46; report compiled by Howard Adelman and Astri Suhrke)

Among the journalists who did cover and analyse the genocide was Stephen Smith. Writing for the French paper *Libération*, Smith reported how the Habyarimana regime had hardened its stance in the early 1990s before developing its 'tropical Nazism'. Increasingly isolated, the regime had 'radicalised and drawn inspiration from colonial racism'; it urged that 'the unity of Hutu, long "subjugated", must reassert itself'. Hutu must close ranks against Tutsi, 'the feudal invader' who had returned carrying arms. The rhetoric of Hutu Power ideologues adopted the vocabulary of German Nazism. Smith wrote:

where Nazis spoke of 'vermin', the anti-Hamitic ideologues call the RPF fighters *inyenzi* – 'cockroaches'. On Radio Mille Collines, calls in Kinyarwanda for the collective murder of Tutsi are made with greater and greater urgency. '*Come on, get out, I need to warm myself!*' urges the sibylline voice of the broadcaster. Then, following news of some local assaults and killings, the incitation to violence becomes more explicit and general: '*The tomb is only half full. Who will help us fill it?*' We thus move on to the project of extermination.[19]

The killings were planned and systematic. They had nothing to do with 'ancient tribal warfare'.

The parallels with Nazi Germany were noted also on other occasions, and they would resurface in late 1996 during the civil war in eastern Zaire. During the mass repatriation of Hutu refugees to Rwanda, Mary Braid reflected on the genocide:

The Interahamwe extremists incited the slaughter. Those who met them, wielding machetes at road blocks during the killing spree or later when they led the Hutus into exile in Zaire and assumed control of the refugee camps, compare them to the Nazis. Just as the Nazis disseminated propaganda against the Jews, the Interahamwe was fed – and fed others – a diet of anti-Tutsi propaganda. It played on deep-seated fears.[20]

International assistance to the Rwandan Hutu refugees was also spoken of in terms of the Holocaust. A senior aid worker in Gisenyi said of the aid to refugees, which came flooding in: 'It would have been no different if the Nazis had fled *en masse* to Austria in 1945 and the Marshall plan had been used to assist their stay there.'[21] Because of the multiple comparisons that could be made, Rwanda became 'Africa's Israel', as another journalist, Chris McGreal, explained in *The Guardian*.[22] Marcus Mabry, of *Newsweek*, concurred: 'If Washington is tight with Kagame, it's partly because he is an English-speaking, US-trained soldier, but also because he is a member of the Tutsi tribe. . . . "These [Tutsi] are the Israelis of Africa," says an administration aide. "They are a minority; they suffered genocide." '[23] Visiting Uganda in March 1998, US President Bill Clinton continued the comparison by remarking how the *interahamwe* had killed 'five times as fast as the mechanised gas chambers used by the Nazis.'[24]

Ideologues and military strategies have also been compared. Ferdinand Nahimana, the disgraced academic who co-founded the pro-genocide *Radio-Télévision Libre des Milles Collines*, and is now being tried by the International Criminal Tribunal for Rwanda (ICTR), has been likened to Nazi Germany's Goebbels (McNulty 1999: 274). When the RPF ignored the international calls for a cease-fire as it closed in on Gisenyi, the London-based organisation African Rights defended the decision: asking for a cease-fire was akin to asking the Americans in 1945 to stop at 'the gates of Dachau . . . and to say: a cease-fire is always the highest priority, try and reach consensus!'[25] Parallels have been drawn, too, regarding the way 'Hutu Power' extremists demonised Rwandans of Tutsi origin, which happened 'in a manner strikingly reminiscent of Nazi images of Jewish people' (Hintjens 1999: 247). These comparisons with the Holocaust, and many could be added, fit into a strategy through which the post-genocide government of Rwanda has tried to sensitise the world to the plight of its people and its own role in the disaster.

Class and the brutal defence of privilege

From the onset of the genocide, informed academics and journalists understood that its context was complex, that the 'ethnic hatred' had multiple origins: in constructions of ethnicity, class, Rwanda's north–south divide, the RPF invasion and war since 1990, and a series of unprecedented economic shocks, some resulting directly from conditionalities imposed by the World Bank/IMF. The class element, though, was not so easily grasped since it required attention to specific ethnographic detail.

One particularly instructive demonstration of how class featured in the geno-cide has come from Timothy Longman (1995), who approached the subject with reference to two localities in Kibuye Prefecture. Longman concluded that 'the massacres represented a calculated and systematic attempt by embattled elites to reassert their social, economic, and political dominance and to eliminate any challenges to their authority' (Longman 1995: 20). Rwanda in 1994 was an extreme yet familiar case of how politicians threatened by democracy may at-tempt to retain their privileges through the fierce construction and exploitation of ethnic difference. Ethnic strife, in other words, is a modern phenomenon, not a remnant of 'ancient' Africa. As Jean-François Bayart observed during the genocide, 'it is politicised intellectuals who are at the origin of the massacres, and not the peasant masses'.[26]

But the grip of the politicised intellectuals had not been uniform in Rwanda, because class discrepancies varied widely. Class domination, as manifested in the boom of illegal land sales, varied not only between regions but also within them. Where socio-economic disparities were wide and the frustration of the landless deep, the killings were 'intimate', i.e. carried out by locals who knew their victims well. Longman highlights this by contrasting Kirinda and Biguhu. In Kirinda, social inequality was acute and the number of landless youth large; the disparity in Biguhu was not so wide. In fact, Biguhu's elite had supported Rwanda's earlier civil society movement and, in 1992, sponsored a local peasant farmer to attend a seminar on civic education. When the embattled elites called for the extermination of Tutsi and Hutu moderates, the two localities responded differently. In Biguhu, exhortations to murder were not heeded; the *bourgmestre* (commune head) brought in outsiders to do the killing. They killed Biguhu's civil society activists – peasants and moderate elites, Tutsi as well as Hutu – and temporarily restored the faltering power of the hardline elite. In Kirinda, on the other hand, the elite organised *a local mob* to kill resident Tutsi. Many Hutu refused to join in, but the landless, unemployed Hutu youth were ready to kill for reward. They butchered a dozen Tutsi men, women and children. The elites thus silenced the criticisms of the poor and temporarily regained control. As elsewhere in Rwanda, and in the Great Lakes region generally, the authorities redirected the hatred and potential violence of the poor – especially of angry, desperate young Hutu men – away from the rich and onto 'the Tutsi', the latter wrongly portrayed as invariably aristocratic and privileged.

The twisted rhetoric, fed by hardline 'Hutu Power' political factions, was well captured by George Balandier, sociologist and Africanist, when he briefed the press:

'More than an [expression of] ethnic conflict in the narrow sense of the term, the massacres have been *experienced* first and foremost as the clash between an aristocratic minority ["the Tutsi"], the holder of privileges, and a mass traditionally linked to it through ties of inferiority. In a certain manner, this has been a class struggle degenerating in terror.'[27]

In Rwanda, this *perception* of the country's 'problem' was part of a collective (Hutu) memory easily resuscitated during crisis. It was inadequate, though, as an evocation of class differentials in Rwanda in the 1990s, because it did not reflect the realities on the ground: the privileged class was Hutu, mainly northern Hutu, not Tutsi. Not being challenged, the perception became an effective weapon to mobilise downtrodden youth against an enemy who was, in more ways than one, imagined.

The Hutu population's deep-seated fear of a return of 'feudalism' may have been the product of propaganda rather than an actual remembering, yet the fear was real and existed against a backdrop of wider regional developments, such as the genocide of Burundian Hutu in 1972, the flight of Burundian refugees to Rwanda in 1988, and the assassination in 1993 of Melchior N'Dadaye, Burundi's first democratically elected president (Lemarchand 1998). The reinstatement of kingship in neighbouring Uganda, notably the return of the Kabaka (king of the Baganda), may also have added to the fears of a return to power of a Tutsi aristocracy which had ruled Rwanda until the end of Belgian colonialism.

It is important, too, to place the rise of Hutu extremism firmly within the context of Rwanda's acute impoverishment of the late 1980s. While some, Bayart included, emphasised that the 'Hutu racial ideology has developed over thirty years',[28] it is also more accurate, if not more appropriate, to acknowledge discontinuities and refrain from vilifying the Habyarimana of the 1970s and 1980s. Alex De Waal is precise on this point:

A *coup* in 1973, announced by its leader, Major-General Habyarimana, as a 'moral revolution', called a halt to anti-Tutsi pogroms and promised development without politics. But since 1990, with simultaneous economic crisis, populist mobilisation for multi-party elections and the threat of the RPF, Hutu extremism has returned in a far more virulent form.[29]

De Waal rightly distinguishes between the achievements of Habyarimana's first decade in power, which brought 'unprecedented stability and genuine moves towards development', and the second decade during which 'Habyarimana's rule became increasingly authoritarian and corrupt; power became concentrated in members of the President's *Akazu* (literally: "little house" or clan) from the north-west, and not only Tutsi but Hutu from other parts of the country were excluded' (African Rights 1994a: 8).[30]

Region: a neglected factor

The significance of Rwanda's north–south divide in the genocide and its aftermath relates to the north-west's historical opposition to rule by south-central Rwanda. This opposition is rooted in conquest, for it was not until the Belgian colonists lent the ruling Tutsi dynasty a helping hand in the 1920s that the Tutsi monarch extended his direct rule over the entire country (see also Chapter 3). Ever since, northern Hutu have viewed southern Hutu as 'Other', as Tutsi, and many despise them for 'sharing a common culture and even kinship' (*Africa Confidential* 35(9)). Relatively dormant in the early days of independence, north–south antagonism peaked after Habyarimana, an army officer from the north, seized power. Before him, President Kayibanda, a southerner, had favoured Gitarama, his home prefecture; now Habyarimana would reverse the process and favour his own north-western region. North and south Rwanda had united in opposing the monarchy during the social revolution of 1959, but, by the mid-1960s, the common enemy was long gone.

Prior to Habyarimana's coup, a UN Commission of Inquiry had reported that the ideals of the Kayibanda government, the first Hutu regime, were fast disappearing: if independence had satisfied Rwanda's ethnic majority, the mid- and late-1960s were marred by terror and discord. Terror was provoked by the growing number of southern authorities who were too preoccupied with personal gain to attend to their public duties (Reyntjens 1985: 390). Rwanda's state marketing board, TRAFIPRO, was at the centre of the intrigue. Launched under Kayibanda and with its headquarters at Gitarama, TRAFIPRO had favoured southern politicians and businessmen. The malaise of the late 1960s was a demonstration of how little had changed in Rwanda since 1959. The revolution had ousted an oppressive regime only to replace it with a system supposedly democratic but equally bent on abusing power (Lemarchand 1970: 492; Reyntjens 1985: 481).

Habyarimana's 'moral revolution'-speak won him sympathisers worldwide, most notably the French president François Mitterand. On taking up office in 1981, Mitterand approved of Habyarimana's coup, applauding not only the end of the malpractices under Kayibanda, but also the northern Hutu ethos famed for its resistance to aristocratic rule. As a consequence, aid to Rwanda increasingly meant aid to the north-west. The long-term consequences for the south would be disastrous. At the time of the genocide, Bernard Lugan, another historian of Rwanda, reviewed the French involvement:

France transferred the part of the University it controlled, from Butare in the south to Ruhengeri in the north. In so doing it delivered several hundreds of students and Tutsi teachers, but equally Hutu from the south, into the hands of northern extremists. France also created the first school for *gendarmes* in the same region, then trained and equipped the presidential guard assassins, all recruited from the President's clan.

Lugan then concluded:

Blinded by their ideology or perhaps just ignorant of Rwandan subtleties, those who un-wisely engaged France in these unfortunate clan politics carry some direct responsibility in the massacres.[31]

Widely supported, the accusation against Mitterand's socialist government must also be set in the framework of French policies in Central Africa, in which

France gave military and diplomatic support to a dictatorial regime, trained government armed forces as part of a cooperation agreement, and intervened to protect a regime against what was then considered to be external aggression. Official policy was cemented by patrimonial relationships between leaders and possibly by secret business, military, or other deals between the two countries. (Callamard 1999: 157–8)

Within this framework of francophone interests, Canada, too, was at times accused of being an accomplice in the genocide. The claim was made in Canada on the Canadian Broadcasting Corporation's English and French networks on 29 November 1994, with the French network accusing Canada of abetting the genocide. The claim may have had validity, yet, as Howard Adelman's inves-tigation later revealed, there was a definite need for caution. Scrutiny of what Canadian officials knew, and of who knew what at what time, led Adelman to conclude 'that the accusation of willful "blindness" or being "*complice du génocide*" [was] unwarranted' (Adelman 1999: 187). Adelman conceded, though, that Canada had erred in the late 1980s when 'linking aid to the process of democratization, a process based on multiparty democracy and the protec-tion of human rights. Political adjustments were pushed on Rwanda at the same time as Canada required Rwanda to adopt a structural adjustment approach to its [crashed] economy' (Adelman 1999: 188). In formulating his verdict, Adelman notes that 'Canada was the only country to reinforce its peacekeepers' once the UN started to withdraw troops from Kigali (1999: 200). Canada, Adelman ar-gues, does have a genuine commitment to peacekeeping: 'If Americans drew the lesson from Somalia that they should avoid peacekeeping, Canadians became even more committed' (1999: 185).

On seizing power in 1973, Habyarimana's northern elite had vowed to re-store the pre-Tutsi culture which several areas had known before the European colonists arrived. The culture to be restored would be dominated by landowners (*abakonde*) who attracted clients (*abagererwa*) through land. But the restoration plan found little support in south Rwanda, where cross-ethnic relations had harmonised and cross-ethnic marriages were common. In this respect, Butare, the south's main town, could be regarded as 'the country's intellectual and spiritual sanctuary, the place where Tutsi and Hutu lived and worked together to give birth to new hopes for the future'.[32]

Death

In 1994, Rwanda's south paid for its aspirations when the presidential guard and *interahamwe* death squads closed in on Butare. The south had shown too great a willingness to share power with the RPF. In *Libération*, Stephen Smith counted the cost.

After the death of the General-President, all these 'moderate' Hutu, whom the almost exclusively northern military considered 'traitors of the race', were subjected to the murderous wrath of the army and the militias of the old regime.[33]

Traitors of the race. The political elite and clique around President and Madame Habyarimana, through the ultra-extremist Coalition for the Defence of the Republic (CDR), deflected public attention away from the issue of class and privilege and onto the allegedly 'more real' problem of ethnicity: the danger of a return to the old order under a Tutsi aristocracy. The essentialist, racist category of 'the evil Tutsi' was restored and operationalised for the sake of safeguarding political privilege.

The ensuing genocide – the word 'genocide' perhaps first being used by Oxfam[34] – resulted in the death of up to 800,000 people, mostly ethnic Tutsi, in just over three months (Joint Evaluation 1996a: 9).

International indifference

On being pressured into accepting multi-partyism and power-sharing with the RPF, Habyarimana lost control; he fell victim to a determined wave of extremism within the *akazu* (the 'little house') of his own in-laws. Habyarimana could thus be described as a double victim: a victim of the international peace industry and of his *protégés*, not in the least the soldiers he had handpicked to serve in his presidential guard.[35]

But the international dimension to the drama was no less significant. Regarding the hasty impositions of the 'peace industry', there had been warnings that the rush for peace could backfire. The country was not ready for the sudden switch to Western-style democracy. In January 1994, Charles Ntampaka, professor of law, had warned:

'Democracy has aggravated tension, because it leads to everyone forming their own groups. . . .

It is true that there's a definite ethnic problem. But the ethnic problem only arises when there is a change of power. The bigger problem is economic – rich against poor, and the rich encouraging the poor to fight.'[36]

There had been warnings, too, in 1993, when Oxfam's David Waller wrote: 'Rwanda stands on the brink of an uncharted abyss of anarchy and violence, and there are all too many historical, ethnic, economic and political pressures that are likely to push it over the edge' (Waller 1993: 60). No one listened. Waller's book was ignored just like a 1992 report by Amnesty International had been pushed aside, the way the 1993 report by the International Federation of Human Rights was pushed aside, the way even General Roméo Dallaire's fax to Lt-General Baril on 11 January 1994 would be ignored. Sent to Baril at the UN Department of Peace-keeping Operations (DPKO) in New York, the fax had detailed the training of the *interahamwe*, the plan for a speedy genocide (killing 1,000 Tutsi in 20 minutes), and the plan to kill Belgian UN troops and thus guarantee Belgian withdrawal from Rwanda.[37]

Why was Rwanda so insignificant? Writing from an NGO perspective, but no doubt reflecting views also in wider policy circles, Anne Mackintosh gave this answer:

it seemed impossible to push Rwanda higher up the agenda – whether in terms of programme funding, or prioritization as a focus for lobbying and communications work. The South African elections were in prospect: in terms of Oxfam's potential to influence parliamentarians and the public, it seemed far more sensible to put resources there. There was just no mileage in Rwanda. (Mackintosh 1996: 48)

While some commentators have played down the impact of the World Bank/ IMF conditionalities, sometimes by arguing that the role of these institutes had been 'essentially one of guidance rather than imposition' (Woodward 1996: 3), one cannot deny that the international community was heavily implicated in Rwanda's vulnerability. Woodward's defence of standard World Bank/IMF practices overlooked the fact that Rwanda's vulnerability had greatly increased following the Arusha Accords. The final blow came in early 1994, when the World Bank and IMF 'suspended credits to Rwanda, stating that the government of Rwanda was now illegal' (Pender 1997: 6). This happened within weeks of the first RPF troops arriving in Kigali under a UN escort. Rwanda had become 'a country with a gun pointed at its head by the RPF, the US, Belgium, Britain, the UN, the World Bank and the IMF' (Pender 1997: 6).

At the UN, too, Rwanda was a low priority, so low that the UN Security Council reached a consensus not to intervene to stop the killings that began in April 1994. The Security Council agreed that the UN 'had a duty and obligation to protect the lives of [its] peacekeepers and that the failure to do so would make it harder to obtain troops for future operations and, perhaps, further the decline in the UN's reputation' (Barnett 1997: 560). In reaching this consensus, the United States of America, through its chief representative Madeleine Albright, had argued most persuasively that the UN troops in Rwanda (UNAMIR) had no business being there (1997: 571). This position was supported by Belgium's Foreign Affairs minister, Willy Claes, who had seen ten Belgian UN soldiers killed alongside Prime Minister Uwilingiyimana – killed as foretold in Dallaire's fax to Baril. UNAMIR's presence was scaled down as the killings intensified.

The UN failure to protect Rwandan citizens at risk prompted France to take unilateral action and send troops under French command. Launched in June 1994, *Opération Turquoise* was 'officially designated as a humanitarian intervention to protect civilians and hinder a mass outflow of refugees, [but it] was launched and executed in a manner suggesting mixed motives' (Joint Evaluation 1996a: 54). French soldiers appeared to have come to Rwanda to protect not so much the civilians at risk as the killers, the *génocidaires*, and to keep pockets of Habyarimana's defeated troops beyond the RPF's reach.[38] Showing no signs that it intended to disarm Rwanda's national army, the French operation made a mockery of the claim that its mission was to protect those at risk of genocide. Sources in Paris later claimed that *Opération Turquoise* had saved tens of thousands of Tutsi in the zone, yet the claim was received with much international scepticism (Joint Evaluation 1996a: 54; Prunier 1995: 292). Some of France's European partners reacted strongly to the unilateral action. Baroness Lynda Chalker, Britain's overseas development minister and close friend of Ugandan President Museveni, the RPF's main backer at the time, later revealed that Britain had offered to help France, but that the offer had been declined.[39]

The aftermath of genocide

Rwanda and the international community

The discovery that Habyarimana's regime had 'fostered the belief that it was the minority's fault they were killed'[40] created such consternation worldwide that it became impossible not to feel empathy with the incoming RPF, which had had the courage to halt the genocide. It was thus that relief workers began to realise they were feeding mass killers, even helping them to rearm. The world of humanitarian aid went into shock, particularly in Britain and the US.[41] This rude awakening, coupled with Western guilt at not preventing the genocide, made many in the international community reluctant to point a finger at Rwanda's RPF and the government it had put in place in July 1994. Many humanitarians, moreover, became impressed with the seriousness with which RPF leaders appeared to be planning a coalition government 'with some opposition parties, led by Hutus who survived the massacres'.[42] That several Hutu in government were respected liberals gave confidence; a broad-based government seemed in the making.

Despite this optimism, the international community was slow to offer direct aid to Rwanda's new government. By the time of the first anniversary of the genocide, most pledges were yet to be converted into hard cash. Even 'though US $537 million had been pledged at the Round Table [in Geneva in January 1995], the Government [of Rwanda] maintained that little of that assistance had been received. . . . Hence, [it] became less inclined "to play the game" as it had done in late 1994 and early 1995' (Kent 1996: 85). Pledges for equipping the Ministry of Justice and generally rehabilitating the justice system had been fulfilled, but little else (see Joint Evaluation 1996b: 75–6). The government of Rwanda felt it was still on its own. The RPF had won the war on its own, stopped the genocide on its own and would now rebuild the nation without significant international help. Worst of all, in the eyes of government, a disproportionate amount of aid earmarked 'for Rwanda' ended up in the camps for Internally Displaced Persons, or in the refugee camps where *génocidaires* recovered and rearmed under UN protection. The crisis and human suffering were sure to be perpetuated. The government's frustration over the lack of international support peaked in late April 1995, when the Rwandan authorities failed to peacefully close down the last of the IDP camps, Kibeho. After RPA troops lost their nerve and fired into the crowd, thousands of IDPs lost their lives; the carnage seriously dented Rwanda's international relations.

Rwandan refugees and their impact on ethnicity in Kivu

After the ethnic violence of 1993, relative calm returned to North Kivu thanks to the mediation of local NGOs and Mobutu's elite troops, the Division Spéciale Présidentielle. But the calm did not last. With the arrival of over a million Rwandan Hutu refugees, whose militias had committed genocide, the fragile peace would shatter the moment refugee leaders, militias and what remained of the national army (ex-FAR) set their sights on Masisi. For the fugitives from justice, the fertile Masisi region, considered to be a part of Rwanda by both Habyarimana and the RPF leadership, promised to be a haven for permanent settlement and impunity. Rwanda's Hutu would achieve the dream of creating a 'Greater Rwanda'. This did not come as a surprise to people in eastern Zaire. Willame recalls:

Representatives of the Nande, Hunde and Tembo tribal associations declare that 'the Rwandans', whether Hutu or Tutsi, 'have never relinquished their dream that one day they would take up arms and conquer eastern Zaire (North Kivu, South Kivu and North-West Shaba) to create a *République des Volcans*.' (Willame 1997: 69)[43]

The refugee presence drove a permanent wedge into the Banyarwanda community. Zairean Hutu militants, often from communities displaced in 1993, now joined forces with Rwandan *interahamwe* and attacked Zairean Tutsi. This happened in Rutshuru first, then in Masisi. Between November 1995 and May 1996, thousands of Tutsi were killed, while some 15,000 fled to Rwanda.[44] The violence in Masisi, however, targeted not just Tutsi but also autochthones. While the *interahamwe* attacked in search of land for settlement, Banyarwanda Hutu used force to (re?)take from autochthones, and increase where possible, the lands they had lost in and after 1981, but especially in 1993. In December 1995, over 400 Hunde and Nyanga were killed in Masisi.[45] By February 1996, some 250,000 autochthones, Hunde and Nyanga mainly, had been forced out (Willame 1997: 70; also Simmance, Page and Guindo 1996).

In these massive displacements, autochthonous politicians saw proof that Rwanda had a habit of 'exporting' its problems to Zaire. The 1994 Hutu refugees had followed in the footsteps of the 1959–63 Tutsi refugees, who themselves had followed various waves of political, spontaneous and assisted migrants. All were unidirectional. As something needed to be done, 'autochthonous' guerila soldiers, Bangilima and Mayi-Mayi, reappeared on the scene by early 1995.[46] These guerillas had a history – a recent history of wanting to rid Kivu of its 'Rwandans' and a somewhat older history of warfare against the Mobutu regime.[47] On resurfacing, the guerillas targeted in the first place the Forces Armées Zairoises (FAZ), the eternal enemy, but Banyarwanda, Hutu and Tutsi, were their second major target. This explains why in May 1996, Mayi-Mayi simultaneously terrorised villages in Rutshuru, where Banyarwanda were numerous, and waged battle with the FAZ.[48]

Not all attacks, though, were the work of Hutu refugees or 'autochthonous' guerillas. In June 1996 for instance, Bunagana, in Jomba parish, was attacked by members of the Uganda People's Defence Forces (UPDF) allegedly in collaboration with the Rwandese Patriotic Army (RPA). Responding to this cross-border attack, local (Zairean) Hutu, helped by Hutu refugees from Katale camp, set upon (Zairean) Tutsi and killed thirty-six people. Some Tutsi escaped to Uganda and Rwanda;[49] no Tutsi remained in Rutshuru. In its report *Forced to Flee: Violence Against the Tutsis in Zaire* (July 1996), Human Rights Watch accused the 'international community' of silence and indifference, and France of continuing its aid to Zaire and the genocidal refugees.

New, shifting alliances also marked the scene in South Kivu, where the presence of so many refugee extremists – armed and rich – made local politicians forget their quarrels and seek out new opportunities. There was more to be gained from an alliance with refugee extremists. Bashi and Warega politicians, previously locked in a high-profile battle, mobilised behind an anti-Tutsi ideology that extended the Hutu–Tutsi antagonism into a much broader African racism: Nilotic or Hamitic against Bantu (Vlassenroot 2000: 273). They raked in the spoils of war and humanitarianism. The new alliances resulted in a 'general campaign against the Banyamulenge, the local Tutsi community' (Vlassenroot 2000: 272). This community, made up of genuine 'Banya-Mulenge', Tutsi economic migrants and Tutsi refugees who had arrived after 1959, was vulnerable because 'their lack of an indigenous citizenship came to be the main argument that they were immigrants without any right to claim national citizenship' (Vlassenroot 2000: 274).

Manipulation by unscrupulous entrepreneurs and local politicians also explained why Babembe turned against Banyamulenge. Ethnic strife, again, was the work of individuals seeking personal gain. While this particular tension might be construed as stretching back to 1964–65, the conflict might not have reignited in 1996 without the shrewd manipulations of Anzuluni Bembe, then the co-speaker of parliament. As ever, ethnicity showed itself to be a latent, emotive force easily distorted and whipped up for individual political gain. Anzuluni linked the long-lasting resentment between Babembe and Banyamulenge with the larger national debate on citizenship. Koen Vlassenroot reflects:

Since Anzuluni was a prominent member of the MPR [Zaire's long-ruling party], he was forced by the democratisation process [of the 1990s] to seek a new power-base, which he found through the exploitation of anti-Banyamulenge resentments in his home area. In April 1995 the *Haut Conseil de la République* (HCR) passed a resolution which was signed by Anzuluni and which treated the Banyamulenge as recent refugees. One month later, the District Commissioner of Uvira made the first moves to put the resolution in action. (Vlassenroot 2000: 274)

Shortly afterwards, in October 1995, *mwami* Lenghe III, customary chief of the Bavira, issued a letter to the effect that 'within his administration, the so-called Banyamulenge are like strangers' (Willame 1997: 90).

Up until the middle of 1996, the question of Banyamulenge citizenship and civil rights had been fought mostly through memoranda and verbal provocations. This changed dramatically the moment Banyamulenge/RPA soldiers crossed into Zaire from Rwanda. While effectively on a mission of self-defence, the campaign was understood to be an invasion because of the massive logistic support received from both Rwanda and Uganda. Anti-Banyamulenge sentiment in South Kivu quickly turned from ugly to insane. Following the first shootout between Banyamulenge and the national army (FAZ) at the end of August 1996, which left several FAZ soldiers dead, Uvira's local authorities declared that only fourteen Banyamulenge families could now be called *zairois*, and the rest should 'return' to Rwanda or face persecution. South Kivu's civil society groups chose not to mediate. On the contrary, they too regarded Banyamulenge as 'unfaithful serpents that [had] abused Zaire's hospitality' (Willame 1997: 95, referring to a Tour Report by Karen Twining, 8–12 October 1996). In the mayhem that followed, many innocent families were harassed and forced to flee to Rwanda. Some were killed. In early October, the FAZ-Banyamulenge skirmishes – *with 'Banyamulenge' now a generic term referring to a newly constituted ethnic group* – developed into war. Armed Banyamulenge clashed not only with the FAZ, but also with Babembe and Bashi.

As with North Kivu, analysts must guard against the temptation of seeing the 1996 troubles of 'the Banyamulenge' as a mere continuation of an 'ethnic hatred' kept alive by the memory of past conflicts or acts of opportunism. Although the close relationship between Banyarwanda (including Banyamulenge) and Mobutu was well 'remembered' in the early 1990s, anti-Banyamulenge sentiment might not have taken on its extreme form if individual local politicians had not been spurred on by the challenge of democratisation and the spoils of humanitarianism.

Banyamulenge uprising and the 'international community'

Lacking their own *collectivité*, Banyamulenge had continued to pay tribute to autochthonous chiefs for access to land, a situation which, especially after 1981, came to epitomise their non-participation in the political process (Vlassenroot 2000: 273–4). Unlike in the early days following their migration from Rwanda, when cattle meant wealth and access to land seemed unproblematic (Depelchin 1974), the absence of a secure territorial base in the late twentieth century seriously weakened Banyamulenge livelihoods and the chance of survival.

Threatened by the Rwandan Hutu refugees, now in league with some Zairean Hutu and autochthonous politicians, Banyamulenge and Banyarwanda Tutsi attempted to overcome their political vulnerability and isolation by claiming membership of a common, vast but unrecognised polity. 'Banyamulenge' became the omnibus term referring to *all Tutsi* who resided in North Kivu, South Kivu and Shaba; a group much larger than the descendants of the original 'Banya-Mulenge'. The reason for the birth of this 400,000-strong ethnic community was political: facing a shared enemy, there was safety in numbers. The number of 400,000 had already been set in November 1995, when Banyamulenge put their problems to the international community in a letter signed by Müller Ruhimbika, secretary-general of the NGO Milima. From here on, Banyamulenge became politically more vocal in demanding their Zairean nationality and civil rights. The high figure and claim to authenticity, which most of the outside world accepted unquestioningly,[50] was a way of telling the world that the rebellion in Kivu was entirely a local product, a movement *supported but not masterminded* by the RPF.

In the same way that the term Banyamulenge appears to have emerged in the 1970s to distinguish Mulenge's Tutsi – true Zaireans – from Rwanda's post-independence Tutsi refugees, so the resurgence of the label, this time in the form of an all-inclusive entity, carried the message that all Tutsi in

Zaire belonged to an authentic Zairean community on a par with autochthones. Banyamulenge were something of a 'lost tribe' not to be confounded with 'the Tutsi' who had taken power in Rwanda in 1994.[51]

Determined not to undergo the fate that had befallen Tutsi in North Kivu, Banyamulenge fought for their civil rights before the insurrection turned into an all-out attack on the Mobutu regime itself. The all-out campaign, presented to the world as a spontaneous fusion of the armed wings of Zaire's revolutionary opposition parties, which had joined 'the Banyamulenge' in solidarity, succeeded in ousting Mobutu in a matter of five months. But it was Rwanda's vice-president, Paul Kagame, who, with Kabila in mind as leader of this civil conflict, masterminded the revolt (see Introduction).

The astonishing success of the alliance, known as the Alliance of Democratic Forces for the Liberation of Congo-Zaire (ADFL), would not have been possible without the assistance of the national armies of Rwanda, Uganda and to a lesser extent Burundi. Informed analysts, however, knew that Kagame was taking a risk. While Kagame and Kabila appeared to share a Marxist-Leninist vision, with Kabila also being good friends with Museveni, Kagame must have had some concern regarding Kabila's lack of popularity in eastern Zaire. If Kabila had any supporters left in Mulenge, they would be *Babembe from certain* collectivités, *but not all Babembe*, and certainly not the descendants of the original 'Banya-Mulenge'. Kagame's choice man for leading the operation needed to work with and lead troops that could be construed as his former enemy. The notion of a Kabila-Banyamulenge alliance was not unproblematic and Kivu's diverse population, whatever the ADFL's spokesmen would claim, was not unanimously behind the uprising.

When 'the Banyamulenge' assaulted the Rwandan refugee camps, they forcefully repatriated some 700,000 Rwandan Hutu. Since the international community had been banned from the battle zone there were no international witnesses,[52] but the attack generated much comment and diplomatic activity, most of which centred around the never-executed plan for a UN-led intervention. To understand this diplomatic activity, one must contemplate the intensifying conflict of interests between the US and France. The former resisted intervention and supported the ADFL; the latter 'allegedly hoped that a humanitarian intervention would use the guise of humanitarianism to place foreign troops in a position to effectively block the rebel advance' (Adelman and Suhrke 1999: xvi). Not only had the French government supported the Habyarimana regime in Rwanda, and intervened to set up a safe haven for the architects and executioners of the genocide, as well as for the passively involved, France had also 'tried in 1990 to rebuild the declining Mobutu regime in order to counter Yoweri Museveni of Uganda, seen as an American ally in the Great Lakes region' (Ngolet 2000: 71). For Mobutu the year 1990, which set Zaire on the road to democracy, had been a year of serious decline. Under the new transitional government, the president had seen his powers wane when the National Conference told him he should rule but not govern.[53]

Five years on, its own role in Central Africa now much diminished while that of the US had grown, France reacted defensively when the ADFL attacked the refugee camps and called for the creation of a 'humanitarian corridor' through which aid could reach the refugees inside Zaire. France's call for intervention was

received with reluctance in Washington and fierce opposition in Kigali. . . . the idea of creating another humanitarian zone was seen by Kigali as a desperate effort by France to help its Hutu allies. The intensification of the rebel attacks in eastern Congo and the resistance of American diplomacy completely ruined this French enterprise. (Ngolet 2000: 73)

Its hands tied, the French government declared it would not send troops without the agreement and cooperation of the US, which was an impossible request. Then, seeing the ADFL advance towards Kinshasa, France's desperate reflex was to recruit Serbian mercenaries hoping that they would boost the morale and firepower of Mobutu's push-over forces. The Serbs bombed Goma and Bukavu from the air, but made no dent in the ADFL's resolve to go all the way.

For its part, the US supported the ADFL campaign through a mixture of open diplomatic and only thinly camouflaged military support: the Clinton administration openly recognised that Rwanda and Uganda needed to secure their borders with Zaire. US support included financial assistance channelled through mining houses that paid court to Kabila and secured lucrative contracts. American Mineral Fields (AMF) and the Canadian-owned Tenke Mining Corporation donated millions of dollars to the ADFL war effort, as well as logistical support with the transportation of troops. US backing for the ADFL, many observers agreed, was linked to Congo-Zaire's vast mineral wealth. Not only the US, but also Germany, France, the UK and Japan were about to enter the twenty-first century critically dependent on imports of chromium and cobalt, valuable materials which Congo-Zaire had in abundance (Fairhead 2000). Not surprisingly, the half-baked intervention plan fizzled out in the days following the mass return of refugees. It died completely when the initial findings of US military reconnaissance flights over Kivu, which had identified several hundreds of thousands of refugees moving deeper into Zaire, were retracted and the crisis was declared over (details in Chapter 5).

Importantly, the reinterpretation of vital imagery was not confined to the results of military reconnaissance. Prior to the mass return of refugees, the government of Rwanda had held public relations exercises aiming to explain Rwanda's 'real' boundaries via yet another rewriting-of-history project, a cartographic representation. To justify the presence of the Rwandese Patriotic Army (RPA) in eastern Zaire, should justification be needed, Rwanda's President Bizimungu showed the media a map taken from Abbé Alexis Kagame's *Un abrégé de l'histoire du Rwanda* (Kagame 1972). This map projected an 'image of homogeneity' by suggesting the existence of a Greater Rwanda at the end of the nineteenth century. Bizimungu argued that the colonial powers had amputated parts of western Rwanda when they fixed the border in 1910. The president had a point, but he applied a modern European framework of *fixed boundaries*, an approach ill-attuned to nineteenth-century realities, which, as seen earlier, were highly diverse. Moreover, President Bizimungu omitted to say that Rwanda itself had not been administratively unified until the 1920s, when Belgium intervened to support the royal court's campaign for political unification. Also left out of the picture was the flight of Tutsi communities from the abusive power of Rwanda's central court, as illustrated in the migration of the original Banyamulenge (Depelchin 1974) and the continual disputes between Rwanda's *mwami* and the inhabitants of Jomba in the late nineteenth century (Fairhead 1989b). These nuanced readings would have cast doubt on the credibility of the president's claim that a Greater Rwanda had existed in pre-colonial days.

Maps can be read and re-read; aerial photogrammetry can be read and re-read; a small community can be 'ethnicised' to become a larger one. These various *interventions* demonstrate the close fit between knowledge and power that lies at the root of much about eastern Zaire and Rwanda that is today taken for granted. The world remains mostly unaware that the readings it was confronted with in 1996 were re-readings, re-presentations, not facts. Conflicts, in other words, give birth to re-readings and make them flourish. It is with this theme, with the power of narratives in conflict, that the present study is concerned.

The power of narratives

In situations marked by conflict, human tragedy, ambiguity, and intersecting local and international interests, one must expect that members of the 'international community' will be used as vehicles for propaganda. Put differently, it is likely that attempts will be made to manipulate the international presence for the promotion of easy-to-grasp, seemingly uncontested narratives which, it is then hoped, will become common currency. Bizimungu's mapping exercise, which looked at the past through the distortive lens of modern parameters, illustrates how a seemingly unproblematic representation may be floated as an instrument for winning over international support. When this happens, it is the unsaid, the void in re-presentation, which demands our attention. The mapping exercise involved one of many narratives running concurrently in which certain erroneous assumptions were made unopposed.

The book's focus is on the pervasiveness and power of clustered narratives that simplify reality to make the post-genocide government of Rwanda and its practices intelligible, rational and legitimate in the eyes of the world. Constructed sometimes with the help of sympathetic outsiders, the interlocking narratives share the common message that rule by the pre- and early colonial royal court was benevolent until destroyed by the European colonial powers. The world today, it follows, has every reason to be confident that the return to power of the Rwandan Tutsi diaspora will herald a new era of righteousness and social justice. To spread this message successfully, Rwanda's post-genocide leaders have tried to persuade members of the international community that the history books need to be rewritten (see Chapters 2, 3, 6), that the country's numerically dominant ethnic Hutu, whose ethnicity was invented by outsiders, have nothing to fear unless guilty of genocide (Chapter 4), and that victimhood bestows the right to dictate to the world how reality is to be understood (Chapter 5). Rewriting history, however, must be done on many levels and in different contexts: rewriting history is left not just to historians and other academics (Chapter 3), but requires the further participation of journalists (Chapter 2), humanitarians (Chapter 4), and policy-makers concerned with rural development and reconstruction (Chapter 6).

Central to this broad participation is the international guilt the government of Rwanda continues to nurture. The argument goes, and there is much truth in this, that the international community over the past century has been guilty of interference when it should have abstained, and guilty of abstaining when it should have intervened. Concretely, Rwandan authorities claim that early European colonists interfered to destroy the harmony of an ancient Greater Rwanda; that independence under Hutu-majority rule was engineered by subversive outsiders who sided with 'the Hutu'; that international scholars interfered after independence to challenge the perception of history which Alexis Kagame and his Belgian collaborator, the anthropologist Jacques Maquet, had recorded once and for all. And when the international community should have intervened, as at the start of the 1994 genocide, it had decided, through the UN, to reduce its presence. The latter observation, irrefutable, is today the starting point from which other, more contestable claims are made.

Kigali's post-genocide regime knows how to make political capital out of the empathy and guilt that exist within the international community. Such guilt is extensive, as Twagiramungu openly stated after his dismissal in August 1995,[54] and makes the international community more receptive to the visions and analyses that emanate from Kigali. The thousands of humanitarian workers which the 'aid industry' brought to Rwanda and the Great Lakes, many on their first mission to Africa,[55] have generally preferred to accept the authorities' easy readings of the highly complex situation they faced. These organisations and individuals, moreover, have actively reproduced and spread, wittingly or unwittingly, a vision of society, economy and history that bears the RPF's seal of approval.

The following example, a statement by Save The Children, UK (SCF), illustrates how RPF-friendly narratives have been (re)produced. In late 1996, when making the case against intervention in eastern Zaire, SCF provided a background sketch on society and history which contained many truths, but which also grossly simplified certain complexities within Kivu. The sketch, a typical narrative, accorded well with President Bizimungu's evocation of a once-upon-a-time Greater Rwanda. In 'Zaire: Military Intervention Is Not The Answer', a news statement released on 6 November 1996, SCF correctly advised the international community not to repeat the mistakes of 1994. These mistakes revolved around the acceptance, indeed encouragement, of Rwandan Hutu refugee camps on Zairean soil; a well-intended humanitarian gesture which had kept alive and fed the spirit of genocide. Regarding non-intervention to be the basis for ending violence and promoting regional stability, SCF urged that the international community help create stability through a) 'support to the displaced and affected local people, believed to number 400,000' and b) 'support for major and rapid voluntary repatriation of the refugees'. Who exactly these 400,000 were was not spelled out: was this a straightforward reference to 'the Banyamulenge' or did the figure include the 250,000 displaced autochthones? Claiming to take cognizance of 'the local dynamics of the situation', SCF provided the following backdrop:

The Banyamulenge in South Kivu and groups such as the Banyarwanda in North Kivu have lived in Zaire for many centuries. Over the past twenty years attempts have been made by the Zaire Government to persecute these groups by trying to deny their rights to citizenship and making various attempts to expropriate property and land. While this situation has persisted for some time, it has been exacerbated in the past two years by the influx of refugees from Rwanda.

The Banyamulenge and Banyarwanda were amongst the relatively better off groups in Kivu province. The Banyamulenge and allied groups lived on the high plateau above the towns of Bukavu and Uvira. The Banyarwanda inhabited the area around Masisi and around Goma. The mass influx of over one million refugees into Kivu has done much to exacerbate economic rivalries and political rivalries and tensions. (SCF 1996)

As with other statements inspired by officialdom, there is always the risk that a statement of this kind says as much through its omissions as through its actual content. SCF's background sketch was broadly correct, except for the claim that Banyarwanda would have lived in North Kivu for many centuries, while the full text contained valuable insights on regional instability: military incursions into Rwanda; unrest in Burundi; the UN failure to disarm ex-FAR and *interahamwe*; Mobutu's exploiting the crisis to save his political skin. The big local issues, however, citizenship and property, appeared in a socio-political vacuum. The non-Rwandophone population was not mentioned, nor was Mobutu's patronage from which 'Rwandan' elites benefited throughout the 1970s, nor was anything said about local views on Banyamulenge joining the RPF in 1990 or about the ethnic clashes of 1993 which had triggered a *complex pattern of internal displacement*. While SCF analysed correctly that the Rwandan Hutu refugees were the catalyst that produced the unbearable tensions that made Banyamulenge revolt, it did not reflect on how the presence of the RPA in eastern Zaire would impact on the 250,000 recently displaced autochthones from Masisi, who were unlikely to be in the RPA's good books. RPA/Banyamulenge soldiers were likely to associate the displaced autochthones with Mayi-Mayi, the hard-to-discipline rebel force with a long history of opposition to Banyarwanda; they were unlikely to show much sympathy. There was no necessary congruence between giving *carte blanche* to the RPA and assisting Masisi's displaced. (SCF's reference to Kivu's 400,000 displaced was, it seems, a straightforward reference to 'the Banyamulenge' and did not include the 250,000 recently displaced Hunde and Nyanga.) Any organisation calling for a *political solution* to a given crisis must thoroughly probe the internal complexities and think them through. The use of unqualified labels that have international compassion appeal – i.e. 'the displaced' – is not acceptable in the absence of contextual analysis. The displaced, too, come with political agendas.

In fairness, SCF did try to demonstrate such awareness. Its strategy for engagement, the public statement said, was 'based on a number of assumptions as to how the crisis [would] develop, recognising both the regional, as well as the local, dynamics of the situation' (SCF 1996: 3). The background sketch, however, showed only a shallow understanding of local dynamics and conformed to what the RPF-led government of Rwanda, as the highest moral and intellectual authority, would approve of. Most of the assumptions SCF worked on seemed probable indeed, except for its key assumption (1996: 4, number 3) that the population of eastern Kivu would wholeheartedly back the ADFL alliance and campaign. Whether SCF realised this or not, the assumption was unfounded in view of eastern Zaire's past history and the recollections of that history. While other assumptions did hold, e.g. that a UN-led intervention would escalate into something 'potentially disastrous for the local population of Kivu' (1996: 5), there could have been no guarantee that the presence of the Rwandese Patriotic Army, while securing Rwanda's border, would automatically bring regional stability.

It may well be, as John Ryle (1998) has argued, that the lack of a systematic interest in the long-term political processes that generate emergencies is typical of humanitarian work (and, he adds, of journalism); agencies lack the institutional capacity and area expertise required to grasp the intricate reality of power relations on the ground. This, however, makes them vulnerable to manipulation by local interest groups. In this respect, we do well to recognise the close relationship between SCF and Rwanda's post-genocide regime. As Ian Linden has written: 'The [SCF] agency moved into Rwanda, as it were, from south-west Uganda, unthreateningly following the path of the RPA' (Linden 1998). SCF thus became an intellectual ally, an organisation willingly inspired by the RPF's vision of society and history. Moreover, and more broadly, we need to acknowledge that the RPF embarked on an extensive campaign to infiltrate humanitarian agencies and organisations as soon as it had established a hold on Rwanda (Gowing 1998: 52).

But we need to go further still. In times of conflict, the international community must not only guard against infiltration and technological interception, it must also come to grips with the origin and power of the narratives and discourses that (re)produce selected visions of society and history. It is here that research on the power of 'oral tradition' needs to be considered; a power which, in the Great Lakes context, often translates as the ability to reproduce history through well-memorised narratives. Research on Burundian refugee camps in Tanzania demonstrates this perfectly (Malkki 1995). In the Mishamo settlement, where Liisa Malkki conducted research in the mid-1980s, Hutu refugees who had fled the mass killings in Burundi in 1972 were engaged in an 'urgent preoccupation with documenting and rendering credible to outsiders the history that had brought them to Mishamo and that they could not escape living' (1995: 53).

In the Great Lakes, the art of 'remembering' the past – living it, re-living it, making it credible – has been eagerly pursued for many generations. In his research on historical transformations in eastern Zaire, mentioned earlier, Depelchin (1974) highlights the vast importance of narratives in Rwandan culture. Impressed with the vividness with which Rwandans remembered their migrations and history, Depelchin reflected:

The way the Rwanda [i.e. 'Banya-Mulenge'] recollect their past through long, unbroken, well-memorized narratives fits the image or idea of what history ought to be. In contrast, the Furiiru – and to a lesser extent the Rundi – have not preserved such well-structured and prearranged narratives. On the surface, the Rwandan historical tradition may seem more 'reliable', but in fact they make the work of the critical historians almost impossible. (Depelchin 1974: 67)

Another historian of Rwanda, Jan Vansina, analyses how Rwanda's royal court used to protect testimonial information by leaving its transmission in the hands of 'specialists [who] learnt by heart' (Vansina 1973: 41). Transmitted texts, mostly in the form of dynastic poetry, may thus have seemed 'reliable', yet they left the historian with the huge task of 'trying to disentangle which aspects of reality relate to the various elements of which a testimony is composed' (Vansina 1973: 77). The challenge lives on in contemporary narratives, because the Rwandan politician's desire to 'get history right' also continues. In April 1998, a government official in Kigali said: '"Our history is not properly written. The young, including Tutsi, don't understand our history"' (cited in Eltringham and Van Hoyweghen 2000: 227).

This book does not advocate conspiracy theory, but argues that Rwanda's RPF-led regime has views about the past, present and future which are being propagated via a wide range of intersecting channels: academic outlets, diplomatic activity, media broadcasting, policy-making for refugees and the writing of rural development policy. In all these activities, outsiders unfamiliar with the intricate interplay of local, national, regional and international dynamics have ended up 'feeling inspired' by the remarkable consistency with which Rwanda's post-genocide leaders have spoken about society, history and economy. Their relatively uniform, easy-to-grasp narratives depart significantly from the findings of those researchers who over the past three to four decades have, in their own ways, 'corrected' the knowledge and imagery inherited from the late colonial period, and they possess a simplicity which newcomers to the region would do well to scrutinise.

Conclusion

The refugee extremists who arrived in eastern Zaire in July 1994 added significantly to Kivu's 'normal' levels of institutionalised confusion. The refugee factor was not an add-on to the conflict scene, but rather a catalyst which reconfigured that scene. The issue, though, is a complex one: while certain killings, notably of Tutsi in Masisi in 1995–96, were clearly 'a continuation of the genocide led by the ex-FAR and interahamwe' and not a continuation of past disputes over who is or is not Zairean (Adelman and Suhrke 1999: xviii–xix),[56] other events such as the aftermath of the Banyamulenge uprising, i.e. the gradual breaking up of the ADFL alliance as originally constituted, cannot be grasped unless one considers events that predate the arrival of the refugees: in this case, the mid-1960s 'Muleliste' rebellion, which opposed Banyamulenge and Bafulero/Babembe/Kabila, and, more recently (1992–93), the clashes between authochthones and Banyarwanda in North Kivu. These prior conflicts, which are always 'remembered', if necessary with distortion and omission, did have a bearing on the 1996 conflict *and its unfolding*. This confirms that the approach to history can never be easy, that it is more likely to be 'impossible' (Depelchin 1974: 67).

Where institutionalised confusion is rife, as it was in Rwanda and eastern Zaire by the late 1980s, complexity becomes a breeding ground for the emergence and flourishing of narratives that may cause further confusion. Regardless of the specific focus of the chapters that follow, each makes reference to carefully worded statements, sometimes prearranged and spin-doctored, about how the past, the present and the future in Rwanda and eastern Congo-Zaire are to be imagined, and imagined internationally. The purpose of this book is to raise contextual awareness about the truth claims the Great Lakes conflict has generated.

2 Mind the gap: how the international press reported on society, politics and history

> We used communication and information warfare better than anyone. We have found a new way of doing things. (Paul Kagame, 8 April 1998)[1]

The thin line between information and disinformation blurs in times of conflict and war, all the more so when fighting restricts access to regions and their people. Journalists, commentators and observers, and those reading their reports, must then weigh the credibility of 'stories' that are difficult and sometimes impossible to verify. Sifting through these stories, they must seek out conflicting narratives and ask why they exist.

In this chapter, which draws from press reports that appeared in the US, Britain, France, Belgium and The Netherlands, we review three episodes in the recent history of the Great Lakes during which narratives about society, politics and history have been 'at work'. We ask how these narratives are structured, and will consider the gap between dominant narratives and established academic perspectives. The episodes covered relate to the end of the war in Rwanda (July 1994), the Kibeho massacre in south Rwanda (April 1995) and the Banyamulenge/ADFL campaign in eastern Zaire in late 1996.

As with other chapters in the book, we shall discover how the research-based script on society and history in the Great Lakes region, specifically Rwanda and eastern Zaire, came to be reconsidered under the influence of the Rwandese Patriotic Front (RPF) and Rwanda's first post-genocide government. The rewriting project, a high priority in Kigali, has benefited from the empathy and services not only of journalists unfamiliar with the region, but also of newcomer academics, diplomats and aid workers. All have helped, although to varying degrees, to popularise and spread an RPF-friendly but empirically questionable narrative. It is the varying degrees to which journalists have toed the RPF line of thought that are examined in the present chapter.

Media coverage of the Great Lakes crisis: existing critiques

Anyone working in zones of conflict is affected by multiple pressures and prone to be manipulated. The outcome – and it makes little difference whether one is a journalist, humanitarian aid worker or political analyst – is that little more than a tiny window on reality can be accessed. Under these circumstances, readers or viewers are presented with *constructs of reality* that rarely capture local people's own understandings of what is going on. John Ryle (2000) quotes a Sudanese informant:

'Who cares what I tell the foreigners as long as the [rebel] authorities do not think I am being subversive?' (Ryle 2000: 95)

The foreigners, however, do not always question what they hear. In the race to be first – first to deliver aid, first to transmit pictures and stories – foreigners may find it hard to admit they are vulnerable to manipulation and deception. Aid workers, journalists and, as the next chapter reveals, newcomer academics are more likely to seek out solidarities and act in partisan ways. Wittingly or unwittingly, they turn into scribes who re-present partial versions of a reality they have just begun to uncover.

It is now widely accepted that the war and genocide in Rwanda (1994) and the conflict in eastern Congo-Zaire (1996–7) have been underreported and misreported because of media manipulation (Gowing 1997, 1998; Hilsum 1995a, 1997; McNulty 1999; Ryle 2000). Regarding the Congo-Zaire crisis, the argument runs that '[the] Rwandan government viewed journalists as a resource to be manipulated through the denial of information' (Gowing 1998: 35). This denial related to the presence of the Rwandese Patriotic Army (RPA) in Congo-Zaire and the perpetration of war crimes and crimes against humanity (Hilsum 1997).[2] In full agreement with this critique, but aware that this manipulation was mostly confined to media coverage in Britain and America, the present chapter adds that the media was also used, albeit with varying degrees of success, to help shape a one-sided perspective on society, history and politics.

To be fair to journalists in disaster zones, we do well first to reflect on the conditions that shaped their dispatches from the Great Lakes: the pressures of satellite technology (from 1996 onwards), the post-Cold War pressures and competition among aid agencies, and the powers of persuasion that warring parties can exert. Regarding eastern Zaire, Nik Gowing, a former diplomatic editor with *Channel Four News* (ITN, London), has produced the most comprehensive critique to date (Gowing 1997, 1998). The international media and the humanitarian community, Gowing argues, were both wrong-footed during the military operation of the ADFL/RPA, because both were vulnerable following their failure to report and help avert Rwanda's genocide (Gowing 1998: 41). Burdened with that conspicuous failure and associated guilt, and generally unable to read local-level politics, journalists and humanitarians 'came to see eastern Zaire through the deceptive lens of moral sympathy with the RPF-led regime in Kigali, the ADFL's strongest backer in the region'. One NGO doctor told Gowing: 'there was an inherent sympathy by the media, NGOs and outside governments for Kagame because his people had been the victim of genocide. It was a moral sympathy. The international community wanted a "moral legitimacy" for Kagame' (quoted in Gowing 1998: 41). Wanting this moral legitimacy, many reporters and commentators readily accepted 'that all Hutus in Eastern Zaire were "extremists" or "genocidal maniacs"' (1998: 41).

The media (and humanitarian community) paid a heavy price for this 'fixation'. Journalists 'did not perceive accurately the hidden military campaign that was unfolding beyond their reach. As a result they never gained the usual upper hand on information that they had come to assume in recent years. They were outsmarted' (Gowing 1998: 6–7). The full cost of the bias, it can be argued, was that 'a high level of officially authorised ethnic slaughter (some went so far as to label it genocide) could ultimately be carried out unseen and virtually unreported, even though the Rwandan government denie[d] that mass killing was the intention from the start' (Gowing 1998: 5). The killings were 'conducted off-camera, in the full knowledge that where there are no images, there is no story' (McNulty 1999: 268–9).

Just days after the ADFL campaign removed Mobutu from power, Lindsey Hilsum (1997) articulated the deception and argued that the dominant perspective on the operation needed correcting. The campaign had been 'more complicated, more devious and, in terms of human wickedness, a great deal worse than [journalists had been] able to convey' (Hilsum 1997). Looking back on the ADFL and its Rwandan Tutsi backers, Hilsum understood that

[the good guys], too, as Tutsis, are prisoners of the political and demographic realities of Central Africa. The Tutsis are a minority in Rwanda, and they know that they can only retain power in the long term by force. They cannot afford virtue.... So their tactic is covert collective extra-judicial punishment. They are confirmed in this course of action by the failure of Western attempts to impose individual justice for the 1994 genocide. (Hilsum 1997)

Besides being unable to access the sites where massacres took place, reporters had particular difficulty with the new doctrine of information control Paul Kagame imposed, a doctrine built around denial. In late 1996, the Rwandan authorities denied that RPA troops were fighting alongside the ADFL. Later, Rwandan officials denied being involved in any atrocities against Rwandan refugees and Zairean civilians. Later still, after Kagame acknowledged the RPA's involvement in Zaire,[3] certain Rwandan officials denied that the vice-president's words would have implied direct RPA engagement (Gowing 1998: 19).

The 'denial machine' (Hilsum 1997) also operated on the international front, where '[s]enior figures from the main supportive non-regional nations denied ... that they had explicit inside knowledge of the operation from the start, despite the close working relationship of their Kigali-based diplomats to the Rwandan leadership' (Gowing 1998: 19). While the latter denials may have been legitimate, as Gowing suggests,[4] those by Rwandan officials could not be deemed credible since subsequent reports by Human Rights Watch Africa (1997a, 1997b), Amnesty International (1997) and the United Nations (UN 1998) have all brought convincing evidence of the presence of the Rwandan military and its role in massacres.

The wrong-footing of the international media in 1996–97 had been possible because of the media's failure to adequately deal with the 1994 genocide. The failure had been profound: not only was the slaughter wrongly portrayed as ancient tribal hatred, but also it was true that 'with the withdrawal of foreign personnel [working in Rwanda] there [had been] a precipitous drop in coverage. When the genocide was accelerating, the Western press virtually ceased to report on Rwanda' (Joint Evaluation 1996a: 46). Moreover, Goma refugees were given centre stage, which made the victims of genocide invisible. When *The Guardian* ran a feature on the cholera epidemic in the camps entitled 'Rwandan Apocalypse', readers may well have gained the impression that the epidemic had erased the bloodbath of the genocide (Chrétien 1995: 15). The bias took its toll and contributed to a skewed understanding of the Rwandan crisis within 'both the Security Council and the Secretary-General', and hence contributed to the withdrawal of UN troops (UNAMIR) on 21 April 1994. In the long run, therefore, 'the Western media's failure to report adequately on the genocide in Rwanda [may have] contributed to international indifference and inaction, and hence to the crime itself' (Joint Evaluation 1996a: 48).

The accusation of inadequate coverage of the genocide, first exposed in Hilsum's contribution to the Joint Evaluation of Emergency Assistance to Rwanda (Hilsum 1995a), has been fully accepted by the international media. The ensuing guilt, which was extensive (Hilsum, personal communication, July 2000), then produced the opposite bias two years later when many tens of thousands of Hutu refugees, now the victims of crimes against humanity, were made invisible in the reporting.[5] Not only had journalists learned next to nothing since being deceived in 1994 by Hutu *génocidaires* who argued that 'both sides' were suffering equally, they were by late 1996 also subjected to the new 'undeclared doctrine of information control drawn up by the new generation of leaders across Central and Eastern Africa' (Gowing 1998: 6).

One high-profile Western disciple of the new doctrine of information control and its 'fixation' is the American journalist Philip Gourevitch, whose book *We Wish To Inform You That Tomorrow You Will Be Killed With Your Families* (Gourevitch 1998) has achieved international acclaim. Certainly, the book deserves praise for conveying the horror of the killings, for bringing together some deeply touching testimonies by survivors who escaped the butchery, and for exposing the dangers and contradictions that continue to dominate their lives. On the other hand, Gourevitch's grasp of Rwandan history is weak, and why the horror happened is left to the reader's imagination. Gourevitch is overly keen to toe the RPF-functional line and thus reproduces the view that all Hutu refugees are genocidal extremists who collectively deserved their fate in eastern Zaire in late 1996. As with his account of the Kibeho massacre (discussed in Chapter 5), he unfailingly endorses Kagame's reasoning that the innocent who died in the camps only have the *génocidaires* to blame.

[Kagame] was not denying that many Rwandan Hutus had been killed in the Congo; he told me that when revenge was the motive, such killings should be punished. But he considered the *génocidaires* responsible for the deaths of those they traveled with. 'These are not genuine refugees,' he said. 'They're simply fugitives, people running away from justice after killing people in Rwanda – *after killing*.' And they were still killing. (Gourevitch 1998: 338)

The argument, in other words, is that only a thorough cleansing of all who were associated with the *génocidaires* – which means a high number of innocent civilians and children – could guarantee a lasting victory over evil. Gourevitch agrees Kabila was right to throw up hurdles and obstruct the UN investigations; he shares the 'feeling . . . that after sitting out the Rwandan genocide, the so-called international community had little credibility as moral referees in the war against the *génocidaires*' (1998: 336). The label *génocidaire* applied to all. Watching the flood of returning refugees, Gourevitch saw not individuals but 'the rout, at least for the moment, of an immense army dedicated to genocide'; an army 'the world had succored . . . in the name of humanitarianism' (1998: 301). Ironically, and not understood by Gourevitch, this logic which speaks of a radical lasting solution is the very same logic to which Hutu Power extremists had resorted in 1994.

Conditions underpinning manipulation

The failure to cover the ADFL military agenda and crimes was rooted in a moral sympathy with the RPF and 'facilitated' by the political doctrine of New Pan-Africanism, which resents every form of Western intrusion whether by governments, humanitarians or the media. The doctrine advocates political regeneration through full participation in global trade, especially in essential minerals, and aims to undermine the effectiveness of the world's monitoring capacity. Upheld by a coalition of African leaders – from Eritrea, Ethiopia, Uganda, Rwanda, Congo-Zaire (then rebels), Angola and South Africa – New Pan-Africanism was optimistic that it could unlock the fortunes of the African continent, reverse decades of misrule, and turn Central Africa into a region attractive to donors and lending institutions. In late 1996, New Pan-African leaders saw a strong connection between the liberation of apartheid South Africa and that of Zaire. Poised to become celebrated post-adjustment states, the two 'giants' would change the course of history and usher in an African Renaissance.

In search of regeneration, New Pan-Africanism also advocated a hard line on justice: if a price had to be paid to cleanse Central Africa and reach the golden age, then the price to pay could be justified as unfortunate but necessary for the greater common good.[6] The vast number of Hutu refugees who vanished in eastern Zaire after the camps were destroyed, and Kabila's effective obstruction of the investigations by the UN and other human rights organisations, confirmed that New Pan-Africanism was ready to pay a very high price indeed.

Receiving strong military backing from Uganda, Rwanda and Angola, as well as extensive logistical support from South Africa and the US, the ADFL, under Kabila's leadership, toppled Mobutu with astonishing speed. One reason for the success was the use of sophisticated military technology, another the firm manner with which the new powers dealt with the 'humanitarian community' and the media. Their strategy was simple but effective: ban outsiders from the battle zone; delay and frustrate their movements; deny any 'rumour' of military excess; withhold information; apply moral argument by blaming the international community for the mess the Great Lakes region is in. Hilsum outlines the strategy:

The officials of Kabila's Office of Information know that journalists have rapid deadlines, limited budgets and a short attention span. If they spin things out for long enough with security scares, with bureaucratic hurdles and impassable roadblocks, the journalists will go away. (Hilsum 1997: 9)

The ADFL threw a cordon around Kivu, played for time, intimidated outsiders and locals alike, and categorically denied any wrongdoings. The end result was 'information shutdown', a move which, Kagame later admitted, had been central to his strategy for eastern Zaire (Gowing 1998: 15). Kagame also acknowledged the importance of his military training at Fort Leavenworth in the US in 1990, when he served in the Ugandan army.[7]

Media dispatches from eastern Zaire were distorted, too, by conditions back home. If media coverage fudged the war crimes and crimes against humanity, this was

partly because of the skill of the Alliance and their Rwandan backers in manipulating journalists, but . . . also a result of the moral simplifications built into the reporting of conflict. To make it story-shaped, there have to be good guys and bad guys [. . .]. Because of the genocide of the Tutsis in 1994, the Rwandan government and its allies have usually been seen as the good guys. (Hilsum 1997: 9)

Although not a new condition, the premium on moral simplification was strongly reinforced by revolutionary changes in information technology. Now using satellite technology, journalists faced a new demand: Western consumers of conflict – editors, viewers and readers – wanted to see and read 'in real time', not days later as had happened in 1994. The 24-hour news cycle imposed 'an inevitable subjectivity and lack of ability to check' (Gowing 1998: 14).

Against this background, we shall count the cost of manipulation not so much in terms of what was not adequately covered – genocide, war crimes and crimes against humanity – but rather in terms of media imaginings about society and politics in the Great Lakes. Journalists, I shall argue, did not only fail to cover ADFL / RPA crimes and tactics, but they also contributed, under conditions of advanced information control, to the active construction of a particular narrative which aimed to legitimatise the ADFL campaign. I do not, however, want to make this a blanket statement. Rather I shall draw up a broad contrast between the reporting in the anglophone world and in continental Europe, and, because such a contrast remains all too crude, I will also separate partisan from analytically more insightful journalism.

Since the above mentioned reviews (especially Gowing 1997, 1998; Hilsum 1995a) offer a full critique of how the international media failed to cover the Rwanda genocide, my starting point here will be July–August 1994, the time when the new RPF-led government was sworn in. The episode brings home that poor, apolitical coverage continued after the genocide, especially in the anglophone press. We then move to coverage of the Kibeho massacre in 1995, when the international media once again turned its gaze on Rwanda. The restrictions journalists faced in Kibeho foreshadowed the subsequent information shutdown in eastern Zaire. Kibeho was a half-way stage in the development of Kagame's doctrine of tight information control.

Covering genocide

Before we proceed, it is prudent to ask about media coverage of the genocide in continental Europe. To what extent does the above critique reflect the content and quality of press reports in say Belgium, The Netherlands or France? While I can only respond in brief, it would seem, especially in the case of the Belgian press, that the indictment of inadequate coverage and analysis does not apply in any general sense. In contrast to Britain and the US, media consumers in continental Europe were not that deprived of insight into the forces and politics behind the tragedy.

In Belgium, the former colonial power, the press generally appeared well informed. Newspapers may have displayed their usual political biases, but reporters and commentators must not stand accused of failure to cover and analyse the genocide. After the second day of slaughter in Kigali, when there was still much speculation about who had brought down the presidential plane, a leading Flemish journalist, Axel Buyse, argued that there were two hypotheses. Writing in *De Standaard*, a paper sometimes accused of being pro-Hutu, Buyse refused to subscribe to the 'obvious' hypothesis that the RPF would have shot down the plane:

it is tempting to regard the death of the two Hutu-presidents as a major step in the realisation of a Tutsi masterplan for regional dominance. Like all conspiracy theory, however, this would be a suggestion of convenience; a suggestion which ignores the differences of opinion that exist among Tutsi. Like Hutu, the latter are just as unlikely to be a homogenous bloc.

The other possibility is that the attack had been planned from within Rwanda's political top by radicals so determined to stall the democracy process they willingly sacrificed the lives of the President and the army's chief of staff. The systematic way in which civil society leaders have been eliminated in recent times supports this second hypothesis.[8]

We still do not know with certainty who brought down the plane, but Buyse's analysis, his supporting the second hypothesis, proves he understood not only Rwanda's internal politics but also the planned nature of the early killings. There was general awareness, too, of the Hutu extremists' propaganda machine, for it had frequently targeted Belgium's ambassador in Kigali. The ambassador had been a regular target on Radio-Télévision Mille Collines, the hate radio directed by Ferdinand Nahimana, the 'former history professor and ex-director of the national information service Orinfor. [Nahimana] had been dismissed from his post in March 1992 after submitting a "pamphlet" to national radio which announced an imminent Tutsi [i.e. RPF] attack. The broadcast sparked off a massacre [of Tutsi] in Bugesera.'[9] Although divided over the issue of the country's relations with Rwanda, the Belgian government had withdrawn its troops from Rwanda one month after the RPF invasion of October 1990 (Prunier 1995: 108). It had also openly criticised Habyarimana following the 1993 human rights report by the International Federation of Human Rights (FIDH et al. 1993).

Close attention to Rwanda's troubled politics was evident, too, in other Belgian papers. Readers of Le Soir and La Libre Belgique, for instance, were similarly kept informed, particularly through Colette Braeckman's dispatches from Kigali. Braeckman, however, strongly supported the RPF and developed theories on the downing of Habyarimana's plane that would later be dismissed as conjectural (see Prunier 1995: 213).

The killing of ten Belgian UN soldiers by Habyarimana's presidential guard, killed alongside Rwanda's Hutu prime minister, Agathe Uwilingiyimana, may have momentarily moved the media spotlight to Belgium's role in Central Africa, and to the evacuation of foreigners, but this did not diminish coverage of Rwanda's own politics. The day news of the UN killings broke, Het Nieuwsblad (12 April 1994) carried an article which highlighted Rwanda's north–south divide, a central factor in the dynamic of the genocide. The training of *interahamwe* militias and the psychology of genocide also received attention. *Knack*, a popular Flemish weekly, used journalist Els De Temmerman's interview with RPF-officer Tony Kabano, who explained how Rwandans had been armed by the *Forces Armées Rwandaises* (FAR) well before they were incited or forced to kill: 'Already by the end of last year, the FAR had trained and armed several hundreds of people in every large commune. Other citizens, however, were forced to participate [in the killings], they had to demonstrate being good Hutu by killing Tutsi, if not they would be judged accomplices and be killed themselves.'[10]

The logic of genocide and the blind obedience it demands, and how this applied to Rwanda, was the focus of a special *Knack* edition even before the massacres spread to south Rwanda.[11]

By early June, De Temmerman's diary was serialised in *De Standaard*. The first-day entry, when De Temmerman renewed contact with the RPF and travelled to its headquarters in Mulindi, covers the systematic nature of the killings and has an interesting interview with RPF leader Théogène Rudasingwa,[12] who declared being opposed to foreign intervention. Undoubtedly referring to France, Rudasingwa said: 'Rwanda's military establishment, guilty of the crimes we are today seeing, has been created through foreign assistance'. De Temmerman's diary was later published in book form (De Temmerman 1994).

In The Netherlands, too, where the general public did not have prior knowledge of the Great Lakes, the interest in Rwanda grew as the crisis deepened. This interest may have been kindled by curiosity regarding Belgium's role in the former colony, but with time, and particularly once the Dutch government emerged as Rwanda's top donor after the genocide, Dutch journalists turned curious about the region's facts and fictions. Dutch media work is of interest because its journalists and commentators were in a position to cross-check their information: anglophone voices could be compared with what was being said in Belgium and France. Here lay the difference with Britain and the US, where public interest in Rwanda was confined to humanitarian assistance and charity appeals, and shaped by information accessed directly from the English-speaking RPF. Some exceptions granted, anglophone journalists mostly relied on relief workers ignorant about the Great Lakes.[13]

In France, Stephen Smith of *Libération* also analysed the build-up to genocide, and challenged the role France had played in arming the Habyarimana regime. Smith, however, cut a lone figure with his analytic efforts. Like most of their English counterparts, French journalists covered intervention issues (Goma refugees; *Opération Turquoise*) but not the genocide itself. At the time of *Opération Turquoise*, as Smith told Hilsum in an interview, 'coverage in France of the French army's "humanitarian mission" was largely positive. "The broad public opinion was that France was the only nation to care about human suffering. They did something and then got out, but by that time everyone wanted them to stay. Most people would say it was a success"' (Hilsum 1995a). Besides detailing Rwanda's 'tropical Nazism' (see Chapter 1), Smith outlined the role of the '*réseau zéro*' death squads, the psychology of genocide, the ever-present colonial legacy, the likelihood of RPF reprisals, and the role of France, which, for Hutu extremists, remained '*notre seul pays ami*'. The French government was paying dearly for its fidelity to Habyarimana.[14] *Libération* also published official letters which showed how France's Ministry of Development Coopera-tion had organised the escape to France of Habyarimana's entourage. Nonethe-less, despite Smith's analysis and the revelations in support of it, the French media continued to focus predominantly on their country's 'positive' relations with Habyarimana's Rwanda.[15]

Facing complex realities

In contrast to the Hutu Power ideologues, who emphasised sharp ethnic contours and the threat of Tutsi hegemony, and grossly distorted social realities, the RPF and its Western sympathisers campaigned to inculcate the opposite view, namely that all reference to ethnicity was nonsense. This ideology drew considerable support, particularly in Britain and the US. Without significant pre-1994 links to Rwanda, but being progressively drawn into the crisis, Britain, the US and The Netherlands were all treated as *tabulae rasae* on which the RPF version of Rwandan history and society could be inscribed. The effort paid off in Britain, where there was no particular school of thought on ethnicity in Rwanda,[16] and worked equally well in the United States, where leading historians on Rwanda and eastern Zaire were sidelined. But it did not work so well in The Netherlands, where exposure to Belgian and French journalists and academics resulted in a more empirically grounded debate.

RPF revisionism, here defined as the campaign to rewrite the tenets of Rwandan society and history as they came to be understood after independence, did not surprise Belgian or French newspaper readers. On the same day the London-based African Rights organisation 'informed' Dutch readers that histo-rians and anthropologists saw eye to eye on the subject of Rwanda's ethnicity and history,[17] Belgium's Axel Buyse reminded his readers of some long-standing disagreements:

The 'ethnic' opposition between Hutu and Tutsi has caused a real little war involving local academics, africanists, former colonists and a whole range of people who, for one reason or other, have something to do with the region. . . . Against the 'Belgian' version of Rwandan and Burundian history [which stressed the pre-colonial roots of ethnic divisions], a 'revisionist' historiography has sprung up over the past few decades. With the support of French academic J. P. Chrétien, Burundian intellectuals – Tutsi – have put forward hypotheses which strongly relativise the 'ethnic fact' and reduce it to an opposition between 'social groupings' whose profiles would have been entrenched by the Belgian (colonial) authorities.[18]

But Buyse did not reject Chrétien's relativist position as such. While he discarded the suggestion, popular among Tutsi intellectuals, that the European colonisers would have invented the ethnic classification, Buyse accepted that Belgian colonists had intensified and 'systematised' (his term) existing ethnic divisions, thereby thwarting any future cross-category movements. On a previous occasion, Belgium's Secretary of State for Development Cooperation, Erik Derycke, had also reminded the press of Belgium's colonial legacy: the administration had fixed Rwanda's already ethnicised social categories.[19] Derycke highlighted that the majority of Tutsi had been poor in pre-colonial and early colonial Rwanda, and warned against romantic interpretations.

Working under tremendous psychological pressures (Hilsum had been caught up in the genocide; De Temmerman regularly had nightmares),[20] gradually becoming aware too that the genocide had been meticulously planned, and aware that certain high-level French authorities protected the genocidal regime through its ambiguous *Opération Turquoise*, it was little wonder that serious journalists often halted their attempts to separate information from disinformation. As conditions demanded empathy, concerned journalists became less likely to ask awkward questions of the RPF, at least for a while, and more likely to embrace its interpretation of the struggle. This process would peak with information shutdown in eastern Zaire some two years later.

The conviction that the RPF produced the more truthful account on society and history was strengthened also by the seemingly watertight logic of the anti-aid lobby within New Pan-Africanism. The thought that emergency aid kept killers alive, even helped them to rearm, nauseated journalists and (many) aid workers alike. It was thus that, particularly in Britain, a politically correct perspective emerged. Slowly but surely, 'the truth' about Rwanda and the Great Lakes began to boil down to a condemnation of the business of humanitarian aid (African Rights 1994c; Uvin 1998). With the tide turning against 'the refugees', a new intellectual climate emerged in Britain and the US, a climate inspired by moral righteousness but crippled by its blind faith in the absolute objectivity of the RPF/government of Rwanda perspective. Critics of the RPF were quickly branded irresponsible, immoral, and in league with *génocidaires* (see Reyntjens 1999b).

It is not my intention to criticise journalists for their lack of ethnographic knowledge, even though many journalists acknowledged its relevance when they first reported the crisis in eastern Zaire, but rather to expose how the knowledge gap came about and was exploited to maximum benefit by the post-genocide regime in Kigali, from where Kagame perfected his doctrine of information control.

Understanding the 'Old' Rwanda

Media ignorance about Rwanda and its past manifested itself early on in the crisis in two ways: first, in the way 'tribalism' entered the reporting; and second, in the way certain journalists acted as scribes for the RPF's rewriting-of-history project. Aptly described as one of Rwanda's priority *development projects* (Jefremovas 1997: 1), this rewriting activity focused mainly on pre-colonial history.

In Britain, the RPF's narrative was most actively nurtured in Fergal Keane's award-winning *Season of Blood* (1995 Orwell Prize), which is an instructive example of how the pressures of war journalism – ignorance about the place, strict deadlines, trauma and empathy – may combine to produce and legitimate a seductively simplistic, distorted version of history as we know it; a version deemed 'politically correct'. Ignorant about Rwandan society and history, ignorant too about the quality of scholarly research since the end of colonialism, Keane was game for the interpretation of his RPF guides. Alerted, rightly, to the racial fantasies found in early colonial writings, Keane went on to assert that *contemporary writings* on ethnicity in Rwanda were 'fanciful nonsense, a carry over from the colonial era' (Keane 1996: 15). Keane's message: dear reader, do not waste your time with anything written between independence and 1990, the point at which the RPF invaded Rwanda and began to educate the world.

Keane's uncritical acceptance of the RPF's version of Rwandan history contrasted starkly with his exceptionally brave and enlightening effort *at the time of the genocide* to get to the heart of the matter. In a BBC Panorama programme broadcast on 27 June 1994, Keane had effectively challenged all received wisdom on the nature of the killings. Starting the programme with an interview of political Hutu moderates whose families had been wiped out in the early killings, Keane threw tribalism out of the analysis. He also interviewed killers, imprisoned by the RPF, who revealed they had known their victims well and had killed for reward. And he confronted the RPF with evidence that their shelling of Kigali did result in civilian casualties and not, as the Front claimed, simply in the deaths of government armed forces and *interahamwe* militias. Most courageously, Keane interviewed Tutsi survivors at Nyarubuye, then took their testimonies to Benaco camp in Tanzania where he confronted the *bourgmestre* who had ordered and taken part in the slaughter. In dangerous circumstances, he showed the interviews and asked: 'Would you go to court if people accused you of crimes against humanity?' It was more than exceptionally courageous. But, and this epitomises the longer-term trend in reporting the Great Lakes, after debunking the myth of centuries-old tribal killings, Keane, in *Season of Blood*, fitted a lens of moral sympathy with the RPF cause and uncritically embraced the world-view of those who had come to represent the victims of genocide.

Dismissing the academic literature off hand, Keane's potted version of Rwandan history boiled down to an account of how one type of clientship, the *ubuhake* cattle contract, had shaped ethnic relations over time, and done so with harmony. The RPF officers in Keane's entourage approved of the cattle focus. Simple to grasp, and a good soundbite too, this focus effectively exposed the arbitrariness of ethnic relations in the modern era. Unfortunately, though, the exclusive focus on cattle obscured those complex yet fundamental developments that had emerged in the second half of the nineteenth century, when King Rwabugiri expanded the central court's rule. Grounded mostly in the loss of rights in land and control over labour, these complex relationships were too unwieldy for media consumption and would, in any case, not have been useful in getting across the message that the incoming RPF was above ethnicity. Only a strongly simplified narrative could convey such a message.

Keane reproduced the RPF's reductionist version of how Hutu–Tutsi–Twa relations had evolved:

What separated Tutsi and Hutu in the past was primarily a matter of occupation and wealth. Thus the Tutsi clan owned large herds of cattle, while their Hutu subjects farmed the land and the Twa subsisted on what they could gather in field and forest. As time progressed many Hutus bought cattle and were assimilated into the Tutsi aristocracy. Some Tutsis became poor and lost their privileged positions. (Keane 1996: 12)

Keane's referring to 'the Tutsi clan' (but which of the eighteen clans was that?)[21] and to 'many Hutus bought cattle' did not stem from empirical research, nor did Keane understand that Rwabugiri broke the power of the land-owning Hutu lineages whose territory he conquered. Once Keane had bought the line that past research amounted to 'fanciful nonsense', he happily but naively reproduced those aspects of history which his RPF guides heralded as defining moments. Thus he accepted the all-revealing significance of 1933, the year Belgian colonists introduced ID cards and took away the 'possibility of elevating oneself from the peasant classes to the aristocracy through the purchase of cattle . . .' (1996: 17). This cattle business, however, as empirical research had shown, was just one mechanism in the development of a complex set of social and political relations under Rwabugiri – and one not all that significant to common people (see Chapter 3).

To his credit, Keane also noted some off the cuff comments by his RPF mentors which revealed the spirit in which three decades of research on society and history was being rubbished. In the heat of battle, RPF officer Frank, the guide of whom Keane wrote that he 'was too intelligent a man to act as a propagandist for the RPF' (1996: 138), once said: '"Now there is only one way to finish this. The killers must be defeated, completely and totally. If you compromise with people like this you are finished. They will be at your throat in a few weeks, maybe even a few days' time"' (Keane 1996: 139). A final solution, no compromise. In another moment of unchecked honesty, another RPF guide also departed from the party line to reveal that '[in] pre-colonial Rwandan society . . . [the] Tutsi nobility that dominated the centre of Rwanda stressed the importance of physical stature, that is, they claimed their tallness and aquiline facial features were synonymous with superiority' (Keane 1996: 12). Such generous clues notwithstanding, Keane fully accepted that the Rwandese Patriotic Front, whose guest he was, had no interest in ethnicity.

Ethnographic ignorance was revealed also in the way the term 'tribal killing' was used,[22] and used over and over again.[23] This happened despite the fact that concerned scholars like Catharine and David Newbury,[24] and Alison Des Forges, had already warned journalists that Rwanda's lethal madness was not a case of centuries-old tribal warfare. In the second week of the genocide, Des Forges wrote in *The Washington Post*:

Politics, Not Tribalism, Is the Root of the Bloodletting. . . . As the piles of bodies mount in Rwanda, commentators are pulling out their generic analyses of violence in Africa: anarchy and/or tribal conflict. Content with ready-made explanations, they overlook the organized killings that opened the way to what has become chaos.[25]

The danger that ethnicity, if understood, might be the sole reference point for analysing Rwanda, also loomed large. The RPF spoke of ethnicity, but what of class? Some journalists knew class to be important in the genocide, but found it difficult to bring class into focus. This could be seen, for instance, in Robert Block's extensive review of the Rwandan tragedy where he referred to the slaughter in Rwanda as 'not exclusively tribal' (so tribal nonetheless), before stressing that 'a shortage of land had been at the core of the Hutu–Tutsi struggle'. Failing to explain the land issue in depth, readers unfamiliar with Rwanda may well have inferred that the minority Tutsi had owned or controlled disproportionate amounts of land.[26] Simple but misleading associations hinting at the interchangeability of ethnicity and class appeared also in major television documentaries. At the height of the crisis in eastern Zaire, the British Broadcasting Corporation (BBC1) ran the following visual:

Tutsi = cattle owners; rich elite; tall

Hutu = peasant farmers; lower class; small (Philo 1998: 36)

By pitting 'rich Tutsi' against 'poor Hutu', the BBC produced a seriously distorted image of ethnic and class relations before the genocide.[27]

There were stumblings, too, in the American press. Assessing the situation in mid-July 1994, commentator William Pfaff (*Los Angeles Times*) both praised the RPF and expressed concern, which gave balance, but failed to grasp the basics of society and history. In an article on *Opération Turquoise*, in which he successfully tackled some 'big questions' on democracy, world order and international intervention, Pfaff gave the impression that he supported the long discredited

Hamitic hypothesis popularised during early colonial rule. The hypothesis held that every trait of civilisation in Africa had originated from outside the continent. Pfaff resuscitated essentialist stereotyping:

> The struggle between Hutu and Tutsi is not simply an ethnic rivalry. The spectacularly tall, cattle-raising Tutsis historically were the rulers of both countries [i.e. Rwanda and Burundi]. They are a Caucasoid people who arrived in the region four centuries ago, probably from Ethiopia, to subjugate the peasant Hutus.[28]

The image of centuries-old tribal warfare, which is what Pfaff upheld despite using the term 'ethnic', was reinforced by Jennifer Parmelee, who wrote from Addis Ababa that Rwanda had been 'wounded by recurrent tribal pogroms'.[29] Entitled 'Clan Rivalries Threaten Africa With Upheaval', the article reviewed thoughts by some eminent historians and political scientists, but made no reference to any research by specialists on Rwanda. The stark reality of newspaper journalism in the US was that American historians of Rwanda failed to make a lasting impact on the media – and this despite their important early contributions.

A further factor in the genocide, the paramount role of Rwanda's north–south divide, also received scant attention in early commentaries in the press, and was certainly not understood in its full historical context. Hilsum provided a useful reference: 'The tensions in Rwandan politics were exacerbated. Being a Hutu was not enough, you had to be a Hutu from the president's northwestern region.'[30] This resonated well with Des Forges' warning that the Rwandan tragedy was not about 'tribal killings'.[31]

Understanding the 'New' Rwanda

If the international press, with notable exceptions, had generally failed to understand and analyse the genocide, how did it report on political developments after Rwanda's new Government of National Unity was sworn in? The period here covered runs from 15 July 1994, when the war was still ongoing, until 1 August 1994, when the government was in place. First we take a look at the continental European press.

In the continental European press

As the 1990–94 war entered its final phase, seasoned Central Africa correspondents exercised caution when pondering the legitimacy of the RPF. Colette Braeckman, although unequivocally supporting the Front, spoke of 'relative legitimacy' and did not rule out that the defeated government might recoup some of its own legitimate power. For that to happen, Braeckman wrote, the former government needed to urge Rwandans still in Rwanda 'not to hurry along the routes of exodus'.[32] In *De Standaard*, Buyse, more sceptical about the RPF, also stressed that the Front still needed to become legitimate. Acting upon the UN call for a cease-fire would be an important first step.[33]

Concern over the RPF's legitimacy was sometimes linked to the idea that the Front itself had played a part in causing the refugee exodus (see also Chapter 5). The Front might therefore need to share responsibility should the crisis escalate *in the region*. The likely flashpoint was Masisi, North Kivu, which had witnessed a spate of massacres the previous year. Buyse commented: 'The influx of hundreds of thousands of Hutu could turn North Kivu into a cauldron far worse than what Rwanda already is.'[34] Similarly, in the Dutch *NRC Handelsblad*, Jannes van der Wijk, a doctor with Médecins Sans Frontières in Kivu since 1992, voiced the opinion that refugees needed urgently to return to Rwanda if ethnic conflict in eastern Zaire was to be avoided.[35] With tens of thousands of *génocidaires* now in Kivu, it was most conceivable that their presence would fuel an already tense situation. Zaire's Banyarwanda Tutsi, many of them 'old caseload' refugees with overt RPF sympathies, could be targeted[36] – which, indeed, is what happened in 1995 and 1996. By flouting the calls for a cease-fire, calls Rwanda's Prime Minister designate, Faustin Twagiramungu, wanted to heed, the RPF cleaned out some very unwanted elements from Rwanda and increased the likelihood of renewed violence across the border. This likelihood, van der Wijk argued, cast a shadow of doubt on the RPF's legitimacy.

In reflecting on Rwanda's new government, the Belgian press also homed in on how the Arusha Accords were being circumvented. Papers allotted space to dissident parties formerly opposed to MRND (Habyarimana's party), and now opposed to the RPF. Joseph Ndahimana, spokesman for the Rwandan socialist party (PSD) in Belgium, listed the main deviations: the five ministerial portfolios earmarked for MRND, now disqualified, had all gone to the RPF; Rwanda's president Pasteur Bizimungu had been appointed for five years instead of the agreed twenty months; the position of vice-president (given to Paul Kagame, already defence minister) had been created *after* Arusha. Kagame's position as vice-president, Ndahimana said, violated the agreement that the military would not be part of government.[37] Arusha was dead. Elsewhere, Nkiko Nsengimana, coordinator of IWACU and also opposed to Habyarimana's MRND, voiced similar concerns.[38]

Heavily criticised, too, was the RPF's plan for re-educating the Rwandan population, particularly its refugees and the numerous intellectuals among them. RPF officers were regularly quoted. Lieutenant Faustin Kaliisa, chief of the RPF's political department in Gisenyi, was reported to have said:

'We shall re-educate the population on its return; lightly in the case of peasants, more profoundly for the educated, for instance through organising a month-long seminar on the political history of our country.'[39]

Quite a contrast emerged between the RPF's easy-going attitude at the border whenever journalists turned up,[40] and the Front's determination that all, and especially educated Hutu refugees, needed to be re-educated. Just before his appointment as the Minister of Rehabilitation, Jacques Bihozagara, then RPF spokesman in Brussels, reinforced that only innocent refugees would return, the rest would be written off as criminals:

'We think we can work out a programme for repatriation. But, there will be some decanting: only the innocent will return, the rest will be guilty of massacres.'[41]

These prophetic words ended a particular controversy in which journalist Braeckman had claimed that the notion of a selective return amounted to *disinformation*. When Jean-Marie Colombani, director of *Le Monde*, had argued that the RPF only wanted to see illiterate peasants return to Rwanda, not intellectual Hutu,[42] Braeckman had responded that she was picking up signs of 'disinformation and manipulation'. She accused Colombani of bias against the RPF.[43]

Journalists also focused on the disinformation Hutu extremists spread. De Temmerman, for instance, recalled an incident following the UNHCR press conference in Goma at which spokesman Ray Wilkinson had said: 'We have received sufficient guarantees that all Rwandans, except those who are responsible for war crimes, will be welcome.'[44] Wilkinson had been challenged by a former minister who alleged the RPF was guilty of atrocities, but this had not stopped a group of refugees from turning their backs on the minister to start the return journey to Rwanda. Not an isolated incident, such defection showed that the camp population was increasingly aware how it was at times being misled by the former authorities.[45] Many returnees, however, had originally been pushed into Zaire against their will; they had fled an escalating war, not the RPF.[46]

Optimism would be dented, though, when civilians inside Rwanda informed UNAMIR and the relief organisations of disappearances and summary executions. In *Libération*, Jean-Philippe Ceppi gave names, dates and places.[47] The subject was so delicate, Ceppi wrote, that UNAMIR soldiers had been instructed not to talk to the press. Braeckman shared the concern over continued RPF exactions, and in *La Libre Belgique* reported extensively on the case of Sylvestre Kamali, MDR president in Gisenyi. In the days before the genocide, Kamali had been linked to the 'Hutu Power' faction of MDR, but after 6 April 1994 had distanced himself from the interim government. While in hiding, Kamali had stayed in Kigali. On 14 July, he was found by the RPF, arrested and taken away. Expressing anxiety over the RPF's way of dealing with justice, Braeckman reflected:

we believed that Faustin Twagiramungu's government had brought with it a justice system that would treat everyone equitably. 'We are going to put in place a credible and reassuring justice system,' the Prime Minister had proclaimed. 'Prejudices and presumptions may exist [within society] but it is the tribunals that will decide.' Since 19 July, however, testimonies confirm that rough justice continues to prevail.[48]

Braeckman also revealed that Kagame, whom she recently had interviewed, was the 'redoubtable patron whose efficacy had been feared even when serving in Uganda, to the point where in 1990 President Museveni had discreetly removed him from the country by sending him [for training] to the United States.'[49]

The multiple concerns which media and aid workers voiced, irrespective of whether they were sympathetic to the RPF,[50] were reinforced when Twagiramungu expressed his own anxieties. He drew a sharp line between the (still to be declared) RPF objectives and what he believed his government should be aiming at. Candidly, Twagiramungu told *Le Figaro*:

'RPF leaders need to be clearer. They have decided on a transition period of five years, but I have no knowledge of the political programme to be installed during that time. Nor do I understand their method for redistributing the population. They justify themselves by referring to the acute need for shelter, but now that the war is finished it is necessary that everyone should be able to return to their region of origin. Why does the RPF not authorise their return? What is the Front waiting for?'[51]

One year later, following renewed complaints and hints that he lacked power within his own government, Twagiramungu was fired from his post.

The continental European press had revealed Twagiramungu's differences with the RPF also on previous occasions, as when he, unlike Kagame, had favoured complying with the UN request for a cease-fire. Kagame and the prime minister were not seeing eye to eye.[52] At this point in their dispatches, many journalists and commentators felt serious discomfort: how could they condemn the genocide and express confidence in the RPF-led government, yet simultaneously help articulate the voices that spoke of continued human rights violations? Were violations haphazard or planned? Would they evaporate with time? Would the differences between Twagiramungu and the RPF be resolved? Newspaper journalists made readers aware of the importance of addressing Rwandan politics.

In The Netherlands, Wim Bossema's search for balance was instructive in this respect.[53] Bossema, a foreign affairs editor, reported the differences of opinion between Twagiramungu and the RPF, but he defended the latter's determination not to hold a cease-fire. Agreeing with the RPF that a cease-fire was inappropriate as long as its demands were not met,[54] Bossema accepted that too much concern with humanitarian issues could cloud one's political analysis. Without a political solution, humanitarian aid was futile. Crucially, however, Bossema also asked: *whose political analysis is clouded?* Is there only one analysis to be considered? Bossema could not agree with everything the RPF said. Extending his reader's political horizon, he warned that the RPF – *not Twagiramungu* – would blunder if the RPF rejected the participation of francophone units in the UN troops that would patrol post-genocide Rwanda (UNAMIR-2). Twagiramungu wanted their participation, including that of French soldiers, but the RPF rejected his request. Although an outspoken critic of *Opération Turquoise*, Bossema maintained a balanced approach by arguing that refugees and IDPs would look with the deepest suspicion on a UNAMIR-2 devoid of troops conversant in French.[55] Rwanda's Government of National Unity was split over the constitution of UNAMIR-2, and Bossema acknowledged the importance of that split.

As Rwanda's new government was sworn in, leading media workers in Belgium, France and The Netherlands declared that Rwanda might be heading towards a better future, but would do so only on condition that the cycle of impunity be broken. They thought direct aid to Rwanda legitimate, particularly if funds rehabilitated the justice system, but saw no reason why the RPF-led regime should be exempt from scrutiny regarding its own violence. Journalists and commentators were under no illusion: Rwanda's new government was not united on every aspect of the struggle, and strong-man Kagame, though he had won the war, had not been greeted as a liberator. No one in the continental European press, not even the RPF-sympathisers, would call the Front a liberating army. The government's legitimacy, it was agreed, was not a given but had to be earned. And the RPF, it was increasingly understood, had a sophisticated, well-rehearsed way with the media.

In the American press

Despite picking up the early signals that spoke of disagreement within the new government, the US press never developed any great interest in Rwandan politics. Disagreements were noted in relation to the time frame for future elections and regarding the role of officials who had served in the former government,[56] but the interest in internal politics faded fast once the Clinton Administration recognised the RPF-led government (29 July 1994) and prepared to send 2,000 US troops to reopen Kigali's airport for relief flights (30 July 1994). Now the prime focus for discussion, the role of the US military, dwarfed all else. America's ambassador to Rwanda, David Rawson, explained that Clinton was sending troops on a 'purely humanitarian' mission: 'Our only objective is to get help to the suffering people as quick as possible and by any means.'[57] Several high-ranking US officers added reassuring phrases for the troops and their families.[58]

Now that continental Europe had begun to understand that something was brewing in Kigali, US journalism dropped the interest in Rwandan politics to dwell on the deployment of US troops. As the troops reopened Kigali airport, Steve Vogel (*Washington Post*) reported from Entebbe on where exactly in the airport the Americans would be positioned. Vogel also reported how America was divided on whether the US should play this policing role in the world. Whilst his job was to cover the expected arrival of US soldiers, not to analyse

Rwandan politics, the dispatches' narrow focus raised questions about how media priorities are set. Media coverage being compartmentalised, the not negligible issue of a country's internal politics is all too easily dropped in favour of some international aspect. That there is a price to be paid for this, often in the form of slippage, became visible in some of the coverage, as when Vogel referred to 'the new Tutsi government in Rwanda'.[59] Ditto for a piece by Keith B. Richburg, the *Washington Post* reporter specialising in African crises who, writing from Goma, also failed to distinguish between the RPF and the Rwandan government.

The [US] troops going to Kigali will be going at the invitation of the government in place, the Rwanda Patriotic Front, which seized Kigali after weeks of heavy fighting.[60]

The word 'invitation' served to allay fears that Rwanda might become another Somalia.[61] The media, it seemed, was being used as a vehicle to convince Americans that Rwanda was like Uganda – safe, worth supporting, and with a future.

Uganda indeed was a focal point in the press. When specialist advice on 'the New Rwanda' was sought, papers readily turned to academic specialists familiar with Uganda but without experience of Rwandan society, history or politics. Almost by definition, specialists were sympathetic to the RPF and the new government, which the US had recognised within hours of the swearing-in ceremony. The mood was partisan. Nelson Kasfir, political scientist and Uganda expert, had this message in *The New York Times*: Museveni and his National Resistance Army (NRA) have shown they can govern, restore peace and bring back stability; Kagame and the RPF, given their close links with Uganda, will do likewise. Emphasising that Twagiramungu and Bizimungu, both non-RPF, had been selected under the Arusha Accords, Kasfir believed that Rwanda's new regime was 'likely to be the start of a broad-based government similar to that of Uganda'.[62]

Likely to be the start. Kasfir also hailed the fact that the RPF held less than half the ministerial portfolios ('I think there can be no more proof of generosity than that') and praised President Bizimungu's ability to understand the importance of inclusion. Of Kagame he wrote:

[The] appointment of Major General Paul Kagame, the front's chief military commander, as vice president and minister of defense, also allows a pattern that General Museveni established in Uganda, the iron fist in the velvet glove. He has allowed much government participation as well as personal freedom in Uganda, but he has kept careful control over the army. The Patriotic Front is likely to do the same.[63]

Likely to do the same. What Kasfir presented to the US public (and later, in translation, to Dutch readers)[64] was analysis by analogy, not a contextualised reading of Rwanda's social and political scene. Rwanda's specific challenge centred around the co-habitation of socially mixed, ethnic groups who share a language; a situation quite different from the set-up in Uganda. Kasfir, moreover, made no reference to the tense relationship between Kagame and Museveni in early 1990, no reference to the likelihood of heightened instability in the Great Lakes region, no mention of the growing concern over arbitrary arrests and disappearances, and no mention of the rift between Twagiramungu and Kagame. The message had to be upbeat – and it was.

The *New York Times* that same day also carried a separate article in which it was claimed:

Specialists plausibly argue that years of living and fighting in Uganda, where ethnic strife has been tamed by reconciliation, has moderated the [RPF] leadership.[65]

Which specialists? Rwanda specialists? Because such questions were not asked, one ended up assuming that Kasfir himself may have been the specialist in question. But the desired effect was produced: with the seal of 'specialist' approval America could rest assured that Rwanda's RPF-led government was a moderate, cohesive body about which no further questions needed to be asked. It was what the RPF and the Clinton administration wanted everyone to believe, and it sounded convincing because media coverage of Rwanda prior to the genocide had been virtually non-existent (see Livingston and Eachus 1999). Rwanda's new government was now increasingly put in a positive light because 'it include[d] a substantial number of Hutu, including the President and Prime Minister'.[66]

In the British press

In Britain, coverage of the RPF and new Rwandan government ran somewhat, though not entirely, along political lines: *The Guardian* and *The Independent* voiced concerns; *The Times* praised Kigali's new leaders. Overall though, and here the reporting paralleled the tendency in the US, there was little focus on Rwandan politics. The focus was on Goma and its refugees, who lived and died in overcrowded camps. This emphasis on the humanitarian over the political and the military, as Hilsum (1995a) later explained, was due in part 'because editors think their viewers and readers have a limited interest in complex political events far away,' and in part because of a lack of political and strategic interest.

How close did newspaper journalists come to understanding Rwandan politics? After the murder of three Catholic bishops in Kabgayi, just as the war escalated, Richard Dowden wrote in *The Independent* that the murders added 'a ghastly new dimension' to the crisis: the RPF's relatively good reputation was tainted. Up to now, the guerilla fighters had 'seemed disciplined and well-organised' and had not perpetrated the massacre of women and children.[67] The Kabgayi murders provoked new questions about the good-guys image, even though the RPF blamed the murders on upset, renegade soldiers. A further blow to the image came when an Anglican bishop gave his first-hand account of RPF atrocities during the seizure of Gitarama, and accused the Front of systematically killing civilians. Chris McGreal commented that 'the bishop, who declined to be named, because he fears for his family's safety, is a Hutu. But his account is substantiated by Tutsis whom he protected from the militias and helped escape to Zaire. None was able to estimate the number of people killed by the RPF, but said the atrocities were not isolated incidents.'[68] McGreal advised the 'international community' not to give the RPF *carte blanche*.

The RPF is not guilty of atrocities similar to the genocide against the Tutsis. But it has carried out systematic summary executions of those it identified as responsible for the slaughter. They often included government officials, whether or not they had a direct hand in the killings.

The RPF has also not shown restraint when civilians get in the way of its military advance. Combined with the [former] administration's vicious propaganda, the effect has been to convince large numbers of Hutus that the RPF intends to exact a revenge as bloody as the extermination of Tutsis.[69]

In 'Rwanda: Question Time', a special feature in *The Independent on Sunday*, Charles Richards reiterated that the RPF had shown restraint during the war, yet he too worried about longer-term developments.

[Given] the bitterness and hatred created in the past three months, on top of decades of mutual resentment, it is hard to see a spirit of reconciliation taking root. On both sides, moreover, there are wild men ready for more killing. The newer recruits to the RPF, many of whom have lost close relatives in the Hutu massacres, may not prove as disciplined as the Uganda veterans.[70]

For a comparative analysis, Richards looked to Burundi, not Uganda, stating that 'neither in Rwanda in the past nor in Burundi at the present have Tutsis ever shown any inclination to share power with the Hutus. Rwanda is likely to exchange one-party majority rule for one-party minority rule.'[71]

The Times, in contrast, took a more benevolent view. For Sam Kiley, Africa correspondent, the political challenge was not how better to discipline the RPF, but how to undo the propaganda of the former Habyarimana regime. Kiley's thoughts diverted attention away from intra-government bickering, much in the way that US papers dwelled on the parallels with Uganda, on the impossibility of a Somalia-BIS, or on opinions within the US. Kiley wrote: 'No evidence of widespread or systematic massacres committed by the [RPF] front has emerged over the past three months', and 'Years of propaganda have convinced the Hutu population that they would be slaughtered if they were overrun by the Front'.[72] The RPF was a restrained, morally superior force. Its 'problem' was that we – all of us, Rwandan and non-Rwandan – needed to acknowledge the Front's moral strength and legitimacy. It was not a question of the RPF needing to build up its legitimacy, a point developed in the continental European press, it was more a matter of restoration, of undoing decades of propaganda and disinformation.

The Times' pro-RPF stance remained firm. In early March 1999, after exiled *interahamwe* killed Ugandan guards and Western tourists in Bwindi National Park in south-western Uganda, *The Times* (4 March 1999) ran a substantial background sketch in which Linda Melvern recalled the rationale and method of the genocide, referring to the '20 years Rwanda was ruled by a clique who came from the north'. Melvern's review bore the stamp of political correctness RPF-style in that she omitted the elements needed for a more comprehensive framework: it said nothing of the 1972 genocide of Hutu in Burundi which preceded those 20 years, nor of the assassination in 1993 of Burundi's first democratically elected president, Melchior Ndadaye, which had sent shock-waves and masses of refugees across the border into Rwanda. Melvern's account of Rwanda's problems did not connect with the traumas, and the interpretation of these traumas, south of the border.

The omnipresence of propaganda and disinformation meant that many journalists turned to humanitarian workers active in the camps.[73] This resulted in a growing awareness that refugees were misled, that their fears of the RPF were unfounded, that the exiled Hutu militias were spreading exaggerated stories of RPF atrocities – 'lies, horror stories' (Ray Wilkinson, UNHCR) – to keep innocent civilians in the camps. These militias, Robert Moore wrote after visiting Goma,

are now destroying their own people. They forced them to flee with apocalyptic warnings of what the Tutsi-dominated Rwandese Patriotic Front (RPF) would do once they won the war. And now the militias – organising in the camps – are trying to prevent the refugees from returning home. In their grotesque logic, it is better to have Hutus dying of cholera in the camps than to have them living within Rwanda reconciled with the RPF.[74]

While Moore's statement applied to the camps in a general sense, care was needed not to exaggerate the power of these horror stories. Disinformation was at work, but, even without the horror stories, many refugees, innocent ones included, preferred not to return to Rwanda (compare de Dorlodot 1996; Godding 1997). And conversely, horror stories notwithstanding, a great many did return to Rwanda (De Temmerman, above; see also Chapter 4).

Refugee-centred reporting, much of it dwelling on heroic humanitarian deeds, meant that newspaper readers did not acquaint themselves with what Twagiramungu had to say on the matter of his government's troubles. Under-reporting on Rwandan politics, which can be explained in terms of the 'lens of moral sympathy' (Gowing 1998) through which journalists had begun to look at Rwanda, was common to most anglophone journalists, irrespective of their papers' political colour. Some journalists, as just seen, did report aberrations by RPA soldiers, but even they do not appear to have paid attention to the tense relations emerging within the new government.

Reporting Kibeho

The distinction between continental European coverage, which regularly looked in on Rwanda's internal political problems, and anglophone reporting, which lacked such a focus, was accentuated with the Kibeho massacre of April 1995. The result was a momentary silencing of anglophone journalists previously critical of the RPA. In looking at media reactions to the massacre I shall restrict myself to a summary of salient points, as I have previously published a review of the press coverage of Kibeho (Pottier 2000).

As the last of the camps for Internally Displaced People (IDPs) to be closed under the UN-led *Operation Return*, Kibeho had sheltered an unusually high number of hard-core Hutu militias. This concentration of criminals was one reason for the high tension preceding the tragedy. The hard core had formed slowly but surely in the days other camps were being closed. While many IDPs had gone home following the closure of their camp, others had simply moved on to camps still open.[75] When tense RPA troops lost patience with the last of the IDPs, who still totalled some 100,000, soldiers fired into the crowd and killed a vast number of people, possibly several thousands. Present in Kibeho, freelance journalist Linda Polman and Julian Bedford of Reuters wrote chilling eyewitness accounts.[76] The exact number of dead would never be established, not even by the international commission of inquiry (see Chapter 5).

Following the Kibeho massacre, the Belgian press showed considerable understanding as to why the tragedy had happened and gave voice to Rwandan officials. Jacques Bihozagara, the minister for rehabilitation, and Prime Minister Twagiramungu, both in Brussels at the time, stressed in their immediate reactions that the campaign to close the IDP camps had not been 'a hidden operation'; the displaced, the UN and the humanitarian organisations had all been informed of the time frame. The claim was generally well received. In *De Standaard*, for instance, often critical of the RPF, it was accepted that expressions of indignation by UNHCR and UNAMIR over the 'short notice' for closing Kibeho were hypocritical.[77]

But, and this did not go unnoticed, the Rwandan ministers in Brussels also held separate conferences at which they articulated opposed views on the number of dead, and on whether the RPA had acted in self-defence. Not challenging UNAMIR's initial estimate of 4,000 fatalities, Twagiramungu accepted that the number, whatever it was, '[exceeded] every conceivable dimension.' An inquiry would be held, he added, to establish whether the killings had been 'a case of legitimate defence or deliberate action'.[78] The following day, interviewed by *De Standaard*, Twagiramungu went further still. Acknowledging there had been no casualties among the RPA troops, the prime minister said:

'the great number of dead gives the impression that the army action was well and truly prepared. In which case we have no option but to condemn the intervention.'[79]

Bihozagara, in sharp contrast, disputed the figure and stressed that IDPs had been used by their leaders as 'human shields', an argument few observers would have disputed. Bihozagara also hinted at the futility of any subsequent 'independent' inquiry by insisting his ministry had already established that only 'several hundred' had died.[80]

Belgian politicians generally shared Twagiramungu's concern about the RPA. In *Le Vif/L'Express*, Senator Claude Bougard (Ecolo), back from a mission to Rwanda, said: 'the RPA is no longer the disciplined army it used to be. Many of the original soldiers have been killed and it has brought into the fold new recruits of the 11th hour who are insufficiently trained.' Journalist Rogeau added that the RPA, omnipresent in Rwanda's towns and hills, had now taken on the roles of policing, political education and prison surveillance.[81]

A mixture of understanding and condemnation also marked the reporting by Braeckman, who regarded the carnage at Kibeho as a disaster that had been waiting to happen.[82] The IDPs had been controlled by hard-core extremists, while government officials had constantly reminded the camp residents that no one guilty of genocide would be spared. These reminders notwithstanding, ultimate responsibility had to rest with those who, for so long, had terrorised Kibeho and its environs. With justification, Braeckman also blamed the overall UN peacekeeping operation; not once had the operation attempted to separate extremists from innocent civilians. The government of Rwanda had repeatedly asked the UN to undertake such a separation.[83]

Braeckman's critical stance against the international community did not mean, however, that she was blind to the escalating security problem posed by the Rwandese Patriotic Army. She acknowledged that IDPs had often left the camps only to return to them later after being 'chased from their communes through fear of the omnipresent army'.[84] Rwandan leaders, Braeckman asserted, needed to share the blame with the international community, and the latter had every reason to be concerned about Kigali's muscle flexing.[85] Her reaction was to plead for more direct support to the new regime, but her condemnation of the massacre was just as strong as that of the Dutch minister of development cooperation, Jan Pronk ('not an incident, but a prepared plan'), or that of Belgium's Eric Derycke, now foreign affairs minister ('brutal and unrestrained action by the Rwandan military').[86] The new government, Braeckman concluded, stood to lose its legitimacy.[87] This mixture of criticism and strong empathy in Braeckman's reporting has to be acknowledged, even though she later 'compensated' with some excessively rosy home-sweet-home return stories involving IDPs from Kibeho. Eager to praise the RPF-led government, Braeckman used the 'happy family' vignette to suggest that not all was gloom and doom for the former IDPs.[88] Her life histories of the glad-we-are-back variety did not necessarily distort the truth, but attentive readers will have noticed the omissions: What about other returnees? What about the innocent now arrested and imprisoned? What about the relatives of the Kibeho dead?

In contrast to Braeckman, De Temmerman presented a more balanced account of the homecomings. Her vignettes shared some of the optimism, and she duly stressed the diversity of experience at the commune level, but she also highlighted the problem of double occupancy (i.e. IDPs finding their homes and farms occupied by 'old caseload' repatriates). De Temmerman explained the serious risk returning IDPs took when pressing for the recovery of their occupied property.[89]

Other journalists also expressed concern that 'the mechanism of denunciation' had begun for the formerly displaced; there was a Rwanda-by-day and a Rwanda-by-night. In *Libération*, Jean-Philippe Ceppi fully acknowledged the grave threat the ex-FAR and *interahamwe* posed in camp and commune alike, but he was equally concerned over the never-ending disappearances and summary executions as the RPA strengthened its grip on the population.[90] By the time Kibeho happened, the rehabilitation of Rwanda's civilian administration and justice system was firmly being steered by the ministry of defence. The army had infiltrated the justice system and posed a threat to any civil servant who disagreed with its orders. The anxieties Ceppi articulated were confirmed in the Dutch press when Hens Kraemer, an anthropologist who had served as a human rights observer in Kibuye in early 1995, argued that the UN peacekeeping force was unable to exert any pressure on the RPA.[91] It was a similar anxiety which had made François-Xavier Nsanzuwera, the public prosecutor in Kigali, flee Rwanda in the weeks before Kibeho. Following the massacre, Nsanzuwera called for more direct support to the Rwanda government, but said his main concern was that 'the Rwandese Patriotic Army and the RPF's political cadres interfere in matters of justice. The judiciary fear the army.'[92] Of the RPF's political cadres, or *abakada*, Nsanzuwera confirmed they were behind '"the resurgence of the phenomenon of disappearances", which were not infrequently linked to struggles over goods, land or houses. The right to property was no longer respected.'[93]

In sum, regardless of their political persuasions, continental European journalists expressed considerable understanding for the pressures the Rwandan government had endured as a result of the failings of the international community. However barbaric, it was possible to comprehend the actions of the

RPA. But equally important, journalists balanced criticising the 'international community' with *highlighting the power struggles that were unfolding within Rwanda.* The presence in Brussels of two ministers at the time of the massacre, preceded by the defection of Kigali's public prosecutor, had helped to achieve this. Even when overtly sympathetic to the new regime, journalists did not feel they had lost the right to criticise. Rwandan politics, readers could appreciate, did have a life of its own.

It is on the need for a dual focus on matters international and internal that coverage in the British and American press took a strikingly different direction. Seemingly still unaware of the ever-tense relations within Rwanda's government, the anglophone press came to be dominated by *a singular concern*: Kibeho's international dimension.

For Sam Kiley in *The Times*, the Kibeho tragedy resulted from two issues. First, '[t]he camp, in which Hutu militiamen were active, was a permanent threat to the Tutsi-dominated government army, whose fellow tribesmen [sic] were the main victims in last year's genocide'[94]. Second, the RPA had cracked under the unbearable conditions the country suffered, conditions resulting from international indifference and dithering. Kiley quoted a long-serving European diplomat in Kigali:

'There is absolutely no excuse for the behaviour of the RPA in these massacres. But they [the Rwandan authorities] have been begging for the international community to help them to break up the Hutu militias inside Rwanda and in the refugee camps in Zaire and Tanzania, and we have done absolutely nothing except make sure that those responsible for the genocide are fed, watered and sheltered. There is no great surprise that the RPA has finally cracked, the pressure cooker blown.'[95]

While the failings of the international community were deservedly underscored, the absence of a critical look inside the Rwandan government was equally striking. There was no mention in Kiley's report of the gaping divide separating Twagiramungu/MDR and Bihozagara/RPF, nor of the deep frustration Twagiramungu had expressed over his government's failure to control the RPA, a frustration shared by Rwanda's ambassador in Brussels.[96] Instead, *The Times* quoted Twagiramungu, now in Paris, where he defended the RPA's action as a 'legitimate response'. (It was hardly surprising that Twagiramungu hardened his tone in Paris. France, after all, had a lot to answer for.) Readers of *The Times*, it seems, remained unaware of the much franker exchanges the prime minister had had in Brussels, so they continued to assume that the Rwandan government spoke with one voice.

Journalists who earlier had been sceptical of the RPF and its agenda also remained silent on political tensions within Rwanda; they explained the RPA excesses solely in terms of the lack of direct international support. Thus McGreal condemned the excessive force ('there was no immediate threat to soldiers to warrant such action'), but deemed the claim to self-defence justified: the RPA had been 'motivated not only by the anger over the past but in defence of the present and the future'. Understanding Kibeho meant accepting that the RPA had wearied of the West's fickleness, that Kagame's soldiers had lost patience, that their discipline had weakened, because they knew 'the outside world [was] more concerned with the human rights of the [genocidal] killers than their victims.'[97] McGreal appeared to have moved across to the School of Political Correctness: helpless Rwanda, under a united government, had every right to feel aggrieved. To understand 'the New Rwanda' one needed only to grasp international politics and attitudes. Of individual politicians and their parties, of the presumed cohesion within government, no questions were asked. From now on, and in line with the increasingly accepted tenets of New Pan-Africanism, Rwanda was to be viewed solely as a casualty of international indifference. McGreal writes

So when the Rwandan government decided to defy the UN and weather the loss of whatever international sympathy there may be by sending the RPA into Kibeho, it knew what it was doing. The government decided the price of international goodwill was no longer worth the cost of allowing the camps to stay open on Rwandan soil. RPA soldiers finally had the chance to take revenge.[98]

The carnage had been rational, calculated, deliberate.[99] And ordered by a government united in its vision on how Rwanda was to be rebuilt.

Coverage of Kibeho in the US press also glossed over matters internal to Rwanda. In the *International Herald Tribune*, Donatella Lorch reconstructed what had happened on the fatal day and stressed that many Hutu had been killed in cold blood. The barbarity of the killings was undeniable. The piece ended, however, with the well-meaning though rather flat words of Shaharyar Khan, the UN special envoy to Rwanda, who said that 'something went horribly wrong in Kibeho'.[100] Strikingly, yet typically of US reporting, there was no analysis of Rwanda's internal political scene. Readers were given a historical perspective on the crisis *generally*, but it did not inform on current affairs. Two days later, when Lorch speculated on the repercussions a possible suspension of aid might have, the impression created was that Rwandan politics did not have a life of its own, and that any sign of internal tension could be remedied with an injection of external assistance.[101] The international dimension dominated. The absence of questions on issues internal to Rwanda was apparent also in Lorch's handling of how Kibeho IDPs fared on returning home. Happy-ending stories, similar to Braeckman's cameos, was the preferred technique. Lorch reported returns free of trouble for the same commune, Gashora, where journalist De Temmerman later interviewed its *bourgmestre*. The latter openly admitted he faced some intractable problems.[102]

Kibeho was a turning point in anglophone reporting on Rwanda. The desire to know what was going on inside the country – in the communes and in government – had weakened considerably. *Rwanda was now imagined as a place where every set-back could be explained exclusively in terms of international indifference.* The guilt which accrued to the failure to cover the genocide, mixed with the considerable psychological pressures exerted on visitors to Rwanda after the genocide, had lessened the appetite for scrutiny. It was not just that journalists used a lens of moral sympathy, but also – as I will show in Chapter 5 – that according to the Rwandan government, the 'international community' had lost the right to an independent view on matters Rwandan. The consequences of this loss would be more clearly understood the following year, when the RPA crossed into Zaire to assist 'the Banyamulenge' with their military campaign.

War in eastern Zaire, 1996–97: Kagame's new way of doing things

Post-mortems on how the conflict in eastern Zaire was reported (Gowing 1997, 1998; Hilsum 1997; Ryle 2000) conclude that the media paid a high price for the moral legitimacy it granted Kagame. Journalists fudged the issue of ADFL/RPA aggression, war crimes and crimes against humanity, and realised only too late they had fallen victim to Kagame's powerful doctrine of information control. The price paid – the 'fixation' that all Hutu were 'genocidal maniacs' – originated in the guilt-ridden failure to cover, and thus to help prevent, the 1994 Rwandan genocide.

Going beyond this critique, yet fully accepting it, I shall suggest that (newspaper) journalists were also actively involved, *albeit mostly unwittingly and only for a short period of time*, in helping to legitimate the ADFL campaign. This they did through arguing, or strongly implying, that the Alliance was homogeneous and representative of all in eastern Zaire, and by ignoring or underestimating Rwanda's role in the Banyamulenge uprising. Like that new generation of instant academics who viewed Rwanda's pre-colonial past as harmoniously balanced (Chapter 3), manipulated journalists ignored evidence about society and history that could cast doubt on the self-image the Alliance projected. The ethnic turmoil in North Kivu just before the Rwandan Hutu refugees arrived, which could have been used better to pinpoint potential rifts within the ADFL, was especially ignored, as were the relationships that had developed in the 1960s between Kabila, Banyamulenge Tutsi, Rwandan Tutsi refugees and autochthonous groups. It is remarkable that most journalists who covered the Banyamulenge uprising and ADFL campaign were *initially* well aware that they needed to grasp local politics and history if they wanted to understand the ADFL *as a movement*. In-depth knowledge was not needed to understand the revolt itself, but was essential if one wanted to make sense of the reception that awaited the ADFL as it approached Kinshasa.

During the 1996–97 crisis in eastern Zaire, the ADFL briefed journalists on its own terms, i.e. on terms that continued the logic of 'moral simplification' already perfected in Rwanda: the analysis of international politics was 'in', and close scrutiny of issues internal to eastern Zaire was 'out'. Not encouraged, in other words, was a focus on land, the very issue at the heart of the (underreported) ethnic clashes of 1993, which had pitted Banyarwanda (Hutu and Tutsi) against the 'autochthonous' groups whose militias were set to join the Alliance. The approach to local history the ADFL did encourage was as follows: events highlighting the persecution of Zaire's Tutsi population were favoured (1981, 1994–96), but not any episodes (1964–65, 1992–93) that might lead to scepticism regarding the ADFL's claims of homogeneity and full local backing. If 1964–65 was brought into the reporting, it was best done in a way that highlighted Kabila's long struggle for justice. Globally speaking, anglophone newspaper journalists took heed and suspended their *initial understandings* of the political history of eastern Zaire. By late November, and now severely constrained in their reporting, many journalists accepted that the ADFL's common agenda – toppling Mobutu, revitalising Zaire – mattered above all else.

The suspension had its price. While it did not affect journalists' ability to probe the root cause of the Banyamulenge uprising, and many journalists did a fine job highlighting the role refugees had played in racialising anti-Banyamulenge sentiment, the suspension did impair the ability to understand the ADFL as a situated political movement. Insufficient knowledge of local politics and history made journalists fall for the simplified 'official' narrative of a representative Alliance-solution, driven by high political ideals and destined to bring democracy to Congo-Zaire. Some journalists, however, would reconsider as the ADFL closed in on Kinshasa.

It was different in the continental European press, especially in Belgium, where journalists and commentators remained more aware that Kivu's complex politics might backfire. Here, the press regularly reminded readers of the fragility of inter-ethnic ties, mostly by referring to North Kivu's 1993 clashes over land. These clashes suggested that the ADFL alliance could have its Achilles tendon. Journalists and commentators also reminded readers of a further potential weakness, namely that Banyamulenge, as 'Banya-Mulenge' in the original sense, had resented and actively opposed the 1964 'Muleliste' rebellion in which Kabila had served. Kabila had had good links with certain Rwandan Tutsi refugees who had fled the pogroms in Rwanda, but these Tutsi were not to be confounded with the Banyamulenge who had lived in eastern Zaire for over a century and more. 'The Banyamulenge' needed unpacking. Pro-ADFL reporting did occur in the Belgian press, notably in dispatches by

Braeckman, but her interviews had such a strong local flavour that attentive readers could easily conclude, as I will here show, that the ADFL was anything but united.

Reporting the origins of the crisis

When news broke of a revolt in eastern Zaire, some continental European journalists and commentators knew they lacked information. In *Le Vif/L'Express*, Olivier Rogeau acknowledged that only a handful of specialists knew about 'the Banyamulenge'. Estimating their number to be between 100,000 and 200,000, even though ADFL spokesman Müller Ruhimbika had already set it at 400,000, Rogeau gave this backdrop:

These cattle keepers began leaving Rwanda at the end of the eighteenth century following a dispute with King Yuhi. With their herds, they moved into unoccupied territory around Uvira, settling at an altitude of 1,800 meters. They decided on their name ('the people of Mulenge', a locality in the region) during the 1970s to end their treatment as foreigners, as Banyarwanda ('people from Rwanda').[103]

Not all in the media recognised the importance of times long gone. One common misconception to which the international community contributed, though perhaps unwittingly, was to regard 'the Banyamulenge' as a large ethnic group, fully indigenous to Zaire and with a population of about 300,000 to 400,000. In the worlds of media and humanitarian aid, many accepted the figure unquestioningly.[104]

Despite the virtual absence of historical references to 'Banya-Mulenge' as an ethnic category – a term which, as Depelchin notes (Depelchin 1974: 70), had lost its 'basis' by the early 1970s – the international community was prepared to accept 'the fact' that Banyamulenge were an ethnic group, large and authentic. In doing so, the community actively contributed to the making of an ethnic group. International opinion, as Reyntjens and Marysse observe,

found itself confronted with a situation it could not easily comprehend. It thus took recourse, notably through the vehicle of the press, to simplistic schemes which ignored the historicity of the situation. For example, international opinion quickly embraced the concept of a 'Banyamulenge rebellion' even though there are no 'Banyamulenge' in North Kivu where most of the military operations were taking place. (Reyntjens and Marysse 1996: 4)

Informed analysts argued, therefore, that 'the Banyamulenge' were an imagined construct that needed downsizing. The Montreal-based *Table de Concertation sur les Droits Humains au Zaire*, for instance, calculated there could only be about 25,000 genuine Banyamulenge.[105] If the ADFL's information officers went for a much higher figure, they clearly aimed to amplify the local character and seriousness of the military operation.[106] Or, as Zairean politicians alleged, the high figure and authentication turned Zaire's Tutsi into a smoke-screen category with which to hide the armed invasion from Rwanda, Uganda and Burundi.[107]

The prosperity of Banyamulenge, area specialist Willame told the press, had been a thorn in the side of Zaire's autochthones, who had 'never appreciated these Tutsi entrepreneurs who continually cross boundaries, control commerce and have obtained from the Zairean authorities immense tracts in Kivu on which to graze their cattle'.[108] The latter privilege had been granted after Banyamulenge assisted Mobutu in crushing the 'Muleliste' rebellion of the 1960s. Willame's sketch may have underexposed the vulnerable side of Banyamulenge society and economy, as suggested in Chapter 1, yet the revelation of a historically evolved tension between Banyamulenge and non-Rwandophone groups in South Kivu was useful to anyone eager to understand the situated character of the ADFL.

Other continental European papers also dwelled on the uneasy relationship between Banyamulenge and autochthones. Thus the *Financieel Ekonomische Tijd* ran a feature in which the Rwandan NGO Traits d'Union Rwanda recalled how the close link between Mobutu and some influential Banyamulenge (and Banyarwanda Tutsi) had backfired during the 1992 National Conference. After explaining that the link had resulted throughout Kivu in resentment and 'antipathy ... against Tutsi in general', a feeling aggravated when Zaire-based Tutsi joined the RPF in 1990, Traits d'Union Rwanda reflected:

At the 1992 National Conference, a crucial moment along Zaire's path to democracy, participants spoke against the Banyamulenge and other rwandophone groups. The conference was in the first instance a settling of scores by the people of Zaire against Mobutu, who still favoured 'the Rwandans'. Moreover, once the RPF had taken power in Kigali, many Tutsi who had always claimed to be Zairean wasted no time moving back to the Rwandan capital.[109]

The resentment Kinyarwanda-speakers faced originated in Mobutu's divide-and-rule politics, which in turn was reinforced by Kivu's steadily worsening scramble for land and other resources. This local context, well highlighted in some Belgian papers, received attention also in *Le Nouvel Observateur* where Claudine Vidal, another area specialist, made some pertinent points. Kivu's problem, Vidal argued,

is very complex.... To say, as is often done these days, that Banyarwanda and autochthones co-exist without a history is incorrect. Since 1965, several hundreds of Banyarwanda – Zaireans of Rwandan origin – have been massacred in Masisi in attacks related to land or cattle but 'ethnicised' by local politicians. The catastrophe began on 29 June 1981, when Mobutu, for purely electoral reasons, had a wicked law passed which deprived Banyarwanda in Kivu and Shaba of their Zairean nationality [granted only a decade ago]. In the wake of this law, which effectively turned Banyarwanda into scapegoats, there was a proliferation of exactions, thefts of land and cattle, lootings, and an escalation of abuse by civil servants and the army. In 1991, massacres began in North and South Kivu. Throughout 1992 and 1993, several thousands of Banyarwanda, both Hutu and Tutsi, were assassinated.

Finally, in 1994, the influx of [Rwandan] Hutu refugees, surrounded by the army and the militias responsible for the genocide, brings real disaster to Kivu. Brutally, an ethnic rift tearing Hutu and Tutsi apart emerges at the heart of the Banyarwanda population. In the summer of 1996, significant massacres of Tutsi are perpetrated by Rwandan militias – Hutu based in the refugee camps – aided by Zairean soldiers.[110]

These Rwandan Hutu militias and the FAZ were sometimes joined by Mayi-Mayi militias who 'represented' (a term to be used cautiously) certain autochthonous groups. In the already mentioned background sketch, Traits d'Union Rwanda clarified that Mayi-Mayi 'aim to expel the Kinyarwanda-speaking population from eastern Zaire, across the border and into Rwanda'.[111] The need to situate the ADFL players in the context of eastern Zaire was particularly important because of a key paradox: autochthonous rebels disliked both Mobutu and Banyarwanda, which implied that their allegiance to the ADFL would be short-lived.

In the early days of reporting the crisis in eastern Zaire, journalists across the board showed a healthy interest in local politics and history. As *The New York Times'* principal reporter, James C. McKinley Jr did a great job explaining the Banyamulenge revolt, showing awareness of the existence of different agendas within the ADFL. McKinley explored the plight of Banyamulenge in relation both to the nationality crisis and to the Rwandan genocide, and suggested there was compelling evidence that RPA troops were operating in eastern Zaire. Approvingly, McKinley quoted an aid official who had said tongue-in-cheek: 'When you put one and one together, there are no Banyamulenge out there in that region.'[112] Demonstrating the improved ability of the American press to cover African affairs (see Ryle 2000), McKinley also knew that the precarious position of Banyamulenge could be explained in terms of the politics of Kivu: 'longstanding feuds . . . over land and cattle'; feuds in which politicians representing groups not of Rwandan origin had gained the upper hand since 1981.[113] McKinley, in other words, acknowledged what Vidal had argued in *Le Nouvel Observateur*: Kivu had its history, and we did well to pay attention.

However, since attention to local society and history was likely to make the reporting excessively complex, McKinley, like other journalists, was forced to opt for easier explanations. Easier, yet still broadly valid. McKinley commented: 'While there are a bewildering number of combatants, all with slightly different agendas, the fighting convulsing Kivu province in Zaire boils down to this: Tutsi forces in Rwanda, Burundi and eastern Zaire have struck back at their enemies and are trying to reassert control over an area that was part of their ancestral kingdoms'.[114] 'Tutsi forces', McKinley had already explained, had lost control 'in 1910, when the European powers arbitrarily changed the border separating Zaire and Rwanda'; a decision through which 'the Banyamulenge [who had] migrated to the fertile high plateaus above Lake Tanganyika's western shore at the end of the eighteenth century . . . became Zairians'.[115]

The importance of McKinley's early reporting is that his initial explorations of local social complexity, his awareness of 'different agendas', was not sustained in the long run. Once it became necessary to ask questions of international import, a necessity which coincided with the ADFL shutting down the war zone, McKinley, like other journalists, would drop his interest in the Alliance's 'different agendas'. His reporting became more partisan, more pro-ADFL.

British newspaper journalism followed a similar trajectory. As the first Western reporter to arrive in Uvira after it fell to Banyamulenge troops, Chris McGreal quoted a rebel soldier as saying: 'We know where Zaire learned to persecute us. We had problems before, but when the Rwandan Hutus arrived after that it was clear we were going to have a lot of problems.' This Mulenge fighter stressed how his 'ethnic group' had been victimised since 1981. McGreal gave a short historical backdrop,[116] then reflected:

once the Hutu militias had settled into the camps they wanted to carve out a territory from which to fight their way back into Rwanda. Their ambition fell on Banyarwanda land [in Masisi], and they found willing partners in the Zairean army and other ethnic groups. Two years of attacks drove 150,000 Banyarwanda from their homes; 15,000 people were killed. . . .

[This happened also in South Kivu, where the] real problems [again] began with the arrival of Hutu refugees. The young militiamen among them exploited simmering resentment at past grievances and the Banyamulenge's relative prosperity.[117]

At this juncture, there was every chance that McGreal's account of the origin of the revolt, an account perfectly adequate, would be enriched with additional information. But this begged many questions. How did 150,000 Banyarwanda come to be displaced? (And were they Banyarwanda, autochthones or both?) Who were the 15,000 killed? Who were the 'other ethnic groups'? And how did the events in North Kivu in 1996 relate to the ethnic clashes of 1993? A more complex analysis beckoned. In the end, though, these issues do not appear to have been probed much further (although McGreal would expose that Kabila lacked popular support in Kivu); not, that is, until about March 1997 when the importance of the ethnic factor resurfaced. The suspension of an interest in local/ethnic agendas may have been due to the ADFL not tolerating such curiosity, or perhaps because detailed knowledge of pre-1994 history was not needed to understand the origins of the revolt, or perhaps because the intervention debate had become so very compelling. In any case, when news broke of the attacks on the refugee camps, along with claims that RPA troops had entered Zaire, the media interest in truly local matters faded quickly. Reporting conditions, with journalists banned from the war zone itself,[118] facilitated the change in focus from local to international issues.

The reporting pattern – an initial interest in local society and history ending abruptly – could be found also in other papers. In *The Independent*, for instance, as Banyamulenge took up arms to fight the FAZ, David Orr offered a close look at recent history, highlighting not only the nationality crisis but also, and perceptively so, the way local Zairean politicians successfully played the ethnic card whenever it suited them. In late October, a good two weeks before the Rwandan refugees returned *en masse*, Orr wrote:

The fighting, which began a few weeks ago, has its roots in animosity between the region's indigenous Zaireans and the Banyamulenge, ethnic Tutsis whose origins in the Mulenge mountains of South Kivu go back 200 years. The settlers, who number about one-third of a million, are widely resented because of their superior wealth in cattle and land.

Since they were denied Zairean citizenship in 1981, the Banyamulenge have become a marginalised force. With elections planned for next year, some of Zaire's politicians have decided to play the ethnic card by whipping up local jealousies. Earlier this month, the Banyamulenge were ordered by the deputy governor of South Kivu to leave Zaire 'or be hunted down as rebels'.[119]

That ethnic relations had been tense *before July 1994* was revealed also in the story of Nyandwi, a young Zairean Tutsi woman who had escaped across the Rwandan border. Nyandwi was persecuted because of her mixed parentage: she had 'a pure Zairean' father and 'a Tutsi' mother. Telling Nyandwi's story in *The Independent*, Mary Braid reflected:

Her separation on racial grounds had come in 1993, before the mass exodus of a million Hutu refugees from Rwanda into eastern Zaire. There had always been local discrimination against Zaire's Tutsis but the influx of so many Rwandan Hutus, many with blood on their hands after the genocide of up to 800,000 of their Tutsi countrymen, escalated tensions.

Hutu extremists, using the UN's Zairean refugee camps as a power base from which to hit at the new Tutsi-led Rwandan government, made local politicians more audacious. A few weeks ago they warned Tutsis who had lived in eastern Zaire for generations to leave or face extermination. The Tutsis chose another path, and for Nyandwi the rebels who yesterday seemed to have taken Goma arrived just in time.[120]

Under difficult circumstances, Orr and Braid, like McKinley and McGreal, worked hard to come to grips with local complexity, 'conceptual hazard' (Ryle 2000), and did so with considerable success. But equally important, what they (and other journalists) had learned about local society and history in the early stages of the reporting seemed forgotten once the ADFL began its long march toward Kinshasa, as will be shown shortly.

With the ADFL assault on the refugee camps, the international dimension of the crisis took over. New questions abounded: Had Rwandan troops invaded Zaire? Should the UN respond? What role, if any, should the international community play? Did the West understand it was embroiled in this crisis? Could France, calling for intervention, be trusted? At short notice, journalists and commentators found themselves at the cutting edge of a new challenging debate regarding the present world order, which, quite naturally, diverted their gaze from local politics and history. ADFL leaders welcomed the debate – and the diversion it offered.

The international dimension

Despite vehement denial by Kigali officials, few journalists failed to report the presence of Rwandan government troops (RPA) on Zairean soil. In fact, it was RPF sympathisers more than anyone else, journalists like Braeckman (*Le Soir, La Libre Belgique*) and Kiley (*The Times*), who seemed least troubled by being open about the RPA presence. Braeckman unreservedly accepted that RPA troops had crossed into Zaire and had done so with US military support.[121] Kiley wrote that Zaire's 'Tutsi citizens' had 'received the backing of about 2,000 Rwandan soldiers from their tribe.'[122] Other journalists concurred: 'the Banyamulenge "rebellion" has more and more the appearance of a concerted operation by Rwanda . . . while the tragedy now unfolding in Kivu looks more and more like an invasion';[123] 'the CIA knows damn well that the war in eastern Zaire was prepared and launched from Kigali';[124] the procrastination over a UN-led intervention initiative 'suits Rwanda's Tutsi leaders perfectly'.[125] In *The New York Times*, McKinley Jr, too, reported that Goma had fallen 'to Zairian rebels and Rwandan troops' and 'that Rwandan artillery and gunboats had helped the rebel advance.'[126] McKinley followed this up with a detailed account of how Mugunga camp, that last bastion of Rwandan Hutu extremism, had fallen in a pincer-movement.[127]

As the fighting intensified and the fate of Rwanda's Hutu refugees became uncertain, the focus of the reporting moved to international responsibilities. It was the moment the humanitarian community became acutely aware of how 'the refugees' it had protected and fed were to be blamed for the escalating anti-Banyamulenge sentiment. Watching what would be dubbed a 'diplomatic ballet' (Reyntjens 1999b), the world media pondered what kind of intervention, if any, could be both desirable and feasible? Should French calls for intervention be heeded? Did anyone understand what was going on in eastern Zaire? Would the US commit troops in the run-up to a presidential election? What should intervention aim at: reaching refugees inside Zaire or assisting them with repatriation? Would a UN-led intervention force disarm the Rwandan Hutu militias and ex-FAR? How could one stop the racism of Zaire's government?

How would Rwanda and 'the rebels' react should an intervention force arrive? The list was endless.

There was also the vexing question of why the UN was taking so long to identify the conflict's belligerents. As Mugunga camp was about to be destroyed, Stephen Smith put it succinctly:

The UN has yet officially to identify the belligerents, the UNHCR yet to condemn those who attacked its camps with heavy weaponry, and the myriad of humanitarian organisations, who with The Vatican call for humanitarian intervention military style, . . . yet to denounce those who effectively prevent them from delivering aid. Why would one send troops if there is no enemy?[128]

Causing serious discomfort among humanitarians, the questions raised were a breakthrough in reporting; a breakthrough which demonstrated how New Pan-Africanism had wrought a paradigm shift in international opinion on aid and intervention.[129] Some journalists had harsh words for the humanitarian international aid effort, now accused of being 'blinded . . . to the long-term consequences of allowing the situation [in eastern Zaire] to fester.' Humanitarians, Michela Wrong argued in *The Financial Times*, may well breast-beat in public but they have learned little from their past sins. Applauding the ADFL rebels' brilliant timing and courage, Wrong praised agencies opposed to the proposed UN-led intervention, especially Britain's Save The Children Fund. These agencies had finally understood they have bad habits, that they 'scream for international action but wash their hands of the implications'. By not screaming, their 'philosophical bankruptcy' could be purged.[130]

Commentators also encouraged comparison. In *The International Herald Tribune*, David Rieff, author of *Slaughterhouse: Bosnia and the failure of the West* (1995), wrote:

From the civil wars in Somalia and Bosnia to the current crisis in Zaire, it has been the international aid agencies that have most strongly and consistently called for military intervention. . . . But to intervene out of humanitarian concern without any idea of *what comes next* often does as much to worsen the situation in the long run as it does to alleviate things in the present.[131]

Rieff's critique raised issues of phenomenal importance. In the Kivu context, however, informed concern, asking 'what comes next?', implied, as it should everywhere, that one is prepared to learn about local realities in some detail and prepared to listen to a plurality of local voices. This barely happened. The debate on the international presence in the Great Lakes became so compelling – and this under conditions of information shutdown and heightened media control – that it diverted the attention away from the local politics which journalists had addressed early on in the crisis. For many, it was the point of no return. When, after the fall of Mugunga, ADFL officers allowed journalists back into Kivu, the media continued to think globally: awkward questions, whether about the 'missing refugees' or the odd make-up of the ADFL, were no longer a priority. If journalists wanted to avoid eviction from eastern Zaire, a real threat, they did well not to upset the powers in the land.

Most journalists chose the easy route: full sympathy with 'the Tutsi', no sympathy with 'the Hutu' (Gowing 1998: 44).[132] Gowing quotes an MSF head-of-mission who believes that the media failed to question the US briefings on 'missing refugees' because '[it] fitted the media perception that Hutus were the problem and needed to be coped with.' As journalists had no way of checking the US aerial photogrammetry and questioning its interpretation, and no desire to challenge the ADFL rulers, they chose to accept. Another NGO representative told Gowing: 'It was not always so much that the Rwandans managed information, but that the media went for the easier stories' (1998: 45). This resonated well with Paul Kagame's own view: 'We knew how the media works. We never told lies [but] we omitted things' (1998: 35).

What did the authorities omit? Information about the existence of conflicting agendas within the ADFL, for instance, or regarding the way the Alliance was perceived in eastern Zaire. Only occasionally did journalists ask; when they did, the answers were frank. To the question 'Kabila, a leader?', one Kivu trader responded:

'He's merely a puppet in the hands of the Rwandan government . . . In reality, it is the Rwandese Patriotic Front which is here. Tutsi have been preparing themselves for some time for this attack on Kivu. . . . It's the region and its riches they are interested in – not Zaire.'[133]

What did others think? One mama in Goma said of 'the rebels', by which she meant Banyamulenge from South Kivu,

'they may have come for Mobutu, but also to take revenge. It's mixed and we, we don't know.'[134]

This mama knew her history.

Situating the ADFL as a political movement

It would be disingenuous to suggest that 'the local scene' in eastern Zaire was ever easy to comprehend. If anything, the scene was often confused and especially so once the Mayi-Mayi had made their entry. When in the midst of battle, six Mayi-Mayi turned up at a Zaire–Rwanda border post, McKinley wrote of eyewitnesses who had seen them 'dancing naked, taunting the Rwandan troops across the border separating Goma from Gisenyi'.[135] Providing context was not easy. Had these Mayi-Mayi really taunted? And if taunting was the right term, had they done so because of irreconcilable agendas or by way of 'celebrating' the newly agreed partnership? – a partnership which everyone knew would not last. It was difficult to tell.

Kiley faced a similar problem of interpretation when telling the story of Cironi Munyangabe, a Tutsi who had fled Sake following an alleged massacre of Tutsi by Mayi-Mayi.[136] Kiley wrote:

Weak with hunger from hiding in banana plantations while the Mai Mai slaughtered Tutsis in his village, including his uncle, Mr Munyangabe swam 15 miles across . . . lake [Kivu] to safety in the rebel-held port of Goma.

'I didn't know much about the Mai Mai. They just came out of the forest, naked, and started shooting. They said they were going to hunt down all the Tutsis,' he said pointing at the bamboo stalks that had saved his life. Little is known about the Mai Mai, other than rumours that they practice cannibalism and believe their magic is so strong that bullets turn to water when they hit their skin. 'I didn't see them eat anyone. But I heard that they did,' Mr Munyangabe said.

Mainly members of the Hunde tribe, they had fought for and against almost every group: they have taken on Tutsi rebels, Rwandan Hutu extremist militia and the Zairean army, apparently driven by little else but blood-lust.[137]

Two days later, Kiley continued with 'the facts':

Mai Mai have emerged as a bizarre but important third force. . . . Their aim is to destroy the Interahamwe, the Rwandan Hutu militia behind the 1994 genocide of a million Tutsis and moderate Hutus. . . . The Mai Mai make odd comrades for the rebels, many of whom are Tutsis, because they have slaughtered hundreds of Tutsis around Sake in the past few weeks.[138]

Sifting through bits of information difficult to reconcile, Kiley argued correctly that Mayi-Mayi and 'Tutsi rebels' were odd comrades. Other information, though, was more difficult to place, especially the allegation that Mayi-Mayi had massacred Zairean Tutsi just now when they had agreed to join the ADFL. Kiley did not explicitly address the likely contradiction, but wrote in terms of magic, voodoo and irrationality: Mayi-Mayi were 'mystical', 'voodoo warriors', and 'driven by blood-lust'.[139] An interest in local history and the scramble for resources would have been useful here, might have eclipsed the militias' 'mystique' and blood-lust, and would have drawn attention to a conflict of political agendas rooted in struggles over land.

Aware of each and everyone's agenda, people in Goma expressed surprise on learning that Banyamulenge and Mayi-Mayi had forged a partnership. Some journalists picked this up: 'Goma's Zaireans do not believe in this partnership because they know Mayi-Mayi aim to rid Zaire of its Banyarwanda.'[140] Knowledge of local agendas made McGreal portray the ADFL as one 'jumble of uneasy partners', a hotch-potch alliance unlikely to have the Kivu population

on its side. From the start of the campaign, he saw through the Banyamulenge–
Kabila link:

Mr Kabila says the murder and ethnic cleansing of the Banyamulenge provided the
foundation for the uprising and his rebels' astonishing success in the past month. But he
has his own reason to resent Zaire's Tutsis. Mr Kabila was a follower of the revolutionary
Pierre Mulele at a time when the Banyamulenge were fighting in support of the Zairean
government to crush this rebellion.[141]

At this stage in the reporting, McKinley, too, was aware of Kabila's past and
lack of popular support within Kivu. In mid-November, in an article in which he
praised the mobility and cohesion of the Alliance troops, McKinley warned that
few of Kabila's former associates believed that he could have masterminded
the rebellion. He quoted one of Kabila's former associates.

'Kabila used to brag about his relationship with Museveni,' said Gen. Nathaniel Mbumba,
the leader of three rebellions in Shaba province in the 1970s and 1980s who is now a
member of the transitional parliament. 'Now, all of a sudden he shows up with his own
army, composed of Banyamulenge, and he expects us to believe that he put this force
together himself. Kabila has never had a popular base in Kivu. This is merely a front
operation for the Rwandans and Ugandans.'[142]

The precariousness of 'ethnic' relations in Kivu was a key point, too, for journalist Mon Vanderostyne (*De Standaard*), who clarified the land situation in a
reader-friendly way:

Many years ago, often in exchange for a calf, Hunde in Masisi leased poor lands to Tutsi
cattle keepers. With time the latter enriched these lands and caused envy among the
original Hunde owners, as can be seen here in the town of Sake. As the original owners
[or their descendants] failed to regain the lands, they called in the Mayi-Mayi to fight
Masisi's Tutsi.

Presently, though, Mayi-Mayi have forged a partnership with rebels who for the most
part are themselves Tutsi. The U-turn partnership may have earned them credibility and
legitimacy – even though, if it proves anything, it may demonstrate above all else the
very precariousness of alliances in Kivu.[143]

What Vanderostyne claimed about Kivu society would also prove true of the
Alliance itself. Not only would Mayi-Mayi be 'thanked' once the battle for
Mugunga was won, but also the role of 'the Banyamulenge' would itself be
questioned, although at a later date.

Other journalists, however, perhaps already influenced by ADFL propaganda,
read political virtue in the 'jumble of uneasy partners'. They regarded the ADFL
as having roots in modern party politics; the Alliance was a country-wide movement, not a narrow Tutsi force out to build its empire. Moreover, the ADFL was
firmly united. Even before Mugunga fell, Mary Braid discerned a unity which
would fast become the Alliance's self-publicised trademark.

the Banyamulenge Tutsis, while they appear to have been the main players in the insurrection's first success in South Kivu, are not the only force. It is not even certain that they dominate what appears to be a coalition of at least four political groups linked by one factor: a hatred of president Mobutu, who has presided over the complete collapse of Zaire during a 31-year rule.

Kabila, who leads the rebel Alliance of Democratic Forces for the Liberation of Congo-Zaire, is not even a Tutsi. A Marxist and life-long successionist [sic], he comes from the mineral-rich Shaba province and fought against Mobutu in the 1960s and in the Shaba uprisings in the 1980s . . . Among the rebel soldiers patrolling Goma this week are many non-Tutsis from Shaba, Kasai and Haute Zaire, north Kivu.[144]

Non-Tutsi from North Kivu. What about their loyalty? Might they have anything to do with the animosity Braid's colleague Orr had revealed in his dispatches some three weeks previously? Already, the interest in local politics was fading. ADFL information officers did not encourage such inquiry. That the coalition might contain autochthones who resented the relative prosperity of Zaire's Rwandophone population,[145] was best forgotten.

As some journalists had forecast, by late November, a mere two weeks after offering their services, Mayi-Mayi faced an uncertain future within the ADFL. André Kisasse Ngandu, a chief commander in the Alliance,[146] said in an interview:

'Yes, we found the Mayi-Mayi here after liberating eastern Zaire. We immediately made it clear they had to stop fighting. Those boys have looted and raped on a significant scale. They have now been regrouped in a camp near Sake where they will be trained with a view to their integration into our liberation army. As you can see, we are well organised.'[147]

Kisasse Ngandu saw a role for Mayi-Mayi, but may have overplayed the discipline-and-solidarity card. For Mayi-Mayi the writing was on the wall; already, they were surplus to requirement.

With the Mayi-Mayi exit, it became easier to conceive of the ADFL as a homogenous, all-Zaire political movement; a movement with pedigree in earlier rebellions. An opinion piece by Victoria Brittain in *The Guardian*, published at a time Western governments were pinning their hopes on Kabila's Alliance, offers a revealing glimpse of how history, in this case the 1960s 'Muleliste' rebellion, was to be remembered. It was a highly selective, 'politically correct' kind of remembering. Brittain explained why in the late 1990s, unlike during the 1960s, Kabila would be successful. Compared with his days in the 'Muleliste' rebellion, Brittain wrote:

two things were different. First, eastern Zaire's population consisted mainly of prosperous Tutsis, who had moved from Rwanda years before because land was scarce, and who were not prepared to give up their wealth to a rabble of Zairean soldiers and Rwandan Hutu killers without a fight. Second, they [i.e., this prosperous Tutsi majority] knew Laurent Kabila, veteran of almost every uprising against President Mobutu since the

1960s, and asked him to lead their fight. Mr Kabila is not a Tutsi – an important detail debunking the Tutsi hegemony theory. Mr Kabila, scarred by the failure of the poorly prepared Cuban-led rebellion of 1965, of which he was part, appears to have rejected another such military adventure and settled for a long, hard slog to create small political cells in towns, and literacy programmes and rural co-operatives in mountainous zones liberated since the mid-1970s. His People's Revolutionary Party of that period is now part of the Alliance of the Democratic Forces for the Liberation of Congo-Zaire, of which he is the political co-ordinator. Over the decades the rebels' demands, like the names, have changed and are now decidedly unrevolutionary: they seek free elections under international supervision, and a new constitution.[148]

Although not written from the field, and thus not directly influenced by ADFL information officers, Brittain's characterisation of the Alliance reflects how Kagame's propaganda warfare generated easy narratives guided by the principle of omission. Three major omissions must be noted in her account. First, in claiming that 'the Tutsi' knew Kabila from the 1960s, it is omitted that a distinction had applied between Tutsi refugees from Rwanda (1959–63) who had joined the rebellion and long-term Tutsi residents (Banyamulenge, genuine *zaïrois*) who had resented that rebellion and helped Mobutu to squash it.[149/150] Masking this fundamental distinction, Brittain's 'they knew Laurent Kabila' fitted the ADFL's insistence that Banyamulenge were a sizeable, fully cohesive ethnic group. Second, no mention is made of the 'autochthonous' groups within the ADFL that resented the prosperity of Banyarwanda. The formidable Mayi-Mayi militias may have been interested in toppling Mobutu but they were no long-lost friends of any Banyarwanda. The importance of their *local agenda* was not something ADFL leaders wanted to draw attention to. Third, Brittain's narrative on the campaign also omits how Kabila's maquis (1967–86) had ended in popular disenchantment. Details about the maquis were at the time hidden in grey literature (e.g. MA dissertations listed in Cosma 1997), so journalists and commentators are not to be blamed for not knowing, but the disenchantment lived on in local memory (see Chapter 1; also McGreal, further down). As ADFL officials and representatives were not going to tell or remind the media of the demise of the maquis, they gave Kabila's past successes an air of dogged, heroic persistence: it had been 'a long, hard slog'.

A later profile of Kabila by Claude Wauthier and Stephen Smith in *Libération* provided quite an antidote to Brittain's propaganda piece. Wauthier and Smith recalled Ernesto 'Che' Guevara's far from flattering impressions of Kabila (often drunk and mostly absent from the maquis); the hostage crisis Kabila orchestrated in 1975 (in which he held foreign research students to ransom); and Kabila's role in the late 1980s as a diplomatic emissary for colonel John Garang, the South Sudanese rebel leader, in which capacity Kabila would sometimes be sent to meet Mobutu. On one occasion, in 1988, Mobutu would have sent a helicopter to South Sudan to pick up Kabila. Wauthier and Smith observed how the ADFL leader was now being absolved of his erratic track record and contradictions by an amnesic international community which desperately wanted to believe that Kabila had 'fought Mobutu all his life and that he really intend[ed] to liberate Zaire, that "museum of repression".'[151]

A liberation narrative

During the ADFL's march to Kinshasa, journalists witnessed a defining moment in Central African history: the fall of a political dinosaur, President Mobutu Sese Seko; the dawn of a new era. There was much optimism; some journalists who had initially asked incisive questions about local society and history now seemed to have forgotten the importance of those questions.

James McKinley's dispatches are instructive. Early on in the crisis, McKinley had shown an interest in how ethnic agendas were played out in the scramble for resources (see above); then a few weeks later, by mid-November, McKinley's search for extra or hidden agendas appeared called off.[152] No longer that 'bewildering number of combatants, all with slightly different agendas', the rebels were now presented as *a homogenous force* made up of 'Banyamulenge', who, once their local uprising begun, had been joined quickly by other locals: 'Hunde and Nande tribes[men]' and 'a rebel group known as the Mai-Mai'. All in this rebel collection, McKinley stressed, had recently 'suffered at the hands of the Hutu guerillas and the Zairian army', which certainly was correct, and all disliked Mobutu, which again could not be denied. Because of these common-enemy bonds, the ADFL movement was thought of as united, truly local and backed by 'the people of Kivu' whose interests the ADFL represented. Partnerships within the ADFL had been unproblematic, long-standing feuds were no longer recalled.

Significantly, as the campaign swept across Zaire, McKinley even came to accept that the widespread popular support for Kabila's campaign had dwarfed the importance of Rwanda's military assistance. This acceptance was enshrined in the testimony of a 22-year-old unemployed youth who had signed up for some seminars in 'revolutionary ideology' run in Goma. He told McKinley:

'When it started, we thought Rwanda was the one attacking Zaire. Later, we found out it was a Zairian struggle. I personally believe in the revolution because it's a revolution sustained by everyone.'[153]

McKinley's reporting had fallen in line with what Kagame's doctrine of information control prescribed: the strength of the ADFL, its cohesion and pure Zairean roots needed highlighting. McKinley did express concern about the reports from Masisi that Hutu villagers were being killed 'in outlying regions by the Tutsi rebels', but the ethnic factor, or how combatants construed the past, seemed to play no further part in his overall assessment of the situation. The ADFL was hailed:

Mr Kabila, from Shaba province and a member of one of the non-Tutsi groups, has brought these groups together under an umbrella – the Alliance of Democratic Forces for the Liberation of the Congo.

One sign of the movement's strength is that tens of thousands of young men have joined the rebel army in recent weeks. Every day truckloads of new recruits, some as young as 14, bump through Goma on the way to training camps in the north. The rebel soldiers are known on the street here [in Goma] as Walinda Amani, the Swahili for 'peacekeepers.'[154]

The more the ADFL closed in on Kinshasa, the more its common cause and homogeneity were stressed and applauded. When the Alliance took Mbuji-Mayi, Zaire's diamond centre, Chris McGreal also praised the rebels for being that 'new breed of African military, with relatively disciplined troops, trained to fight, with a cause to fight for, underpinned by a revolutionary philosophy contemptuous of the generation that took Africa to independence'.[155] Zaire's new dawn seemed imminent. With the excitement of the historical moment, there was little time to doubt; optimism regarding the outcome of the ADFL campaign was mostly stronger than the fear of any lingering divisive agendas waiting to resurface. No one could deny that with every town they took, the rebels were greeted as liberators.

The liberation narrative the ADFL had spin-doctored stressed that not too much should be read into the presence of Rwandan and Ugandan troops on Zairean soil. Semantics played its part: these troops had not invaded, they had come to assist. Under scrutiny, journalists and commentators, especially in the anglophone media, began to portray the ADFL movement as entirely home-grown. Unlike in November 1996, when he had kept an open mind on whether or not the war was foreign sponsored,[156] by mid-February 1997, McKinley ruled out foreign sponsorship. The idea of foreign sponsorship, he now argued, was something Mobutu had invented.

From the beginning, Mr Mobutu and his aides have tried to portray the rebellion as a foreign-sponsored attack from Rwanda, Uganda and Burundi, not as an indigenous uprising. He has accused those countries of sending troops to fight beside the rebels and supplying weapons, a charge all three deny. Though there are many ethnic Tutsi among the rebels who speak Rwandan, there has been no independent confirmation of Rwandan or Ugandan troops fighting in Zaire.[157]

The denial machine was in full swing. McKinley had moved away from his previous understanding that Rwandan artillery and gunboats had helped the ADFL advance.

A similar shift occurred in *The Times*, where Kiley also argued that the notion of external aggression against Zaire should have no place in analysis. Despite his earlier statement that 2,000 RPA troops had crossed into Zaire, Kiley now attributed the suggestion that Rwanda had invaded to French propaganda. On 11 March 1997, Kiley wrote:

The imminent collapse of Kisangani to rebels, who have been supported by English-speaking soldiers from Rwanda and Uganda, has sparked a wave of propaganda in France. Yesterday *Libération* alleged that Rwandan Hutus had been massacred by advancing Tutsis in a 'second genocide' aimed at annihilating the Hutu tribe. France sees the rebellion as a question of external aggression by Zaire's neighbours rather than an uprising against the rule of President Mobutu.[158]

And the people of Zaire, Kiley stressed, firmly rejected this French propaganda: 'France is becoming increasingly unpopular on the streets of Kinshasa as Mr Kabila's popularity has increased.'

McKinley, for his part, reconsidered somewhat in early March 1997, when he reported the anxieties 'liberated people' felt about being recolonised. After the ADFL had taken Kindu in typically swift fashion, and the population had cheered, McKinley gave voice to local doubters:

some [locals] say they are wary of the rebel soldiers. Along with Zairian Tutsi and other local people, there appear to be some Rwandans and Ugandans among the rebel forces, including the commanding officers, local people say. In private, some people are expressing reservations about becoming a 'colony' of Rwanda and Uganda.[159]

Still, these same locals were also 'impressed with the steps the rebel administration [had] taken since the city fell into their hands'.[160]

Despite giving voice to local doubters, through which McKinley reconnected with his earlier interest in the politics of eastern Zaire, *The New York Times* remained upbeat. From Kinshasa, correspondent Howard W. French reported that the country's five-month-old rebellion was an attack not just on Mobutu but on an entire political class. The dominant mood was that Kabila would 'copy one of his principal sponsors, President Yoweri Museveni, whose own insurgency seized power in Uganda in 1979, ending years of misrule as catastrophic as any that Zaire has known under Mr Mobutu.'[161] Kabila's agenda would not differ from that of the Ugandan and Rwandan mentors with whom he shared the ideals of New Pan-Africanism. Uganda remained the key point of reference.

Kiley, too, towards the end of the ADFL campaign, acknowledged that Kabila's triumph in Lubumbashi, where a tumultuous welcome awaited him, had not been entirely euphoric. He writes:

some people were anxious yesterday that [Kabila's] Tutsi officers, many originally from Uganda and Rwanda, should not take government positions, and insisted the rebels should hold local elections as they had in Kisangani.

'Tshisekedi [Zaire's chief opposition leader] may be a bit of a joke, but he is at least purely Zairean. He will be a significant factor in the future of the country. We do not want to be ruled by Rwandans and Tutsis; we hate them,' a senior businessman in the capital said.[162]

But Kiley remained optimistic. By referring to the Tutsi officers as 'originally from Uganda and Rwanda', he upheld the image of a military campaign purely internal to Zaire. The rebels, Kiley asserted, were no puppet force even though the operation had 'involved "lending" large numbers of experienced Tutsi offi-cers and guerillas from the Ugandan and Rwandan armies'.[163] With an effective metaphor, Kiley expressed his belief that the ADFL rebels were holding up 'the healing knife' that would cure this sick Zaire.[164] Uganda and Rwanda would remain truthful to their original ambition, which was 'to clear eastern Zaire of Ugandan rebel groups and armed Rwandan Hutu refugees who were destabi-lising their own countries, and to prevent a threatened mass slaughter of Tutsis within eastern Zaire'.[165] Readers could safely assume that the two neighbour-ing states would soon acknowledge Kabila's graduation and scale down their presence in Zaire.

In the anglophone press, serious reconsideration of Rwanda's role in the civil war came only after journalists had seen Kabila openly flirt with the powerful mining houses, not only with De Beers but also with its rival, American Mineral Fields. It was time to ask questions about Kabila's relationship with his backers. Would Kabila stay loyal to Kagame and Museveni? Had 'the Banyamulenge' really asked Kabila to lead their fight, as Victoria Brittain had claimed? It was time to rethink. McGreal writes:

Mr Kabila was plucked from obscurity to head the 'revolution'. He had a longstanding relationship with Uganda's president, Yoweri Museveni, and was known to Rwanda's army chief, General Paul Kagame. . . . [From the beginning of the campaign,] Rwandan troops have led the Alliance's fight to the gates of Kinshasa. . . .

The unanswered question as victory looms is the extent to which Mr Kabila has shaken off his handlers. Rwanda's soldiers continue to call the shots on the ground. The rebel leader's movement has no unifying cause other than Mobutu's overthrow.[166]

Other journalists also expressed doubt. Some ten days after Kiley claimed that the idea of an invasion from Rwanda amounted to French propaganda, Michela Wrong acknowledged in *The Financial Times* that Kabila was adept 'at manipulating the Western media and ensuring a "clean" image of the civil war is presented to the world'. She reopened the case: questions about Rwanda's involvement and longer-term interests in Zaire were still necessary. On 22 March 1997, Wrong wrote that 'analysts have been pondering to what extent Mr Kabila is his own man, to what extent the instrument of the Ugandan and Rwandan governments. The question is prompted by Mr Kabila's career'.[167]

As the ADFL closed in on Zaire's capital, Wrong felt Kinshasa's pulse; it was too early to be confident about what the ADFL stood for. She noted how Kabila always carefully played down his past and often grew irritated when pressed. Perceptively, Wrong suggested that simple dichotomies – especially 'invasion' versus 'pure civil war' – were inadequate. A more open-ended global framework was needed, *the ADFL was still in search of an identity.*

Membership currently ranges from Tutsi fighters from east Zaire's Mulenge Hills to former Katangese soldiers, from veteran bush fighters to academics who recently returned from exile in South Africa, the US and Germany.

'We get the impression it is a very disparate movement, full of opportunists who have been living abroad and want to come back as ministers,' says a Kinshasa-based politician. 'Maybe we can't know what the ADFL stands for until it has worked that out for itself.'[168]

Kinshasa was in the grip of 'an obsession with conspiracy theories', with those still loyal to Mobutu arguing that 'the rebel advance [was] . . . entirely a conspiracy by Washington, in cahoots with puppet governments in Uganda and Rwanda'.[169] Wrong's personal inclination was to play down Washington's alleged interest in Zaire and to reduce the interests of Uganda and Rwanda to being merely the providers of 'heavy tactical support'; Kabila was his own man and the ADFL campaign a strictly internal civil war. Yet, and to her credit, Wrong also articulated Kinshasa's (and the country's) growing fear that Zaire was about to be recolonised.

For the ADFL, the hardest part will not be simply the storming of Kinshasa . . .

They will have to win the hearts and minds of Kinshasa's 5m residents, who have a strong sense of national identity and are sensitive to any suggestion that their new rulers are a Rwandan movement lurking beneath a cosmetic Zairean front. 'A lot of people are saying we want Kabila to bring about change, but we don't want him to take power,' says a businessman. 'We want a real Zairean to lead the country. We are not going to be ordered around by a bunch of Tutsis.'[170]

Fear of colonisation by Rwanda should not be seen as simply a figment of the imagination. There was more to it, although, under the conditions that governed reporting, it was hard to say what.

Questioning the liberation narrative

In the continental European press, the issue of Rwanda's active involvement in Zaire and local people's reservations about the ADFL had never been much in doubt, nor had the cohesion of the ADFL ever been much presumed. As for Kabila's past, there were no illusions about that either.

Never losing sight of the ADFL's faultlines or the lack of popular support in Kivu, journalists queried *early on in the campaign* whether there would be a place for Kivu's autochthones in the new administration.[171] Even more crucially, the question was asked whether Banyamulenge would have a role in Kabila's Congo . . . The difference between anglophone and Belgian reporting was that the former noted the oddity of certain relationships yet stressed the common bond forged by victimisation and hatred against Mobutu, while the latter sensed that the ADFL might not survive under the weight of its irreconcilable agendas. Less than two weeks after Rwandan refugees returned home, journalist Vanderostyne wondered whether Kabila might not jettison the Rwanda/Banyamulenge support to which he owed his success. First, though, Kabila would deal with 'the Mayi-Mayi, . . . who in some newspapers feature prematurely as partners to the rebels. These naked warriors, in actual fact, are the henchmen of just about everyone who is too weak or too lazy to do the fighting themselves.' Next, Vanderostyne argued that 'we may presume that in the very near future they will be ousted as idiots whose usefulness is spent, just like the Banyamulenge might only play a temporary role as catalysts in the conflict'.[172]

Why did Vanderostyne also question the future of Banyamulenge? The reason, simply, was that caution was advised when considering Kabila's link with 'the Tutsi'. Generalisations were not helpful, one needed to distinguish between recent Tutsi immigrants (1959 onwards) and true-Zairean Banyamulenge. Articulated very clearly when Zaire had granted Banyarwanda their citizenship in 1971 (see Bisengimana's declaration in Chapter 1), the distinction was often overlooked, as in Victoria Brittain's adoption of the ADFL narrative. Others, too, were confused. Foreign affairs editor Wim Bossema, for instance, presumed a positive link between Banyamulenge and Kabila going back to the 1960s. Referring to Kabila's past life as a gold smuggler, Bossema told his readers how all that suddenly changed

with the revolt of the Banyamulenge-Tutsi. In the revolutionary 1960s many Tutsi fought in the ranks of Kabila's revolutionary people's party (PRP) and these old ties have now been reactivated. This explains why Kabila suddenly sprang back from oblivion to become spokesperson for the Alliance of Democratic Forces for the Liberation of Congo-Zaire.[173]

Bossema was right that Tutsi had fought with Kabila in the 1960s, but he confused two groups: Banyamulenge who had suffered during the 1960s rebellion and the post-1959 Tutsi immigrants from Rwanda, some of whom had joined the rebellion. The error resulted from manipulation. By November 1996, the officials who put spin on the ADFL campaign had made sure that challenging episodes from the past would be reframed: 'the Banyamulenge' had always been a large ethnic group inside Zaire; all it needed to sound convincing was for journalists to accept this and spread the message.

The uncertain link between Kabila and (genuine) Banyamulenge was picked up, too, in an interview Colette Braeckman had with Kabila in which he revealed that his Banyamulenge force was just one element of the Alliance. Braeckman wrote:

Without minimising the support of the Banyamulenge who enabled him to launch his offensive from Kivu, Kabila nonetheless insists that they are only a minority and that they have been joined by Zaireans from all over the country. 'Right now we are receiving letters of support from every corner of Zaire and even from the diaspora . . .'.[174]

Kabila may have been playing his New Pan-Africanist card here, claiming the movement was above ethnicity, yet he also hinted uncannily that he might have 'plans' for those who had spearheaded his 1996 rebellion.

The possibility that such plans existed transpired even more clearly in an interview ADFL Commander André Kisasse Ngandu gave to Marie-Laure Colson of *Libération*. Kisasse's tone matched Kabila's. After dismissing the links with Rwanda – 'A small neighbour like the rest with whom one has to cooperate' – Kisasse had turned rather talkative:

'This war has no link with the Banyamulenge question. Who are these Banyamulenge? An ethnic group, just like the Bretons are where you come from. In Zaire we have more than 500 ethnic groups. Do you really think such a small ethnic group could possibly conquer such a vast territory?' The Alliance of Democratic Forces for the Liberation of Zaire, of which Banyamulenge are a part, surpasses all ethnic cleavages, Kisasse asserts. 'In 1965, we fought for Bafulero democracy against the same guy [Mobutu] whom we are fighting today.' . . . 'Laurent-Désiré Kabila and myself, we share the same past.'[175]

And who had assisted Mobutu? Colson did not need to ask.

These interviews with Kabila and Kisasse were hugely important in forging the idea that Kabila and Kagame might be on a collision course. On one level, the interviews were clear demonstrations of how the ADFL's 'denial machine' operated (Rwanda and Banyamulenge? not important); on another level, they contained remarks that eerily reminded of where Banyamulenge had stood in 1965. It had not been forgotten. The denials, therefore, carried significant *double entendre*.

The importance of the 1960s, as a memory not erased, came to the fore when Babembe militias attempted to block the southward progression of the Banyamulenge/ADFL. Already in late November 1996, one Belgian paper reported that the Banyamulenge push towards Shaba was thwarted by Babembe militias.[176] In view of Anzuluni Bembe's campaign against Banyamulenge in 1995 (see Chapter 1), it did not come as too great a surprise that some of Kabila's former friends from the maquis, recruited mainly from among the Babembe population, had risen up against him. They were easy to manipulate since they had not taken too kindly to Kabila's 'selling out' to Banyamulenge. On 28 December 1996, *La Libre Belgique* reported:

according to mail received in Belgium from Zairean refugees in Tanzania, Babembe would strongly resist the rebels in the Fizi region (South Kivu), where Kabila held his maquis after 1965. Babembe aim, one letter explained, to prevent 'the Rwandans from reaching Kalemie' (North Shaba, between South Kivu and Moba). The same source alleges that Babembe have killed some 400 'Rwandans' in Fizi.[177]

A place of many histories, Kivu was not united behind the Banyamulenge/ADFL campaign. Yes, everyone disliked Mobutu, but this did not mean they had to like one another. No wonder Kabila always spoke in terms of the solidarity of political parties. The technique, as one French journalist noted in Goma, masked the likelihood of future ruptures appearing within the ADFL: 'No ethnic groups, hence no need for revenge.'[178]

Interestingly, the most compelling evidence that the ADFL was prone to fragmentation and not above ethnicity came from the pen of Braeckman, whose detailed dispatches revealed, though perhaps not intentionally, how the ADFL had far from overcome its internal differences. Braeckman made strong claims regarding ADFL cohesion and local support, but the interviews she conducted in eastern Zaire spoke clearly of internal suspicions and tensions fed by memory. For Braeckman, the fall of Mugunga camp had been a double victory: not only had some 700,000 refugees returned to Rwanda in apparent peace, but there was also the added bonus that Nyanga, Hunde and other autochthones would be ever-grateful to 'the Banyamulenge' for starting the war. One headline read: 'As [Banyamulenge] rebels continue their offensive in Masisi, Hunde, Mayi-Mayi and Kasindi breathe again.'[179] This headline fully captured the shared suffering at the hands of Hutu extremists, but did not address the question of how autochthones and Banyarwanda had been positioned just prior to the arrival of the refugees. A sigh of relief among autochthones? Fear is more likely. Autochthones had every reason to be worried, for the ADFL leadership, they knew, would waste no time before declaring that Mayi-Mayi needed to be disciplined. Braeckman's headline, though, will have pleased the ADFL and its Kigali backers, since it 'confirmed' that the people of Kivu backed the rebellion as one.

Other interviews by Braeckman also allowed readers to see through the smokescreen of a united rebel front. Thus, one Mayi-Mayi commander who explained the solidarity within the ADFL in terms of the common 'Rwandan Hutu' enemy (and perhaps also with reference to Mobutu), let it slip that he could not read the minds of his Banyamulenge allies. Braeckman explained:

[The commander] appreciates the help of the Banyamulenge and, as he says, that of the Rwandans from across the border. But, like everyone else around here, he also wonders about the latter's true intentions. For him, one thing is clear: Tshisekedi [Zaire's opposition leader] and Kabila must reach an agreement, and there must be no question of annexing Kivu [to Rwanda].[180]

The commander's 'no question of annexing' was a reminder that Mayi-Mayi, besides fighting the FAZ, aimed to rid Kivu of every form of Rwandan presence and influence.[181]

Equally revealing, several days before she interviewed the Mayi-Mayi commander, Braeckman was informed by (genuine?) Banyamulenge that they, too, were uncertain about Kigali's intentions. Fearing annexation, one of the fighters had said:

'Those who attacked us [i.e. Rwandan Hutu militias] had forgotten that we have fighting experience, that in the 1960s, our fathers, weapons in their hands, had chased the Muleliste rebels, and that many among them subsequently served in the Zairean army. You write that Kigali supports us, arms us: be assured that we have no need of that support, and that we are sufficiently numerous and trained'.[182]

The implications of this frank statement may have eluded Braeckman. Whilst she attempted to use the soldier's testimony to cast Banyamulenge in the role of self-reliant liberators who did not need RPA support, a good line which again must have pleased the authorities in Kigali, she also allowed the soldier to remind her readers that Kabila, a second-rank commander in the 1960s rebellion, was no long-lost friend of the people of Mulenge.

The news in early 1997 that the alliance between Banyamulenge and Mayi-Mayi had ended was not surprising. In fact, outright war had broken out. The two groups, the claws of the pincer movement that had obliterated Mugunga camp, clashed in Butembo. Receiving widespread attention in Belgium, news of the clashes came with the warning that Kabila's version of events was not the only one. One Belgian paper wrote that 'those in Kabila's entourage claim that Mayi-Mayi have tried to murder his local commander, André Kisasse, somewhere near Bunia. Other sources, however, believe that Mayi-Mayi are no longer prepared to tolerate the authority of Banyamulenge-Tutsi within Kabila's rebel organisation.'[183] Kabila's version of events was straightforward and cloaked in military language: fighting broke out after Mayi-Mayi had attempted to kill Kisasse in retaliation for the threat that they would be disarmed and 'retrained'. The refusal to comply resulted in two weeks of skirmishes that left thirty dead. The alternative explanation, however, had more depth: given their strongly opposed long-term political agendas, it was unthinkable Mayi-Mayi would serve under Banyamulenge command. Another Belgian journalist commented:

Back in 1995, Mayi-Mayi declared war on 'the Rwandans', whom they intended to chase from Kivu. . . . The current alliance is unnatural, since there is no love lost between Mayi-Mayi and the Tutsi in the ADFL, nor between Mayi-Mayi and the Rwandans who support the ADFL.[184]

According to one humanitarian worker in the region, the whole of the Goma-Walikale-Bukavu triangle had become a war zone.[185] Mayi-Mayi had resumed their main political agenda; they attacked Butembo on 20 February 1998, then Beni. By late May, both centres had become 'dead towns'.[186]

Coinciding with these clashes, the new governor of South Kivu announced that several 'Banyamulenge' had taken advantage of the confusion of war to move into high-level positions. He told them to step down and make room for autochthonous zaïrois.[187] Continental journalists and commentators had anticipated that Banyamulenge might face trouble (Vanderostyne, above). In fact, already in late November 1996, and much earlier than in the anglophone press, continental European papers had begun to suggest that within the ADFL two agendas might collide: one, an old revolutionist's dream, in which Mobutu and the FAZ featured as the common enemy but in which Rwanda's role might become marginalised; the other, the 'Banyamulenge' quest for recognition of their civil rights, a quest entwined with Rwanda's need to secure its borders and eliminate the threat of another genocide by Hutu. Interviewed in *La Libre Belgique*, Filip Reyntjens commented

that the agenda of 'the Zaireans' does not necessarily coincide with that of [Banyamu-lenge] 'Tutsi'. 'What binds these two is in the first instance an alliance of convenience. There is undoubtedly a divergence of objectives, with one party aiming to overthrow the Mobutu regime and the other fighting for the defence of their community rights. It is not excluded that some [in the Alliance] will soon aim their weapons at their allies of today.'[188]

The issue could not be separated from Kagame's plans either, since he, after all, had invited Kabila to head the Banyamulenge revolt. In *Libération*, already at the time of the refugees' return migration, Colson had made it clear that it was Kagame, not the Banyamulenge (as Brittain later claimed), whose idea it was that the guerilla veteran should head the rebel force: 'Banyamulenge, Tutsi of Zaire, have risen up against central government. These rebels are supported by Rwanda, which has appointed Laurent Kabila as their leader.'[189]

It took anglophone newspaper journalists a little longer before they too (not all of them, and not all of the time) acknowledged, i.e. rediscovered, local agendas and how these might collide. It was not until well after the January clashes between Banyamulenge and Mayi-Mayi, for instance, that Michela Wrong told her readers how the ADFL was not as cohesive as had appeared in late 1996. Mr Kabila was struggling to cement his crumbling alliance.

Nothing, it seemed last year, could halt the Alliance of Democratic Forces. Three months on, prospects seem a lot more daunting for Mr Laurent Kabila. . . . his multi-ethnic coalition is in danger of splintering.

Wrong conceded that despite looking 'surprisingly strong at the outset', the ADFL was in reality 'very much a marriage of convenience between disci-plined, Rwandan-trained Banyamulenge Tutsis, rebels from Shaba and Kasai provinces and local Mai-Mai warriors, traditionally hostile to Tutsis'.[190] This is not to say, however, that Wrong came to doubt the cohesion of the ADFL. Its information officers, Wrong acknowledged, had a polished, friendly-but-firm way with journalists;[191] so it was perhaps unavoidable that doubt and optimism should oscillate. In early March, after quoting a diamond dealer who said he had heard that life in liberated areas was good, Wrong seemed once again fully confident about the success of the campaign. Zaire *was* behind Kabila.

Rebel victories in the east have coincided with a radical shift in public attitudes towards the fighters' cause. Last October, when the revolt by the Banyamulenge . . . first burst into life in South Kivu province, Mr Kabila was generally regarded as a puppet of the neighbouring Rwandan government. His uprising was viewed as a foreign invasion . . . Since then Mr Kabila has been adopted as the people's hero.[192]

More incisive was McGreal's reconsideration of his earlier claim that the ADFL was 'underpinned by a [new] revolutionary philosophy'. After the rebel ADFL took Lubumbashi, McGreal reconnected with his in-depth knowledge of the region's politics and reminded readers of how easy it is for politicians to rekindle old rivalries.

Laurent Kabila, the rebel leader, is promising all the usual reforms – elections, order, an end to corruption. But Zaire's ethnic and factional rivalries, manipulated so successfully by Mobutu, are not about to disappear; nor are the fundamentals of an economy described by one observer as 'a kleptocracy in which officials and employees, from top to bottom, have survived by bribery and theft'.[193]

The ADFL liberation narrative, in other words, had merely appropriated concepts popular within New Pan-Africanism: breaking with the past; good governance (a new political philosophy); forms of political solidarity transcending ethnicity; a home-grown civil war. Behind the rhetoric, McGreal knew, contradictions and disparate agendas still lurked.

When Laurent Kabila finally arrived in Kinshasa, McGreal reconnected with local politics and history in eastern Zaire. Kabila, the 'rebel in crocodile shoes', had a 'worrying past'; he was 'remembered by many as a brutal and opportunist autocrat'. McGreal explained:

buried deep in the east of the country are a group of people who have first-hand experience of Mr Kabila's rule, and they would not recommend it to anyone.

Mr Kabila armed and ruled the Bembe people on and off from 1964 until the late 1970s. . . . The Bembe accuse Mr Kabila of brutal killings, such as burning alive at the stake those he suspected of betraying him, or of using witchcraft. They say he used them to mine gold which ostensibly went to fund his obscure and, at times futile, revolution.[194]

Diplomatically, McGreal left it an open question 'whether the Bembe's judgement [was] harsh', but stressed that 'an undisguised hatred of Mobutu [would] not sustain a government.' Kabila, though, did have the right to speak.

[Mr Kabila] casts his revolution as about 'changing the face of Africa'. It is, he says, no longer influenced by foreign ideologies but rather the pan-Africanist roots which first drew him into politics and then rebellion.

And the years of obscurity in the hills were far from a waste of time. 'My long years of struggle were like spreading fertiliser on a field. But now it is time to harvest,' he says.

But what kinds of seed had Kabila cast? 'Traditional' or 'hybrid'? – which in political terms translates as stable and reliable or seasonally to be renegotiated, repurchased. It appears that Kabila's seeds were of the latter type. What came to mark the ADFL campaign was a complex web of ever-shifting alliances. Some journalists came to grips with this essential phenomenon. Kabila's late-in-the-day 'switch . . . to the Bembe's old foe, the Banyamulenge – Zaire's Tutsis' (McGreal) gained in importance as Kabila established his rule. After a good year in power, Kabila did indeed jettison his Banyamulenge/Rwandan backers. Hilsum brought news not only of the demise of Rwanda's influence on Kabila, but also of a further shift in his loyalties.

The Congolese hated the idea of being controlled by Rwanda – as one broadcast last week called it, 'a country so small you can't find it on the map'. To gain political support at home, Kabila distanced himself from his Tutsi backers. He sent home the Rwandan Tutsi soldiers who were the backbone of his military power. On the principle that my enemy's enemy is my friend, he appears to have aligned himself with Hutu extremists who wish to exterminate the Tutsis.[195]

If Kabila had earlier been praised for preventing the break-up of Zaire, a fear which haunted the US, the Alliance leader soon fell foul of both the international community and his own people. Kabila disappointed his foreign investors and the US (American Mineral Fields, for instance, saw its contracts terminated); he failed to introduce significant democratic reform and dismissed the national conference; he blocked UN attempts to investigate the alleged atrocities by the ADFL/RPA against refugees and Zairean civilians; last but not least, he marginalised his Rwandan backers, who left hugely disappointed. Public opinion, as seen in the reports from Kinshasa just before its fall, had been sensitive to the presence of so many 'Rwandans' within Kabila's close circle of advisers. Anti-Tutsi sentiment in the streets of Kinshasa, a problem also marking the end of Mobutu's reign, fed not only on malicious stereotyping but also on the actual presence of Rwandan and Ugandan troops.

Kabila, it seemed, had bowed to public pressure. And yet, as had transpired from several interviews during the ADFL campaign itself, he, with Commander Kisasse, may well have planned this scaling down of the 'Rwandan' presence for some time. After reducing 'the Tutsi' presence, Kabila brought in some old friends from Katanga and continued the ethnic nepotism for which dictator Mobutu had been renowned. Rwanda's political leaders were incensed. As François Ngolet (2000) analyses:

Kabila failed to meet the expectations of Rwanda which by helping him conquer power expected to see the end of persecutions of the Tutsi-Banyamulenge, the problem of their citizenship resolved, and their full integration to the Congolese nation taking place with harmony. This mistreatment of the Banyamulenge coupled with Kabila's lack of gratitude and incapacity to secure the Congo-Rwanda border was another source of disappointment in Kigali ... The same disappointment was shared by Kabila's former allies such as Uganda and Angola, whose borders with Zaire were frequently crossed by forces hostile to regimes in Kampala and Luanda. It is this global dissatisfaction with Kabila's performance by his former allies, and the feeling of betrayal shared by the Tutsi minority that have caused the war to begin again in eastern Congo on August 2, 1998. (Ngolet 2000: 77)

By launching the second war, Rwanda and Uganda demonstrated that their presence in eastern Zaire was not restricted to the need to secure their national borders. Their interests, without a doubt, were political and economic (Ngolet 2000: 80–2; Reyntjens 1999).

Conclusion: information warfare and political correctness

At the time Rwanda's Government of National Unity was sworn in, the continental European press, taken as a whole, achieved a balanced combination of empathy with the RPF and scepticism concerning the Front's intentions. There was a clear focus on Rwanda's internal politics: the RPF-led government of Rwanda deserved to be assisted internationally, yet still needed to earn its legitimacy. Importantly, the uneasy relationship between Kagame and Twagiramungu was clearly noted, as were its consequences. This interest in Rwandan politics was not shared by the majority of US and British journalists and commentators, who opted to read Rwanda through the lens of international failure. It was as if Rwandan politics did not have a life of its own.

With the Kibeho massacre, the anglophone press confirmed its tendency not to focus on Rwandan politics: scrutiny of the RPF/RPA agenda or army abuses was inappropriate, was taken to mean the critic sympathised with 'the other side' or did not understand the horror of genocide. While continental European journalists declined to accept they had lost the right to look inside Rwandan politics, the British and US press (and many humanitarian workers) came to follow the 'politically correct' view that Rwanda's problems were best understood as resulting exclusively from international indifference. It became widely accepted, as we shall see in Chapter 5, that the failures of the international community deserved to be sanctioned with the loss of the outsider's right to an independent opinion on politics in Rwanda. It was time to stop criticising the new government and hand the media-conscious RPF, which controlled government, the monopoly on knowledge construction. If there was anything worth knowing about Rwanda and the Great Lakes region, Rwanda's government, from which Twagiramungu and other Hutu ministers were about to be expelled by hardliners, would tell the world what it was. Reporters had their first experience of Kagame's doctrine of information control.

By late 1996, Kagame's way of controlling information had matured: the international media was told in no uncertain terms how to read the crisis and its solution. 'Correct' readings did away with local complexities and set the beginning of relevant history at July 1994, the time of the Hutu refugee crisis. Reference could be made to 1981, when Banyarwanda lost the right to Zairean citizenship, or to Kabila's decades of struggle against Mobutu, provided certain 'details' were omitted. Moreover, there was to be no historically informed scrutiny of who 'the Banyamulenge' were; they were only to be imagined as a large entity, homogenous and settled in Zaire for a very long time. Blocking out Kivu's complex history did not impair the analysis of the Banyamulenge uprising, a point which needs to be stressed, yet it did prevent a contextualised understanding of 'the solution' which existed in the shape of the ADFL campaign. The manipulation had its greatest impact on the anglophone press. Despite some clear initial interests in Kivu's social and political history, anglophone newspaper journalists and commentators ended up imagining eastern Kivu to be a closed book; at best a place with a history too complex to mention, at worst a place without a history. Certain (late) exceptions granted, mainly in writings by McGreal and Wrong, the anglophone press pasted over the faultlines within the ADFL and the tensions known to analysts aware of Kivu's struggles prior to the arrival of the Rwandan refugees. The RPF-led government in Kigali, through its propaganda machine, was at work to tell the world that the ADFL campaign was home-grown, distinctly Zairean and anti-ethnic.

In contrast, the continental European press, particularly in Belgium, maintained a more steady focus on conflicting 'local agendas'. Ironically, the work of one of its most ardent pro-RPF/ADFL journalists (Braeckman) turned out to be so richly detailed that the relevance of the past in eastern Zaire, and how that past was remembered, could not remain hidden. The focus on conflicting agendas, most clearly maintained in work by Smith, Colson, Buyse and Vanderostyne, culminated in an *early questioning* of Kabila's allegiance to those whose support had ensured him victory. The moment Kabila installed himself in Kinshasa, the country's perpetually 'ethnicised' reality resurfaced with a vengeance.

As auto-critics have argued (Gowing 1997, 1998; Hilsum 1995a, 1997), the international media and humanitarian world were wrong-footed in eastern Zaire. The review in this chapter corroborates the verdict but warns against blindly applying it to the continental European press, which, particularly in Belgium and through the dispatches of Smith and Colson in *Libération* (France), maintained a more solid, continuous focus on 'local issues'. This included paying attention to interpretations of local history that were in danger of being overshadowed by the historical magnitude of Mobutu's demise.

3 For beginners, by beginners: knowledge construction under the Rwandese Patriotic Front

Having escaped world attention right up to the moment of genocide, Rwanda was a country waiting to be 'discovered'. What kind of a place was it, *really*? What kind of a place might it become? But the world did not start from scratch. While Central Africa was not well known in the West, the region nonetheless was 'enveloped in a century of powerful imagery – ranging from "Heart of Darkness" to the "Noble Savage"'; it was a region outsiders felt they 'knew' well (Newbury 1998: 76).

In this chapter we consider how the new guardian of Rwanda's culture and destiny, the victorious Rwandese Patriotic Front (RPF), made its own contribution to the crafting of an intellectual image about the place and its heritage; an image which the world, the anglophone part especially, would be encouraged to embrace. The portrayal was easy to grasp, reconnected with a classic study translated into English, Maquet's *The Premise of Inequality* (1961), and was, as would become clear in late 1996, politically convenient. To help popularise its preferred vision of history, the RPF secured the support of sympathetic journalists and aid workers uninformed about the region, and academic scriptwriters without research experience in Rwanda. This chapter deals with RPF-functional academic representations, including statements on the crisis in eastern Zaire, parts of which the post-genocide authorities in Kigali regard as the legitimate extension of the Rwandan polity.

The mobilisation of academic RPF supporters, and the consistency with which they ignore or misrepresent post-independence scholarship on Rwanda, took British academia by surprise – and storm. Nowhere was this better demonstrated than in Didier Goyvaerts' book review of the edited volume *L'Afrique des Grands Lacs: Annuaire 1996–97* (Marysse and Reyntjens 1997), which appeared in *African Affairs* in October 1998. Goyvaerts, who at the time he wrote the review had yet to produce his first research-based publication on the history and politics of the Great Lakes (Reyntjens 1999a: 122), accused the contributors to the *Annuaire 1996–1997* of treading the Belgian government line on the emergence of ethnicity in Rwanda. The accusation stunned the contributors and editors of the *Annuaire*, since such a government line does not exist. Goyvaerts, moreover, charged the contributors with 'waging their personal war against the

Tutsi, whom they utterly detest' (Goyvaerts 1998: 578), a charge curiously coated in essentialist language. Goyvaerts' 'arguments', Reyntjens demonstrated in his reply to the review, were based on political correctness and a desire to commit 'character assassination', but not on scholarly research or debate.[1]

While Goyvaerts' review is a rather extreme example of academic revisionism, guidance by the RPF generally works in rather subtle, more persuasive ways. It is to such guided arguments that we must now turn.

Rewriting ethnicity in Rwanda

In the aftermath of the 1994 genocide and RPF victory, a discarded, idealised representation of Rwanda's pre-colonial past resurfaced. This model originated in a functionalist anthropology nurtured by the colonial desire to justify indirect rule, and conjured up an idyllic, integrative society devoid of ethnic divisions and tension. This pre-colonial Rwanda enjoyed harmony, so the story went, because its chief social institution – *ubuhake* cattle clientship – had facilitated social mobility across fluid occupational categories. Status was a fact of life, but negotiable. The brainchild of a colonial research effort by Jacques Maquet (1954, 1961), a Belgian anthropologist, and Abbé Alexis Kagame (1952, 1958, 1972), a member of Rwanda's *nyiginya* Tutsi aristocracy, this functionalist representation was discredited in the decades following independence.

After independence, new research showed that clientship in pre-colonial Rwanda ('clientship' being the term preferred to 'feudalism') had not been restricted to *ubuhake*, the so-called cattle contract, but that a plurality of patronage forms had existed. It emerged, moreover, that the vast majority of the population, Hutu and Tutsi, had had virtually no control over their land and labour power. The seeds of this inequality, and the severe poverty caused among both Hutu and Tutsi, had been cast when King Rwabugiri, of the *nyiginya* dynasty, imposed his administration and harsh rule on formerly autonomous local lineages. The king confiscated their lands and broke their political power. Pursuing a kind of assimilation policy, Rwabugiri institutionalised ethnic divisions, mainly though not exclusively through the bonded labour service known as *uburetwa* – from which all Tutsi were excluded (see Chapter 1). European colonisers later adopted this central institution for their own political purposes. In post-independence research, the importance of *uburetwa*, through which mobility between social/ethnic categories came to be severely curtailed, emerged as the hallmark of pre-colonial Rwanda. It was the end of an era (late colonialism) during which 'the Old Rwanda' had been conceptualised through an *elitist* filter.[2]

The integrative representation, which excessively reduces the complexity of Rwanda's pre-colonial past, resurfaced during the RPF war in Rwanda (1990–94) as an ideological antidote to the more diverse picture that had emerged after independence. By focusing on the 'easy terms' of cattle *ubuhake* at the expense of promoting an understanding of the conditions created by different forms of land clientship, but especially *uburetwa corvée* labour, the pro-RPF discourse resuscitated an idealised representation of Rwandan society and history. This representation glossed over significant social complexities, not only to mask the *pre-colonial origins of ethnicity in Rwanda*, but also to intellectually justify a system of leadership by Tutsi minority rule. As this chapter will show, the RPF's extensive academic campaign, which spread selective information about pre-colonial Rwanda, aimed to rewrite history and make the world believe that ethnicity was a non-issue within RPF ranks. The effort complemented the campaign involving certain journalists.

Appraising the idyllic version of pre-colonial Rwanda

The academic vehicle used for resuscitating the functionalist, aristocratic vision of Rwandan history consists of an ongoing series of statements regarding the roots of ethnicity by mainly anglophone analysts, who have neither research experience in Rwanda nor any great understanding of its vast literature. In these comments, 'instant experts' confidently proclaim that the Hutu–Tutsi distinction in ethnic terms was the invention of the European colonisers, a force which had destroyed the 'reciprocity in Hutu–Tutsi relations that had diluted the latter's dominance' (de Waal 1994a: 1). Or as Vassall-Adams put it, colonial indirect rule had 'destroyed the *checks and balances* of the feudal system and deprived Hutu of all their social entitlements' (Vassall-Adams 1994: 7).

This particular interpretation of ethnicity derived from research by Maquet, who had declined to work with Hutu Informants because 'the more competent people on political organisation were the Tutsi' (Maquet 1961: 3). To justify his position, Maquet had argued that his 'aim was not to assess the opinions and knowledge of the whole of the Rwanda population on their past political organisation, but to discover as accurately as possible what that organisation was' (Maquet 1961: 3). The protégé of Alexis Kagame, the abbé-ethnographer whose great-uncle had commanded a formidable army under Rwabugiri, Maquet had worked in partnership to vindicate Kagame's aristocratic representation of pre-colonial Rwanda (Vidal 1991: 54). Maquet romanticised about the harmony of the pre-colonial past by over-emphasising the significance of cattle *ubuhake* while ignoring the land contract and the degrading *uburetwa* institution. Some anthropologists interested in the Great Lakes region during the final decade of colonial rule, when the Tutsi aristocracy aspired to continue to rule, adopted Maquet's idealised version of patron-client relations (Gravel 1968; Vansina 1963), but others strongly opposed it (De Heusch 1966; d'Hertefelt 1964).

It took a new generation of historians and anthropologists to talk to the Hutu population and give the historical record more substance and balance. The challenge they faced and their achievements have been succinctly summarised by Villia Jefremovas:

Although early clientage ties, especially those contracted between elites, may have had an element of reciprocity, the process of the centralisation of power and the expansion of the state into the peripheries and to all levels of society in the precolonial period forced the majority to accept ties which were more exploitative than reciprocal. Recent analyses of clientage and other precolonial structures in Rwanda have all emphasised this point and discredited the ahistorical approach taken by the early anthropologists (Newbury, M.C. 1974, 1978, 1988; Vidal 1969, 1973, 1974; Rwabukumba and Mudandagizi 1974; Codere 1962; Meschy 1973, 1974). (Jefremovas 1991a: 53)

Despite uncertainty about the exact use of ethnic labels in nineteenth-century social and political discourse, there is today certainty that the European colonisers were not the first to rule Rwanda along divisive ethnic lines. Overt ethnic friction may not have existed at the close of the nineteenth century (see Grogan and Sharp 1900: 119), but the ethnic divisions and, according to Grogan and Sharp, 'obvious hatred' toward the Tutsi overlords, were well entrenched by 1898, the time Germany colonised Rwanda. The crux of the argument is that the mid- to late nineteenth century was a period of tremendous upheaval during which social and ethnic divisions began to crystallise.

Rwabugiri's administration not only rigidified social distinctions in ethnic terms, but also engendered a process of ethnic self-consciousness among groups of Tutsi in Nduga, central Rwanda, where the court's rich oral literature and ritual, embodied in the Esoteric Code (Kagame 1952), 'served as effective catalysts in the ideologization of Tuutsi identity' (Newbury 1988: 208). Tutsi self-awareness would be nurtured further under Belgian rule through the writings of educated Tutsi, notably those of Alexis Kagame. Belgian colonists contributed to the ideology of (elite) Tutsi self-consciousness an explanation of 'physical difference' in terms of ancestral migrations – for which there was no firm empirical basis – and they made *all* Tutsi superior, *all* Hutu inferior. Twa formed the bottom group in the hierarchy. The hierarchy became fixed in the 1930s when Belgium introduced ID cards, created schools for training Tutsi administrators and set up 'native tribunals' headed by Tutsi (Des Forges 1969: 198; Hoben 1989; Lemarchand 1970: 73). The interventions were racist, but the seeds for a racialised ethnic division had well germinated by then.

How the idealised representation of ethnicity resurfaced

After the horror of the 1994 genocide, it is easily overlooked that ethnic polarisation, and more generally the politicisation of ethnicity, was instituted under Rwabugiri. This oversight may stem from ignorance about Rwanda's complex past, but, as this section will show, this ignorance was most convenient to the

RPF, which was keen to turn the clock back to the representation of Rwanda popularised in late European colonialism.

At the end of Rwanda's 1990–94 war and genocide, some well-known Africanists expressed empathy with Rwanda's new regime by obliterating three decades' worth of historical research. Among them was the much respected historian Basil Davidson, who championed the idyllic, aristocratic representation without as much as a glance at the work of those researchers who had interviewed the descendants of the oppressed. Davidson was adamant that Maquet had done the job once and for all. He told readers of *De Morgen*:

By the 1930s, there was a full body of literature on Rwanda, excellent studies, including work by the Belgian anthropologist Jean-Jacques Maquet, through which the history of the old kingdom had been fully documented.[3] . . . When the Germans became involved in the 'scramble for Africa' in 1890, they found in Rwanda and Burundi no trace of tribalism. Those who lived there spoke one language, were one people, divided over occupational groups. No classes!

Food producers called themselves Hutu, they grew bananas – a tremendous crop, on top of which you just need some protein. [But] the Tutsi had spears, so the Germans saw in them a ruling class. . . . The Tutsi thus became the ideal instrument for Indirect Rule. . . . Because the Tutsi first needed to be isolated – it was necessary to intervene in the relations as they had evolved. . . . The Germans fashioned a ruling class and a class of serfs. Forty years later, the Tutsi hated the Hutu, and vice versa.[4]

Davidson's argument that European colonialism *created* the divisions that later resulted in ethnic conflict is not supported by empirical research. As research in the 1960s and 1970s has shown, it is a fallacy to believe that European administrators would have 'invented' ethnic divisions. With the exception of Rwanda's north-west and some pockets in the east, where Belgium effectively helped to install rule by Nduga, European colonial authorities built upon existing social institutions, including ethnic divisions.

An acknowledgement of the colonial campaign to racialise social and economic relations does not mean one has to erase from memory what preceded the arrival of the European colonists. Such erasure, however, is what post-genocide revisionism[5] aims to achieve through the services of 'instant experts' who now write of pre-European inter-ethnic harmony. Resuscitating the aristocratic representation, Basil Davidson wrote in 1992 that

the manner of [the] nineteenth-century dominance [by aristocratic Tutsi] was mild, and was regulated by 'lord and vassal' relationships which had some resemblance to the simpler forms of European feudalism. 'The rich man in his castle and the poor man at his gate' appear to have been the outward and visible forms of *a mutually acceptable* relationship between Tutsi and Hutu; at least in principle these forms represented *an agreed sharing* of rights and duties. Colonial enclosure changed all that. (Davidson 1992: 249; emphasis added)

There is truth in the statement that European, mostly Belgian colonialism 'changed all that', for the Belgians did indeed racialise Tutsi–Hutu relations. On the other hand, Davidson's portrayal short-changes us by omitting the de-tailed, contextualised historical research undertaken in the 1960s and 1970s. *A mutually accepted relationship? An agreed sharing of rights and duties?* Post-colonial research, by Rwandan scholars and outsiders, has given us a more dynamic portrayal of the late nineteenth century, and de-emphasised the wholesale benevolent nature of the various forms of Tutsi–Hutu clientship. As Jefremovas writes,

> when we turn to the recent historical, political, geographical and anthropological work done on precolonial Rwanda, we find a 'history' far more complex. . . . The image of 'mild dominance' is shattered by the turbulent transformation in land, labour and power relations. . . . Davidson's bland 'move towards more emphatic forms of central-ized power' (Davidson 1992: 249), [thus] becomes a longer and more violent process through which land and power were centralized into the hands of a tiny aristocratic elite. (Jefremovas 1997: 3)

While Westerners working in/on Rwanda after the genocide eventually under-stood that Hutu and Tutsi were socially constructed ethnic categories which assumed their full emotive force under European colonialism, they generally remained puzzled by Rwanda's socio-political complexity, and the diversity of social formations in space and time. The chief obstacle to understanding the past was that the media-conscious RPF fed Westerners the line that pre-colonial re-lations could be understood through recourse to a single principle, the *ubuhake* cattle contract. Other contractual forms of a forced nature, that whole plethora of exploitative 'contracts' grounded in the appropriation of land by the royal court, were of no importance.

Examples of the uncritical acceptance of a pre-European social harmony delicately poised on the cattle contract are plentiful. Consider the following:

> The feudal system, exploitative as it was, had none the less established reciprocal obli-gations and allowed for a degree of social mobility. The ruling class had clear respon-sibilities towards the underlings, and Hutu could rise to the status of Tutsi by acquiring wealth in the form of cattle. (Vassall-Adams 1994: 8)

And also this:

> Indirect rule, under first the Germans and then the Belgians, who took over Rwanda and Burundi at the end of the First World War, destroyed the checks and balances of the feudal system and deprived Hutu of all their social entitlements. (Vassall-Adams 1994: 7)

'Checks and balances' is a phrase Joseph Mullen also uses in his account of pre-colonial Rwanda. Mullen, though, approaches Rwandan history not by carefully reading the literature, but by *comparing* Rwanda's past with other times and places. For example, he writes:

Though possessing the physical force to suppress or eliminate the Hutu and the Twa (as white settlement in Australia or North America has done in relation to the aboriginal population) the Tutsi chose to enter into a mutually complementary system of relations of production. The Tutsi devised an intricate and sophisticated system of *checks and balances* which permitted capital accumulation, encouraged a controlled degree of social mobility, gave a common sense of belonging to all three groups and ensured that they had a stake in the economic system. (Mullen 1995: 31; emphasis added)

This is yet another example of 'Maquet recycled'; recycled for beginners, by beginners. *A common sense of belonging and ownership?* – as if Alexis Kagame never wrote the Esoteric Code, as if Rwabugiri never confiscated lineage-owned lands and appropriated the labour power of those he subjugated.

Mullen does not deny that there was exploitation within Rwanda's pre-colonial 'feudal' system, but stresses there was a 'unified national conscious-ness' and a 'communality of interests' in which all three ethnic groups shared. And again the focus is on cattle, *as if the Hutu masses were involved in ubuhake cattle clientship*. Mullen states that

The peasant Hutu masses and the Twa became clients based on a form of pastoral service contract called '*ubuhake*'. A Hutu client gained the protection of a Tutsi overlord by supplying him/her with services in labour and goods, and the overlord in turn gave the client cattle on a leasehold basis to the client. This protection included support in litigation against other Tutsi, advocacy in the case of representation in the court of the *mwami* (king), contributions to bride wealth and widowhood and overall provided a general social safety net. (Mullen 1995: 25)

Adopting the Maquet/aristocratic-Tutsi view, Mullen believes that the advan-tages and disadvantages of the system were in balance. He accepts the system was exploitative because Hutu/Twa clients could see their contracts terminated at any time, yet he also detects a much valued 'measure of mutual comple-mentarity in a unified economic system run by pastoralists and agriculturalists' (Mullen 1995: 25–6). Naively, Mullen asserts that it is this 'communality of in-terests [which] the current wave of Hutu extremism . . . totally ignores' (Mullen 1995: 32). Such an assertion misconstrues people's experience of the past (see De Heusch, below; also Malkki 1995).

A similarly simplifying, idyllic vision of pre-colonial times appeared in the first report on Rwanda by African Rights:

When the first Europeans arrived a century ago, they found a true nation: the Ban-yarwanda people. The Banyarwanda were divided in three groups: Tutsi, Hutu and Twa. The three shared the same language, the same customs, the same political institutions, and the same territory. What made them distinct was not that they were distinct 'tribes', but that they were distinct categories within the same nation. (African Rights 1994a: 7)[6]

Acceptable so far. Less acceptable is the additional claim that Hutu–Tutsi relations were marked by a 'reciprocity' which 'diluted [Tutsi] dominance', a reciprocity later 'destroyed by Belgian rule', through which 'a rigid system of tribute and exploitation was imposed, creating deep grievances that underlie today's violence' (de Waal 1994a: 1). This statement, too, overlooks the land-centred transformations Rwabugiri introduced, as well as the active involvement of *local elites* in making social relations fully rigid under European rule. The portrayal of a pre-colonial 'true nation', differentiated by occupational and political status, may at a glance seem broadly correct, but it misleads in its tendency to generalise conditions that applied primarily to Hutu and Tutsi elites and which, in any case, were not found in every corner of Rwanda.

The intellectual challenge academics face today is that they must see through the smokescreen of sameness (same territory, same clans, same political institutions, same language) and must appreciate the divisive institutions and practices which preceded European rule. Against this background, the notion of reciprocity (i.e. vast amounts of land, labour and produce for different types of protection) loses much of its appeal. True, there was a structure of reciprocal surveillance in place through which the (mainly Tutsi) cattle chiefs and army chiefs needed to listen to complaints put forward by the (mainly Hutu) land chiefs, which could result in 'dilution', but this structure existed in a context of severe socio-economic inequalities. To portray Rwanda's ethnic divisions as a German or Belgian 'invention' is to read too much into the fact that Tutsi and Hutu speak the same language, have the same religion, inhabit the same geographical space and belong to the same clans.

The duties of the aristocracy were also poorly implemented. Take, for example, the pledge that the royal granaries – to which the peasantry contributed so generously at harvest times – could be used as a source of emergency food aid when hunger struck. Rules and realities were not the same thing. While the exactions (of grain and beans) were more than generous, redistribution in times of need could be very disappointing. Despite the vast quantities of tribute food that went into the royal granary (*rutsindamapfa*) or into the granaries of local patrons (food grown in designated fields, *intore*), the poor would in times of distress receive only very small amounts. And the aid was conditional. Food distributed from the royal granaries, which may have been comparatively generous (i.e. more generous than that distributed by local court representatives), had to be replaced after the next harvest (Vanwalle 1982: 73).

History, ethnicity and the perfect soundbite: 10 cows

Post-genocide anglophone representations of the 'Old Rwanda' treat the *ubuhake* cattle contract as if it had been the catch-all institution. Once one knows about *ubuhake*, one knows everything there is to know; land is not an issue. Even when informed aid workers explicitly ask how land features in that world of presumed pre-colonial harmony, they find it difficult to deal with land conceptually. Work by Anne Mackintosh shows this remarkably well. In her otherwise excellent analysis of the antecedents of the Rwanda genocide, Mackintosh (1996) clearly struggles to put land in perspective: the land conquest under Rwabugiri is acknowledged, but not built into the analysis. And so once again, *ubuhake* is the all-important social leveller. Mackintosh writes that

> by the late nineteenth century the Tutsi were at the top of the social hierachy, with Hutu and Twa at the bottom, though there was *considerable mobility* in between. . . . When the Belgians introduced identity cards in 1933, all Rwandans were classified according to how many cattle they had: *if you owned more than ten cows, you were counted as Tutsi; less than ten cows you must be Hutu* (if you were a mere potter, you were Twa). Thereafter, it was the father's ethnic group that determined his children's group identity; the stratification was complete and irreversible. (Mackintosh 1996: 49; emphasis added)

Mackintosh duly notes that the ethnic classification existed before the Europeans arrived, but the idea of 'considerable mobility' overrates the number of Hutu who moved up the social ladder. Social mobility had existed in pre-Rwabugiri days, under *ubukonde* (Newbury, Chapter 1), but had by and large vanished after Rwabugiri labelled all cattle-owning lineages as Tutsi. Under Rwabugiri, the much impoverished Hutu majority remained unaffected by the cattle contract, *a point Maquet himself emphasised* (Maquet 1961: 150; also Vidal 1991 on how rare inter-marriage was); other, more important 'contractual' forms of clientship became prevalent. After Rwabugiri's *nyiginya* dynasty expanded its sphere of influence, broke the power of local landowning Hutu lineages and instituted *uburetwa*, the capacity of ordinary Hutu to amass wealth was so reduced that only a handful of 'token Hutu' could be called upwardly mobile. The social mobility offered through cattle clientship 'never affected more than a small percentage of Rwanda's population' (Newbury 1988: 134) and 'affected mainly (though not exclusively) those of Tuutsi status' (1988: 140; Vidal 1969). Pre-colonial reciprocity involving wealth in the form of cattle had been mostly an affair between elites.

De Waal, too, failed to provide the required historical context and depth:

> In the 1930s, the Belgians conducted a census and issued an identity card for each individual, which specified whether they were Tutsi, Hutu or Twa. Such was the slender basis for the racial typology that the census takers were obliged to use ownership of cows as a criterion: those with ten or more were Tutsi, those with less were Hutu, in perpetuity. On the basis of a cow or two hinged the status of overlord or serf, and with it access to education and every other privilege bestowed by the administration.[7]

The seductively neat 10-cows theory ignores the existence of clientship forms anchored in land expropriation and misconstrues the severe inequalities grounded in ethnicity which existed already in the second half of the nineteenth century. The distinction between overlord and serf did not hinge on 'a cow or two'.

All too often, Rwanda's history is collapsed into a few easy-to-remember lines. Here is another example. When Rwanda featured in the *Guardian Education* (1 November 1994), its history was again presented as a simple linear progression from a time about one hundred years ago, when 'Tutsi and Hutu lived in relative harmony', to a transformative colonial episode during which the

colonial powers [Germany, then Belgium] turned the traditional Tutsi-Hutu relationships into a class system. The minority Tutsi were given privileges and western-style education, while the Hutu, usually farmers, were given nothing. The Belgians even introduced identity cards, which still exist today, showing people's ethnic group.[8]

Not only is the suggested transition from 'harmonious' to 'class-based' relations misleading in that it suggests that Hutu and Tutsi belonged to different classes prior to the 1994 genocide,[9] but the emphasis on privileges being 'given' suggests that the Rwandan elite was not actively involved in running the country: the elite was a victim of external aggression, passive and manipulated. The notion that pre-colonial elites were invariably duped, now rather outmoded among scholars (see Moore and Vaughan 1994), is alive and well in RPF-functional renderings of Rwandan history. But the blame-it-all-on-the-European-colonisers position[10] is a denial of agency, a denial of the fact that Rwandan elites 'largely determined the ways in which colonialism influenced the transformation of clientship ties' (Newbury 1988: 59). Tutsi victimisation in the genocide, it seems, is now being projected back in time: the good Tutsi elite at the royal court had been unable to continue with its benevolence, after the arrival of the colonialists.

The history of how ethnic relations evolved in Rwanda is highly complex and requires a focus on land as well as cattle, on rich Tutsi and (the majority) poor ones, and on the diversity of contracts Rwabugiri introduced, especially *uburetwa*. Once this complexity is adequately highlighted, it becomes more difficult to be positive about the so-called mutual benefits of the clientship systems. To depict socio-economic relations in pre-colonial Rwanda through the single focus on cattle may appeal, because it makes 'Rwanda' instantly intelligible, but the depiction also gives people unfamiliar with the country the false sense that today the clock can easily be turned back to those harmonious times before the Europeans arrived 'to change all that'.

If 'instant academics' propose views and theories that ignore the findings of some three decades of post-colonial research, where did they obtain their information from? Right from the onset of the RPF's military campaign, its spokesmen keenly spread the 10-cows thesis. Time and again, commanders would tell journalists that the 'silly business' of ethnicity was just a question of cows, a colonial mistake – and that was all they needed to know.

'If you have more than 10 cows you can become a Tutsi,' says Captain Diogène Mudenge, the RPF commander at the eastern Rwandan town of Gahini. 'Hutu simply means "servant" in our language. Somebody with lots of cows has the right to have servants. Tutsi just means rich. It was during the 1950s and the 1960s that the difference became politicised.'[11]

The 10-cows soundbite is an exceptionally effective way of conveying to the world that the RPF is above ethnicity. Just weeks before the genocide, Tito Rutaremara, RPF political leader, told journalists that the Front's soldiers

'hardly know their country; hardly know the difference between a Hutu and a Tutsi. Yet they are there, in the bush, fighting the war.'[12]

De-emphasising social complexity may raise morale, may even persuade foreign diplomats and donors to have confidence in the new regime, but serious analysts, whether aid worker or academic or journalist or diplomat, cannot justify turning a blind eye to complexity. In this age of high-tech communication, seductive soundbites are all too enthusiastically recycled. An interesting example of this recycling is McNulty's assertion, popularised by the RPF, that 'despite attempts by colonists and post-colonial sectarian regimes to prove otherwise, there is only one ethnicity: Rwandan' (McNulty 1999: 276). Although he earlier referred to 'Newbury 1988' as just one of two pre-1994 works on Rwanda in English (1999: 272), McNulty had clearly not digested Newbury's thoughts on ethnicity. To support the hypothesis of a single ethnicity, he approvingly quotes the social geographer Dominique Franche who told Le Monde: 'Tutsis, Hutus and Twas live together ... They speak the same language and share the same culture and religion. They used to specialize in certain areas of the economy, but not systematically ... The conflict [1994–96] can't be described as ethnic, since there's only one ethnic group in Rwanda, and that's Rwandan' (interview by Langellier, Le Monde, 12 November 1996; cited in McNulty 1999: 276).

In 'Genocide and Obedience in Rwanda' (1997), Hintjens also reproduces the RPF-functional line that the Hutu–Tutsi classification in ethnic terms was the invention of European colonialism. The Belgians did not understand Rwanda and imposed their own categories in desperation. Imagining pre-colonial Rwanda to be marked by 'relative flexibility and social mobility', a balanced socio-economic system 'lost in successive rereadings of the country's history by outsiders, and then by Rwandans themselves', Hintjens comes out in full support for the RPF's claim that Rwanda's troublesome ethnic categories have no raison d'être other than the short-sightedness of the colonial administration. The Belgians panicked, then counted cows.

When the Belgians introduced identity cards in 1931, ... they could not decide who was Tutsi and who was Hutu. They therefore decided to use a strictly economic system of identification. Anyone with more than ten cows at that time became Tutsi, and all (his) children, grandchildren and so on. Anyone with less than ten cows became Hutu, or

Twa. With their fear of complexity, the Belgian colonial administration thus 'tidied up' Rwandan identity in a banal, surreal process of pseudo-racial classification. The tidiness had lasting consequences. The reason . . . one in ten Rwandans are Tutsi, is that one in ten men owned cattle in 1931! (Hintjens 1997: 3)

It would be wrong to ignore the racial theorising that influenced so much of colonial history, early colonial history in particular. But it is equally wrong to conjure up a timeless pre-colonial Rwanda. The 'tidying up' of ethnic distinctions was a process, not an event. Why ban Rwabugiri from history? The terms 'Hutu', 'Tutsi' and 'Twa' may have denoted flexible relations of superiority and dependence in pre-Rwabugiri days (before 1860), but their meanings changed under Rwabugiri when ethnic identities rigidified.

'Instant experts' would do well to return to the time Maquet launched his functionalist model, which was *immediately criticised* by researchers like d'Hertefelt and De Heusch. These scholars were highly aware of the evil of Belgium's racialised approach to ethnicity, but they also understood that Rwanda's ethnic terms had pre-colonial antecedents. In 'Mythes et idéologies', d'Hertefelt (1964: 219–20) exposed the fantasy of the Hamitic theory that Rwanda's Hutu–Tutsi–Twa classification would have had a 'natural' origin. He also attacked the idea that 'the Tutsi' would have arrived in Rwanda as the representatives of a superior civilisation to which the other two groups spontaneously submitted themselves. The Hamitic myth, which saw Tutsi as a branch of the Caucasian race (and for which the British explorer Speke had been a great 'propagandist', see E. R. Sanders 1969: 521), was soundly thrown out. D'Hertefelt's work on Rwanda's eighteen clans, each of which might have Hutu, Tutsi and Twa, was an important contribution to debunking the Hamitic theory. But d'Hertefelt's research on clanship did not predispose him to embrace the structural-functional model. On the contrary, he wrote:

both the published literature and new research show that, on a number of important points, the model embodies ideal norms, even imaginary ones, more than it reveals reality. (d'Hertefelt 1971: 17)

De Heusch also contested Maquet's model, which he found wanting on empirical grounds. De Heusch could not bring himself to pretend (to use Mullen's words) that there would have been any significant 'communality of interests' between Tutsi elites and the majority poor, whether Hutu or Tutsi. Reflecting on the various Tutsi elites whose armies fought one another in pre- and early colonial days, De Heusch was emphatic:

one cannot without naivety or in good faith speak of the 'positive interests' of the Hutu and Tutsi members of an army when that army is entirely devoted to Tutsi conquests and the maintenance of Tutsi domination over Hutu. (De Heusch 1966: 134)

It is worth recalling, too, that Maquet's model, did not apply to all of pre-colonial Rwanda, i.e. Rwanda in its present shape. By the end of the nineteenth century,

Rwanda consisted of a central nucleus directly administered by the *mwami* and his court, peripheral zones under the nominal control of the *mwami*'s representatives, and zones where central government exercised a certain influence but without effective control. (Reyntjens 1985: 95)

This diversity of levels of control and influence meant that at the beginning of European rule, the legitimacy of the central court was particularly weak in the regions of the north and north-west (Lemarchand 1977: 78). Some areas, moreover, were ruled by Tutsi elites opposed to Nduga: Gisaka, for instance, and parts of Kinyaga. Within this climate of armed conflict, it does not make sense to speak of a 'common sense of belonging' (Mullen 1995: 31).

Today's instant experts are not bothered by what Maquet's critics had had to say when *The Premise of Inequality* was published. Such experts also fail to pay attention to the diverse picture the historical record presents us with. Instead, they suggest that whatever we learned over the past three decades was nothing but propaganda, a deliberate attempt to undermine the purity of pre-colonial days. Nowhere is this message more strongly articulated than in Fergal Keane's rubbishing of post-colonial research (see Chapter 2), but newcomer/ partisan academics have tried equally hard to discredit this research. De Waal, for instance, tried to convince newspaper readers in Britain and The Netherlands that thirty years of post-colonial research on Rwandan history was best represented by a single referent: the career of Ferdinand Nahimana, the Hutu historian who became director of the extremist Radio-Télévision des Libres Milles Collines and is now on trial in Arusha.[13] Not containing his revulsion, de Waal reminds us that Nahimana's research on Rwanda's pre-colonial Hutu kingdoms of the north-west 'appear[ed] in scholarly publications'. As for other scholarly work, notably Catharine Newbury's meticulously detailed *The Cohesion of Oppression*, this work too is dismissed by de Waal with the claim that its *raison d'être* was above all 'to explain the "social revolution" of 1959'. Deemed 'a valuable addition to the literature', and no more, the book's chief merit was that it 'challeng[ed] the previous orthodoxy that patron-client ties imbued the whole of Rwandese society'. This superficial comment could not have been based on a close read of the many subtle arguments Newbury had developed. Linden's *Church and Revolution in Rwanda* (1977) received the same treatment: written to justify the events of 1959.

To write about Nahimana as if he were the sum total of research on ethnicity in post-independent Rwanda is disingenuous. Hintjens' (1997) attack forms a neat parallel to de Waal's. By referring to the racial theories of Nahimana as presented in the *Independent on Sunday* (8 January 1995),[14] Hintjens restates the RPF line that the past three decades of historical research on Rwanda do not deserve to be looked at. Post-colonial research was nothing but 'a rewriting of Hutu pre-colonial history [spearheaded] by Ferdinand Nahimana, . . . [and] part of [the] reinvention of tradition' (Hintjens 1997: 7). The notion of a '*rewriting* of Hutu pre-colonial history' is odd: who researched the region's political system before Nahimana? And, if anyone did, was the account really that different? Hintjens backs her argument by referring to Lemarchand's conclusion in 1970 that the 'Revolution of 1959' was not the end of tyranny for Hutu, but rather the beginning of a period in which a new governing elite stepped in and 'borrowed from the past the tools to shape the future' (Lemarchand 1970: 492, quoted in Hintjens 1997: 7). Hintjens contends that Nahimana's research can be dismissed because the 1960s proved him wrong.

But why is Lemarchand invoked? (This is puzzling since Lemarchand's conclusion is widely shared among the historians Hintjens accuses of reinventing tradition.) Lemarchand's point does not invalidate the academic research to which Newbury, Vidal, Meschy, Reyntjens and Lemarchand himself all contributed. While one may be critical of certain aspects of a colleague's research (see e.g. De Heusch 1995 on Vidal, or Reyntjens 1985: 29 on Lemarchand), these differences of opinion have never before resulted in anyone suggesting that post-colonial research merely aimed to reinvent tradition. Nahimana's extreme version of the racist 'Hamitic hypothesis', which indeed fed Hutu Power propaganda in the early 1990s (see Chrétien 1995), is easily dismissed on the basis of the historical evidence which emerged after and even before Rwanda's independence (d'Hertefelt 1964, above). One cannot, therefore, use Nahimana's lethal racism of the 1990s to discredit all post-independence research on Rwandan history.[15]

Not all academic newcomers to Rwanda, though, have acted as scribes willing to produce RPF-functional narratives. Mahmood Mamdani, for instance, was not so easily persuaded and exposed the contradiction between official RPF rhetoric and casual conversations involving prominent RPF members. About his visit to Rwanda in 1995 he wrote:

I was nonplussed to be told over and over again by leading people in the RPF: 'We speak the same language, have the same culture, and live on the same hills; we are the same people.' But in casual conversation and out in the street, some of the same individuals would readily identify Muhutu and Mututsi. Sometimes by physical appearance. (Mamdani 1996: 5)

Mamdani also recalled that before the RPF invaded Rwanda in 1990, 'one of the issues hotly debated in the Rwandese Alliance for National Unity (RANU), formed by refugees in Uganda in 1979, was whether the difference between Bahutu and Batutsi was one of class or ethnicity' (1996: 5–6). In an interview with *Le Monde*, Jean-Damascène Ntakirutimana, who was Twagiramungu's chief of staff during his time as prime minister, confirmed the contradiction: 'The RPF denies that there is any ethnic problem today with the same energy it used in denouncing the ethnic imbalance of the old regime.'[16]

Rethinking the 1959 Hutu social revolution?

The academic rewriting encouraged by the RPF also focuses on the 1959 social revolution. And here, as well, an important historical epoch is being re-imagined. Essentially, the RPF and its sympathisers have resuscitated the old theory, spread by surprised Tutsi aristocrats and Belgian administrators alike, that the pro-democracy movement of 1959 was merely the work of isolated individuals. It was 'Hutu leaders [who] incited the population' (de Waal, below). Hintjens, too, promotes this opinion. While acknowledging that the Bahutu Manifesto (February 1957) expressed 'fears of Tutsi dominance' – fears articulated by 'the Hutu elite, led by Abbé Kagame and the future President Grégoire Kayibanda', i.e. one Tutsi aristocrat and one southern Hutu – Hintjens nonetheless claims that the grievances expressed were 'overshadowed by the elitist, Northern-dominated anti-Tutsi ideology' (Hintjens 1997: 7, 12). There is some truth in the proposition: the revolution was not devoid of northern influence, since *ubukonde*, at the time still prominent in the north, not only survived the abolition of other forms of clientship but had its authenticity confirmed (see Chapter 1). On the other hand, domination by the north did not come about until Habyarimana's coup in 1973; and his rule ensured inter-ethnic stability until the late 1980s.

The problem with the RPF-friendly gloss on 1959 is that the emphasis lies not on abolishing the monarchy, but on Tutsi ethnicity. Reconsiderations of what happened in 1959 are couched in essentialist ethnic terminology – 'anti-Tutsi ideology', 'Hutu leaders incited' – which plays down both the objective of the revolution (abolishing the monarchy) and the inter-ethnic partnership through which this objective was realised. This partnership is revealed when one considers the involvement of the Kabgayi-based Tutsi clergy in the build-up to the revolution. Alexis Kagame may not have played too great a role in advocating social change – in fact, a colleague lists him among the more conservative clergy – but he did acknowledge that 'the reality of Rwanda's ethnic relations could not be denied' (Kalibwami 1991: 445). Kagame realised that 'the Tutsi' had been elevated and privileged by the Belgians, unlike 'the Hutu', whom he regarded as 'the great sacrificed', *les grands sacrifiés* (1991: 390–1, referring to Kagame 1975).

Recalling his personal experiences as editor and director of *Kinyamateka* (1955–63), then Rwanda's leading publication,[17] Justin Kalibwami stresses that the church did not suddenly drop its allegiance to the Tutsi aristocracy that it had supported for so long. In contrast to the Belgian administrators and Rwandan

Tutsi aristocracy, both of whom were surprised by the 1959 uprising and then blamed it on Hutu individuals, church leaders understood that the struggle for democracy had been in the making for some time. For church leaders, this was a people's struggle: in *Kinyamateka*, 'the people certainly invested their hope of liberation' (Kalibwami 1991: 372–3). Rwandan journalism at the time may have been 'directed by men of the church', yet, from 1953, the paper published 'critiques directed at the Rwandan authorities and the country's political regime' (1991: 370). Clerics contributing to the journal refrained from expressing personal opinion, but 'they did try to instil in the public spirit the conviction that the monarchy was a human institution which depended on the will of men, and which did not confer any superhuman power and dignity' (1991: 372).

It was the Tutsi aristocracy and monarchy, not 'the Tutsi', which *Kinyamateka* and the social revolution aimed at. In the latter half of the 1950s, the Catholic church could no longer be equated with the racial fantasies and advice of Mgr Classe, the pre-World War II veteran. These fantasies had long been challenged by a new breed of clergy, by figures like Mgr Perraudin and working-class European priests sensitive to the inequalities of class and race (1991: 439). Despite differences within the church (the conservative Bigirumwami opposed Mgr Perraudin), Kalibwami maintains that 'globally, the Church, Catholicism, favoured the kind of social change which the Hutu movement demanded' (1991: 446; see also Linden 1977; Newbury 1988: 289 note 71). Certainly, the voice of the Catholic church contributed to the overthrow of the monarchy, but it was a multi-ethnic voice that reflected a broader public aspiration. The situation within the Catholic church was that pro-democracy as well as pro-monarchy factions were ethnically mixed: 'Among the Tutsi priests, some openly supported the Hutu cause; in contrast, among the Hutu priests, quite a number publicly defended the ideas of the *mwami* and the Tutsi aristocracy' (Kalibwami 1991: 445). To conceive of 1959 in terms of an exclusive anti-Tutsi ideology is to deny Tutsi clergy their role in the Hutu democracy mouvement; even Alexis Kagame knew the pro-democracy movement was justified.

Today's 'anti-Tutsi' take is essentialist and potentially dangerous, because it fosters the view that the racist theories of Mgr Classe and the Belgian administration had driven an irreversible wedge between Hutu and Tutsi. This was not the case. An essentialist reading of the events of 1959, pitting Hutu against Tutsi, ignores that the architects of the revolution, among them Hutu and Tutsi clergy, brought down a monarchy.[18] A better informed, more detailed reading of pre-colonial and colonial history, and church history in the final stage of colonialism, shows the pitfalls of essentialism. The 1959 anti-monarchy uprising was both legitimate and backed by some cross-ethnic solidarity among its architects, at least among the clergy, much in the same way that some northern Hutu later joined the RPF before it invaded Rwanda in 1990.[19] These Hutu came mostly from the same northern area as the popular Colonel Alexis Kanyarengwe, then the RPF president.[20] Kanyarengwe had fled Rwanda in 1980 after being accused of plotting to overthrow Habyarimana.

Today, the 1959 revolution is discredited by presenting it in essentialist terms devoid of any inter-ethnic solidarity; an approach often accompanied by ignorance about the differential interests which the colonial state and the church pursued in the late 1950s. African Rights proposed the following gloss on 1959:

Unable to adapt, the [rigid, politicized class] structure shattered as independence approached. The Roman Catholic church and the Belgian rulers switched their support to the Hutu, recognizing that the Tutsi could not retain power in any democratic system. In 1959, following the unexpected death of Mwaami (king) Mutara Rudahigwa, who had been a force for moderation, Hutu leaders incited the population against the Tutsi. Over the following seven years, perhaps 20,000 Tutsi were killed in a series of pogroms, while about 150,000 fled the country. The Tutsi population in Rwanda was halved. (African Rights 1994a: 7)[21]

There is more than a touch of simplification here. While Belgian administrators and some 'first generation' church leaders were clearly responsible for 'discrimination based on racism' (1994a: 27), and spreading fantasies about race, it is incorrect to portray the Catholic church as a static, perpetually cohesive, opportunistic force.

In the interest of achieving national reconciliation, serious scholarship must recognise that there was important cross-ethnic solidarity in the run-up to the revolution of 1959–62, as Kalibwami confirms. Moreover, 1959 remains a revolution through which 'control over the allocation of land passed to the majority . . . and freedom of labour for the Bahutu peasantry' was re-established (Mamdani 1996: 33). This is not to claim that 1959 was a total success. After all, Mamdani argues, it 'did not change the institutional character of the state apparatus. Power remained as fused and authoritarian as before' (1996: 33). Those who today get involved in rewriting the script of 1959 would do well to reflect on the land issue: despite continued control by (new) elites, redistribution was also much in evidence. Mamdani concludes correctly that Rwanda's post-genocide government cannot legitimately rewrite the significance of 1959 by calling it anti-Tutsi.

To deny the legitimacy of the 1959 social revolution is to dent the programme for reconciliation, for how can there be reconciliation without a shared understanding of history? Consensus will not be easy. Mamdani reflects:

I met Bahutu figures, including some in the present cabinet, who uphold 1959 as a 'social revolution' which emancipated the majority. Today history is no longer being taught in schools in Rwanda, mainly because there is no account of 1959 that is acceptable to both Bahutu and Batutsi, even to those inside the government. Is not to exclude the non-violent proponents of Hutu Power from the broad base tantamount to undercutting the process of reconciliation by declaring their account of 1959 illegitimate? (Mamdani 1996: 32)

Prunier (1997) echoed this perspective when Prime Minister Twagiramungu and Minister Sendashonga were dismissed from the first post-genocide government. Their expulsion, and the murder of Sendashonga in May 1998, was an enormous setback for Rwanda's reconciliation process.

Reconciliation will not be possible without a nuanced, shared understanding of history (Lemarchand 1998), a process which includes the intellectual challenge of learning more about the production and reproduction of social memory (compare Fisiy 1998; Malkki 1995). The challenge in Rwanda today is complicated further in that the official discourse on the 1994 genocide maintains in practice the ethnic division which the RPF-led government denounces in theory: only Tutsi are victims of genocide; moderate Hutu are victims of politicide who died in massacres (Eltringham and Van Hoyweghen 2000: 226). The distinction has an implied moral hierarchy.

Rewriting ethnic history in eastern Congo-Zaire

In late 1996, African Rights argued that the attempts to justify intervention in eastern Zaire were anchored *not* in the 'realities in eastern Zaire, [but] ... in the institutional imperatives of the humanitarian international' (de Waal 1997: 204). The long and the short of the crisis, African Rights held, was that '[the] humanitarian agencies needed money', and with Christmas coming up what could be a better time for fundraising? After 700,000 refugees returned to Rwanda and the US declared 'the crisis' over, African Rights tried to reassure analysts that the real tragedy had been a Fundraisers' Catastrophe:

Events on the ground in eastern Zaire were not out of control: rapid political progress was being made (albeit by military means), at remarkably low human cost. It was the disaster relief agencies that were out of control, and they nearly succeeded in inflicting the disaster they were predicting on eastern Zaire. (de Waal 1997: 212)

This analysis has given humanitarians a lot to think about, and rightly so. On the other hand, an analysis which has no room for 'the history and politics of eastern Zaire', and which mentions relevant aspects only 'in passing' yet goes on to conclude that 'the crisis in Zaire was the beginning of a solution for the residents of central Africa' (1997: 204, 212), does not pass the test of ethnographic scholarship.

De Waal writes about 'the local Zairean population' (1997: 211) as if it was/is a fully cohesive body whose sole enemy was/is the Hutu refugee extremists. While the actions of these extremists were paramount in triggering the 1996 crisis, the impression of a cohesive population united in struggle against a common enemy is misleading. Had de Waal exposed how Mayi-Mayi and 'Banyamulenge' pursued diametrically opposed agendas, had he detailed the military role Banyamulenge had played in crushing the 1964 rebellion in which

Kabila fought 'on the other side' supported by Babembe (who were not good friends with genuine Banyamulenge), had he revealed how certain Babembe and Bashi opposed the ADFL's southward advance in late 1996, it would have been impossible to sustain the image of a cohesive 'Zairean rebels offensive'. This could not be allowed, however, since attention to such ethnographic details would have made readers question the RPF's narrative that the crisis had found a 'local solution' backed by all in Kivu and beyond (see also Chapter 2).

While the broad criticism levelled against 'the business' of humanitarian aid must be valued (African Rights 1994c), it is unacceptable that such a critique should be substituted for empirical political analysis. Critiquing international intervention is one thing, understanding local politics quite another. The critique of the international aid effort does not contain any grounds (and certainly not after treating Kivu's politics and history merely 'in passing') for claiming that a liberating dawn had arrived for 'the residents of Central Africa'. In 'Eastern Zaire, 1996 – The Fundraisers' Catastrophe', the population of eastern Zaire is muted, packaged and presented to the world as homogenous and fully supportive of that equally homogenous, but in reality quite divided, collection of rebels.

Other RPF-supporters tried equally hard to depict a new dawn. In a maverick comment on eastern Congo-Zaire, Goyvaerts suggested in 1998:

For the first time in a long time, peace has returned to the Lake Kivu region. . . . The area has regained its balance thanks to the ultimate victory of the RPF. . . . Thanks to the military actions of the regime in Kigali, the problem of ethnicity has by and large been neutralised, so much so that a new *endogenous* explosion of violence appears to me to be virtually impossible. (Goyvaerts 1998: 90)

This is far-fetched. No sooner had Kabila seized Mobutu's throne than the political realities of eastern Zaire revealed their dynamic: the 'new dawn' was not what it had seemed from the vantage point of the anti-aid lobby. As seen in the previous chapter, even before Kabila seized the throne, the new governor of South Kivu declared that several Banyamulenge had taken unfair advantage of the confusion of war to move into high-level positions.[22] The fraught relationship between Banyamulenge, now an omnibus category, and 'autochthonous' groups also came to the fore rather swiftly.

Kivu was not at ease with the outcome of 'its' rebellion; the area's political faultlines, temporarily masked by the manipulative ADFL alliance, continued to vibrate.

Conclusion

In a meeting in 1995, Anastase Gasana, Rwanda's then Home Affairs minister, confirmed that one of the priorities of the new government was to rewrite the history books.[23] When newcomers to Rwanda, diplomats especially, expressed

surprise at this priority, which they often did (Jefremovas 1997: 1), they revealed not so much their incredulity as a profound ignorance of the political
centrality of Rwandan 'history'. Rewriting history, with the helping hand of
sympathetic academics or (as in the previous chapter) journalists, stands high
on the government's agenda.

The concept of 'hiring' scriptwriters for the task of re-imagining Rwanda
and its links with eastern Zaire is not alien to Rwandan officials. Major Wilson
Rutayisire, director of the Rwanda Department of Information, for example,
referred to the hiring of scriptwriters when he denied the RPA's involvement in
the killing of Rwandan refugees in eastern Zaire. The allegation, Rutayisire said,
was 'based on superficial conclusions charged with malice'. Rutayisire argued
that 'Rwanda's connection in the alleged massacres in the Congo is the creation
of the powerful who can hire the services of human rights groups to keep
their "moral high ground" afloat.'[24] Rutayisire referred here to (powerful) Hutu
extremists in Zaire and the (serving) human rights groups which had reported
the killing spree. He targeted four groups: Human Rights Watch, based in New
York; the Canadian Center for Democracy and Human Rights; the Paris-based
International Federation of Human Rights; and the Congo-based African Zone
Association for the Defence of Human Rights. These organisations had accused
a special RPA unit of slaughtering thousands of refugees;[25] an accusation later
corroborated by the findings of the UN Secretary General's Investigative Team
(UN 1998).

Hutu extremists may well have hired scriptwriters, for they certainly have
sympathisers in the West,[26] but the charge that 'the powerful' recruit partisan
writers can be levelled also at the RPF leadership, which ever since its invasion
of Rwanda has mustered sympathetic academics (and some journalists and aid
workers) to write its version of how Rwanda's history and ethnicity should be
understood.

Although teaching history was suspended in Rwanda after the war and genocide, the fact is that *history is being rewritten* – not just Rwanda's pre-colonial
and early colonial history, but also that of modern eastern Zaire-DRC – and
this is being done both in Rwanda and in the West. The horror of the 1994
Rwanda genocide must never be forgotten, but if reconciliation is to take place
in Rwanda then a broader, more detailed and historically informed contextualisation of the drama is required. Under conditions of partisanship, whether with
the RPF or with Hutu extremists, an agreed version of Rwandan society and
history will not emerge, and autocratic rule will 'present itself' as the Rwandan
government's only conceivable solution to end ethnic strife. Already, the die
appears cast. The now advanced national programme for a total restructuring
of the country's physical and social landscape, the focus of Chapter 6, suggests that the search for a commonly agreed reading of society and history may
already have been called off.

Grasping Rwanda's complex history is not a luxury; it is essential if the international community is to retain an informed presence in the Great Lakes. Yet one must ask how independent a voice the highly diverse international community can hope to have. This massively important issue will be dealt with in Chapter 5, which scrutinises certain key encounters between the government of Rwanda and international representatives.

4   Labelling refugees: international aid
     and the discourse of genocide

The last two chapters have shown how academics and journalists with strong
RPF sympathies, but mostly without prior knowledge of the Great Lakes region,
have embraced and spread the Front's idyllic, harmonising perspective on pre-
colonial society and history. An important aspect of the discourse, however, is
that the Front's claim regarding the social construction of ethnicity – or 'the
mistake' of ethnicity – is easily combined with assertive, essentialist statements
on identity: outsiders as well as insiders readily resort to 'the Hutu' or 'the Tutsi'.
The former are 'perpetrators' of genocide or, in the case of those who died in
1994, 'victims of politicide'; the latter are 'survivors' or 'victims of genocide'.
    The present chapter continues the debate on contemporary representations
of social identity with an analysis of how Rwandan refugees were perceived
during the crisis of 1994–6. Using field data from 1995, I demonstrate how
Western humanitarian practices reinforced the essentialist discourse on ethnicity and in doing so reinforced the notion of a collectively guilty refugee body.[1]
The profound horror of genocide, the data suggest, combined with the *normal
practice* of labelling refugees, i.e. combined with the habitual denial of refugee
identities and voices, in such a way that all were deemed guilty. This collective labelling has become an important cog in the mechanism that perpetuates
violence in the Great Lakes.

Interpretations of ethnic violence

In an attempt to overcome the limitations of the term 'ethnic hatred', analysts
now regard conflict as a kind of text, a violent text, a violent attempt to tell a
story. Or, as Paul Richards has put it, conflict is a violent attempt by belligerents
'to "cut in on the conversation" of others from whose company [they] feel
excluded' (Richards 1996: xxiv). This textual perspective implies that violence
is a mode of interpretation (Apter 1989: 23), a view eminently applicable to
Central Africa's ongoing crisis.
    One key aspect of the textual approach to ethnic violence in the Great Lakes is
the recognition that 'Tutsi elites [tend] to substitute collective guilt for individual
responsibility, and to affix the label "génocidaire" to the Hutu community as a

group' (Lemarchand 1998: 8; also Eltringham and Van Hoyweghen 2000). This tendency – understandable since the perpetrators of genocide always suspend their personal morality to allow the state to take over (see Zur 1994: 12)[2] – was most forcefully illustrated in late 1996 when Rwanda's 'missing refugees' were collectively criminalised by the government of Rwanda and its representatives. Inside Rwanda, certain Tutsi survivors also applied a logic of guilt by association: to be a Hutu was to be presumed a killer (Mamdani 1996: 22–3). Such essentialist labelling is a prime ingredient in the perpetuation of violence throughout the Great Lakes. As Lemarchand explains,

an ominous parallel emerges between the discourse of Tutsi extremists in Rwanda, within and outside the army, and their counterparts in Burundi: by attributing responsibility for genocide not to individuals but to a whole community – lumping together the perpetrators of genocide and innocent civilians, including those Hutu who risked their own lives to save those of their Tutsi neighbors – the result has been to create those very conditions that impel some Hutu to become rebels, and ultimately 'génocidaires'. (Lemarchand 1998: 8)

The purpose of this chapter is to look at a complementary aspect of, and reinforcing mechanism for, the tendency to substitute collective guilt for personal responsibility. The phenomenon under investigation is the way the international aid effort construed the Rwandan Hutu refugees *as a collectivity*, as a 'blur of humanity' (Malkki 1996: 367) which should have no say in its own destiny. Against the standard view that the UNHCR and its implementing NGOs enabled 'the killers' to recover and continue the genocide, a critique fully justified, we also need to consider how aid organisations habitually label 'the refugees' as an amorphous mass of people-in-need, a labelling which, in the case of the Rwandan camps, made the notion of collective guilt – and hence disposal – more acceptable. The labelling may have been *business as usual*, but the impact went beyond the usual degrading. The aid community's refusal to approach refugees as differentiated individuals, as thinking human beings, as professionals, as people prepared to take an active part in the everyday running of the camps, reinforced the legitimacy of an essentialist stereotyping through which blame for the 1994 genocide was apportioned to 'the Hutu' collective.[3]

My specific argument is that a collective label ('the refugees', 'the Hutu') was applied in four major ways. First, the professionalism and skills of a great many refugees went unrecognised, along with their ability to analyse camp-related problems. Crudely put, refugees were treated as dumb and dependent. Second, refugees became a degraded mass through the food they received. This food was mostly of poor quality and culturally inappropriate, while agricultural activity was curtailed. Third, Rwandan refugees were treated as if they had lived in a unified Rwanda. With few exceptions, aid workers were unaware of Rwanda's north–south divide, a historically evolved political gap critical during the genocide. Fourth, although aid workers recognised that the majority of refugees were not guilty of any actual killings during the genocide, they all came to be labelled as 'hostages' collectively trapped under the claw of unrelenting extremists. This perception does not fully square with the repatriations recorded over the two-year period in exile.

Camp realities: Goma, 1995; Ngara, 1995

On 23 July 1994, spokesman Ray Wilkinson declared: 'UNHCR is convinced that [Rwanda's] new government is enough in charge to reasonably guarantee [the refugees'] safety.'[4] All refugees, except those responsible for the slaughter, were welcome to return. He added: 'UN envoy [Michel Moussali] has spoken with former government leaders here in Goma. "We are prepared to go home and to take the people with us," they have said.'[5]

These two statements may have seemed unproblematic, yet they could hardly be taken at face value since they invited (or should have invited) several further questions. Such as, what does the RPF mean when it refers to 'those who are guilty', and how long does it take to establish guilt? Are there agreed, guaranteed guidelines regarding the procedures for lawful arrest? (Answer at the time: no.) And what do former government leaders mean when they say they are 'prepared to go home and take the people with them'? Might this not be a veiled reference to some hoped-for retaking of Rwanda by military means? Without the guarantee that the Rwandan government intended to invite former authorities to debate the country's political future, which was an impossible guarantee, there was no way members of the former government could be serious about an imminent return by peaceful means.

That situations on the ground, both inside Rwanda and in the camps, were more complex than assumed would become clear in early 1995. As the prospect of a constructive relationship between the government of Rwanda and the international community ebbed away, a British ODA mission concluded: 'Inside Rwanda, security has deteriorated in past weeks and confirmed reports of arbitrary arrest and ill-treatment are causing increasing concern' (quoted in *The Independent*, 21 March 1995). The knock-on effect, *The Independent* spelled out, was that a growing number of former refugees were now doubling back into Zaire. At the time, the UNHCR estimated that some seventy to eighty people were returning to Kibumba camp every day.

'I went home to Byumba [in northern Rwanda] with my family in January,' Jean Sakufi, a Hutu living in Kibumba [camp], said. 'When we arrived we heard my mother-in-law had been killed by Inkotanyi [RPF soldiers] so we came back to Zaire. We're not going home again until our safety has been guaranteed by the international organizations working here.'[6]

It is voices like Jean's which could have made the international aid effort more aware that many refugees did have genuine concerns about safety and justice in Rwanda, that refugees were not a mass of murderers all unwilling to face the reality of genocide. The doubling back into Zaire was not simply a victory for Hutu hardliners, but confirmation that life in Rwanda continued to be highly insecure. Significantly, too, many would-be returnees knew whether their homes were occupied and what chances they had of successfully reclaiming their property. Among those who walked back to Rwanda in November 1996, many knew what awaited them.[7] The flow of information 'from home' had been facilitated by the maintenance of the familiar commune structure in the camps.

That the basic engagement of humanitarian agencies with refugees was marked by incomprehension and confusion came into the open when, one year into the crisis, two major organisations, UNHCR and Médecins Sans Frontières (MSF), issued contradictory statements on whether refugee intimidation by ex-tremists continued. Released on the same day in July 1995, the positions were as follows:

UNHCR: According to Carol Faubert, *the intimidation of 'ordinary' refugees* by leaders of the old Rwandan administration *'no longer occurs'*, even though the extremists in the camps continue to spread propaganda and disinformation most effectively.

MSF: *The instigators of the genocide* are taking control of the camps in an increasingly systematic way, and *block the return of the refugees.* . . . 'They [the instigators] are free to come and go between camps, and manipulate the refugees through controlling the flow of political information.'[8]

While the statement by MSF may have reflected the hardening of extremists towards innocent civilians at a time when aid flows were drying up, it is dis-concerting that such a contrast should have existed. More than anything else, the contrast epitomised the aid organisations' general inability to comprehend the everyday-life experience of camp politics. The contrast confirmed what other analysts had experienced in refugee situations elsewhere: the *de facto* approach routinely taken by UNHCR and the implementing agencies often ap-pears 'dictated more by hand-to-mouth response to donor pressure than a set of established principles *or detailed knowledge of the local situation*' (Allen and Morsink 1994: 5; emphasis added).

Of course, we must not underestimate how difficult it is to situate the actors in a refugee drama, particularly when that drama follows war and genocide. Identification will never be easy. As I have written elsewhere,

[it] may seem straightforward to be introduced to a *Président du Camp*, to the *Président de la Société Civile* or to representatives of a Rwandan NGO, but it is not. Who are these actors in the drama? How are they linked? What is the status of leaders who say they were democratically elected? What are their links with the old regime, with the

military? Can anyone speak freely? Who are the civilians I cannot identify? And how was everyone embroiled in the genocide? Many such questions I could never resolve, nor could the aid workers I consulted. (Pottier 1996a: 404–5)

To outsiders, the term 'civil society' may appear synonymous with 'NGOs', but the question arises whether the term can denote political independence under an oppressive regime. As Mahmood Mamdani cautions, civil society must be understood *analytically* in its actual historical formation, and *not programmatically* as an agenda for change (Mamdani 1995: 224).

Having dealt with this methodological problem elsewhere, I shall here focus on the cost incurred when organisations fail to differentiate 'the refugees', fail to see them as group members or individuals with life-stories to tell: stories about trauma, fear, anger, hope and aspiration; stories about skills learned before the flight into exile; stories about contributions made to the smooth running of camp life. An ethnography of camp life must not be limited to an appreciation of commune-level politics; the interest must extend into the politics of everyday life, which means, for instance, that analysts must learn to understand the effects of shifts in people's social status. In this respect, elderly men who possessed land in Rwanda were dealt a severe blow when it was known their farms were occupied. Without land, they lacked political leverage *vis-à-vis* the junior adult relatives over whom they used to have control. It was the same for older women who had become separated from adult sons and daughters. Without the support of junior family, the elderly had few entitlements.

Unrecognised skills: initiative-taking, professionalism, ability to analyse

Initiative-taking unrecognised

When gatekeepers control the flow of information in a camp, which is common, it takes a special effort to access the views of so-called 'ordinary' refugees. This became clear in the course of my fieldwork when a group of women in Lumasi camp, Ngara (Tanzania), related that many unaccompanied minors had been fostered by refugees. There were over 7,000 such children in Ngara region, nearly all with foster families; the women were proud of this. Problems to do with fostering did occur, but were mostly resolved without recourse to the authorities.[9] The women's positive view on fostering was countered, however, by the Rwandan representative of Norwegian People's Aid (NPA), the NGO responsible for community services. Taking a *social services* attitude, this community worker deplored the absence of 'a proper orphanage' in the camp. Strongly authoritative, her words ended our discussion that day. Afterwards, though, several women who had participated in the discussion revealed in private how their community leader tended to indulge in assistance by outside NGOs.

But NPA's expatriates defended the position of their Rwandan counterpart. Not referring to fostering as such, but to 'the total breakdown of community relations' within the camps, one expatriate said: 'Although we must fight the refugees' recipient mentality, it is still too early to move towards self-reliance. People are used to hand-outs (free water, health and food), so when it comes to community development they do not quite see why their own resources should be harnessed.'[10]

What matters here is the labelling of refugees as lacking initiative. The standard approach applied: refugees do not take initiative, do not have skills, and are happy or forced by circumstance to be dependent (see also Houtart, UNHCR, pp. 139–40).

Not all NGOs, however, were insensitive to self-help. In Musuhura camp, adjacent to Lumasi, two NGOs, Christian Outreach and Tear Fund, in collaboration with UNHCR staff, supported programmes initiated by refugees. Among the initiatives were projects to share food with vulnerable groups; micro-credit projects to aid small, collectively run businesses; and youth training schemes. Another manifestation of initiative-taking, but one rarely reported, was the removal of troublesome community leaders, especially at the *secteur* level. Such initiatives were often supported by committed NGOs. Christian Outreach actively promoted the refugees' search for new, responsible leaders in Musuhura. These leaders – 'community mobilisers' and administrators – had come forward in response to specific social and economic problems, such as unfair food distributions, or because former leaders were absent or had left under pressure. A contributing factor to the success of these NGOs had been UNHCR's decision, in February 1995, to halt the payment of 'incentives' to commune leaders. This suspension had followed the discovery that over-registration and food diversions continued unabated.[11] New leaders, I was told, were less likely to interfere with community-based initiatives.

The example of self-help in Musuhura paralleled the success which the NGO Concern had had in Lumasi when it set up its own food distribution system. Initially, Concern's independent workers had been harassed, but the problem did go away. (When there was just one huge camp at Benaco, food distributors had been appointed by established commune leaders, causing diversions and hunger among poor refugees.) When Lumasi started up, and Concern took charge of food distributions and camp management, the organisation stamped out these diversions by appointing its own distributors. The demands previously made by old-regime authorities were greatly reduced and food came to be distributed directly to households. The transition to fair distributions took time, yet succeeded with some ease relative to the time it took in the camps around Goma (Pottier 1996a: 414).

When I interviewed war widows from Muvumba commune (Byumba Prefecture), widows initially displaced because of the RPF invasion of October 1990, they appreciated Concern's support and recalled their earlier experiences:

In Benaco we remained one week without food. Some of us ate grass or mud. None of us had taken food across the border. It rained, but there were no plastic sheetings nor did we get blankets. After one week we received the first food – beans – from the Tanzanian Red Cross. We also began to regroup according to commune. But the Tanzanian Red Cross handed the food to the commune leaders (*bourgmestres*), who then divided it up according to *secteurs*. There was no justice. The rations widows received were small, we got pushed aside and often received nothing at all. Young people snatched food away from us.

After one month in Benaco, Concern and CARE took charge of food distributions and built distribution centres. *Secteur* leaders became more involved and supported the weak. But the distributors were men and often good friends with the *bourgmestres*. When they did not know you, they cheated, they gave you whatever they liked, which was always much less than what you should receive.

The big change came after we moved to Lumasi camp where Concern appointed new distributors, men and women. They were known to us and we trusted them. Food was no longer diverted, we received our fair share.[12]

Despite the positive difference the change in food distribution strategy made, some new problems surfaced. As with the provision of other services (employment, water, health), refugees were very sensitive to the *regional origin* of those in charge of food distributions. Many refugees were concerned about the regional identity of both the food distributors, who handled the scoops, and the loaders. For instance, distributors serving Rukira commune (Kibungo Prefecture) were all from Rukira itself, which meant they were known and had to be fair, but not so the men who fetched the food. These loaders, who transferred food from the EDP (External Delivery Point) to the chute from which Rukira was served, were from Byumba, not Kibungo. They were northerners.[13] This caused resentment and allegations that loaders diverted bags. Rukira people said Concern had been informed and planned to move Rukira to a different distribution centre.

These experiences in Musuhura and Lumasi showed that community mobilisation for non-political purposes was a feature of camp life and that it paid – economically, socially and psychologically – to support these initiatives. Nonetheless, community mobilisation was rarely encouraged, and certainly not on any significant scale. In Lumasi, the emphasis remained on 'social services' and working through established structures. Despite the *bourgmestres*' 'salary' cut, UNHCR and the *bourgmestres* continued to meet once a week, together with Concern and other NGOs, to discuss a variety of social and economic issues. These meetings reinforced the position of established leaders or, more accurately perhaps, reinforced an established authority structure. The outcome was that humanitarian aid was not used to support the alternative structures that had arisen or might arise. As a result, it became harder to create an atmosphere of trust, a prerequisite in the promotion of dialogue on sensitive topics, including the politics of repatriation.

In Mugunga, too, there was no shortage of self-help initiatives. Most of these came from women, and many took place within organisational frameworks that had existed before the flight. Women's groups, however, like other Rwandan NGOs, had signed the Goma charter of the Collectif des ONG (on 4 July 1994), a charter few humanitarians will have regarded as politically neutral.[14] The Collectif des ONG (NGO Collective from now on) stated that its members were independent from the warring armies, the interim government (then in power), the RPF and political parties generally. This neutrality seemed honourable. On the other hand, while the NGO Collective advocated support to the displaced, it remained silent on the subject of genocide. Its preoccupation was with buttressing 'self-help activities among the displaced' and strengthening the 'partnership between Rwandans and the outside world' (*Traits d'Union Rwanda* 3: 17). Crucially, the NGO Collective recognised the legitimacy of other NGO collectives, including the network CCOAIB (Le Conseil de Concertation des Organismes d'Appui aux Initiatives de Base) which had given its support to the 'traditionalist' NGOs allied with Hutu Power (*Traits d'Union Rwanda*, Special Edition 2: 21). This strong indication that the NGO Collective was not as neutral as it claimed to be is likely to have contributed to the UNHCR's marginalisation of the twenty-one NGOs which had signed the charter. The latter felt ignored by the international community and left out of the planning decisions.

The finding from the Tanzanian camps that self-help activities abounded, yet struggled for recognition and financial support, also applied to Goma. Within Mugunga, for instance, the NGO Collective aimed to promote the refugees' right to self-initiative. One way in which this was done was by running seminars to which UN agencies and NGOs were invited. Members of the NGO Collective said that it was difficult to ensure the cooperation of these outside organisations as the latter were still learning how to appreciate the refugees' intellectual patrimonium, but they gladly reported that a recent seminar on refugee struggles for survival (17–19 June 1995) had been attended by representatives from UNHCR and several international NGOs. Allegedly, this was the first time that international aid workers had attended. Although the NGO Collective knew that UNHCR-Goma was suspicious of the motives underlying self-help, motives perceived as political, its members believed that UNHCR, WFP and major NGOs had begun to appreciate the contribution that the NGO Collective could make to camp management. The German development organisation GTZ, responsible for sanitation and firewood, and the American Refugee Committee (ARC), responsible for health, were singled out as organisations genuinely interested in working with refugees: 'They do try to follow up our suggestions, which we value.'

Members of the NGO Collective stressed that UNHCR should understand that working through the refugees' own resources must inevitably lead to important financial savings, since refugees are invariably cheaper to employ than expatriates. The NGO Collective added that working with human resources, refugees in this case, was a moral obligation for UNHCR because implementing organisations often pulled out of emergencies at very short notice. One representative said:

UNHCR has a moral duty to prepare refugees for that moment of departure and must work towards a partnership relationship with them. We appreciate many of the initiatives UNHCR has taken, including its efforts to accurately assess the camp population and democratise access to food aid, but we also want to receive recognition for our own initiatives. Often it is *our* suggestions that result in improvements *they* make.[15]

This opinion deserves further attention.

Professionalism unrecognised

Professional skills also went unrecognised. While the recruitment of medically skilled Rwandans appears to have been a routine priority early on in the crisis in Goma,[16] 'traditional birth attendants' (TBAs) in Lumasi camp complained they had been ignored for too long and forced to practise 'illegally' and without remuneration. In a future crisis, they argued, UNHCR, or the World Health Organisation or any designated health NGO, should screen refugees with medical skills as a matter of urgency. TBAs had been particularly frustrated during the early months of turmoil when they were often unable to help with difficult births because they had fled without their professional certificates. It was not until they had arrived in Lumasi, after an initial stay in the *Zone Turquoise*, that TBAs learned that a health NGO, the International Rescue Committee (IRC), was interested in registering them. Before arriving in Lumasi, they had assumed there was no structure within which they could practise their profession.

Educationalists were likewise frustrated, because secondary education does not feature among UNHCR's priorities. With reference to Ngara, Tanzania, the following statement aptly summarises UNHCR's policy:

Under UNHCR coordination, the Community/Education NGOs have encouraged refugees to be more involved in various aspects of their camp life (. . .). In Ngara (. . .), it has been agreed that with the exception of primary education where UNHCR, UNESCO, UNICEF, GTZ and the Community Services NGOs have been more pro-active, other activities should be initiated by the refugees themselves. (Houtart 1995a: 2)[17]

The lack of assistance with secondary education, together with the frustrating isolation which intellectuals and many skilled professionals experienced, led elite refugees to talk in terms of 'intellectual genocide'. As with other issues, the deteriorating food supply for example, the problem was again perceived in terms of the prospect of a forced, premature return to Rwanda.

The refusal to support secondary education can be justified on political grounds, since UNHCR did not want to be seen as encouraging permanent camps, yet these camps brimmed over with young people. With 60 per cent of residents under twenty-five years of age,[18] every youngster was a potential recruit for the next round of war and genocide. Jean-Pierre Godding, Caritas worker and former development counsellor in Gisenyi, clarified:

'Youth are not a priority for HCR. This is understandable. HCR is concerned with refugees and its basic position is that refugees need to return as soon as possible. In contrast, our [Caritas'] starting point is that a good section of the refugees will never return, either because they have blood on their hands or because their homes and farms have been taken over by Tutsi returnees.'

Addressing the international aid effort, Godding continued: 'Our efforts must not end with the provision of food aid. We must build bridges between the Rwandans inside and outside Rwanda, provide correct information, and help youths develop a perspective for the future. If the approach to humanitarian aid remains as it is, then we will indeed be preparing for a new conflict tomorrow.'[19] Godding accepted that the task of building bridges did not have to fall to UNHCR, or to UNHCR alone, but, he insisted, the UN agency had a duty to facilitate initiatives that aimed to make correct information available.

It was on the issue of information that the views of UNHCR and of the refugee majority stood diametrically opposed. Wishing to be seen to be neutral, UNHCR launched a Refugee Information Network restricted to themes aimed at normalising life *inside the camps*. UNHCR made information available, for instance, concerning the weekly content of the refugee food basket or regarding the measures to improve health and sanitation. In sharp contrast, many refugees expressed concern over conditions back home (related to justice, imprisonment, loss of property, etc.) and demanded to be informed about the obscure political processes that sought to determine the modalities for repatriation.

Anxieties caused by the lack of information regarding international negotiations ran deep and were not just a politician's preoccupation. UNHCR, though, did not want to hear about them; information about the political process of repatriation was not a priority because 'ordinary' refugees were thought not to be interested. UNHCR's community services coordinator for Ngara, Myriam Houtart, explained in a circular:

By having fled their country, refugees have lost control over many aspects of their life which is making them *very insecure and dependent*. Information about camp management, the problems faced by the aid workers and the refugee community, the daily events, *and eventually about [the] Rwanda situation whenever [that may be] possible . . .* is giving them more tools to face and understand the reality and situation of camp life. (Houtart 1995b: 3; emphasis added)

At the field level, UNHCR claimed that the majority of refugees had no need for information about the political processes that determined their future. Distinguishing clearly between politicians and the rest of the camp population, Houtart claimed:

According to refugees consulted, the word reconciliation seems to have political connotation and should be left to politicians to deal with. They would prefer for the time being to talk about peace, unity and cooperation *within the camps*. (Houtart 1995b: 4; emphasis added)

This neat dichotomy between politicians and non-politicians is not helpful. While it appears to reflect the wishes of 'the refugees' (but who and how many were consulted?), it would have been more realistic to accept that the bulk of the refugees did have a strong interest in politics and, therefore, a need for up-to-date information of a political nature. In 1995, especially following the Kibeho massacre, these interests and needs were greater than UNHCR conceded. In this respect, a Mugunga initiative worthy of note was the setting up of a reading centre (*centre de lecture*) where refugees could read on aspects of the crisis and how it was being dealt with internationally. Launched by the NGO Collective, this reading/resource centre was selective in what it displayed, which was hardly surprising, but its call for more information was legitimate – and a right UNHCR should recognise. The claim that ordinary refugees were not interested in the politics of reconciliation rested on a rather narrow conceptualisation of what repatriation entailed. As refugees understood the terms, repatriation and reconciliation entailed a range of concerns: not only about bringing the killers and ringleaders to book, but also about the appropriation of property by Tutsi repatriates.[20]

Analytical skills unrecognised

During field research I was regularly made aware of just how difficult it is for humanitarian agencies and organisations to appreciate refugee perspectives, and how frustrated refugees feel when their insights are ignored. Aid organisations, as the NGO Collective put it, had difficulty appreciating 'the refugees' intellectual patrimonium'. Key areas where the refugees' analytical skills went unrecognised included water, fuel, food aid and health. Through the reflections they shared, refugees showed they were well aware of the nature of these problems and the many cross-cutting issues involved.

The pressures the refugee crisis exerted on the environment, with clear consequences for water, are a good starting point. The water situation in Lumasi, exceedingly precarious by mid-1995, provided an excellent example of how refugees, whether 'intellectual' or not, analysed camp conditions. In Lumasi, where the number of boreholes was negligible and the supply of tankered water erratic, women from Muvumba commune commented that water distributions should be organised like food distributions, with reliable timetables. The women complained that not only did the water tankers arrive at irregular intervals, but also they had to queue all day and sometimes got no water at the end. One woman said: 'People nowadays start queuing at 3 a.m. or 4 a.m., because they are desperate. But unlike with food, no matter how early you start queuing [for water], it is never certain that you will be served.' To add to the frustration, Lumasi had four boreholes only, one of which had broken down while another was shared with Lukole camp, where Burundese refugees lived.

A frequent elaboration on the water problem was that shortages had worsened in the second quarter of 1995 because of the poor quality of the food aid received. Water consumption, Lumasi refugees argued, had doubled following the arrival of poor-quality maize and beans. A teacher said: 'Provided they can collect that much in a day, a family of 4 or 5 who used to go through 15 litres a day, now probably uses 30 or 40 litres.' Poor beans and maize meant more water, more firewood. The hard beans were dubbed *rumarinkwi*: 'it takes too much firewood'. These old, hard beans were 'low end' supplies taken from stocks held by the International Federation of the Red Cross (IFRC); they needed 'rotating out'. The gift had been convenient since the World Food programme (WFP) was by now struggling to secure new donor commitments.[21] It was the increase in cooking time which explained, refugees said, why they needed to queue for water so very early every morning.

But refugees saw a link not only between poor-quality food aid and the increased pressure on scarce resources, but also between water insecurity and the lack of personal protection; a link which, some people argued, had resulted in a surge of assaults and rapes. This link was articulated in several interviews and, in a separate interview, confirmed by Anglican pastors. Referring directly to the increase in rape due to the water shortage, but mentioning also the increasingly hazardous long walks to collect firewood, the Anglican pastors said they could not understand why UNHCR, Concern (in charge of Lumasi's management) and the Tanganyika Christian Relief Service (in charge of water) had not tried harder to resolve the appalling situation.

Refugees in Lumasi were also concerned that the agency responsible for assuring the supply of firewood (CARE) seemed to show no interest in tackling the need to replenish the dwindling resources. Although firewood programmes were often presented by NGOs as part of their sensitisation campaign, refugees regularly contested the claim that sensitisation on environmental matters was actually needed. 'We know how to take care of the environment,' a middle-aged man said, 'because we have a saying in Rwanda that "for every tree you cut down you must plant two saplings." ... The solution is for UNHCR or CARE to make saplings available so we can plant. Two saplings per *blindé* [shelter] would be enough.

We *do* want to reverse the damage we have caused, because no one here knows how much longer we will be staying. It is not in our interest not to replant the hills we have laid bare. Emergency workers do not seem to understand that this is how we feel, they just accuse us of not caring about the environment. That's wrong. Right now, we help ourselves [to scarce resources] because we struggle for life (verb: *kwirwanaho*), but we can just as easily be mobilised to replace these trees, perhaps by doing *umuganda*.'[22]

While it is only fair to acknowledge that Rwandans have practised intensive agriculture and anti-erosion measures since at least the end of the nineteenth century (Grogan and Sharp 1900: 118–19; Honke 1990: 16),[23] NGOs, perhaps on the pretext that they faced an emergency, had little time for refugee views on environmental degradation or to follow-up on suggestions for action. This meant that the outsider, the relief worker, could step in as the enlightened, indispensable 'sensitiser'.

The question must be asked, though: are these expatriates really equipped – technically, culturally and politically – to act as agents of change? And is change indeed what is needed? That expatriate personnel recruited for the purpose of sensitisation often arrived totally unprepared is revealed in the following 'confession' by Yann Jondeau who, at the age of twenty-two, had arrived in Goma to work for MSF-France. His experience was not an isolated one. In an interview with *Le Figaro*, Jondeau recalled that as he headed for Kibumba camp, where he would sensitise the population in matters of health, he realised he had

'no inkling of what was going on. There were two ethnic groups, Hutu and Tutsi, but apart from that ... When by the end of the second week we understood that we had come to the rescue of the militias who had carried out the massacres, we all got a good smack in the face. The perpetrators of the genocide controlled everything in the camps. And worst of all, because we were French they actually liked us!'[24]

Jondeau also revealed how emergency aid imposed its own authority structures and recreated undesirable hierarchies: 'We behaved like colonial patrons. When you're white it is hard not to do this in Africa, because that's how you are perceived, whatever you do. I as well, I began to speak of "my" employees. At the age of 22, I had 200 people working for me.'[25] This relief worker may have been technically competent, yet he had no understanding of the political and cultural context he had come to work in. It hardly mattered to the aid business: he was there to sensitise, not to practise philosophy.

An interesting perception regarding cleanliness around shelters (*blindés*) during the rainy season, when it is hard to keep that space free of puddles and mosquitoes, also revealed good analytical skills. To act prophylactically, refugees needed hoes to dig drainage canals and cut down weeds, but hoes were not at hand. 'If only NGOs paid more attention to camp agriculture,' some refugees said, 'we might have better access to hoes and improve conditions around the *blindés*.' Health and agriculture, sectors so often delinked in development policy (Pottier 1999b), were firmly connected in the minds of camp residents. Whether medically skilled people or mere 'clients', refugees repeatedly stressed that health policy required an integrated approach.

Refugee voices were not heard; UNHCR and many NGOs preferred a top-down approach justified in the name of 'emergency'. A group discussion with Rwandan staff at a health post in Mugunga, a post closed at short notice, kept harping back on the central issue that UNHCR had difficulty accepting that refugees could be intellectuals. One staff member said, 'UNHCR knows how to turn intellectuals into beggars.' UNHCR-Goma, his co-workers stressed, had a habit of 'hiding behind Geneva' as if no decision was ever made in Goma itself. 'Geneva has cut your salaries, Geneva is closing your hospital ... UNHCR is not used to the idea that refugees think.' It is conceivable that UNHCR's position had been exacerbated by the genocide factor, i.e. that the organisation may have used the genocide to justify that refugees should be intellectually marginalised. On the other hand, it seems equally valid to argue that UNHCR was simply not prepared for its encounter with such a well-organised 'body' of refugees and the very high percentage of intellectuals living in the camps.

Refugees are refugees: food culture denied

For refugees, the clearest sign that they were treated as a mass of undifferentiated, unworthy people came in the form of food aid. Refugees in the camps received yellow maize, both as a grain and flour, even though maize is not a preferred food and maize flour not a preferred flour. Rural Rwandans prefer root crops over grains, and cassava flour over maize flour. The 'problem of maize' was most serious in the camps of Ngara, where 83 per cent of the distributed maize was in the form of whole grain (Pottier 1996b: 328; also Jaspars 1994: 25). By mid-1995, war widows displaced since the 1990 RPF invasion had become accustomed to maize, both yellow maize grain and flour, but they preferred white maize as it could be pounded by hand. 'Yellow maize is no good for the poor and vulnerable, for only those with money can afford to have it ground' (Group discussion, July 1995). White maize had been distributed earlier on in the crisis, in Benaco camp (Jaspars 1994: 5), but not for very long.

The predominance of maize grain over maize flour in Lumasi was much disapproved of, even by those accustomed to eating maize porridge. The cost of milling was a factor in this. Refugees found it disappointing that WFP was allowed to distribute maize grain to camps where grinding mills were insufficient and at a time when most people struggled to secure even the smallest amounts of income. The milling fee of twenty Tanzanian shillings for every kilogramme of maize ground was beyond the means of the majority poor. They would either sell the grain or, more commonly, boil and undercook it. 'Undercooked maize,' women said, 'causes kwashiorkor, because lactating mothers do not produce enough milk.' The over-emphasis on maize was widely regretted.

In Mugunga, too, the over-emphasis was a talking point. Refugees acknowledged that people from northern Rwanda were more used to eating maize porridge, because of the years of displacement and external assistance, but everyone suffered when maize grain rather than flour was distributed. Although the problem was not half as bad as in Lumasi, refugees, here too, requested better milling facilities. When only maize grain was available, women knew they would undercook the grain, which, they said, causes diarrhoea in children. Women claimed there was little they could do given the limited supplies of firewood. The only way around the problem was to work for cassava flour on Zairean farms. For a day's work, a refugee woman received 1,500 New Zaires or one bowl (*ingimere*) of cassava flour. Women mixed cassava and maize flour to make food supplies in the camp more palatable and longer-lasting.

In both Lumasi and Mugunga, refugees also drew attention to the low quantities of food they received, especially in the case of beans. For the bean-loving Rwandans, the target allocation of 120g of beans per person per day, rarely achieved anyway, was a painful joke. Refugees argued that WFP/UNHCR needed to adjust their international standards to fit local cultures. 'Does WFP not know we are bean eaters?' Refugees also wondered why they so rarely received rice. The absence of rice from the food basket, like the maize 'overdose', was mostly interpreted in terms of an international conspiracy which aimed to starve the refugees and force them back to Rwanda. They had similar views on the poor quality of some of the other food items. Rotten beans, hard maize, and old and bitter CSB[26] were all interpreted as unmistakable signs that the international community opposed the refugees' presence outside Rwanda's borders. As refugees saw it, Rwandan food culture, and hence their identity as a people, was blatantly ignored.

Rwanda's north–south divide: importance not grasped

Although Rwanda's north–south divide had been a key factor in how the genocide had spread southward in April 1994, few aid workers understood its continued importance in the camps. The ignorance was symptomatic of the tendency everywhere to treat refugees as a homogenous group without history (see Malkki 1992). Ethnic diversity and multi-partyism being absent in Lumasi (or, in the case of multi-party politics, invisible), agencies mistook these absences as indicative of social homogeneity. Sometimes though, as in Lumasi, the regional divide was strongly reflected in the pattern of arrivals. With an estimated camp population of 70,149,[27] Lumasi had 65 per cent of refugees from around Byumba and 35 per cent from Kibungo. Unlike the Byumba refugees, the newcomers from Kibungo had not had any prior experience of refugee life and were in much poorer health. To summarise:

Byumba = northerners + early arrivals + experience in IDP camps inside Rwanda since the early 1990s. Largest commune: Muvumba.

Kibungo = southerners + late arrivals + no previous camp experience. Largest commune: Rukira.

Health services is another area where aid organisations showed how little they understood of the politics of everyday life. In Lumasi camp, refugees were generally impressed with the technical delivery of the health services rendered by the International Rescue Committee (IRC), yet they expressed concern regarding the social matters that expatriate health workers overlooked. With several NGOs scaling down their activities by mid-1995, refugees voiced disappointment with what they thought were *social costs not visible to the majority of aid workers*. In particular, when certain health facilities run by NGOs were closed down and alternatives were proposed, refugees became highly conscious of 'the others', that is the other refugees, on whom they would now depend. This was especially so when 'the others' came from the other side of the north–south divide. For example, when the African Education Fund (AEF) hospital in Kibungo closed down, its patients were told they should now seek treatment at a hospital staffed with people from Byumba. Knowing they would not be welcome at this alternative site, Kibungo refugees strongly resented the change.

Refugees from southern Rwanda were also reluctant to share water points with northerners because such sharing often led to conflict and tension. Kibungo refugees said they would rather go to the nearest borehole in the valley, where the water was dirty, than queue at standpipes nearer their shelters but located in the communes of Ngarama and Muvumba (Byumba prefecture), where they risked harassment or a fight. A group of *cellule* leaders from Rukira voiced the opinion that UNHCR, or the NGO in charge of camp management, should be better informed about and sensitive to Rwanda's regional division, since aid worker ignorance easily resulted in frustration or fights.

Programmes for primary education, likewise, were commented on in terms of employment opportunity and cost, i.e. the number of jobs they provided and who snapped them up. A group of women from Rukira (south Rwanda) pointed out that most of the primary school teachers in their area were from Byumba, north

Rwanda. These teachers had been recruited by Norwegian People's Aid (NPA) at a time when the people from Kibungo (late arrivals) were still 'learning how to be refugees'. The women from Rukira had raised this matter with NPA, which then resolved that teachers who asked to be replaced would be replaced only by teachers from south Rwanda. Lumasi refugees were sensitive to job recruitment patterns, which was one important criterion by which they judged the performance of NGOs, whether in education or other sectors. UNHCR-appointed security guards, recruited when Lumasi opened, also featured in the debate on assistance and regional origin. Most of these guards were northerners, an imbalance to which refugees from south Rwanda objected. It was the same for other jobs: NGO workers, latrine diggers, toilet slab makers and night watchmen were mostly 'professional refugees' from the north.

Crucially, aid worker ignorance about regional politics convinced refugees that UNHCR's judgement regarding conditions in post-war Rwanda could not be trusted. How could Western aid workers fail to understand camp politics, something so central to everyday life, and then claim they knew that the conditions for a safe return to Rwanda were guaranteed? With very few exceptions, refugees were nonplussed by UNHCR's cavalier attitude towards repatriation; its ambivalent attitude had been all too blatant during the first year in exile. The succession of contradictory messages – safe, go back (mid-August 1994); unsafe, do not go (mid-September 1994); safe again, go now (mid-December 1994) – was understood to stem from the combination of two forces: first, the humanitarian workers' ignorance of Rwandan politics; and second, frustration over their inability to bring squalid camp conditions and the risk of major epidemics under control. Refugees intuitively knew it was camp conditions rather than an informed reading of the political scene which dictated UNHCR's positive disposition towards repatriation. Aloys Rukebesha, president of the Société Civile en Exile at Mugunga, once said: 'Repatriation is not just a question of logistics, of trucks and leaflets. No, it's deeper than that. But HCR does not seem to understand.'[28] For many refugees, UNHCR's easy-to-reverse stance on the conditions for repatriation also indicated that its loyalty lay with the new authorities in Kigali. Western readings of Rwandan politics were regularly questioned: did UNHCR not know about the deepening rift *within* Rwanda's 'government of national reconciliation'? Did UNHCR not know what every refugee had known since December 1994, namely, that Prime Minister Twagiramungu had openly held the Rwandese Patriotic Army responsible for the insecurity inside Rwanda?[29] On that memorable occasion, Kagame had countered that the prime minister was acting irresponsibly.

In August 1995, when Twagiramungu was forced out of office, he unequivocally exposed the international community's profound ignorance of contemporary Rwandan politics. The root of that ignorance, he stressed, lay in the guilt which had overcome the community after it failed to stop the genocide. Hardliners in the RPF-led government expertly globalised and exploited that guilt.

'That the international community did not prevent the genocide has hit her deep in the stomach,' analyses Twagiramungu. 'She feels guilty and in debt to the RPF – which did end the genocide – and eases her conscience with a variety of aid programmes. Simultaneously and without critical reflection, the international community accepts the RPF's position that all its followers are innocent victims while all refugees are to be regarded as murderers.'[30]

Burdened by this globalised guilt, the international community did little to scrutinise Rwanda's internal political and economic adjustments in the first year the RPF took power. There were reports of human rights violations – some serious, some dubious – but few within the international community showed any interest, for instance, in repossession, which was a key factor in repatriation.

Only in the second half of 1995, when Zaire set an ultimatum for the return of refugees, did aid agencies voice concern over the right to reclaim property and over the arbitrary nature of many arrests, often linked to the problem of double occupancy. In a report released in Nairobi, in July 1995, Médecins Sans Frontières warned that the conditions for repatriation were not in place in Rwanda, because 'the spirit of revenge [was] stronger than the desire for justice'. MSF portrayed the judicial system as extremely weak, not so much because of the slow resumption of direct aid to Rwanda, but because of the RPA. The few Rwandan judges in office did not have a grip 'on certain sectors of the army, which powerfully influences the *de facto* functioning of the judicial system.'[31] MSF excluded an early voluntary return of refugees. UNHCR, on the other hand, remained optimistic, hoping to assist 3,000 returnees a day.[32] One month later, and falling well short of its target, UNHCR blamed the high levels of anti-RPF propaganda in the camps for the low level of repatriation, but accepted that three-quarters of the refugee population would return if there were transparency in Rwanda on matters of arrest, detention and the entitlement to reclaim occupied property. UNHCR was now caught between its newly found concern over the absence of transparency and its admitted failure to introduce into the camps an information system that told 'the truth about the current situation in Rwanda'.[33] This was quite a U-turn on what UNHCR believed ordinary refugees were interested in.

In the long run, however, and despite Twagiramungu's warning about conditions in Rwanda, UNHCR maintained that the reason why refugees did not return was because they were being held hostage by Hutu extremists and the ex-FAR. It was not the conditions in Rwanda which kept them in exile; it was 'the Rwanda of their perceptions . . . that led the population to reject the option of repatriation' (Connelly 1997: 6). These perceptions had resulted from the *interahamwe*'s two-year long campaign and terror. Without belittling the formidable ethical difficulties UNHCR faced, the point must nonetheless be made that the political reality of the camps had not been one of uniform or constant terror. The extremists' grip on camp residents had had its ups and downs, and there had been times when ex-FAR officers despaired because of low troop morale and dwindling support among refugees (Pottier 1996a: 162–5; also Claudine Vidal, *Le Nouvel Observateur*, 21–27 November 1996). The notion of an unwavering hostage crisis is misleading. The point against generalisation was also made early on in the crisis by Rwandan sociologist Placide Koloni, in relation to the return home of refugees from the north-west. As with the killing pattern during the genocide (see Longman, Chapter 2), so too the possibility of an early return from the camps depended on the 'quality' of the leaders who had fled with the Hutu population. Some authorities terrorised their people, others did not. In early August 1994, Koloni explained that it was especially people from Gisenyi who returned, and notably from the Bugoyi region. Koloni explained the phenomenon

in terms of the activities of the exiled prefect of Gisenyi, Come Bizimungu, who was a moderate. For some time now, Prefect Bizimungu has made sporadic visits to Gisenyi, where he negotiates with the new authorities. This creates confidence. In contrast, from Bushiro, the other region within Gisenyi, which happens to be the home area of the assassinated Hutu-president Habyarimana, no one returns home. 'The Bushiro authorities in exile terrorize their people.'[34]

Labelling and collective guilt: paying the price

After some 700,000 refugees returned to Rwanda in November 1996, and the US military claimed that only 'the warring parties' remained,[35] Rwandan officials declared the crisis was over. When asked about the remaining refugees, Manzi Bakuramutsa, Rwanda's ambassador in Belgium, offered this quick arithmetic: 'Rwanda estimates the number of returning refugees to be about half a million. That means more or less *everyone*. What remains in Zaire are the criminals.'[36] Anastase Gasana, the Home Affairs minister, concluded similarly: all but 'a few stragglers' had returned to Rwanda.[37] 'The real problem,' Paul Kagame added, was 'that no one has ever known how many refugees were in those camps, but I guess – and my guess is just as good as anyone else's – that most refugees have now returned to Rwanda.'[38] An indifferent US ambassador in Kigali agreed: there were just a few tens of thousands of Rwandan refugees left; certainly no masses.[39] Kagame's humble logic was backed by findings – revised findings (see Chapter 5) – obtained through US aerial reconnaissance. Those who remained, the RPF-functional logic went, 'were the routed extremist army [ex-FAR] and its camp followers, who scarcely warranted the privileges extended to refugees' (de Waal 1997: 211). Kigali officials called them 'intimidators'.[40]

Used to dealing with refugees in aggregate terms, world politicians and opinion makers, particularly in Britain and the US, followed suit. They agreed that those who remained in Zaire were indeed criminals and hence an acceptable human price to pay for the liberation of all 'real' refugees.[41] The same leaders who in 1994 had wanted to save the image of the UN at all cost (Barnett 1997) now seemed just as desperate to have an RPF-led 'African solution' whatever the cost. The 'African solution' did save lives, UN soldiers' lives, but it also resulted in the massacre of tens of thousands of refugees and Zairean citizens (UN Secretary General's Investigative Team, Report 29 June 1998). An acceptable sacrifice? Only when the globalising label of 'the genocidal refugee' is accepted.

The 'certainty' and 'moral justification' for arguing that there was no one left to worry about rested on the premise that the UN and other aid organisations had a habit of inflating their figures for the population of the refugee camps. The aid world was self-centred and immoral, which gave the RPF its lever and absolute right to hold the moral high ground. And the refugees were one mass of people who spoke with one (extremist) voice. They were collectively guilty, as de Waal had argued earlier in an interview with *NRC Handelsblad*. Guilt accrued to the Hutu identity: 'Once begun the slaughter has to be justified. So everyone must take part, because that is an essential aspect of the ideology, of Hutu-ness.'[42] Collectively guilty, collectively disposable.

The claim by the US military that practically all refugees had returned to Rwanda – a claim considered in the next chapter – gave the ADFL/RPA its licence to kill in eastern Zaire: those who remained were *génocidaires* on the loose. Shortly after the crisis was officially declared over, the first reports of a killing spree in eastern Zaire reached the world outside. On 26 December 1996, Chris Tomlinson, the Associated Press correspondent in Goma, reported:

Not only from North Kivu do we hear of systematic liquidations, cries of alarm are also reaching us from South Kivu where 'groups of heavily armed, English-speaking men have slaughtered hundreds of refugees along the Bukavu-Walungu-Shabunda road.'[43]

As for UNHCR, High Commissioner Sadako Ogata was never very precise in her public statements. A week before refugees returned *en masse* from Goma, she thought corridors possible, in Zaire and in Rwanda, but this would require protection by a neutral military force and human rights observers.[44] This neutral force, she accepted, would need to have the power to disarm the Hutu militias and ex-FAR.[45] Not very realistic, she knew. Ogata's position, one might infer, was that UNHCR sided with the Rwandan government and that the corridors had to be 'humanitarian return corridors'. Ogata admitted that she did not know how exactly the refugees could be persuaded to return, nor did she have a firm idea about how extremists and the ex-FAR could be disarmed. These uncertainties indicated it was unlikely that Ogata would not have been aware of the military plan Kagame had hatched for eastern Zaire.

Conclusion

Humanitarian agencies, whether UN or foreign NGOs, deal with a bewildering diversity of refugee situations and must, in any given crisis, constantly ask *Who's Who?*, often without much hope of receiving any clear answers. Or the question is not asked, in which case humanitarians hear only the voices of extremist leaders who routinely distort information. Whichever way it goes, there is likely to be reinforcement of the cliché that all refugees are the same: a blur of dependants, voiceless and politically insignificant (see also Malkki 1996: 393). In situations of extreme violence, the cliché is likely to be extended further to the perception of collective responsibility for the violence. In the case of the Rwandan refugee camps, it was through its *normal procedures*, through the usual clichés and ways of dealing with refugees, that the international aid effort reinforced the notion of globalised Hutu guilt. This tacit reinforcement made Paul Kagame's plan for eastern Zaire more acceptable on the diplomatic front. (The next chapter continues this discussion.)

The importance of my argument must be set in the context of how violence reproduces itself through the mechanism of interpretation. By upholding the image of an undifferentiated Hutu collectivity, UNHCR and the implementing NGOs encouraged and reinforced the notion that it was all right to essentialise about ethnicity; by clearly siding with the RPF-led authorities in Kigali (e.g. mostly accepting that the refugee return should be unconditional), the international aid effort indirectly promoted the notion of a Hutu collective guilt, a notion straight out of 'the fantasy-land of official mythologies' (Lemarchand 1998: 14). In eastern Zaire, the price paid was the sacrifice of tens of thousands of Hutu refugees all labelled *génocidaires*, many women and children, and thousands of Zairean civilians, who died at the hands of the RPA/ADFL troops once the camps were dismantled. In Rwanda today, the notion of a collective Hutu guilt continues as a major obstacle in the quest for national conciliation.

5   Masterclass in surreal diplomacy: understanding the culture of 'political correctness'

The normal procedure of labelling refugees as a helpless, amorphous body, I have argued in the previous chapter, made it easier for outsiders to conceive of 'the Rwandan refugees' as voiceless and collectively guilty of genocide. Refugees are a lump of humanity at the best of times, and against the background of genocide Rwandan refugees could not become the exception. Still, it remains striking how easily the world forgot the 'missing refugees' and, how easily some Western commentators accepted the killings as a small price to pay for justice. Why were the dominant voices in the international community so quickly persuaded? The short answer is that the RPF-led government of Rwanda had by then won the moral argument. Kigali's new leaders had convinced the world that they – and they alone – had the right to know and determine what was going on in those parts of the Great Lakes region they now controlled.

How did they convince the world? This chapter examines the argument and cultural mechanism through which Kigali's new leaders silenced the international community. The perspective I develop complements, *but does not replace*, the standard analysis of why the UN decided against intervention. France's lead role in calling for intervention, the ghost of the disastrous 1992 UN mission in Somalia, the strongly felt need for an African solution, and Western interests in Zaire's mineral wealth were all crucial in arriving at that decision. To complement the analysis, this chapter focuses on the culture-specific strategy Rwandan leaders deployed to reinforce the notion that only they had the right to determine how the Great Lakes region should be understood and rebuilt. The strategy revolved around concepts of morality, guilt and punishment. Non-intervention, I argue, resulted from *the combined force* of international level-headedness (political and economic) and a sustained, well-directed strategy pursued by Kigali's authorities, who used moral argument to corner diplomats, and those who might influence diplomats, into a humiliating, though by no means uncomfortable, checkmate position. To ease whatever discomfort was felt, Kigali allowed its chief international backers in the West to prepare for intervention in the full knowledge that *realpolitik* would prevail.

Geopolitics, diplomacy and the ADFL

As seen in Chapter 1, the scramble for Zaire's valuable mineral wealth, which includes cobalt, niobium, gold and tantalum, is one key explanation as to why the US backed the ADFL, and why the Alliance progressed towards Kinshasa with such astonishing speed. American Mineral Fields (AMF), which controls many cobalt mines in Canada, fought hard to gain the monopoly over Zaire's cobalt deposits; it paid out substantial sums to the ADFL and lent Kabila its executive Lear jet. After toppling Mobutu, Kabila formally thanked the US for its assistance.

During the campaign itself, economic ties between Congo-Zaire and North America were forged or reinforced through seminars for businessmen that ran parallel to a steadily intensifying diplomatic engagement on the part of the US. Dennis Hankins, a US diplomat in Kinshasa, visited the ADFL headquarters in Goma when the war was still at an early stage. In his footsteps followed the US ambassador in Kigali, who

frequently visited Kabila in Goma, at a moment when the rebels' strategy moved from a regional insurgency to the drive to overthrow Mobutu (IG 1997). These diplomats were not operating on their own account. In his interview with *The Washington Post* in July 1997, Paul Kagame not only admitted that Rwandan military officers led the ADFL, but also revealed that he informed Washington about the military campaign in the eastern Congo. In August of 1996, the Rwandan leader even traveled to New York and Washington to highlight his plans to the Clinton administration (IG 1997). (Ngolet 2000: 70)

US diplomatic efforts were much in evidence just before Mobutu's demise. George Moose, US assistant secretary of state, and others met Kabila in South Africa when President Mandela attempted to broker a peaceful end to the war. Most conspicuous was the US shuttle diplomacy of Bill Richardson, the US ambassador to the United Nations, who successfully applied pressure on both Mobutu and Kabila to prevent the ransacking of Kinshasa.[1] Despite decades of Cold War support to the Mobutu regime, the US stood firmly behind Kabila.

South Africa's economic interest in Zaire's diamond fields in Mbuji-Mayi, where De Beers managed to continue its operations, also translated into political support for the ADFL leader. Already in late February 1997, a spokesman for Mandela told the press: 'The intention is to encourage Kabila to play the role that President Mandela believes he is capable of playing in Zaire. Kabila is obviously a very important player.'[2]

Given that high geopolitical stakes demanded full respect for Kabila and other New Pan-Africanist leaders, the prospect of a UN-led intervention in eastern Zaire had always been a non-starter. At the height of 'preparations', the US flew reconnaissance planes to assess the number of refugees still in Zaire, an exercise which turned extremely controversial when the US military retracted its initial figures. In his review of the circumstances surrounding the retraction, Nick Gowing explains that the reconnaissance

operations were set up as a fig leaf to justify an eventual high-level, international po-litical decision not to go ahead with any kind of significant military intervention by a Multi-National Force (MNF). One senior MNF officer [told Gowing]: 'It was clear from Day One in mission planning that began in Germany that when the One-Stars [Brigadier-Generals] came in there was an acceptance that the mission would never happen. Still, planning went ahead up and down through the national structures.' (Gowing 1998: 58)

Planning went ahead on the understanding that there was no real problem to address.

The ADFL's masterstroke came some four days before refugees returned to Rwanda *en masse*. As UN Secretary-General Boutros Boutros-Ghali agonised over 'genocide by famine',[3] ADFL commander Kabila feigned impatience with the international community and made it clear that if the UN did not hurry up and send a force prepared to disarm the Hutu militias and ex-FAR, he would have to go in himself.[4] Kabila knew the international force would not be mobilised, which gave him, and Kagame, further ammunition with which to humiliate the UN. On this occasion, Kabila and Kagame spoke with one voice. Kagame said: 'If you [the international community] will not do this, . . . we shall have to do it ourselves.'[5]

These final warnings came when the AFDL and Rwandese Patriotic Army (RPA), supported by Ugandan and some Burundian troops, were already oper-ating in Zaire and poised to take Mugunga camp; they coincided with the UN Security Council announcing it was to delay *for another ten days* its decision on whether to intervene. Those dragging their feet were the US and Britain. France, on the other hand, decided to send 120 troops to Congo (Brazzaville).[6]

Despite the no-go position adopted within the UN, world powers would go through the motions of preparing for an intervention in which Canada would take the lead. Canada's interest in peacekeeping operations was very genuine, as Adelman and Suhrke (1999) argue,[7] yet Canada also had a strong interest in Zaire's mining operations. James Fairhead recently highlighted the unique relationship between Congo-Zaire and Canada, revealing that the two countries, along with Cuba, hold nearly all of the world's cobalt reserves (Fairhead 2000). Canada was not just watching the show. One of its former prime ministers, Brian Mulroney, a director of Barrick Gold, was actively involved in the corporation's successful attempt to sign mining agreements with Kabila. Barrick Gold's other directors include George Bush Sr (former CIA director and president of the US) and Richard Helms, also a former CIA director. Canada's commitment to peacekeeping may have been genuine, but so was its interest in cobalt.

However, it is unrealistic to assume that relations between post-genocide Rwanda and its non-African backers would always be clear-cut and unambiguous. Such unavoidable ambiguity was the impetus for my writing this chapter from the perspective of morality. In this respect, when gauging the level of US military intelligence about the Great Lakes, Gowing has asked us not to jump to conclusions.

[Regular] contacts between foreign diplomats and Rwandan officials several times a week both in Kigali and in the field did not necessarily mean that non-regional governments were briefed either automatically or fully on Kagame's strategy for Rwanda and the Alliance inside Eastern Zaire. Indeed, Kagame says he withheld information (cf. interview with Kagame in *Weekly Mail and Guardian*, 8/8/1997). Similarly, it can be argued that the coolness of the US in particular to the deployment of a Multi-National Force in November 1996 must not be seen necessarily as an expression of open support for Kagame and Kabila, and the campaign of ethnic revenge.

Rwanda confirms this more qualified view. 'People expected US involvement, but the reality was different,' said Vice President Kagame [in an interview with the author, 8/4/1998]. 'The fact that we did things so well is seen as a sign of very close co-operation.' But he says that such an impression was wrong. (Gowing 1998: 20)

Kagame's assertion could be just another denial. On the other hand, there have been times when the US warned that Rwanda must restrain itself, as when the ADFL prepared to take Kinshasa. This begs the question of how – in moments of uncertainty – the Rwandan authorities maintained their grip on broadly sympathetic, yet somewhat nervous foreign backers. The answer is that the Rwandan authorities expertly generated and manipulated feelings of guilt, which they did on an international scale. This process, gradual but with strong cultural underpinnings, is what the rest of this chapter aims to unravel.

On morality, guilt and punishment

I begin my argument with an ethnographic flashback on fieldwork carried out in Rwanda in the mid-1980s. Via the story of Ferdinand, a young man tried and convicted for stealing banana bunches from a grove, I introduce certain Rwandan notions pertaining to morality, punishment and patronage. Morality and patronage are inseparable. The ethnographic story deals with the consequences of Ferdinand's proven theft.[8]

Ferdinand

In October 1985, Ferdinand, convicted of theft, brings a mild complaint to the weekly meetings of his cooperative (cf. Pottier 1989b). My personal/Western view is that Ferdinand's complaint is entirely reasonable, but other members of the cooperative ridicule it. Ferdinand feels humiliated (verb: *gusuzuguza*). Among those who give him a really hard time is Gaspard, *chef de secteur*, a local official of whom everyone 'knew', though this had never been proved, that he regularly embezzled money.

Several weeks later, the incident seemingly forgotten, Ferdinand plucks up courage and approaches his *chef de secteur* with beer and money (*ruswa*, a sweetener), requesting help with obtaining access to a plot of (state-owned) marshland. Ferdinand succeeds, and later tells me how lucky he is and how 'indebted' (verb: *kugira umwenda*) he feels towards Gaspard.

A few months go by, then it is Gaspard's turn to stand accused at one of the weekly meetings. Two members of the cooperative make an oblique reference to the rumour that *notre chef* has 'borrowed' (verb: *kwiguriza*) from the cooperative fund. As members discuss the case, Ferdinand picks up a cue from Gaspard, a long hard stare, then comes to the rescue: 'borrowing isn't theft', he proffers, 'even though it may be some time before one can return that money' (*kwiguriza s'ukwiba n'iyo byafata igihe imbere yo kwishyura*). The gathered members understand that Ferdinand, a man of low moral worth, has been 'coaxed' (verb: *kwitabaza*) into speaking up for the troubled official.

The situation Ferdinand finds himself in is a common one. It is commonly captured by the saying *akibo kajya iwamungarurire*, i.e. one makes the (borrowed) basket return.

The parallel with the international community in post-genocide Rwanda is that it, too, like Ferdinand, had been caught red-handed (verb: *gufatanwa itonga*) – that is, caught failing in its mandated duty to protect civilians. And caught twice: a first time when the UN reduced its military presence at the onset of the genocide (April 1994), and a second time when Operation Return ended in the Kibeho massacre (April 1995). For people caught red-handed, whether petty thieves or members of the international community, Rwandans can only feel contempt. Such people have lost face, must not be taken seriously and can be lied to. Moreover, as the case of Ferdinand shows, people caught red-handed can be roped in by their patron, who will 'remember to make the basket return' should he, the patron, need face-saving assistance.

The relevance of this well-known local cultural strategy to the international scene is that Rwanda's president, Pasteur Bizimungu, used it to good effect after world leaders condemned the government of Rwanda over the Kibeho atrocities. As this chapter shows, the morally discredited Western dignitaries came to troubled Bizimungu's rescue in Kibeho when the president needed to save his own government's credibility. As representatives of an international community judged corrupt and indifferent to Rwanda's suffering, these discredited dignitaries were 'surprised' (verb: *gutungurwa*) when called upon, then 'became servile instruments' (verb: *kuba ibikoresho*) in the service of Rwanda's president.

That the international community, the aid community especially, was perceived as a thief caught red-handed was something Rwandan and ADFL leaders regularly stated. In November 1996, as the ADFL campaign gathered momentum in eastern Zaire, Kabila reminded the world he had seen 'too many embezzlements. "The people of UNHCR and the NGOs have been caught red-handed."'[9]

My argument is that the continual humiliation of the international community subsequent to the 1994 genocide, a humiliation made infinitely worse with Kibeho, contributed to the international community turning into a servile instrument at the beck and call of the Rwandan authorities. This is not to diminish the overriding importance of geopolitics, but to explore the mechanism for inducing servility and to spell out how it was operationalised. On a deeper level, one could argue that this politico-cultural mechanism, highlighted in the case of Ferdinand but found throughout the Great Lakes region, lies at the root of that 'culture of impunity' which makes repeated mass killings and genocide possible.

A legacy of international failure and guilt

Seven weeks after the beginning of the 1994 massacres, UN Secretary-General Boutros Boutros-Ghali admitted that it was genocide and that the UN had failed to mobilise the 5,500 UN troops he had promised to send to Rwanda. Apparently troubled by this failure, he publicly expressed regret and globalised the blame:

'We are all responsible for this failure, not only the world powers but also the African countries, the NGOs, the entire international community.'[10]

The failure had multiple aspects. Not only had the UN ignored clear warnings of the impending genocide, it had also taken its time before using the term genocide. The term had been avoided because it invokes legal responsibility under international law. Once Boutros-Ghali publicly admitted the guilt of the UN, however, the international community was caught as good as red-handed and would be made to pay.

Like Ferdinand in the case study, the guilt and debt of the international community, expertly exploited by the Rwandan government, meant that Westerners lost the right to ask 'awkward' questions of the RPF and its agenda. An early example of that loss was the shame of the UN-commissioned but suppressed Gersony report, which had detailed widespread, systematic killings by RPF soldiers in 1994; another was the 'scientifically revised' UN estimate of how many IDPs had died at Kibeho (see below). About Gersony, Prunier wrote that 'in late 1994, UN consultant Robert Gersony had estimated RPF killings in the Northwest and in Kibungo at about 30,000. In its desire to have good relations with the new government in Kigali, the UN then [suppressed] the report it had commissioned, creating a doubt about its very existence' (Prunier 1997: 360). Providing documentation of UNHCR's firm denial that the Gersony report ever existed, Alison Des Forges has argued that 'the UN decided to suppress it, not just in the interests of the recently established Rwandan government but also to avoid further discredit to itself' (Des Forges 1999: 726). Des Forges added: 'The US, and perhaps other [UN] member states, concurred in this decision, largely to avoid weakening the new Rwandan government' (1999: 726).

Although sections of the report were leaked to the international press (Des Forges 1999: 730; Joint Evaluation 1996b: 46), the suppression raises the question of *how* dissenting international voices are silenced. The dominant mechanism, as this chapter shows, unfolds in two broad stages: first, remind your critics of the moral bankruptcy of the international community; next, 'remember to make the basket return', i.e. implicate the international community, make it 'work' for you. Prunier highlights the first step in the sequence: 'any hint that the RPF might be guilty of massive human rights violations is immediately countered ... with an indignant reminder of the genocide' (Prunier 1997: 362).[11] But this is only the first step. Then, after you have reminded the guilty, you must implicate them in your scheme and turn them into 'instruments' at your service (*ibikoresho*).

The first sign that international guilt could be converted into strong support for the RPF came within hours of the swearing-in of the new government in Kigali. As the driving force behind the UN decision to withdraw troops from Rwanda in April 1994 (see Barnett 1997), US president Clinton atoned by immediately recognising the victorious RPF and the government it installed. In an apparent show of strength, Clinton insisted that this RPF-led government be broadly representative, committed to restoring law and order, and determined to forge national unity,[12] yet he did not take long to express satisfaction. Delighted with the prompt recognition of Rwanda's new government, *The New York Times* called upon all Americans to back Clinton: 'The President needs and deserves public support at home.'[13] Clinton also called for the *immediate repatriation* of refugees, proposing to send a full contingent of troops to safeguard returning refugees under the banner of 'Support Hope'.[14]

Despite the serious concerns voiced by Médecins Sans Frontières,[15] UNHCR joined Clinton and declared Rwanda safe for innocent refugees who wished to return.[16] Even before the RPF took Gisenyi, UNHCR had already announced it was prepared 'to "help" the RPF to stabilise the people in their villages'.[17] Boutros-Ghali added his weight by calling for a doubling of humanitarian aid to Rwanda; he urged all refugees to 'Go Home Now'.[18] Such signs of international solidarity were much appreciated in Kigali, where political cadres worked with the media to promote their 'good guys' image.

How did other donors react? The Netherlands, a newcomer to the Great Lakes but poised to become Rwanda's No.1 donor, was just as accommodating as the Clinton administration. Jan Pronk, the Dutch minister for Development Cooperation, urged the international community to recognise Rwanda's needs and provide direct aid.[19] Importantly, however, direct support did not mean Pronk felt restrained in voicing concern about the RPF agenda. On studying the battlefield situation, for example, Minister Pronk expressed reservations about the new government's intentions *vis-à-vis* the refugees, arguing that the RPF should accept joint responsibility for pushing civilians across the border. The RPF had pursued an exodus strategy 'by cordoning off the towns while leaving open an escape route',[20] Pronk said. Not burdened by any colonial past in Africa, the Dutch government could afford to be both supportive and critical of the new regime.

By late July, when there was optimism that refugees would start returning to Rwanda in high numbers, British aid to the region totalled £40 million. One month later, when Britain decided to have its own ODA officials in Kigali, funding had reached £60 million.[21] Aiming to make Rwanda 'a magnet to attract people back', Britain committed direct funds to the Rwandan government for health care, seeds and agricultural tools for home-bound refugees.

The French reaction, predictably, was less accommodating. Speaking on Radio-Télévision Luxembourg (RTL), Alain Juppé, the Foreign Affairs minister, was downright arrogant: 'I appeal to this government: are you able today, yes or no, to reassure the people who will be returning? Can you really guarantee their safety in your country, Rwanda?'[22] Juppé knew of divisions in the new government; he was aware there was no agreed perspective on how to tackle the displacement issue and promote reconciliation. He knew, too, that tens of thousands of refugees, perhaps one hundred thousand, had blood on their hands. Without implying that there existed clear-cut blocks in Rwanda's new government, the basic division was between moderates, who recognised that IDPs/refugees had legitimate fears about arbitrary revenge and harassment, and hardliners, who argued that the reluctance of the displaced to go home meant they had participated in the genocide (Kent 1996: 71, 75). Initially, neither block had wanted to alienate the international community, for Rwanda urgently needed assistance, but alienation would set in during early 1995, as optimism over Operation Return dissipated.

Whereas during the first six weeks of Operation Return high numbers of refugees had gone home, their subsequent experiences of harassment and insecurity meant that, by mid-February 1995, they steadily trekked back to the camps (Kent 1996: 73). For this failure, government hardliners blamed the international organisations. By the time of the first anniversary of the genocide, anti-Western feelings ran high. When six thousand corpses were reburied alongside the remains of Agathe Uwilingiyimana, the assassinated Hutu prime minister, the mood was sombre. It was also distinctly anti-UN and anti-international community. Rwanda's military leader and vice president, Paul Kagame, reminded the world of its guilt, of how it had failed to stop the genocide, and said that this moral failure now needed converting into a moral commitment to help rebuild Rwanda.

'Everything we see here today is symptomatic of a serious sickness which had eaten our society for a very long time unchecked . . . Despite all the speeches made here there is not a single person who has effectively answered for his involvement,' [Kagame] said.[23]

Five days later, certain Rwandan officials hardened their stance against the international community. They made inflammatory speeches at anti-UNAMIR demonstrations where anger was directed against the Human Rights Field Operation in Rwanda, HRFOR (see Office of the Humanitarian Coordinator 1995: 3). Rwandan state radio accused HRFOR of 'stray[ing] from its original mandate' (1995: 3). UN monitors had shown too much interest in the RPA, its disregard for the rehabilitation of Rwanda's civil justice system and predilection for instant justice. Deprived of the aid they had hoped for, Rwanda's new leaders began to argue that no one outside Rwanda should have the right to criticise the regime. By the end of 1996, after Rwanda had invaded eastern Zaire to solve the crisis there and improve its own security, the official argument would be articulated in the clearest of terms (Gahima, see p. 177).

Following the Kibeho tragedy, staff at the Ministry of Rehabilitation and Social Integration (MINIREISO) gave their version of what was wrong with international assistance.[24] All claimed to be speaking as individuals, not as members of the Ministry, but they shared a common perspective. Their concerns were as follows:

i) Rwanda was overrun by useless NGOs; many were small organisations that could not survive without UN contracts. These NGOs were not committed to assisting Rwanda in its transition from a state of emergency to long-term development.

ii) The business of sub-contracting to western NGOs meant that funds earmarked for Rwanda were pocketed by non-Rwandan interests. Millions of emergency-aid dollars never reached Rwanda.

iii) Adding insult to injury, UN agencies and NGOs kept the perpetrators of the genocide alive and healthy, thereby contributing to the region's continued destabilisation. The UN and the humanitarian organisations were interested only in their own survival.

iv) Most hurtful was the presence of NGOs that restricted their Rwanda operations to supporting internally displaced persons (IDPs) or former IDPs. Such exclusive assistance was tantamount to rewarding criminals for their role in the genocide.

MINIREISO staff insisted they were not against the presence of the UN and the NGOs, they even tolerated NGOs that continued to defy the government's plea for registration and collaboration, but they found it perplexing and immoral that so little of the funding destined 'for Rwanda' was being spent on people *inside Rwanda*.

Given the lack of area expertise among diplomats (Chapter 1), and given that the UN had publicly admitted its guilt and shame at failing to halt the genocide, it is time now to ask how regional ignorance and guilt were dealt with after the RPF seized power. The answer, as Prime Minister Twagiramungu revealed in September 1995, was that the RPF knew how to exploit the international guilt to maximum benefit. It is time now to explore a critical moment, a tense diplomatic encounter during which the Rwandan government effectively 'remembered to make the basket return'. The encounter, being one among many similarly structured meetings, ensured continued diplomatic cooperation under hostile circumstances.

Kibeho's graveyard: masterclass in surreal diplomacy

Confirmation that the morally discredited international community had lost the right to criticise Rwanda's new government came in the wake of the Kibeho massacre, when President Bizimungu invited western diplomats and NGO representatives to join him on the site of the tragedy. For the Westerners who attended, the day turned into a most bizarre, surreal spectacle. In *Rwandan* diplomatic terms, however, the *journée surréaliste*[25] was part of a clearly identifiable sequence of strategic moves – moves characteristic of the Rwandan way of 'doing' politics.

Masterclass

Minuet in 338   Five days after the massacre, on Thursday 27 April 1995, President Bizimungu (re)visits Kibeho in the company of foreign ambassadors and NGO representatives, whom the Ministry of Foreign Affairs and Cooperation had 'cordially' invited 'to a meeting with the Head of State in KIBEHO.' Facing worldwide condemnation because of the barbaric killings, Bizimungu opens the proceedings by announcing that an independent commission of inquiry will be set up.[26] To rid this initiative of the suspicion that it might be a whitewash, Bizimungu solemnly proclaims: 'Truth must explode!'[27] He then promises that 'all corpses will be exhumed, counted and examined to determine the cause of death'.[28]

Bizimungu's next move stuns the diplomats, as the exercise begins at once. The eminent visitors are caught unawares, are cornered, become implicated. Acting as UNAMIR's provost-marshal, British Major Mark Cuthbert Brown leads President Bizimungu 'to the place where the "blue berets" had dug mass graves. Immediately, some ten Hutu civilians set about the task, powerfully wielding the hoe. Bloated and blanched, the first corpses appear.'[29]

As human remains are exhumed and counted, Home Affairs Minister Seth Sendashonga, a Hutu with two brothers in prison accused of genocide, talks to the IDP hard-core (some 2,000) still in Kibeho. In Kinyarwanda, he urges

that they 'must be reasonable', that they have 'nothing to fear', that 'only those who participated in the genocide will face the law and account for their acts'. To sound more convincing, he adds: 'Those now back home have already found work. It's going well for them.' The besieged – who for the past six days have received neither food nor water – respond with grunts.[30]

The IDPs know the extent of their participation in the genocide; they know, too, that justice does not necessarily prevail in the home communes. As for jobs, who is Sendashonga trying to fool? (In late February many former IDPs had trekked back to the camps.) The reply of the hard-core IDPs is to deride the impotence of the UN. Using a megaphone, they recall that their friends had died, last Saturday, in front of impotent 'blue berets'. They reaffirm fearing for their safety should they be made to return to their villages, and demand to join the 1.2 million Hutu refugees in Zaire.[31]

Now comes the first diplomatic (and media) coup. The foreign diplomats, ill at ease, are roped into the active recruitment of would-be returnees from among the remaining hard-core. As bodies are exhumed and counted, Sendashonga brusquely turns to the ambassadors

and asks them to collect the names of those prepared to go home. In an instant, the diplomats understand the purpose of their invitation. The Rwandan government – sick of the [international] criticisms – wishes to implicate them in the management of this crisis.[32]

The German ambassador, August Hummel, is game. 'We are here to guarantee that you will not be killed,' he says in French. 'I beg you, come with your children. There is no future here for you!' Instantly, two young men pull away from the crowd and demand to be taken to their home commune. They want to know what is going on. . . . Jumping at the chance, the minister and ambassador lead the young men to a waiting car. The village is not far. On returning, the men explain that 'since the return of the IDPs all has been fine' in their commune. The German ambassador gives the 'V' for victory and invites the crowd to make a move. Fiasco. One young person with a broken arm, one old man and one woman with her baby leave the ranks. Two thousand stay put.[33] Sendashonga explains that the IDPs are directed by extremists, who hold women and children hostage.

But the show is not over yet. Second media coup: the body count is carried out, there and then, and set at 338. After two hours of surreal spectacle, the Foreign Affairs minister, Anastase Gasana,

takes stock: 23 corpses in one grave, 13 in another, 41 elsewhere . . . That should be a total of 338 corpses buried in Kibeho.[34]

The day ends with an emphatic victory for President Bizimungu, who now throws down the gauntlet for those who had earlier spoken of several thousand dead. The President's voice rises. 'It is 338 corpses. If you pretend there are more, tell me where they are, show them to me!' Intimidated, the UN ambassador to Rwanda accepts that the figure of 338 has 'good indicative value' and declares himself reassured 'that the "international mission of inquiry will provide conclusions to suit all the parties involved"'.[35]

338. The figure would never be verified, not even by the independent inquiry.

Aftermath   Part of Bizimungu's victory that day was that he and the UN ambassador had now set the (real) terms of reference for the inquiry that was to follow: the world must not expect anything that would challenge the president's word. All the world could hope for were 'conclusions acceptable to all parties', excluding IDPs. Bizimungu's ritual enactment of the sorry state of the Rwandan justice system had been poignant; a convincing display of how 'the conspiracy of silence' continued in the Great Lakes. 338. No one objected, no one dared to. The international community accepted its impotence.

The technique used for winning over the ambassadors received no comment in the press, yet it was a recognisable, politico-cultural manoeuvre – one very similar to that used in the case of Ferdinand. The sequence: make someone caught red-handed, with proven guilt, feel truly uncomfortable; catch that person off-guard and implicate him/her in a way not anticipated; then make him/her your accomplice. The technique worked; the diplomats never expressed second thoughts.

Hardliners in the Rwandan government must have rejoiced when Bizimungu's assertive statement on fatalities, of which the UN ambassador had approved, caused UNAMIR to declare it had held a 'more scientific' recount through which the number of fatalities had been reduced from its own minimum of 4,050 dead to just about 2,000. UNAMIR gave no information on the 'scientific' method used. Issued via the Integrated Operations Centre (IOC), the statement NR-95.27 read as follows:

Kibeho Camp Situation Update. The UNAMIR Force Commander, Maj.-Gen. Guy Tousignant visited the Kibeho camp and Butare today. He met with Ministers of the Rwandese government, officers of the Rwandese Patriotic Army monitoring the situation and representatives of various Non-Governmental Organizations. After taking a more scientific count of the number of deaths, the figure has been revised to approximately 2,000. The number of wounded and injured is estimated at more than 600. (UNAMIR NR-95.27)

While nowhere near the president's own figure, the 'more scientific' recount confirmed in Rwandan eyes that the UN and humanitarian agencies and organisations did indeed have a habit of inflating their figures.

One week later, however, UNAMIR issued a confidential report in which it accused the RPA 'of digging up and secretly removing corpses from the Kibeho camp in order to conceal the exact number of fatalities in the massacre of

22 April'.[36] The accusation echoed the position of the Fédération Internationale des Ligues des Droits de l'Homme (FIDH) and Human Rights Watch/Africa (HRW/A), both present in Kibeho during the massacre. In a joint statement released on Monday, 24 April 1995, the organisations had reported eyewitness accounts of how 'RPA soldiers quickly buried corpses during the night of April 22–23, and in the early morning of April 23. Soldiers also threw corpses into latrines' (HRW/A and FIDH 1995: 2). The statement concluded that the truth about the number who died would never be known. But HRW/A and FIDH rejected the assertion that fatalities would be around 300, the number officially circulated. In fact, the day after the massacre, with the masterclass in surreal diplomacy still several days away, Bizimungu had already visited Kibeho to set the number of fatalities at roughly 300 (see also Bihozagara, Chapter 2). In setting the number, he had given journalists a taste of the medicine being prepared for diplomats and NGO representatives. Contending that the massacre, the weekend's 'incident', had been provoked by Hutu militiamen who fired on the RPA, Bizimungu

told journalists that the blame for the incident rested with the armed Hutu who had hidden in the camp. According to Bizimungu, there could be no more than about 300 dead. 'People talked of 8,000 dead. Did you see them?', Bizimungu asked. Some journalists were visibly shocked by the president's claims, for he spoke against the backdrop of a hill still strewn with corpses.[37]

One diplomat present on the day, Shaharyar Khan, the UN special envoy to Rwanda, has recently confirmed how President Bizimungu, misinformed by the local RPA commander (later punished for his role in the carnage), confronted the UNAMIR officer – a Zambian captain   who had informed the press he personally counted 1,500 dead bodies on 22 April. Asked by Bizimungu why he had lied to the media, the Zambian UN captain stood his ground and confirmed his observation, then was 'jostled by the RPA officers for his impudence' (Khan 2000: 112). Khan also recalls other false accusations that fitted neatly into the 'smear UNAMIR' campaign.

Reporting on Kibeho, FIDH and HRW/A were not to be intimidated either:

In those areas where the UN personnel were permitted access, they established a detailed count of 2,000 dead and an estimated total of 4,050. Rwandan military and civilian authorities have stated that 300 were killed. The hasty burial of the victims makes establishing a confirmed death toll impossible, but given the duration of firing, the kinds of weapons used, and the high population density of the crowd, it is certain that the victims number substantially more than 300. (HRW/A and FIDH 1995: 2)

The Rwandan government reacted strongly to any suggestion that the president's figure was misleading, and once again seized the occasion to portray itself as victim:

These allegations are totally absurd. The United Nations are unhappy that we have closed down the IDP camps and sent the displaced people home, claim[ed] major Wilson Rutayisire, spokesman for the government. The UN are engaged in propaganda against the government.[38]

Rwanda's state radio also denounced '"the [anti-government] campaign of certain NGOs and the international media". Radio France Internationale, the BBC, CNN, UNAMIR and MSF-France are all spreading disinformation. In short, Kigali is up against a formidable campaign orchestrated by the international community.'[39] Within the logic of Rwandan morality and politics, the discredited international community had no right to challenge the word of Rwanda's president. How could anyone put the word of the UN above that of the president, the official spiritual guardian of the survivors of the genocide? In the eyes of Rwanda's new leaders, this was unthinkable. The UN had been caught red-handed more than once, had admitted guilt and suffered humiliation; the only honourable way out for the UN was to serve the new leaders, and do so unquestioningly.

It did not follow, however, that all Rwandans agreed with their government that the international community should be gagged because of its guilt. For to accept that gagging was the appropriate penalty was to play into the hands of government hardliners and the RPA. Genuine survivors were aware of the danger. Ever vulnerable because of the latent accusation that they survived through collaborating with the *interahamwe*, survivors were mostly scared of the RPA, and would have felt hurt had the international community stopped monitoring political developments and abandoned civilians to the whims of the military (see also Mamdani 1996: 23). The persistent tension between Rwanda's civil administration and the RPA was something even Rwandan NGOs were trying to come to terms with and remedy. In an interview with Marie-France Cros,[40] the Association rwandaise de défense des droits de l'homme (ARDHO) agreed that many among Rwanda's then 17,000 detainees were innocent victims of disputes over property or attempts to acquire property by unlawful means.

Before we turn to the war in eastern Zaire, during which the Rwandan government exercised its monopoly on truth, it is useful to say something about the initial international response to Kibeho and the independent inquiry that followed.

How did donor governments react to Kibeho?

Initially, the RPA's barbaric use of violence in Kibeho drew sharp condemnations from South Africa's President Nelson Mandela, the OAU's Secretary-General Salim Ahmed Salim, Dutch Minister Jan Pronk (development cooperation) and Belgium's Minister for Development Cooperation, Erik Derycke. Angered that the RPA had ordered all foreign organisations out of Kibeho the day after the massacre, for their own safety, Pronk condemned the Rwandan government for breaking the agreement that the evacuation of IDP camps was to be undertaken without force or recrimination (also Kent 1996: 72). Pronk said Kigali must shoulder full responsibility for the shame of Kibeho, even though he acknowledged that the camp had held some of the country's most dangerous criminals.[41]

The European Union reacted by freezing its direct aid and reminding Rwanda's leaders that aid depended on respect for human rights and on doing more to promote reconciliation. The freezing of aid affected mainly infrastructural assistance (water supply, roads and electricity) and law and order services. Certain long-term grants and risk capital from the European Investment Bank were also suspended.[42] Bilateral aid to Rwanda, too, came to a grinding halt, but not necessarily in all sectors. Thus Belgium suspended its direct aid, but not its emergency aid nor its assistance for rehabilitating the justice system. Rwanda 'regretted' Belgium's decision, which, Paul Kagame believed, was misguided because 'based on inaccuracies and exaggerations by the media'.[43]

But donors did not speak with one voice. Within the international community a split occurred between Britain and the US, on the one hand, and mainland Europe on the other. Abstaining from the protest over Kibeho, Britain's Conservative government backed the Rwandan government's version of events and, as The Times put it, reacted in a 'measured' way. The Times defended the decision to continue direct aid on the grounds that it reflected 'the wider context of events'.[44] Baroness Chalker put the blame for Kibeho on the Hutu extremists, reiterating that the RPA troops had 'undoubtedly panicked'. She told The Times: 'These camps are full of Hutu extremists with weaponry who were breaking out at night, terrorising the villages where people have resettled.'[45] The RPA panic had been provoked. Chalker regurgitated the claim by Christine Umutoni, head of the government programme for rehabilitation and social reintegration, who alleged that one of the Kibeho residents, a major in Habyarimana's army, had organised an attack against the RPA on the morning of the massacre.[46] This allegation, by the lawyer who later represented Rwanda in the commission of inquiry, 'confirmed' that the RPA had acted in self-defence. Chalker accepted the government's hardline version of what had happened in Kibeho rather than that of Prime Minister Twagiramungu, who had agreed that premeditation by the RPA could not be ruled out (see Chapter 2). There was no question of Britain reducing its aid package.[47] Fighting the European Commission's plan to suspend funds earmarked for rehabilitation, Foreign Office officials in London defended Britain's position as being 'in line with the views of charities and UN organisations, such as Unicef, which is lobbying hard for aid to continue'.[48]

Britain did not condemn the European partners, but SCF, a popular NGO in good stead with the Rwandan government, took up the baton to defend the politically correct view on Kibeho. Coming at a time when the Belgian public had just received confirmation of the rift between Kagame and Twagiramungu, SCF director Mike Aaronson's condemnation of the EU's position came as a bolt from the blue. What shocked was not that Aaronson, speaking in Brussels, pleaded for the continuation of direct aid – there was, after all, agreement that certain types of aid should continue – but that he accused the Belgian and Dutch governments of *not understanding Rwanda*. Addressing the general assembly of European NGOs, Aaronson voiced the opinion that the decisions by 'Belgium and The Netherlands "aim to influence public opinion in Europe, but do not take the situation in Rwanda into account".'[49] The intervention may have seemed courageous to those unfamiliar with the Great Lakes region, but it also echoed how Britain unwaveringly backed the Rwandan government and ignored the growing rift between Twagiramungu and Kagame, i.e. ignored the hardening of extremist attitudes. Was this tension, then, not part of 'the situation in Rwanda'?[50]

At the general assembly, the Dutch NGO Novib was more level-headed and warned that a fast growing faction within the RPF had had enough of the leadership's moderate elements. The Novib director, Van den Berg, reminded the assembly that several Rwandan ministers had recently asked him in private to exert pressure on the RPF to improve their country's human rights record and to stop extremists from gaining the upper hand.[51]

Like Britain, the US government also reaffirmed its allegiance to the Rwandan government. Under-secretary for Foreign Affairs, George Moose, said he was 'extremely concerned' about Kibeho and called on Rwanda's government to punish the commander(s) responsible for the bloodbath. But there was no condemnation. This was not the time, Moose said, to halt direct aid. A US diplomat explained: 'Our view right now is that the US does better to continue its direct aid, because ... much [international] aid goes directly to the displaced in the camps.'[52] While it is too simplistic to suggest a sharp contrast between anglophone and francophone worlds (Oxfam, for instance, disagreed with SCF's position), it emerged in the aftermath of Kibeho that the US and the UK governments stood firmly behind the 'official explanation' issued by Kigali's more hardline authorities. Already, the two governments were indicating that they had relinquished the right to an independent view on matters Rwandan.

A so-called independent inquiry

The conclusions of the international inquiry were presented to the Rwandan government and Kigali-based diplomats when they were 'hardly drafted'.[53] The report accused the RPA of 'disproportionate' reactions that violated international law, but concluded in rather woolly language that the tragedy of Kibeho neither resulted from a planned action by Rwandan authorities to kill a certain group of people, nor was it an accident that could not have been prevented. (Brisset-Foucault 1995: 12)

The blame for Kibeho needed to be shared. 'There is sufficient reliable evidence to establish', the report stressed, that 'unarmed IDPs were subjected to arbitrary deprivation of life and serious bodily harm in violation of human rights and humanitarian law by RPA military personnel' (1995: 13). On the other hand, similar crimes had been 'committed by armed elements among the IDPs themselves' against fellow camp residents. RPA soldiers and criminal IDPs were both to blame. The report explained that 'logistic and time constraints' had prevented the commission from determining the exact number of dead, but it suggested that 'it is apparent that the numbers are more than those formally counted' (1995: 10). The commission also criticised the UN for its slow command structure and pointed to certain (unnamed) NGOs for 'actively contradict[ing] the policies of the government of Rwanda by encouraging IDPs to remain in Kibeho camp' (1995: 11).

Inside Rwanda, reactions to the report were favourable. Major Wilson Rutayisire, Rwanda's Director of Information, called the report 'balanced despite certain omissions. Among the latter, he noted the absence of any reference, in the conclusions reached, to "the right to legitimate defence by the army", which, he added, had been "attacked by criminals".'[54] Rutayisire's positive verdict was shared by the RPF's London-based intellectual apologist, African Rights, which, just before the Kibeho massacre, had claimed that Rwanda was not suffering from any real breakdown in law and order. African Rights asserted that what we were witnessing was not a breakdown but a *perception of breakdown*.[55] Quoted in *The Independent*, African Rights clarified that 'arrests [were] not arbitrary and [that] the guilty [were] not being pursued with sufficient vigour. Rakiya Omaar [the organisation's co-director] said the *perception of a breakdown* in law and order arose because Rwanda's judicial system had collapsed and the government lacked resources to prosecute the guilty.'[56]

After the vigour of Kibeho, African Rights hailed the results of the independent inquiry and, toeing the dominant government line, argued that the killings had been an incident misrepresented by humanitarians who should now apologise for their bias. De Waal, co-director, summarised as follows:

the relief agencies [one of whom, Goal, had suggested up to 8,000 dead] almost achieved impunity. Despite the independent commission's findings, no agency made a retraction or a public apology for its erroneous statements, nor even a correction in subsequent public reports. (de Waal 1997: 202)

African Rights applauded the commission's reference to 'overestimation of the initial fatality counts and estimates' (de Waal 1997: 202, quoting Brisset-Foucault *et al.*, 1995: 10).

The positive reactions by Major Rutayisire and African Rights contrasted sharply with the way certain commission members reacted to their own report. Members raised objections regarding the inquiry itself (no bodies counted) and the report's generally euphemistic language. One commission member expressed concern that the conclusions reached '[did] not contain half of what we found',[57] while another, law professor Koen De Feyter, Belgium's representative, criticised the lack of area expertise among members, as well as the censorship inflicted: 'Besides noting the fact that the members of the commission were "technicians without any concrete knowledge of the country", Mr De Feyter signals that the investigation was slowed down by the commission's Rwandan representative, Christine Umutoni.'[58] In his interview, De Feyter went on: 'It was important to establish the existence of caches, but impossible to examine systematically the 2,000 latrines within the camp', even though the commission's mandate had included verification of the number of dead.

Amnesty International, for its part, expressed satisfaction that an inquiry had taken place, with findings published, but it, too, regretted the gaps and shortcomings of a report merely thirteen pages long. The report 'failed to satisfy the strict international standards for such inquiries and . . . also failed to make adequate recommendations to prevent further human rights violations in Rwanda'.[59]

Despite the shortcomings of the inquiry and its report, diplomats were relieved that it was all over: they had a document, no matter how watered down, acceptable to both the Rwandan government and the (now faceless) international community. Less than a fortnight later, diplomats were also relieved to hear that two RPA commanders had been suspended; the resumption of aid could now be considered. By early June, in a joint statement with the European Commission, '[t]he fifteen development ministers [of the EU] decided . . . "to engage in political and technical dialogue with the Rwandan government", with a view to resuming the partially suspended aid'.[60] Bizimungu's masterclass in diplomacy had had its intended effect; Kigali knew it could now rely on the cooperation of an increasingly compliant international community. As for the NGOs and human rights organisations who remained sceptical of the 'independent' inquiry, they soon learned that their critique was understood to mean they were 'against Rwanda'. In December 1995, the Rwandan government 'finally took its only effective sanction, and . . . expelled 38 agencies (114 remained)' (De Waal 1997: 202). The agencies were not surprised. Following threats by RPA soldiers against MSF workers and a raid on Red Cross houses within a week of the Kibeho disaster, many aid workers knew their time was up. One senior official said after the raid: 'We are on the verge of being expelled because of our outspokenness. Our people feel their lives are in danger because the government mistakenly feels that we are against it.'[61]

How Kibeho could be understood within a framework of 'correct' outspokenness was later demonstrated in Gourevitch's (1998) blockbuster account.

Despite the varied reactions to the Kibeho Commission report made at the time, Gourevitch writes that

the commissioners managed to annoy everybody involved at Kibeho – the government, the UN and the humanitarian community, and the *génocidaires* – by distributing blame for the catastrophe fairly evenly among all three parties.

. . .

The message was clear: the Commission considered the continued existence of the Kibeho camp 'an important obstacle to the country's efforts to recover from the devastating effects of last year's genocide', and found that both RPA personnel and 'elements among the IDPs' had subjected people in the camp to 'arbitrary deprivation of life and serious bodily harm'. (Gourevitch 1998: 203–4)

Based on interviews with traumatised UN soldiers and aid workers, Gourevitch's account of what happened at Kibeho creates the misleading impression that the commission was right to share the blame. He makes a lot of the machete deaths and mutilations prior to the full-scale RPA attack, and dwells on how the 'emergency wing . . . set up for Kibeho casualties' at the Butare hospital had treated mainly people wounded by machete. Visiting Butare three weeks after the massacre, and on his first visit to Rwanda, Gourevitch was told that the thirty or so casualties still left in the wing were 'all machete cases'.

'Want to see?' one of the nurses asked, and led the way. Twenty or thirty cots were crowded beneath weak neon light, in a stench of rotting flesh and medicine. 'The ones who're left', the nurse said, 'are all machete cases.' I saw that – multiple amputations, split faces swollen around stitches 'We had some with the brain coming out', the Norwegian [nurse] said quite cheerily. 'Strange, no? The RPA don't use machetes. They did this to their own.' (1998: 194–5)

Gourevitch does not hide the RPA atrocities, but 'illustrates' how the Kibeho deaths were caused by bullets, machetes and UN incompetence. All on a par. His story is a *chef d'oeuvre* of obfuscation.

The 'evidence' that blame must be shared equally leads Gourevitch to argue that the loss of life in Kibeho will one day be likened to the criminal excesses near the end of the American Civil War or to the executions in France, immediately after World War II, of between ten and fifteen thousand people accused of collaboration with the fascists (1998: 187–8). For Gourevitch, 'the whole story' of Kibeho is the story that lies beyond (and elsewhere): the Kibeho killings, too, will one day be remembered as 'purifying to the national soul'. Whilst such comparison is not inappropriate, Gourevitch omits to ask how people in the Great Lakes region *understand and remember acts of violence*. As Malkki (1995: 63, 72) has shown so very clearly regarding the memory of Hutu deaths in Burundi in 1972, the massacres may be remembered in purifying terms, but they are terms that purify the victim's ethnic identity, Hutu in this case, and not Burundi's multi-ethnic national soul.

How the international community continued to play the game: Zaire, 1996

The revolt by Banyamulenge in late 1996, the presence of RPA troops in Zaire and the subsequent destruction of the refugee camps gave Rwandan leaders the opportunity to demonstrate that they had won the mind-war over reality construction. Confident that the masterclass in Kibeho's graveyard had sent the irrefutable message that only the Rwandan authorities had the right to decide what was 'really' going on, and confident too that the international community had accepted this position, President Bizimungu and Foreign Affairs minister Gasana now made their next move: Rwanda, the international community needed to accept, had a legitimate presence in eastern Zaire.

Although the Rwandan government vehemently denied that its troops were deployed in Zaire, despite confirmation from reliable sources, its officials spun an imaginative, seemingly convincing yarn about Rwanda's historical links with eastern Zaire. Anyone craving for instant, easy-to-grasp knowledge was impressed. Minister Gasana proved he was a master at the game. Gasana argued that Europe had inflicted lasting damage on the Great Lakes when the colonial powers had gathered in Berlin in 1885 to draw up international borders. By acting irresponsibly in Berlin, the international community had caused Kivu's 'Rwandan populations' to be at risk a century later. Differently put, if 'the Banyamulenge' suffered persecution in 1996, one should blame not only the Rwandan refugee extremists and their international protectors, but also the decisions Western leaders had taken over a hundred years ago. It was a diplomatic masterstroke: the international community had been morally defunct for over a century.

At a first glance, Gasana's clear and well-detailed message seemed convincing: as Rwanda's *real borders* included large tracts of Kivu, which President Bizimungu enthusiastically confirmed on a map paraded in front of the media, Rwanda had a duty to protect '[the] rights of the populations of Rwandan origin established in Kivu'.[62] Supporting this portrayal of the pre-colonial past, President Bizimungu evoked a 'Greater Rwanda' which included the highlands where Banyamulenge lived and where, he claimed, they had lived for some 600 years before 'the white man' arrived. This Greater Rwanda, the president suggested, had enjoyed excellent relations with its Bahunde neighbours.[63] It was this harmoniously balanced 'Greater Rwanda' which the Western colonial powers had cut in half: first in 1885, then a second time in 1910. Journalist James McKinley Jr reported Bizimungu's lesson in history.

Waving placards and maps depicting the Rwandan kingdom of the nineteenth century, Mr Bizimungu pointed out that the Tutsi now living in Zaire had been part of an ancient Tutsi kingdom. Their lands became part of Zaire in 1910, he said, when European powers redrew the map. '[Banyamulenge] are in their homelands', he said, 'and if somebody wants to uproot them, if someone wants to disown them, let that country [i.e. Zaire] disown the land as well.' Despite his hinting at a Greater Rwandan kingdom, Mr Bizimungu took pains to emphasise that Rwanda was not interested in annexing eastern Zaire. The president said that Rwanda did not have the resources to intervene in the conflict and that other countries had responsibility to stop what he called a genocide against Zairian Tutsi. 'Morally I support these people,' he said. 'Between extermination and fighting, I would advise them to resist.'[64]

Bizimungu's reconstruction of the past, however, was both factual and imaginative. Correctly, he recalled that the present border between Zaire and Rwanda had resulted from the 1910 tripartite convention which had involved Belgium, Germany and Britain. At the convention, Rwanda, then under German occupation, had lost North Kivu and Idjwi island to the Belgian Congo.[65] The Belgians knew there would be local opposition, so they forced chiefs to pay taxes to them rather than to the Rwandan *mwami* (Fairhead 1990: 83). Bizimungu had sound reason for referring to North Kivu as a lost area which could be 'part of the solution'. But Bizimungu went further; he called for the return of Banyamulenge territory as well. What this request overlooked, however, was that the Banyamulenge homeland in South Kivu, where 'Banya-Mulenge' had moved in the nineteenth century, had never been part of the polity controlled by Rwanda's central court. Bizimungu was building his 'imagined community' (Anderson 1991).

Not only had Mulenge not been wrenched from Rwanda in early colonial days, but it was also the case that pre-colonial Rwanda itself had been far from politically unified. Pre-colonial Rwanda had been made up of several Tutsi dynasties (Rwanda, Ndorwa, Gisaka, Bugesera, Burundi) which regularly fought one another. Belgium, in other words, had snatched North Kivu and Idjwi, but it had also co-created the modern Republic of Rwanda. Finding himself on a slippery slope, Bizimungu remained silent on Belgium's assistance to Rwanda's central court in the 1920s. A further problem with Bizimungu's perception of a Greater Rwanda was that no clear-cut boundary had existed at the end of the nineteenth century. Rather than being marked by fixed territories and boundaries, the region's political map at that time had been a mixture of diverse engagements with Rwanda's central court ranging from full occupation with complete administration to instances where tribute was paid or in which ritual ties were maintained and situations best described as raiding (Vansina 1962: 90–1; Fairhead 1989b).

The fiction of a unified 'Greater Rwanda', which Bizimungu promoted map-in-hand also at other opportune moments, was the president's way of saying that if RPA troops were fighting in Zaire – an allegation he denied – these troops were in fact operating on home turf.

In an earlier muscle-flexing speech, in Cyangugu on 10 October 1996, Bizimungu had also obscured the situation in Masisi at the time of the 1994 Rwanda war and genocide by suggesting that RPF soldiers could have gone all the way but had refrained from doing so because the leadership had respected Zaire's sovereignty. Bizimungu explained:

> The Banyamulenge, so much talked about, are the relatives with whom we used to share Rwanda. From about 1960–63 onwards, however, with the creation of the Organisation of African Unity, we have subscribed to the principle that frontiers are inviolable. This is why, when we were fighting the genocide and the massacres, we stopped at the border [with Zaire] and did not come to the rescue of the Masisi populations, even though we had the capability. We respect the sovereignty of another country.[66]

The claim deserves comment. First, in July 1994, Masisi was relatively calm. The question therefore arises as to who exactly needed saving; an issue clouded by the term 'the populations'. During the so-called ethnic clashes in North Kivu in 1993, there had been a roughly equal number of fatalities and IDPs on either side of the conflict – that is, among autochthones and Banyarwanda – while autochthones had made no distinction between Banyarwanda Hutu and Tutsi. Banyarwanda Tutsi, moreover, would not have referred to themselves as Banyamulenge. Second, the Tutsi pastoralists who crossed the Ruzizi river before the Europeans arrived, and who were genuine Banyamulenge, may have been 'relatives', but their departure from Rwanda was likely to have been caused by discontent (Depelchin 1974).

Not constrained by the polite formalities of international exchanges, Bizimungu, speaking in Kinyarwanda, turned Gasana's 'duty to protect' into 'the right to exterminate'. The president told the people of Cyangugu:

> I am telling the Banyamulenge they must teach a lesson in history and etiquette to all those who persecute them . . .. I am also telling them to set an ultimatum for the departure of those Lucifers who want to exterminate and expel Banyamulenge from their country. . . . He who says he wants to kill you, he who says he wants to exterminate you without reason, gives you the automatic motive to utilise every possible and imaginable means for it to be you who exterminates him so the nuisance can stop.

In Rwanda, preparations to come to the rescue of 'the Banyamulenge' were already well under way.

Conscious of the high geopolitical stakes and genuinely eager for a local solution, the West, minus France, was not going to challenge the Rwandan government's evocation of this mythical past. Nor was the West going to thwart Kagame's plan for eastern Zaire. In fact, any tension that might have resulted within the European Union because of the plan was quickly eased. This was most visible during the Bordeaux Anglo-French summit at which British

Prime Minister John Major, supported by Foreign Secretary Malcolm Rifkind, went out of his way to argue that France and Britain had no fundamental disagreement regarding the situation in eastern Zaire. For some journalists, this news came as a surprise. *The Times* wrote that 'Mr Major's comments . . . seemed to represent a significant shift in the British position. [Two days ago,] officials appeared to play down the prospect of military help. Yesterday Mr Major said it was "premature" to decide now, but he did not rule out the "option of assisting in a military operation".'[67] There was, however, no question of a real shift, for Major had added that necessary touch of *realpolitik*: 'On the question of troops we need to know what the host government thinks and what the neighbouring governments think'.[68] The thoughts of the authorities in Kigali and Goma were well understood. Britain would comply with Paul Kagame's perspective on the situation.

Compliant governments, it is worth noting, were allowed space back home to express their concern over 'the refugees'. Kagame and Kabila were tolerant. Western powers committed to *realpolitik* would not be criticised for continuing to play the old game of *moralpolitik* and pretending they might still work with France on some future plan for intervention. Michael Portillo, Britain's Secretary of State for Defence, thus appeared to come out in support of intervention. In the House of Commons, Portillo enthusiastically conjured up visions of a crusade in the name of civilisation.

'The House will rightly ask why Britain should become involved in a place far from our country and where no vital national interest is engaged; because we are a civilised nation.'

Mr Portillo indicated the British force would take a tough line with any militia attempting to prevent delivery of humanitarian aid. 'If our objective is to enable aid to reach the people who are starving, and if people stand in our way, then those people must be prepared to face the consequences of their actions', he said.[69]

Tough talking in the House? No, just words, just indulging in some old-fashioned *moralpolitik*. Portillo knew, as did other politicians and diplomats, that the dice were cast. One could debate intervention and make the concerned public feel better for it, but the option was not on the cards. Five days later, and still assuming (in his own words) that 'between half a million and one million refugees [were] unaccounted for', Portillo said the plans were now on hold. Rwanda's Foreign Affairs Minister, Anastase Gasana, had had the last word: with the exception of 'a few stragglers', there were no more Rwandan civilians in eastern Zaire.[70]

US politicians acted likewise. Kigali-based diplomats said no-go; the politicians back home prepared for action. Already in early November, Robert Gribbin, the US ambassador to Rwanda, had stated categorically that there was 'no need for an external military force'.[71] Back home, though, US politicians played a different, more humanitarian tune. Nicholas Burns of the US State Department gave the impression that the Clinton administration was still committed to *moralpolitik*. Not only did Burns claim that the US was neutral in this conflict,[72] his department also went through the motions of preparing for a UN-led intervention after Clinton gave his 'tentative "yes"' to the idea of a multinational force.[73] The parallel with Britain was neat. The US military even solved the problem of having US troops operate under foreign (Canadian) command,[74] and they sent a military delegation to the Great Lakes to ascertain the situation.[75] US politicians denied the US was against intervention.

UNHCR also called for an early end to the idea of a UN-led intervention. In line with what it had claimed most of the time (that is, that Rwanda was safe to return to), UNHCR became optimistic when seeing huge numbers of refugees roam about independently of leaders and militias. Four days before the mass return, the UN refugee agency issued this statement: 'Our information tells us there are big concentrations which move independently of the militias, often in groups of forty to fifty. We can reach them first, after which they will speedily return to Rwanda without there being any need for an international intervention force.'[76] For UNHCR, the separation of extremists from ordinary, mostly innocent refugees, had become a fact. This put paid to its support to the intervention plan.[77]

Key international players readily agreed that the mass return of refugees to Rwanda was a success and the intervention plan could be folded. They did so in the comforting knowledge that panic-ridden predictions, notably of 'genocide by starvation' (Boutros-Ghali) and massive deaths from hunger, thirst and disease (by MSF and Oxfam staff amongst others),[78] had been exposed as grossly exaggerated once the refugee mass started to return to Rwanda. The refugee chapter could now be closed. In Gribbin's opinion, 'most of the people who are Rwandan refugees and who want[ed] to return home [had] done so';[79] all thought of intervention, his staff claimed, was now 'bullshit'.[80] Justification for dropping the plan existed in the findings of US aerial reconnaissance photogrammetry, on the basis of which US commanders in Kigali were adamant that the 'missing refugees' should be forgotten. America and Rwanda saw eye to eye. After UNHCR (re)considered that the situation remained critical, Seth Kamanzi, political adviser to President Bizimungu, asserted: 'We challenge the UNHCR to give us proof of where those [remaining] refugees are. Nowhere do the American satellite photographs show up any significant refugee concentrations.'[81]

Their moral credibility seriously undermined, some NGOs went on the offensive. Thus Oxfam staff accused the US military of 'losing' refugees and deliberately backtracking. In a widely circulated statement, Nicholas Stockton, the Emergencies Director at Oxfam UK and Ireland, recalled the following sequence of events:

On 20 November [1996] Oxfam staff were shown the original US aerial reconnaissance photogrammetry that confirmed, in considerable detail, the existence of over 500,000 people distributed in three major and numerous minor agglomerations. (Whether these were refugees or displaced Zairois could not be determined.) This information, also made available to the United Nations, was the non-attributed source of the UNHCR press release of 20 November that also identified the whereabouts of a very large proportion of the 'missing' population. Yet, incredibly, in a press conference in Kigali on 23 November, the US military claimed that they had located only one significant cluster of people which 'by the nature of their movement and other clues can be assumed to be the ex-FAR and militias'. The press were given reassurances that this population appeared to be in 'good shape'. On the basis of this information and repeated assertions of the predominantly military composition of this group, proposals for the deployment of an international military force began to collapse . . . We were asked to believe, and many did, that all the remaining Rwandese and Burundian refugees and displaced Zairois had disappeared from eastern Zaire without trace.

However, on the basis of the quality and authority of the information received by Oxfam on 20 November, we feel bound to conclude that as many as 400,000 refugees and unknown numbers of Zairean displaced persons have, in effect, been air-brushed from history. (Stockton 1996: 2)

The US military top did not budge. Instead, its commanders assumed an aggressive 'prove it' position, which chimed well with Paul Kagame's doctrine of information control.[82] The 'prove it' insistence was adopted especially by Lt-General Baril, the military man who had failed to respond to the fax which had warned of Rwanda's impending genocide (see Chapter 1). Journalist Nik Gowing later commented:

Those working in the Multi-National Force say Lt-General Baril was insistent that any claims of refugees must be backed up with clear evidence. . . . [As] one MNF insider put it: 'Baril would say: "Prove it to me." The Humanitarian Community would say: "We have heard . . ." The general would insist that's not proof'. . . . One highly placed source believes Baril was 'told to lose 160,000' refugees to reinforce the overall international imperative not to get involved. (Gowing 1998: 60)

The primary aim of the aerial reconnaissance, Gowing concluded, 'was to use the imagery and intelligence interpretations to ensure no multi-national intervention took place that might obstruct Kagame's determination to remove the Hutu threat' (1998: 62).

It is in the denial that significant numbers remained in eastern Zaire, and in the acceptance that those who did remain were all criminals, that the US showed most clearly that only the authorities in Kigali had the right to determine what was going on 'out there'. British officials were more careful not to get drawn into the numbers game, but they too knew how strongly Kagame opposed the intervention. The day Britain's own aerial reconnaissance team was due back home, which was before the mass exodus was completed, the Armed Forces Minister, Nicholas Soames, made his position clear:

'It is grossly irresponsible just to send troops flying all over the world in search of some will o' the wisp.' He added: 'We're not going to go unless there is a clear mission to undertake. If there is still a humanitarian job to do, we will go. If there isn't, we are not going to knowingly send them off on a wild goose chase.'[83]

The airbrushing from history of a vast number of refugees, all labelled *génocidaires*, was a case of Kibeho revisited.

Conclusion

International compliance with Kagame's military activities in eastern Zaire in 1996 could be explained in terms of international fatigue or indifference. As one EU diplomat said, 'Clinton is in full transition, and it is not easy for him to decide, as the first decision of his second mandate, to send American troops to Africa . . .'[84] Compliance could also be explained in terms of geopolitics. Journalist Colette Braeckman put it thus: 'Rwanda and Burundi are two tiny countries that represent . . . gateways to the immense Zaire, whose eastern provinces are a vault hardly opened but rich in strategic minerals.'[85] Alternatively, from the perspective of moral sympathy, compliance may be explained in terms of the persistent comparing of 'the Tutsi tribe' and the people of Israel; a comparison which regularly features in the international media (see Chapter 1). Those who represent the victims of genocide are not to be challenged.

Indifferent and fatigued, locked in moral sympathy, or gagged by the promise of riches? While all three interpretations may apply, the 'moral sympathy' dimension undoubtedly outweighed the others; there will always be times when sympathetic outsiders need to be reassured of the moral righteousness of those they support. (For instance, when it grew uncertain about Kabila's intentions, the Clinton administration stepped up its diplomatic pressure to ensure a peaceful entry into Kinshasa.[86]) My argument, therefore, has been to propose a reading of the situation which complements the above perspectives. I have suggested that the continuous humiliation of the international community subsequent to the genocide, a humiliation made so much worse with the Kibeho massacre, rendered the international community mute when it came to challenging Kigali's perspective on aspects of the crisis in eastern Zaire. This was seen clearly, initially, in the acceptance of a narrative on history which fantasised about the past while legitimating Rwanda's military presence in Zaire (which Western diplomats did not protest) and later, in a more gruesome manner, in the international acquiescence regarding the disappearance of such a vast number of refugees. By late 1996, key forces within the international community had accepted that they had lost the right to an independent opinion on Rwanda and eastern Zaire.

Predictably, the day some 700,000 refugees marched back to Rwanda, incidentally also the day the UN Security Council gave the all-clear for a scaled-down and strictly humanitarian intervention, 'interested' UN parties withdrew quickly. No one had ever believed an intervention would take place – and it would not because the RPF-led government of Rwanda, skillfully occupying the moral highground, continued to call the shots. Rwandan officials had warned that an international intervention force would only be welcome if invited.[87]

Even before Mugunga camp was 'liberated', Raymond Chrétien, the UN special envoy in the Great Lakes region, conceded

that two years after the genocide, Rwanda had 'the right to impose conditions' and that he would 'at the very highest level take [Kigali's] preoccupations into account'.[88]

Chrétien had put his finger on it: the RPF, which had stopped the genocide and taken Rwanda, had been elevated to a morally superior force; the UN accepted its moral inferiority. Kigali was in charge: in eastern Zaire, Rwandan troops were fighting 'at home'.

Outsiders, as the Kibeho masterclass in diplomacy had established, or confirmed, no longer had the right to challenge the RPF-led regime on its interpretation and handling of Central African affairs. Gerald Gahima, secretary-general of Rwanda's ministry of justice, confirmed this loss during a conference statement on reconciliation. Referring to the mounting international concern over human rights violations in Rwanda, Gahima argued emphatically:

So there are human rights violations, but *it is still not right for outsiders to pass judgement on Rwanda today.* If the international community had acted [to stop the genocide], the Human Rights violations of 1994 would not have taken place. It was possible to stop. It only needed a strong show of force. Sophisticated weapons were not used as in the case of Serbs and Croats. (Gahima 1997: 5; emphasis added)

An end to the genocide at this early stage would have lifted the RPF's 'moral obligation' to intervene, and the international community would still have been entitled to its own opinions.

An ethical minefield now looms: is there any realm left where outsiders can pass judgement on Rwanda today? Must outsiders remain mute in the face of narratives that simplify reality and justify a reconfiguring of socio-political space? And is asking such questions still considered moral? Awaiting the debate that will enlighten us on where exactly we stand, let me recall how the Rwandan government converted its moral superiority into analytic monopoly. In the mid-1990s we have witnessed a very Rwandan way of 'doing politics': catch a thief red-handed, humiliate him or her, let that thief off the hook, then remember 'to make the basket return'. In late 1996, the basket was returned, full to the brim.

Rwanda's interest in a reconfigured socio-political space, however, was not confined to a 'redrawing' of the country's border with Zaire. Within Rwanda itself space was being reconceptualised and utilised in drastically altered ways. It is this problematic, for which 'history' once again provides justification, to which we must now turn.

6   Land and social development: challenges, proposals and their imagery

The resuscitated, functionalist narrative on Rwandan society and history is also 'at work' in the design of policy initiatives for rural reconstruction. This chapter focuses on land reform and its rationale, and shows how the policy documents that justify reform portray allocative practices in the past, present and future. The aim of land reform, I argue, may well be to rationalise existing practices and boost production, as officials and experts claim, yet the discourse of reform also acts as an instrument which, through its representation of the past, helps to legitimate the present. A second aim of the chapter is to contrast post-genocide policy guidelines with the lived reality of land allocation and use. Via an empirical look at two sets of policy guidelines – first, on the repossession of temporarily vacated property; second, on land tenure reform and villagisation – I will suggest that policy *implementation* is more likely than not to be a matter of policy *interpretation*.

This chapter begins with a general appreciation of 'the trouble' with land and an account of how Rwanda's 'traditional' systems of land access and use evolved in the earlier part of the twentieth century. A discussion of post-genocide challenges and solutions then follows, before we conclude by considering the role of policy discourse in the rewriting-of-history project: a development priority on which earlier chapters have also focused. The rewriting upholds allocative practices that favour returnees and the regime they represent.

The trouble with land

In 1995, a report by Michigan State University (MSU) argued that rural Rwanda had been entrapped in a downward spiral of regression since the mid-1980s. Three factors were responsible: unsustainable land use (i.e. intensification without investment in soil fertility and land improvement), lack of off-farm employment, and rapid population growth (Clay *et al.* 1995: iii). This decline could be reversed, the report suggested, through the following: (1) greater use of organic matter, which requires an increase in the number of cattle owned by subsistence farmers; (2) more purchased inputs like chemical fertiliser and lime; and (3) a more secure tenure system, which requires an overhaul of Rwanda's (barely existing) land laws. While the need for political stability was said to be paramount, the emphasis of the report was on the promotion of income-raising activities, through either cash cropping or off-farm employment, and on the need for more secure land tenure.

Reforming Rwanda's land laws, the Michigan report noted, meant first and foremost reducing 'the risk of appropriation, and [inducing] the right to transact land' (1995: 105). Both the old ban on poor people selling off small parcels of land, commonly ignored by the late 1980s and the rental practices that resulted from the ban were said to cause productivity decline. As farmers seldom invest in land they do not control, renting land meant low conservation investments and fertility. The detrimental impact, the report stressed, was most visible in south-central Rwanda with its high level of absentee landholdings (1995: 108). This contrasted with the land situation in the country's north-west, where previous surveys by the Division of Agricultural Statistics (DSA/MINAGRI 1984–94) had found a high level of land acquisition through purchase, even though land sales caused by economic hardship were officially prohibited (1995: 108).[1] The report echoed the position of both the World Bank and the Rwandan government: Rwanda must rationalise and privatise.

Shortly after the completion of the Michigan study, 'the people of Rwanda', a much used cliché, began to request the right to transact land. This was clearly demonstrated in *Kibungo Experiments and Experiences* (Karake 1997), a local publication sponsored by the Lutheran World Federation. The article on land first reiterated the official view on the problem of land, which ran along the same lines as the Michigan report, and then confirmed that the right to transact land must be sanctioned by law. Privatisation of land was not only essential, but it was also, the article claimed, the people's will. The backdrop for this debate was that, under current law, land in Rwanda belongs to the government, except for a few tracts leased to individuals and religious orders since colonial days. The vast majority of Rwandans 'do not own land titles, and the government takes land at will and compensates only development on land' (1997: 8).[2]

The article went on to say that recent seminars in Kibungo, which had brought together a cross-section of the population under the leadership of the prefect, had

requested that once and for all, let there be land laws so that land is a commodity that can be exchanged, used as a collateral or freely be developed. These same feelings were expressed by a national workshop on land tenureship organised by the then Ministry of Agriculture and Animal Husbandry held . . . in December 1996. (Karake 1997: 8)

Other participatory seminars in Kibungo had recommended likewise: 'that Rwanda must have clear land tenureship laws – so that land can be freely exchanged' (1997: 22). The people's wish, in other words, conformed with the World Bank's recommendation that Rwanda must move towards 'granting full property rights instead of simple usufruct' (Banque Mondiale 1998: 3).

Before the war and genocide, land ownership, access and use were not regulated by statute. Where regulations did exist, there was confusion, either because of the provisional character of the law or because of non-implementation (Larbi 1995; Platteau 1992). Ephrem Gasasira, who wrote the guidelines for repossession (Gasasira 1995), confirmed this by referring *inter alia* to April 1961 when the Ministry of Home Affairs had prepared a circular with directives to *bourgmestres* concerning land distribution (no. 661/ORG). The circular was never published. Gasasira describes Rwanda's post-colonial attitude to land legislation as a game of wait-and-see (Gasasira 1995: 7).

Reflections on land and social development must therefore begin with the appreciation that in Rwanda 'custom' has prevailed. Legal texts on land ownership and use do exist, but they have no practical significance since nearly all pertain to 'foreigners and religious missions', whose rights were granted during colonialism (Barrière 1997: 10). Ordinary Rwandans have no interest in these written land laws; what matters to them is that the land is there to be used. Barrière quotes Muhayeyezu: 'Whether the land is registered or not makes no difference to a Rwandan. It is his land, and that's it' (Muhayeyezu 1996: 6). It's a pertinent observation.

Importantly, the laws that exist are rarely implemented. For example, while the Constitution of 1962 stipulated that all land sales or gifts had to be approved by the Minister of Agriculture, few who obtained land ever registered their transactions because the procedure was too long or risky (Larbi 1995: 23). The prohibition of distress sales was easily circumvented; unlawful sales of land escalated in the late 1980s (André 1995; von Braun *et al.* 1991). Regulations were also circumvented in the case of Rwanda's resettlement schemes (*paysannats*), which for some time had remained the country's most important strategy for countering land scarcity and emigration (Silvestre 1974).

In line with the Michigan study, the National Seminar on land reform in Rwanda (République Rwandaise 1998) has argued that Rwanda's post-independence land tenure system – a dual system, with near total state control and limited privatisation – does not offer 'the peasant any secure access to land since the state remains the ultimate owner. Experience shows that the public management of land and environment often results in failure, because local actors fail to take responsibility' (1998: 99). This diagnosis is both accurate and well documented (see e.g. Nkundabashaka and Voss 1987). To change this situation, the government of Rwanda has embarked on a drastic re-organisation of rural space which will do away with dispersed settlements and farm fragmentation, practices considered detrimental to rural productivity. Government strategy is to go for full-scale villagisation (*imidugudu*), and this despite the failures of such a strategy elsewhere in Africa.

It is useful, though, to remember that the debate on spatial reorganisation is not new in Rwanda (Prioul 1976; Twagiramutara 1976). Indeed, the late

President Habyarimana himself had been very critical of the pattern of dispersed settlement and farm fragmentation. He was of the opinion that '[the] traditional system of random landholdings and scattered homesteads blocks the development of the countryside' (quoted in Nezehose 1990: 38). Habyarimana would not have had anything as drastic as villagisation in mind, but he was aware that farming practices, driven as they were by 'tradition', stood in the way of an optimum utilisation of the land resource (Nezehose 1990: 39).

To understand the full context in which the recent proposals for land reform developed we must now turn to early colonial and pre-colonial times and ask how, with a few exceptions, land came to belong to the state. The historical process demands our attention because it is 'remembered' in contemporary proposals for reform.

Access to land: a historical perspective

In writing about pre-colonial times, historians distinguish between those regions of contemporary Rwanda that came to be ruled by the Tutsi *nyiginya* central court before the twentieth century (Nduga and surrounding areas, Kinyaga) and those which at that time remained outside the central court's influence, especially the north-west and the Hutu kingdoms of Bukunzi and Busozo. These regions did not come under Nduga rule until the 1920s, when Belgium intervened (see Chapter 1).

Before this administrative unification, land was held by corporate lineages in a system of clientship known as *ubukonde*. The term denotes a plot of land cut from forest and collectively owned at the level of the lineage. As the first occupier, the lineage head (*umukonde*) allocated some land to his parents and clients (*abagererwa*), and some to potential clients from outside the lineage (Smets 1960). A non-lineage member

could request land from the lineage head. He would then become a tenant on lineage land; in return for use of this land, he would transmit prestations (usually sorghum or banana beer) to the lineage head from time to time, and would *sometimes* work in the latter's fields. (Newbury 1981: 139; emphasis added)

Labour prestations were not onerous. As a rule, clients pledged loyalty to the *umukonde* and made annual prestations, mostly hoes and a certain amount of beer, *but only occasionally pledged labour* (Reyntjens 1985: 487–9; Ruhashyankiko 1985: 72–6). With time, good clients would themselves become lineage heads (*abakonde*) and attract their own political followers, all of whom were eager to acquire land. Where a client became head, which meant that the relationship with his own *umukonde* had flourished, the prestations would be dropped. The downside of *ubukonde*, however, and particularly where it existed as an institution in the north-west, was that the land allocated to clients could be reduced at any time should the *umukonde* wish to reclaim some. This might be done, for example, so that the head could settle members from his own extended family. A specific source of frustration with this system was that the reduction in arable land did not lessen the clients' annual prestation.

Regions that came under Tutsi rule were governed by a different agricultural system, *isambu*, in which land belonged not to the 'first occupier' but to the divine Tutsi king (*mwami*). The king distributed large tracts to relatives and political clients, but, unlike under *ubukonde*, he did so in return for prestations in kind *and labour*. The extraction of labour power marked the difference between the two systems. The central court, moreover, ruled that only the Tutsi king had the right and power to decide on how land should be distributed. This constituted another fundamental break with one of *ubukonde*'s central features, namely that the land rights of an *umukonde* – as lineage head – could not be alienated (Barrière 1997: 6; also De Meire 1928). Although central court officials appear to have used *ubukonde* as the model for building their own forms of clientship (Newbury 1981: 139), King Rwabugiri rejected the principle that land could be collectively exploited under arrangements that honoured the rights of the first occupier. He broke the power of the landholding lineage heads, then enhanced the state's extractive capacity by appointing land chiefs who were given the means to requisition *uburetwa* labour.

After the Belgian authorities moved in to help unify Rwanda's administrative map, Rwanda's north-west witnessed the arrival of political *abagererwa*, Tutsi notables sent by the court to replace the original *abakonde*. The displacement meant that *abakonde* lost not only valuable land, but also important annual prestations (Reyntjens 1985: 489). In Ruhengeri, for example, the Tutsi authorities 'appropriated landholdings of between 5 and 70 hectares, thus reducing the land left to an individual *umukonde* or his family to small properties of around 3 hectares or less' (Ruhashyankiko 1985: 73–4, referring to the *Séance du Conseil Spécial Provisoire du 7 mars 1960*). *Abakonde* often retaliated by augmenting the prestations they themselves demanded of their clients (*abagererwa*). Ruhashyankiko refers to research by Reisdorff (1952), the Belgian ethnographer-administrator who documented the excessive levying of the *abakonde* of Rwankeri and interpreted the excess as a sign of political weakness.

Belgium's particular brand of indirect rule not only spread *uburetwa*, but also altered the practice in two major ways. First, the labour prestation was amplified to suit the extractive needs of the colonial administration. By the 1930s, Hutu *ubuhake* clients (*abagaragu*), previously exempt from the labour prestation, 'were compelled to perform manual labor for their patron in some areas of the country' (Newbury 1981: 142). Their patron's labour needs had become more acute after the Belgian colonists encouraged chiefs to become coffee entrepreneurs. This transformation made *uburetwa* more onerous and more resented (1981: 143), particularly in regions not brought under the control of the central court until the arrival of Belgian rule. 'It is no accident', Newbury writes, that these areas 'manifested the strongest anti-Tuutsi sentiment in the politics of the 1950s' (Newbury 1981: 144).[3] Second, rule by Belgium made *uburetwa* the responsibility of individual adult males. *Uburetwa* ceased to be an obligation met at the lineage level, as had been the case in Rwabugiri's time. Adult males were now 'called upon more frequently and more regularly to perform *ubureetwa*' (Newbury 1981: 142). There was also more emphasis on money payments.

But 'double colonialism' did not mean that the alliance between Belgium and the Tutsi central court was smooth.[4] Belgian colonists may have helped to extend court rule, but they also undermined it by dismantling the divine powers of the Tutsi king. Despite being in a partnership of clear mutual advantage, the European colonists imposed a set of 'civilising measures' that sapped divine rule. Measures included the withdrawal of the *mwami*'s right over life and death, the introduction of modernity and Christianity, and the prohibition of court rituals that renewed the *mwami*'s divine origins and legitimacy. While this transformative process took time, it was clear already by the mid-1920s that the Belgian Administration occupied centre stage and that Rwandan notables had begun to pay court to the Europeans rather than their own king (Des Forges 1972: 333).

As the modern state took over, a 'rational' approach to land distribution and utilisation was advocated, especially through the colonists' scheme for assisted settlements (*paysannats*) in sparsely populated areas.

Land and livelihood security from independence until 1994

While independence democratised access to land for the majority of Rwanda's (male) household heads, it soon transpired that the steep rise in population density, combined with the continuous fragmentation of land through inheritance (all male descendants inherited), made farms too small to be viable. The non-viability of farms then resulted in a steep increase in the incidence of distress sales by very poor farmers, which in turn gave rise to conflicts over land. In the course of their fieldwork in the north-west in 1993, André and Platteau (1996) recorded such conflicts on an almost daily basis.

A related livelihood problem has been Rwanda's inability to create sufficient off-farm income generating activities. Land being an exceedingly scarce resource, studies of food security have long stressed how off-farm income can help to maintain and boost food and livelihood security (Loveridge 1992; Pottier 1986, 1993; Vis *et al.* 1975; von Braun *et al.* 1991). The benefits of off-farm income for food consumption have been most clearly demonstrated in the case of the fertile, high altitude Zaire-Nil Divide (von Braun *et al.* 1991).

However, while the benefits of secure off-farm income cannot be doubted, the following must also be observed. First, off-farm income opportunities in the 1980s were mostly in the hands of male farmers (von Braun *et al.* 1991: 12); second, opportunities were heavily dependent on the continuous support of external donors. In the less fertile south, this heavy dependence on donors often led to unsustainable practices (Pottier 1993: 19). As the search for off-farm employment is a recurrent nightmare in Rwanda, the main conclusion of von Braun's study remains valid: the country needs 'rapid expansion of off-farm employment opportunities along with yield-increasing technological change in agriculture [as] the prerequisites for assured entitlements to food for the poor' (von Braun *et al.* 1991: 58). Post-genocide recommendations for kickstarting productivity in rural Rwanda all make a similar point.

In the absence of viable income-generating activities, cultivators in the 1970s had turned to Rwanda's many under utilised lands, especially the marshes and valley bottoms (Nezehose 1990: 52). So essential to survival was their exploitation that access came to be regulated on a collective basis, i.e. through membership to cooperatives. Parastatal marshland projects were also launched.[5]

Despite the flurry of donor activity in Rwanda after independence, it was clear by the late 1980s that Habyarimana's regime was not committed to ensuring food and livelihood security for all. When the struggling poor sold their land in desperation, Habyarimana's elite were there to buy it up; when hunger hit south Rwanda in 1989, food aid remained stockpiled in the OPROVIA warehouses in Kigali (personal observation); when OPROVIA ran into anticipated financial difficulties, the regime did nothing to meet its financial obligations (see Chapter 1). The overriding attitude within Habyarimana's government was that food security had been, and would remain, a strictly local issue, a personal affair grounded in face-to-face patronage. The state did not accept responsibility.

Today, the Rwandan government proposes to ensure the well being and livelihood security of every citizen via a thorough restructuring of the way land is distributed (see Barrière 1997). The chosen approach to reform, villagisation (*imidugudu*), which has a strong surveillance function, was launched in December 1996 and heralded as a rational response to the old problem of low agricultural productivity. Whether the commitment to food security for all will be actualised without recourse to localised or ethnicised forms of favouritism and clientship remains to be seen, but first soundings suggest that Tutsi repatriates (a.k.a. 'old caseload' refugees) may benefit more than other social groups (Hilhorst and van Leeuwen 1999; Van Hoywcghen 1999). This favouritism has two origins: first, repatriates can exploit policy loopholes, as will be shown with reference to the repossession of property; and second, policy prescriptions are routinely interpreted with recourse to a strong moral discourse, which will be demonstrated with reference to both *imidugudu* and the plight of widows.

Repossession

A conversation I had in Butare in 1995 throws light on the sensitivity of repossession. Following research during the mid-1980s in Tumba-Cyarwa, a *secteur* of Butare, I paid subsequent visits in 1990, 1993 (a tense time), 1994 (after the war and genocide) and 1995. On this last visit, I met up with Grégoire and Médiatrice (pseudonyms), brother and sister, whom I had known well in the mid-1980s. With the weight of the genocide upon them, our exchanges were brief. Here, in parenthesis, are a few lines.

A Conversation

Grégoire [to Johan]: 'Yohanni, times are difficult. Of the three brothers who shared this farm, I'm the one who remains. Father passed away before the war, you know this, the others have fled, I do not know if they are alive. The farm is smaller too, we have new neighbours, we do not know them.'

The new neighbours, repatriates from Burundi, had claimed a share of the farm. They once lived here, they said. Grégoire now cultivates the plot that remains with Médiatrice, the sister whose Tutsi husband was killed in the genocide. She was at home nursing her young son, Espoir. When I knew Médiatrice in the 1980s, she was still unmarried and lived at home.

Médiatrice: 'You see how it is now, I am back home. My husband, whom you never met, passed away in the genocide. Now I live here and work some of our father's land. Do you want to see?'

As I used to know the family well, I said I remembered how Sébastien, the youngest of the brothers, had returned home in 1986 after losing his job in Cyangugu. To give him his share of the land, the brothers had all 'moved up a bit' (verb: *kwisuganya*). As there was good understanding in the family, they had proverbially made the rabbit skin stretch to cover five (*ah'umwaga utari uruhu rw'urukwavu rwisasira batanu*).

Médiatrice: 'Now Grégoire has moved up for myself and Espoir. Grégoire says had father known about these terrible times, and how my husband would be killed, he would have taken pity and given me *ingaligali* land.'

Johan: 'You even have some banana trees on your plot . . .'

Médiatrice: 'Yes, I am very lucky, one day they will be Espoir's.'

Médiatrice was indeed among the lucky widows. Her brother supported her, she had a son, there was still some land to share. The vast majority of Rwanda's hundreds of thousands of genocide and war widows are not so lucky. As for the new neighbours, Médiatrice and her brother agreed, it was better not to disturb them.

In contrast to Rwanda's much publicised agricultural disaster at the end of the 1994 war,[6] the problem of how farms and other property would be repossessed when the 'new caseload' refugees returned from Zaire and Tanzania was regularly dismissed by officials as secondary and unproblematic. In their dealings with the international community, officials routinely assumed that repatriates returning from exile would mostly move into the homes of those who had perished in the genocide. Pondering the number of properties required to house the repatriates, Augustine Iyamuremye, then Minister of Agriculture, reflected in January 1995:

It is a somewhat sinister calculation. We start by observing that one million people have returned from exile in Uganda and Burundi, but that this figure contains some forty percent non-farmers. Further, we believe the number of dead farmers to be around half a million, and we take account of the fact that a number of new refugees will not return. In sum, we believe that between 500,000 and 600,000 [vacant] properties will be found. The government also plans to designate particular zones that belong to the State and which could be distributed for resettlement.[7]

Statistically balanced, Iyamuremye's assessment suggested that repatriates could be slotted-in, there should be enough vacant property to go round. The narrative, however, omitted that by early 1995 tens of thousands of farms belonging to refugees in eastern Zaire and Tanzania had already been taken over by repatriates.

When a million and more Hutu refugees returned in late 1996 and early 1997, many found that Tutsi repatriates now occupied their farms. For the past two years, these repatriates had worked the land, enriched the soil and, importantly, had built alliances with the new authorities; the latter often themselves repatriates. In combination, these factors increased the likelihood that squatter-repatriates would stay put whatever the guidelines on repossession might say (see Gasasira 1995). Would double occupancy cause problems? Officials did not think so, at least not when they faced the media. Rather, they voiced optimism. When the repatriation from Goma got under way, Christine Umutoni, the assistant minister for rehabilitation and social integration, was not daunted by the prospect: 'We have sufficient capacity,' she said, 'to absorb the refugees. There is land for them. Some houses are occupied by other people, but the local authorities will ensure that properties return to their rightful owners. . . . The real problem is [neither land nor property, but] social integration'.[8] Official optimism was particularly reflected in the ruling that returning Hutu refugees would repossess their properties within a fortnight, a ruling Umutoni confirmed.[9] Vice-President Kagame was equally confident. He put it boldly: 'Twenty percent of Rwanda is unoccupied because that space used to be reserved for hunting. Why would we not use that space?'[10]

Beyond the calculations and optimism, the more serious question was this: what exactly were the rules for repossessing property? The Arusha Accord of 1993, still binding, stipulated that only

the repatriate who left the country ten years ago or less has the right to recuperate his properties even when they are presently occupied by a person or the state. (Gasasira 1995: 14)

As the guidelines Gasasira had produced on behalf of MINAGRI/FAO could not be clearer, optimism reigned. Unlike in 1994, when the government tolerated the portrayal of Rwanda as a helpless country ravaged by war, by 1995, and amidst growing tension between the government and international donors, the world was told it should not worry. Repossession would be sorted out *internally*, and speedily.

This optimistic narrative, however, did not consider the complexities of every-day life; something Gasasira himself had anticipated. Repossession would not be so easy, he knew, when the property had been expropriated by the state for reasons of public interest or when the property had changed hands on previous occasions. Likewise, repatriates absent for over ten years might still find they could overturn the ruling that they must not reclaim. This might happen, for instance, when the property to be returned had been 'momentarily unoccupied' (Gasasira 1995: 15), which was common during the 1994–96 refugee crisis, or when a former occupant had died during the civil strife (1995: 17). In the latter case, the officially endorsed solution was to prioritise the repatriate, 'since nothing is as dear as the land of one's ancestors' (1995: 17). Reclaiming property momentarily unoccupied would be allowed according to the following logic: first, that land ultimately belongs to the state (it still did); second, that the state would provide alternative accommodation when the 'new caseload' refugees returned; third, that the purpose of all land is to put it to use. In a country facing economic uncertainty and food shortages, this third principle promised to be effective where repatriates made claims not in the spirit of the Arusha.

In summarising these obstacles to smooth repossession by 'new caseload' refugees, Gasasira did not doubt that thousands of repatriates, disqualified in principle, would be allowed to make strong claims. Gasasira, and MINAGRI/FAO by implication, condoned level-headed circumvention:

People need to understand first and foremost that all land belongs to the state. It is the state which grants use rights to individuals, and which withdraws these rights should the individuals no longer be able to properly exploit the land in question. *The development of the land must be the final goal of every land concession.* We cannot afford to have arable land that is not under cultivation because the land is there precisely to feed society. (Gasasira 1995: 21)

UNDP/FAO consultant Olivier Barrière (Barrière 1997) would step in at a later date to develop this principal point (see pp. 196–9, this chapter).

Even should repatriates wish to leave the property on the return of the 'new caseload' refugees, the latter could not hope to move back in until the field crops were harvested. This sound rule would be honoured. Gasasira states:

Those who have crops in the fields of other people must be allowed to stay long enough so they can harvest. This is the least we can do.

The 'new caseload' refugee who returns will therefore need to await the end of the harvest before he can reclaim his property. We believe that this measure is the only means at our disposal to ensure that people [i.e. repatriates not living in their own homes] actually produce food. If we do not do this, we are heading for a killer famine. (Gasasira 1995: 21)

When some 700,000 refugees came back from Zaire, they did so at a time when key field crops had just begun to grow. The timing of their return, November 1996, meant it was impossible for the majority simply to go home and reclaim property there and then. Facing the media, however, officials continued to assert that repossession would happen 'within a fortnight'. It was another demonstration that Rwanda's new leaders were savvy about the media. Despite this official confidence, people inside Rwanda knew such statements belonged to the realm of fantasy. Unless their land had been looked after by relatives, which had happened in a number of cases,[11] returning refugees knew that the end of the harvest, another two months away (January–February 1997), would be the earliest they could realistically hope to repossess homes and farms.

A further reason why (Tutsi) repatriates might oppose repossession claims was that the guidelines acknowledged that some pre-genocide occupants had been 'undeserving', i.e. had acquired their properties without ministerial authorisation. Given the prevalence of unauthorised land sales in the 1980s, and given also that so many commune records were destroyed in the war, it was only to be expected that thousands of repatriates disqualified by Arusha would argue that the properties they were moving into had previously belonged to 'undeserving occupants'.

In short, despite significant official optimism, there existed several good reasons to believe that repossession claims and counterclaims would be made and resolved not through recourse to the guidelines but through palavers *at the commune level*,[12] where repossession would be tackled with the protocol, wit and intrigue so typical of local-level debate (compare Pottier 1989a, 1989b, 1994b). Most importantly, repatriates would argue their cases before commune-level authorities with whom they had already built relationships, so there would be no need to follow Arusha to the letter. Where 'new caseload' returnees challenged repatriates, which was not risk-free,[13] they might expect to see the legal battle drawn out over long periods of time. Much would depend on how well the repatriates got along with the commune authorities (not infrequently repatriates themselves) and on whether government was in a position to provide alternative shelter and farmland. Where such alternatives were not forthcoming, which was common, it was the 'new caseload' refugee rather than the 'old caseload' repatriate who was more likely to end up in need of a home.

In fairness, though, it would be wrong to assume that repatriates were always favoured, for to assume this is to overlook the relative autonomy of communes. This autonomy had already come to the attention of the Ministry of

Rehabilitation and Social Integration in 1994, albeit in a negative sense, when the Ministry learned that long-serving commune leaders were reluctant to let go of the coveted privilege giving them control over the allocation of marshlands (Gasasira 1995: 7). Some commune leaders had also tried to hide that there was 'vacant land' in their communes. Their reluctance, Gasasira suggested, could be blamed on the absence of rigorous land laws; legal laxity had made the authorities believe that they themselves owned the vacant lands (1995: 8).[14]

This mixture of clear guidelines and scope for commune-level interpretation explains why repatriates often remained uncertain about what would happen if and when 'new caseload' refugees returned. Their anxiety over tenure was much in evidence during a visit I paid to Muvumba commune, Mutara Prefecture, in 1995.[15] At the time of this visit, some 60 per cent of Muvumba's original population was absent in Lumasi camp, Tanzania,[16] yet farms in the commune were occupied at roughly 80 per cent (local agronomist: personal communication). Not working their own land and fearing the return of its rightful owners, Muvumba's new farmers exploited the land to no more than 30 per cent of its capacity (UNREO 1995: 3).[17] An assessment mission which visited Muvumba at the end of the war had concluded that agricultural production remained deficient despite seed distribution, because there was extensive uncertainty over land tenure and a general lack of inputs (WFP/ARP 1994: 9).

The under-achievement in food production suggests that the dynamics of repossession did not always favour the Tutsi repatriates. This could be explained in part, as just seen, by the repatriates' genuine fear of a mass return of the 'new caseload' refugees,[18] and in part because many commune-level authorities did want to see justice done. Despite the noted loopholes, 'new caseload' refugees often reclaimed land successfully, especially in communes where resettlement was implemented with speed and cooperation (Hilhorst and Van Leeuwen 1999: 29–30) or where they had relatives who had looked after the property.

Law, land and women's rights

Women's rights in land, and the question of whether these rights can be actualised, are issues not unlike repossession. Broadly, legal entitlement is one thing, lived reality another. Women's rights, even when backed with new legislation, do not necessarily translate into *de facto* access to resources.

The Rwanda genocide altered the ratio of men to women to roughly 30:70. For the areas hardest hit, available statistics show that between one third and one half of all women were widowed (Joint Evaluation 1996c: 14; World Bank 1995: 7, 140). These widows and their (female) children had no right to inherit the land they used to farm, as it was controlled by the male relatives of the deceased husbands. The exception, until recently, used to be land bestowed as *ingaligali* land. Pottier and Nkundabashaka (1992) clarify the concept:

Women cannot inherit land, but a woman, married or not, may receive land as a gift (*urwibutso*) from her elderly father. The gesture is denoted by the verb *kuraga*. This kind of land (*ingaligali*) is usually set aside for emergencies, at the time a family farm is divided up among the male children. A troubled daughter (*indushi*) will be given such land and will have access to it for as long as she is deemed in need, if necessary for life. After her death, however, the land will be reclaimed by her late husband's nearest patrikin. (Pottier and Nkundabashaka 1992: 165)

The practice of bestowing *ingaligali* land was still common in certain parts of Rwanda in the early 1990s (de Lame 1996: 122, 144–5), even though the brother of a 'troubled daughter' was by now more likely to pressure his sister into relinquishing the land at an early opportunity. This was in contrast to the mid-1980s, when brothers might tease a troubled sister but would refrain from bullying her. Today, land being exceedingly scarce, 'troubled daughters' are unlikely to benefit from the gift of *ingaligali* land. Women without husbands will be women without land, except where they have grown-up sons.

Following the war and genocide, the policy challenge was to change the 'judicial guidelines and legal interpretations of laws pertaining to property, land and women's rights' (Joint Evaluation, 1996c: 14). As with repossession, the challenge and the solution were sufficiently clear. A national seminar (République Rwandaise 1998) proposed amendments to the law to strengthen women's control over land. These included:

- The widow is subrogated *vis-à-vis* her husband's land rights.
- The unmarried woman who finds herself the sole surviving descendant of the patrilineal group, to the second degree or as a parallel cousin, is entitled to inherit the land rights of the group.
- The married woman who has neither brother nor sister can inherit the land rights of her parents. (République Rwandaise 1998: 106)

Clear enough. What is less clear is how such guidelines, which became law in November 1999 (AVEGA 1999: 2), will be *interpreted* in local settings. Interpretation occurs because the widow's problem is not just about the loss of a husband, it is also about the status of her marriage and children. The likelihood exists that the new law governing access to land will be circumvented through local debate on whether individual women can be said to qualify. There will be legal and not-so-legal widows; widows who married with bridewealth and others who did not, and the latter may well be told that the legal changes do not apply to them. There is the linked problem that 'many rural widows are not aware of [their rights to family inheritance] and therefore do not know how to recover their husband's property from male relatives' (1999: 2).

In this context, development workers must recognise that the local-level discourse on public morality is replete with gendered stereotypes through which men and women comment upon or explain the problems and attainments of others.[19] In Rwanda, women are especially prone to be negatively affected by the discourse. Referring to gender inequality within households, Jefremovas puts it thus: 'stereotypes of women as loose women, virtuous wives or timid virgins are used by both men and women to interpret, manipulate, validate or negate control over labour, resources and surplus' (Jefremovas 1991b: 379). 'Virtuous wives', however, is a social category which today requires further unpacking, since, as research in north-western Rwanda has shown (André 1995), questions are now being asked regarding the status of a woman's marriage.

Catherine André's research exposed the inner workings of the discourse of public morality and stereotype that produces and marginalises vulnerable groups. In the early 1990s, vulnerable groups and individuals had seen their entitlements to land vanish, rapidly and fiercely. Those losing entitlements included individuals deemed illegitimate (especially widows not married with bridewealth), divorcees and their children, and migrants returning to their communes after long spells away from home. Also marginalised were second wives in polygamous marriages, along with their children, and young men who lacked status. An ethnographic example of the latter, showing how low status impairs a young man's capacity to claim land, exists in Danielle de Lame's ethnographic study of Munzanga in west-central Rwanda. Here, Josefu, a young unmarried man, orphaned and without brothers, struggled to save from the clutches of his uncles the land he had legally inherited. Lacking status in the extended family, Josefu failed to keep his land (de Lame 1996: 122–3).

In Rwanda's north-west, the category of widows married without bridewealth (*inkwano*) grew considerably in the 1980s (André 1995: 87). Proper transactions had become so expensive that a groom's father often needed to sell land in order to raise the bridewealth. Rather than sell land needed for security in old age, parents preferred to see their children marry in a non-customary way, i.e. without the required exchanges of *inkwano* and the essential counter prestation, *indogoranyo*.[20] By the late 1980s, the problem of bridewealth had also affected eastern Zaire and other parts of Central and East Africa (Pottier and Fairhead 1991; Pottier 1994c). Women's vulnerability was also conspicuous in the case of divorce, even when the union had been sanctioned by bridewealth. Gripped by poverty, a divorcee's family was now highly unlikely to offer any support in the customary manner, e.g. by allocating *ingaligali* land in her father's commune (André 1995: 87). The point is that even before the 1994 genocide and war, poor people, mostly women, were increasingly barred from actualising their land inheritance rights. Given this expansion of vulnerability and social exclusion, it is oversimplistic to approach the question of the Rwandan widows' rights to land purely in terms of widowhood resulting from civil strife and genocide. A more comprehensive analytic framework is needed.

The power of the local discourse(s) on public morality and exclusion continues to be strong in Rwanda, so much so that public opportunities for debating poverty and social exclusion are regularly shunned. While the Rwandan government clearly intends to take social engineering to new heights, officials on the ground use coded language (verb: *guca amalenga*) when it comes to discussing poverty-linked rights at local levels. Or they fail to engage. In reviewing the Bugesera-Sud Water Project, for example, Han Seur (Seur 1999) became aware that officials from the Ministry of Public Works (MINITRAP) shied away from discussing 'hot issues' like destitution and widowhood whenever they dealt with commune leaders or the population at large. Seur writes:

Issues like poverty, economic differentiation, access to land, single headed households, widows, orphans and *personnes indigentes* [i.e. destitutes], were gradually removed from the agenda or, whenever mentioned, caused irritation. MINITRAP refused to discuss the issue[s] with the *commune* or during meetings with the population. Apparently widows and orphans, especially if there are too many, did not fit into a post-war, post-emergency discourse. (Seur 1999: 25)

Rather than confront these issues with transparency, the common response within the Bugesera-Sud Water Project was for officials to call in a sensitisation team mandated to change the people's long corrupted mentality of always wanting to receive free hand-outs (1999: 25). Responsibility was thus offloaded directly on to the disempowered who, when too numerous, were blamed for the corrupt mentality they have acquired.

The implication for Rwanda's 'troubled daughters', widows and female orphans, is straightforward: new legislation regarding land is most welcome, but if their plight is left off the public agenda, we may expect 'custom' to prevail.[21]

Imidugudu

Guidelines, autonomous local authorities, strong discourses of public morality and exclusion are elements also found in planned resettlement, or villagisation (*imidugudu*), the programme *par excellence* for solving Rwanda's twin problem of low agricultural productivity and continued insecurity. How was *imidugudu* conceptualised? how implemented? and what are its built-in biases?

Given longstanding official concern over dispersed settlement and land fragmentation, it is not too surprising that today's villagisation programme continues an agenda begun before the war and genocide. The inspiration for *imidugudu* has come from the Rwandan NGO ARAMET, founded in 1988, which floated the idea that 'the core problem of Rwanda was not overpopulation or land scarcity in itself, but a lack of proper planning. . . . The central tenet was that the socio-economic pressure could be resolved through better land use planning, better settlement patterns, and economic growth outside agriculture' (Hilhorst and van Leeuwen 1999: 14). Adopted by the post-genocide government, ARAMET's perspective turned into a grand scheme for villagisation; a scheme officially regarded as 'the only alternative we have' (Hajabakiga, MINITERE, October 1999). A straightforward narrative accompanies the programme. Patricia Hajabakiga, secretary-general in the Ministry of Lands, Human Resettlement and Environmental Protection (MINITERE), specifies: 'The policy is clear. In rural areas, every Rwandan is to move into a village for the purpose of proper land utilisation and the provision of basic services' (IRIN, 13 October 1999).[22]

Initially, *imidugudu* received much international criticism, since similar schemes elsewhere (Tanzania, Mozambique, Ethiopia) had failed. But this attitude changed following the mass return of 'new caseload' refugees. Their return meant *imidugudu* could be reframed – imaginatively – as an emergency plan. The programme began to look more attractive/urgent and raked in the funds: UNHCR lent its support, as did a host of international NGOs. *Imidugudu* could also be thought of as contributing to national reconciliation, which again increased its international appeal.

Inside Rwanda, however, there was vagueness and confusion, since different ministries issued different instructions on how to implement the policy (Hilhorst and van Leeuwen 1999: 11); *imidugudu* turned into 'a multimillion-dollar programme in the midst of vagueness' (1999: 6). A major concern for donors was that *imidugudu* had low levels of popular consultation, with little sign of voluntary participation, and implementation rates and practices that differed enormously from one commune to the next. This variation not only reflected Rwanda's long history of local political autonomy, it was also built into the programme. On launching *imidugudu* in December 1996, the cabinet of ministers had declared it would strengthen the capacity of local authorities to re-organise their rural space.

Hilhorst and van Leeuwen's study of villagisation in Gisenyi *secteur*, southeast Kibungo, confirms that local authorities do exert their right to give *imidugudu* a personal touch. Hilhorst and van Leeuwen interviewed Rwandans who had been forced out of their *paysannat* and into an *umudugudu* (singular) in the summer of 1997. The *paysannat* had been abandoned in 1994 when residents fled to Tanzania, at which point repatriates ('old caseload' refugees) had arrived. When the most recent residents ('new caseload' refugees) returned in late 1996, Gisenyi's councillor (*conseiller*), himself a repatriate, told the repatriates to stay put, while the former residents were told to share their house plots. This sharing of plots appears to have been relatively trouble free and may indeed, though it is too early to confirm, have stimulated reconciliation. Problems arose, though, when everyone was told to vacate the *paysannat* and build an *umudugudu* several kilometres away. When the marching order came, repatriates often ignored the property rights of the original occupiers and took building materials and furniture to the new site. The original inhabitants were unable to prevent this. At the new site, repatriates received land, which they welcomed, while the original *paysannat* dwellers were told that they would, for the time being, continue to work their old – but now distant – gardens. The original inhabitants complained bitterly, pointing out that the *imidugudu* programme was being implemented in Kibungo Prefecture with marked variation; a drastic uprooting like that experienced in Gisenyi had not occurred elsewhere. In other communes, people had been allowed to stay in their old houses. One informant said: 'My old house was close to the road, but it had to be destroyed.' This informant alleged that the inter-commune differences reflected the personalities of *conseillers* (Hilhorst and van Leeuwen 1999: 43).

Importantly, too, the involuntary nature of participation in *imidugudu*, stressed in several interviews, meant that the problematic of land utilisation was not fully addressed (1999: 44). Hilhorst and van Leeuwen admit that Gisenyi *secteur* was unique in several respects (high refugee numbers; high number of genocide victims), yet they regarded the failure to address land distribution and productivity as characteristic of every resettlement. This gives cause for concern, since the *imidugudu* policy officially aspired to solve the problems of excessively high people to land ratios and agricultural decline (Hilhorst and van Leeuwen 1999: 6; also Barrière 1997). When the cabinet of ministers had decided to end dispersed settlement, they had claimed, along the lines of the 1995 Michigan report (see p. 179), that villagisation would rationalise agriculture. Regrouping into villages would free up fertile land for cultivation as villages would be built on poor-quality land (Van Hoyweghen 1999: 363).

Crucially, in its implementation, *imidugudu* policy resonated with the public discourse on morality, i.e. with dominant views on who deserved access to arable land. In Saskia Van Hoyweghen's research in Butare, 'old caseload' refugees often expressed the sentiment that they deserved land more than others because they were, in their own words, 'willing to work' (1999: 364). In contrast, 'new caseload' refugees were labelled lazy, as they had 'lost the habit' of farming because of their pampered time in the camps. Responding to this moral discourse and labelling, the authorities in several Butare *communes* allocated fields to people deemed 'willing to work', which not infrequently meant Tutsi repatriates who were in a position to buy land from those in distress (1999: 365). Poor people desperate for cash would sell them land, or let their banana groves, often for a fee below the value of the crop. It was a newcomers' market.

Observations in Bugesera also suggest that the population was being streamlined in terms of moral worth. On studying two settlements in Bugesera, Hilhorst and van Leeuwen found that residents in Mayanga, exclusive to 'old caseload' refugees, had received cultivation plots of up to two hectares per household, admittedly at some distance from the *umudugudu*. In contrast, Gahembe, the second settlement, housed 'vulnerable groups' who were being denied access to land. Not having had access to sufficient land in their original homes, Gahembe's vulnerable peasant farmers had expected to benefit from the redistribution, but instead ended up disappointed on discovering they would not receive any land

(Hilhorst and van Leeuwen 1999: 31). These undeserving poor belonged to a new social category to be 'attracted' out of agriculture and offered 'more rewarding income opportunities in rural areas' (Van Hoyweghen 1999: 368).

Much of what Van Hoyweghen (1999) and Hilhorst and van Leeuwen (1999) have found corroborates the suspicion, still strong within many international NGOs, that *imidugudu* aims to compensate genocide survivors and 'old caseload' refugees for not being allowed to repossess property under the Arusha Accord. If this hidden (or maybe not so hidden) agenda is confirmed, and Gasasira's reflections on repossession suggest that officials are not trying too hard to hide the loopholes, then *imidugudu* could stand accused of increasing ethnic polarisation and delaying reconciliation. Agencies reluctant to sponsor the programme harbour that fear. *Imidugudu*, moreover, looks attractive to local authorities who have some capital to invest.[23]

The bias in favour of survivors and repatriates suggests that *imidugudu* may carry a political message not just about Rwanda's future but also about its past. In this case, we may expect to find traces of the discourse on public morality and exclusion in the consultancy documents that support the plan for nation-wide villagisation. The influential UNDP/FAO document on land tenure reform (Barrière 1997) has the key.

Post-genocide proposals for land reform

In broad agreement with the tenor of the Michigan study (Clay *et al.* 1995), all proposals for land tenure reform (Banque Mondiale 1998; Barrière 1997; République Rwandaise 1998) suggest that Rwanda can increase its productivity through a change in land use, a change which will break with 'the logic of subsistence farming' and adopt a market-oriented approach. In real terms, this means investing in large landowners through extending agricultural credits. As the approach is already being implemented, the FAO can be said to be 'targeting the "richer" farmers for seed distribution' at the expense of poor ones. Hence, farmers who are 'likely to eat their seeds, are [now] less likely to receive any' (Van Hoyweghen 1999: 367).

UNDP/FAO's assistance with the official search for ways in which land utilisation can be improved has resulted in two important policy documents. Before the mass return of new caseload refugees, the FAO studied and reflected on property and the repossession of property (Gasasira 1995, reviewed above); after the mass return, FAO studied the land problem and suggested a strategy for reform (Barrière 1997). The latter study, by consultant Olivier Barrière, has become an authoritative document. In March 1999, it was still the only proposal for land reform to have been made public (Hilhorst and van Leeuwen 1999: 11).

In the opinion of UNDP/FAO, the World Bank and the Rwandan government, the international support to Rwanda's better-off farmers must be accompanied with a commitment to land consolidation, the rationale for which is that poor people's minute farms have reached their maximum production capacity. So what should be done? Barrière's starting point is that under (what he calls) 'the traditional system', the (male) cultivator 'does not acquire a space but . . . the right to that space or any other resource; a right which in theory can be reclaimed' (Barrière 1997: 20). A close reading of the full document reveals, however, that Barrière equates 'the traditional system' with *isambu*, the agrarian system introduced by the central Tutsi court under Rwabugiri. *Isambu* superseded *ubukonde*, which conferred non-alienable rights to autonomous lineage heads. (I shall return to Barrière's historical sketch later.)

Barrière recognises that Rwanda today is no longer a country inhabited by cultivators alone. Rwanda is different now, more diverse, more like it was during the time before independence. It is therefore reductionist to believe, Barrière argues, that only cultivators should have rights. Rather we must think

in terms of livelihood security for pastoralists, foresters, fishermen, hunters. . . . Cultivators are no longer the only actors who enter into the dynamic exploitation of the environment. The competition means that rights are being reclaimed, and this requires a global organisation which recognises the need to protect the environment for the sake of sustainable development. (Barrière 1997: 24)

This concept of environmental protection for sustainable development holds out various challenges and imperatives. For Barrière, there are two major rules to be obeyed and implemented. First, given the renewed plurality of economic interests, the authorities must move towards a land tenure system which acknowledges both the role of the state as guarantor of justice and sustainable development, and the role and rights of individuals. (This notion of a state-guarantor did not exist under *ubukonde*.) The second basic rule must be that 'land is the patrimony of the people of Rwanda. The State is the guarantor of the perpetuity of this cultural and biological patrimony' (1997: 30). Second, the notion of land as cultural patrimonium does not mean that private interests go unrecognised. Sustainability, Barrière insists, cannot be achieved unless 'the family estate' becomes legally indivisible (1997: 32). This suggestion, however, has been rejected by the World Bank, which advocates the continuation of customary inheritance practices but with proper registration of land titles.[24] Despite the controversy, Barrière's (UNDP/FAO's) reasoning is perfectly compatible with that of the World Bank, since he unequivocally embraces market liberalisation and privatisation. This sits well with the call by the Rwandan government (and the World Bank) for moving public enterprises into the private sector, a move which should lessen the state's budgetary commitments (République Rwandaise 1998: 98).

Within this logic, Barrière endorses *imidugudu*, which, he says, makes good eco-developmental sense. He praises the scheme, because 'its goal . . . is to make optimal use of the agricultural space, to facilitate the relationships between different localities, and to provide better security for the population at large' (Barrière 1997: 41).

Of policy-makers and history

In view of the recent accusation that the international community is viewing *imidugudu* more as a political than a technical programme (Hajabakiga, MINITERE, October 1999),[25] it is instructive to scrutinise Barrière's vision of Rwanda's agrarian past. Can a clear line be drawn between the technical and the political?

Barrière's UNDP/FAO report upholds the image of a harmoniously balanced pre-colonial past, yet is shaky on several counts. For a start, *ubukonde* is presented as if the system operated only in Rwanda's north-west (Barrière 1997: 6); there is no hint that the system had existed elsewhere, nor that it preceded *isambu*, for which it may have served as a model. Barrière is also economical with the truth – i.e. with the information available – when describing how *isambu* spread northward. Without presenting a timeframe, he suggests that *isambu* spread because of demographic pressure. The encroachment of *isambu*, on *ubukonde*, which began in the middle of the nineteenth century when Rwanda was still thinly populated, thus appears to have been 'natural' rather than the product of conquest. Within south-central Rwanda, Barrière claims,

demographic pressure led to the progressive seizure of lineages on the periphery, who became political clients of the central court whose aim was to impose the *isambu* regime on communities based on the principle of first occupier [*lignages défricheurs*]. Progressively, the authority of the lineage chief made way for that of the *mwami*, even though it did not entirely disappear. (Barrière 1997: 6–7)

To explain the imposition of *isambu* in terms of a progressive demographic pressure is not in line with Rwanda's well-documented historical record. Military conquest is the more appropriate reference point.

Barrière, moreover, describes the impact of *isambu* on *ubukonde* in neutral or presumed positive terms. As the much hated *uburetwa* labour prestation – an essential feature of *isambu* – is not referred to, we end up with a less than insightful philosophical comment on the nature of Rwanda's 'customary law' (a singular concept!). Barrière makes it sound as if Rwandans today, northerners included, would remember the spread of *isambu* as the arrival of a benevolent system. It is only with the demise of *ubukonde*, Barrière contends, that Rwanda moved to a fairer system, *isambu*, in which land became alienable (by the divine Tutsi king) and its use more sustainable (Barrière 1997: 6). Before *isambu*, the utilisation of resources depended on the allegedly idiosyncratic judgement of individual *abakonde*.

The political significance of Barrière's reconstruction of Rwanda's customary land rights is that he fails to discuss *uburetwa* as part of *isambu*. This allows him to present *isambu* and rule by the *mwami*'s central court as the uncontestably superior regime for all of Rwanda. By banishing *uburetwa* from the discussion, in the manner of instant expert journalists and academics (Chapters 2 and 3), Barrière contributes, though perhaps unwittingly, to the stubbornly persistent misconception that 'the Rwandan client system consisted of a benevolent protective form of integration, not exploitation' (Newbury 1981: 140). As early as the late 1970s, Newbury complained about this misconception and its persistence in 'secondary works' on Rwanda. Curiously though, Barrière mentions *corvée* labour, but he sees *corvée* as a feature of land distributions under *ubukonde*: entering into *ubukonde* engendered 'an allegiance marked by the offering of prestations in food, drink *and labour* which expressed submission' (Barrière 1997: 7; emphasis added). The reference to 'labour prestations' under *ubukonde* is misleading. As seen at the beginning of this chapter, loyalty to one's *umukonde* was expressed through the gift of hoes and a certain amount of beer, but did not involve *corvée* labour on a scale comparable to *uburetwa*. To add to the confusion, Barrière refers to *uburetwa* as something even *abakonde* had to do, but without making it clear that he has moved on to a different timeframe, i.e. that he is now referring to *uburetwa* as a labour prestation imposed by the political *abagererwa* dispatched by the central court. This misconception that *uburetwa* would have existed in *ubukonde* proper, that is prior to the imposition of rule by the central court, was first corrected during the administrative unification of the 1920s (see De Meire 1928), when the misconception was attributed to an error by German administrators. By being imprecise about timescales, Barrière perpetuates a very old, erroneous impression.

Through Barrière, UNDP and FAO lend support to the (mis)conception that fair-and-sustainable land tenure rules did not exist in Rwanda until land practices everywhere came to be governed by *isambu*. The return to a pre-Tutsi (pre-*isambu*) political culture after the 1959 social revolution, much reinforced under Habyarimana, was therefore to be seen, Barrière hints, as the return to a system of 'absolute property right', i.e. undemocratic and unsustainable.[26] With the coming to power of the Rwandese Patriotic Front, the time is right, Barrière insinuates, to turn the tables once again. There will be one difference, though: the emphasis now is on state protection *and privatisation*, through which a more productive future will be secured.

Conclusion

Regarding Rwanda's agrarian crisis and the need for solutions, UNDP/FAO, the World Bank and the government of Rwanda have produced some smooth but simplistic policy narratives: double occupancy of farms is unjust, so repatriates will vacate within a fortnight; land is under utilised, but full villagisation will rectify this; hundreds of thousands of widows lack access to land, so laws facilitating access can be passed and implemented; off-farm income needs boosting, and resettlement is the prerequisite; land management suffers from farm fragmentation, so the answer is to consolidate and privatise, which allegedly is the people's will. Not unlike some other contemporary messages about Rwanda, reviewed in previous chapters, these 'easy readings' are representations destined for the eyes and ears of an audience foreign and insufficiently informed. They are clear examples of the anti-politics machine seen at work in other parts of the globe (Ferguson 1994).

Not surprisingly perhaps, the World Bank's own study of poverty in Rwanda (Banque Mondiale 1998) shuns the issue of how wealth differentiation and class, which contributed so much to setting off the tragic events of 1994, can be controlled. The Bank's study does not avoid politics entirely, since it calls for popular consultation on *imidugudu*, but it leaves the prospect of continued class differentials and poverty outside its analytic frame. Through this omission, the theme that matters most is not presented for (public) reflection.

Simplistic policy narratives may be normal business in development work, yet they also reflect, in the case of post-genocide Rwanda, the already mentioned rejection of perspectives and judgements independently arrived at by outsiders. Hidden from the (chosen) outside expert's gaze is any detailed consideration of real-life scenarios and their complicating factors, such as the existence of a strong public discourse of morality through which policy directives are locally (re)interpreted. Also hidden from view is the commonly high degree of political autonomy at the local level. In addition, as a close reading of Barrière's proposal reveals, policy arguments may contain subtexts to strengthen the legitimacy of the post-genocide regime in power. Newcomers to Rwanda do not detect these subtle manipulations.

Several policy suggestions – legislation for widows' rights in land; resettlement of the population and privatisation of access to land under state supervision; and participation in all of this by Rwandans on a voluntary basis – have acquired an aura of rationality. The message seems to be: Government and donors know what they are doing. Those suggesting new policies, however, take little account of the likely impact that discourses of public morality and social exclusion will have on how policies are actualised. This suits the Rwandan authorities who want to see Rwanda imagined, and internationally imagined, as a place where rational choices are made and implemented. Rarely do officials admit that it is not that simple. The exception is Gasasira who, providing realistic context, offers more than a glimpse of social complexity. He freely admits there will be significant local interpretation; it would be unwise not to heed his argument.

There is, fortunately, some hope that planners at MINITERE,[27] who are mostly 'Kigali-based "outsiders" who do not know Rwandan rural realities well', have begun to appreciate, in the words of the Kibuye Prefect, that 'only the people themselves can find true solutions' (the Kibuye Prefect, speaking at the National Land Policy workshop, 2–3 November 2000; cited in Palmer 2000). Along with the workshop's openness on sensitive issues (e.g. land grabbing by new elites; absentee land owners), the prefect's statement inspires confidence that MINITERE is taking consultation with peasant farmers seriously. The deeper challenge, though, will be to transcend the country's institutional culture which favours a top-down, male-biased approach to problem solving. It will not be easy to reverse this. As Robin Palmer, Oxfam (GB) land policy adviser, wrote in his recent report on the National Land Policy workshop: 'Given that women now comprise 62 per cent of Rwanda's population, there seemed to be amazingly little recognition of this, or reflection on this, nor was there any pressure from women's groups' (Palmer 2000: 5). The ethnographic complexity of Rwanda's rural realities, which, as this chapter shows, revolves heavily around discourses of morality, has yet to enter the planners' field of view.

Conclusion: representation and destiny

Since April 1994, numerous journalists, aid and relief workers, diplomats, politicians and academics have involved themselves with Rwanda and embarked on a mental crusade to make sense of a situation seemingly drained of every form of logic and morality. Searching for instant understandings, the majority of crusaders, particularly from the anglophone world, have come to embrace a model of Rwandan society and history which simplifies complex relations and obscures relevant contexts. The model is rooted in the political doctrine of the Rwandese Patriotic Front, which, as Rwanda's post-genocide spiritual guardian, displays exceptional skill at converting international feelings of guilt and ineptitude into admissions that the Front deserves to have the monopoly on knowledge construction. Once in a while, opinion makers have asked questions about their received wisdom and its source, as when John Ryle exposed the dubious relationship between humanitarian aid and media coverage,[1] but few commentators, if any, have examined in detail the investigative apparatus which produced their perspectives. It seemed better not to examine. Because of the urgency of the situation, which for many meant coping with the refugee crisis or talking diplomacy or reporting to the world, the outsiders could not take time off for a more in-depth study of Rwanda's present and past. They thus found it convenient and practical to accept the new regime's message that post-independence research on Rwanda amounted to 'fanciful nonsense' (Fergal Keane), a theme which some newcomer academics elaborated with apologistic zeal.

With this book I have sought to dislodge and (re)contextualise the simplifying narratives to which the international community has become accustomed, thus providing a more grounded reading of the antecedents and the aftermath of Rwanda's tragedy and, to a lesser extent, that which befell eastern Congo-Zaire, now renamed the Democratic Republic of Congo (DRC). As an antidote to the easy readings that obliterate context and detail, I have eased a number of complex voices back into the debate. They are the voices of people who have nuanced stories to tell: Rwandan farmers whose lives are socially constructed (an issue not picked up in policy recommendations for economic recovery); Rwandan survivors of genocide whose complex lives cannot be reduced to the fact of their survival; Rwandan refugees whose voices were silenced under the crush of standardised emergency measures and the discourse of collective guilt; people from eastern Zaire who remind that the ethnic tensions they endure cannot all be brought back to the Rwanda genocide; long-serving scholars – Rwandan, Zairean and Western – not afraid to challenge simplified versions of reality and willing to stand up against the use of essentialist terminology, but whose voices, too, were smothered under the weight of an emerging hegemonic discourse. I have called for more receptivity to voices that contextualise their accounts, and for greater awareness of how representation is always a matter of ethics. Anyone interested in the social and political dynamics of Rwanda and the Great Lakes region must move away from simplicity and become better prepared to face outbreaks of violence, including the search for solutions, with adequate knowledge of context and complexity. Since the 1994 genocide and war, Rwanda and eastern Zaire-DRC have been forced into an intellectual crisis, as well as a human and political one. Depictions of reality have come to be led by political visions and ideas, not by empirical study.

The hiring of social scientists for the purpose of warfare or 'development', activities often hard to distinguish, is nothing new. In 1992 David Ludden wrote with reference to India: 'Development regimes hire historians to make themselves look good' (Ludden 1992: 278, quoted in Bose 1997: 58). Similar observations have been made regarding the role of social and natural scientists in colonial Africa (see Asad 1991; Cooper 1997; Moore and Vaughan 1994; Vaughan 1996). So what of Rwanda? We can usefully begin to consider the case of Rwanda by turning first to V. Y. Mudimbe's (1985) seminal paper on African gnosis, philosophy and knowledge. Aware that early anthropological and missionary representations had resulted from the unequal power relations between North and South, Mudimbe praised the brilliance of Abbé Alexis Kagame, whose *Philosophie Bantu-Ruandaise* (1956) had attracted international attention. Mudimbe highlighted how Kagame had 'demonstrate[d] that contrary to anthropologists' and missionaries' accepted opinions, his people had always had a well-organized and systematic "philosophy"' (Mudimbe 1985: 161). The culture of the people of Rwanda was not 'pagan', and missionaries needed to heed the warning. The rupturous emergence of an African 'We-Subject', the '"Nous-Sujet" africain' (Eboussi-Boulaga 1977. 339), testified that Kagame's demand for an anthropology with dignity was being met from both within and outside Africa. But Mudimbe did not stop here. He was interested, too, in the political contexts that produced knowledge. And here he was concerned. Mudimbe stressed that the African discourse he saw emerge through the publications of Eboussi-Boulaga (1977, 1981), Kagame and others, was a cultural hybrid tainted with ambiguity. Accordingly, and acknowledging work by Ralibera (1959) and Foucault (1980, 1982), Mudimbe offered questions for urgent consideration: who, in a text, is speaking? from which institutional position? according to which grids? With reference to African gnosis and phi-losophy, Mudimbe called for a more careful consideration of the relationship between African ethnography and the politics of religious conversion.

More recently, similar questions have surfaced in the related context of Alexis Kagame's relationship with the colonial ethnographer Jacques Maquet. On re-searching the nature of their intellectual partnership, the kind of partnership common in colonial settings marked by indirect rule, Claudine Vidal (1991) learned that Kagame's political project had been to found a constitutional monarchy. Vidal writes:

> Between this political project and an ethnography influenced by functionalism, a lasting harmony developed. When measured in terms of citations, references and paraphrases, Kagame's *Codes* dominated Rwandan ethnography for a long time: they inspired visions of the past that were timeless and idealising.

> J. Maquet was the first [anthropologist] to transcribe this aristocratic representation of pre-colonial Rwanda in refined ethnographic language, and he managed to make it pass as highly objective because, in contrast to Kagame, he maintained a perfectly distant tone throughout his work (Maquet 1954)....On the basis of Kagame's manuscript, Maquet designed a questionnaire for the ageing notables who lived in various parts of the kingdom (Kagame 1975: 220). According to Maquet, who was very precise on the conditions under which the questionnaire was administered, nearly all the 'notables' were Tutsi: they belonged to the central court....It was thus that, in the footsteps of the "White Father" historians, a young anthropologist authenticated Kagame's objectivity. (Vidal 1991: 54)

Half a century later, the Rwandese Patriotic Front enrolled a new, but more diverse generation of 'instant experts' to authenticate its version, a reproduc-tion, of how beautifully integrated Rwanda-without-the-white-man had been. Maquet revisited: the 'outsider' and the 'other' once again working in tandem; the categories 'outsider' and 'insider' once again locked in solidarity. This is not unusual. As Abu-Lughod reminds us: 'the outsider self never stands outside; he or she always stands in a definite relation with the "other" of the study [. . .]. What we call the outside, or even the partial outside, is always a position within a larger political-historical framework' (Abu-Lughod 1993: 40). What was unusual, though, was that the 'instant experts' of the mid-1990s achieved and spread perspectives at the end of an era in which social scientists had asked some very searching questions on how they were 'positioned' in their research.

The return to the colonial model of Rwanda's pre-colonial past, along with its skewed representation of society and history in eastern Zaire-DRC, could well be defended on the grounds that the model can be considered 'post-Oriental', i.e. produced by a subordinate minority which after protracted struggle overcame the relations of domination which had kept it in exile. A defence along such lines has merit. The problem, however, is that this minority's representations and discourses (now widely popular in international circles) reconnect with the views of a privileged, colonial elite – that is, with colonising outsiders and insiders – whose biases were exposed through empirical research in the 1960s and 1970s. The idealising narrative of Rwanda's pre-colonial past, the return to the work of Kagame and Maquet, is therefore also a return to the 'Oriental' depictions that colonial anthropology helped to produce. Today's fashionable interpretation of Rwandan society and history, which strips away complexity and timeframes (failing, for instance, to distinguish between *times before and after* king Rwabugiri), is perhaps no more than an unintended copying of the master narrative that grew out of the cooperation between 'outsider' and 'insider' colonists; a narrative which aimed to legitimate 'possessive exclusivism' (cf. O'Hanlon and Washbrook 1992: 157). On the other hand, the present coterie of impressionable scriptwriters is not just copying a classic anthropological monograph, but also has managed to 'improve' on some of its findings. Today's common claim, for instance, that mobility across social categories was smooth and frequent in pre-colonial days (see Chapters 2 and 3) does not square with Maquet's contention that such mobility was very limited. 'It is certain,' Maquet wrote, 'that the number of Hutu and Twa assimilated to Tutsi because of their holding of political offices or because of their wealth, *has always been tiny*' (Maquet 1961: 150; emphasis added). In the hands of instant experts, this tiny participation has been inflated to the order of 'considerable mobility', which would have involved 'the peasant Hutu masses and the Twa' on the basis of 'an agreed sharing of rights and duties'; a situation resulting in 'many Hutus [being] assimilated into the Tutsi aristocracy'. Once appropriately described as 'a recurrent poison in Rwanda's body politic' (Linden 1998), this interpretation of Rwandan history has clearly moved up a gear.

Ethnographic representations may be approached, by way of a working hypothesis, as economies of truth made possible because of powerful 'lies' of exclusion and rhetoric (Clifford 1986: 7). According to this approach, truth is distorted through the mechanism of exclusion: some data are selected, others discarded. Clifford's perspective applies to writings colonial and post-colonial, and provides us with a fine tool with which to reflect on conflict scenarios and intellectual warfare. Useful too, from the same edited volume on writing culture (Clifford and Marcus 1986), is Crapanzano's take on 'lies'. Crapanzano likened the ethnographer to Hermes, Zeus's messenger, who had 'promised to tell no lies, but did not promise to tell the whole truth' (Crapanzano 1986: 35). This meant that when the messenger spoke, one needed to ask: how much of what is said excludes, ignores, censors and de-values other spheres of people's multi-faceted lives? Asking these questions of RPF-functional renderings of Rwandan society, economy and history, as I have done in this book, helps us to appreciate what great care the Front has taken, and continues to take, to engage with all major modern channels of information: news media, academe, humanitarian aid, diplomacy and development – all channels increasingly reliant on mediascapes.[2] Not just in Rwanda but in the world over, the scope for imaginative borrowing has become vast. Imagination as social practice is nothing new in itself, and certainly not in times of conflict, but the speed with which and the scale on which global media processes now produce imaginings and re-imaginings is unprecedented. Events in Rwanda and the Great Lakes region show what possibilities exist when imagination is used as a tool to forge a new social order.

It is against the backdrop of new electronic capabilities and possibilities for exercising public imagination that the challenge of a better future for Rwanda, through reconciliation, becomes truly awesome. Lemarchand appreciates the magnitude where he writes: 'there can be no reconciliation . . . without justice, and no justice without truth' (Lemarchand 1998: 3). He warns, however, that

[it] is doubtful that the full truth will ever be known about the circumstances and scale of the atrocities committed in former Belgian Africa. [But] unless a concerted effort is made to get closer to the facts and move out of the fantasy-land of official mythologies, the collective memory of Hutu and Tutsi will continue to enshrine the same myths, with little hope in sight that the killings may stop. (Lemarchand 1998: 14)

The space between fact and fantasy-land is yet to be charted and agreed upon. And agreement will not be reached unless the complexity of 'ordinary' people's lives is acknowledged by everyone involved in shaping Rwanda's (and Burundi's) destiny: from government official to journalist, from politician and diplomat to the academic who 'discovers' the region through her or his first review essay. The complexity of people's lives, and especially of people not guilty of genocide, is truly extraordinary. As Prunier appreciates:

Innocents have guilty relatives – and can be victimized because of them. Tutsi survivors have been accused by Tutsi 'returnees' of being 'collaborators' because they survived. The families of Hutu moderates, who have been ravaged by the genocide in the same way as Tutsi families, are not considered 'true' survivors because they are seen as tainted by the general guilt of the Hutu in post-genocide Rwanda. (Prunier 1997: 359)

Against this appreciation of complexity stands the force of essentialist discourses. What happened in Nyamata, Bugesera, when 'the Hutu refugees' came home in late 1996, is revealing. The *bourgmestre* of Nyamata, a commune which had seen some of the worst genocide atrocities, did what was expected of him: he called a public meeting before the refugees returned and instructed that 'those who lived in a house belonging to Hutu returnees had two weeks to vacate. If not, the commune authorities would make them leave.' Whether the *bourgmestre* would actually be able to implement the ruling was quite a different matter. One survivor told the press: 'The Tutsi of Nyamata, both the survivors and the repatriates, have neither forgotten nor forgiven.' He, Grégoire, summed up how his Tutsi friends felt: 'All Hutu are guilty. The men killed, the women protected the killers, and the children went out looting.' Clearly, Nyamata had become a place where survivors and repatriates had decided – and who could blame them? – that returning Hutu refugees had forfeited every right to land and property.[3] Whatever the national guidelines on repossession prescribed, and they allowed for local interpretation, this locality's dominant moral discourse would construct its own guidelines. Nyamata had its own context, its own rationale.

Analytic efforts to appreciate context and complexity, however, are today hampered by the Rwandan government's insistence that outsiders should have no opinions of their own. Outsiders have lost the right to judge what goes on in Rwanda. Today, reality is what Rwanda's political leaders, as moral guardians, tell the world what it is. And what the world needs to know is an old story, a 1950s story, a highly simplified story. It is the story of a Rwanda imagined by diaspora-scholars who have finally made the long trek home.[4] It is also a story that suits 'beginners', one which many outsiders have come to own, reproduce and spread.

The 'new generation' of international post-genocide commentators on Rwanda – a transnational body of experts whose 'area expertise' is mostly non-existent – operates predominantly in ways that mimic the relationship of mutual advantage which had developed in colonial times between Alexis Kagame and Jacques Maquet. The insider offers enlightenment to the outsider; the outsider returns the gift by offering the prospect of international recognition and legitimacy. Moreover, just as the colonial experts synchronised their discursive understandings of colonial situations, so contemporary experts tune into the discourses of their 'disaster colleagues' who may, just may, know that little bit more. The result is a chain of 'interanimated' adjustments to the utterances and viewpoints of other professionals; positions rarely grounded in sustained empirical research. Political, social and economic landscapes are thus simplified, streamlined and misread: post-war farmers with diverse experiences become 'famished seed eaters'; the heterogeneous world found in refugee camps becomes 'the refugees'; those targeted in the social revolution of 1959 become 'the Tutsi'; that multitude of pre- and early colonial clientship relations becomes 'the cattle contract'; those who masterminded and carried out the genocide become 'the Hutu'; the various Tutsi social groupings in eastern Zaire are collapsed into 'the Banyamulenge'; and so it goes on. Since Rwanda's war and genocide, the world has seen a burgeoning of essentialist categories and viewpoints likely to delay the search for a shareable account of society and history.[5] This will keep the Great Lakes region divided. Without a broadly agreed account, or (better perhaps) without a vision of the past which acknowledges that different interpretations of history will exist, Rwanda and eastern Zaire, and the Great Lakes region generally, will remain entrapped in an official discourse which legitimates the use of violence and makes some, leaders and led, *génocidaires*.

Appendix

ZAIRE – DEMOCRATIC REPUBLIC OF CONGO (DRC):

mid-nineteenth century	Rwandan Tutsi migrants move into Mulenge (eastern Congo)
1910	International borders imposed. Congo gains North Kivu and Idjwi island from Rwanda
1937–45	First assisted migration of Banyarwanda to North Kivu (25,000)
1949–55	Second assisted migration of Banyarwanda to North Kivu (60,000)
1960	Congo independent (changes name to Zaire in 1971)
1964–65	'Muleliste' rebellion in eastern Congo; rebellion quashed and leaders, including Kabila, go into exile
1967	Kabila returns to set up maquis
1972	Citizenship for all Banyarwanda living in Zaire since 1950; Tutsi refugees from Rwanda's 1959–62 revolution are excluded
1973	Bakajika law legalises private land ownership; causes confusion over land rights
1979	End of Kabila's maquis; rebels disperse
1981	Citizenship law (1972) annulled
1987	Banyarwanda boycott elections in South Kivu
1992	National Conference bans Banyarwanda participants
1992–93	Banyarwanda (Hutu and Tutsi) killed in ethnic clashes in North Kivu; displacement of 350,000 Banyarwanda, mostly from Masisi
1994	July onwards. Over one million Rwandan Hutu refugees, including the perpetrators of the genocide, set up camps around Goma, Bukavu and Uvira; 100,000 Masisi Hutu remain displaced

1995	April. Zaire's Haut Conseil declares that all Banyamulenge – now a generic term for Tutsi living in Zaire – are recent refugees
1995–96	November to May. Thousands of Masisi Tutsi killed by Hutu refugee extremists and their local allies; 15,000 Tutsi flee to Rwanda; 250,000 autochthones (Hunde, Nyanga) flee Masisi and become internally displaced
1996	August. Supported by Rwandan and Ugandan troops, Banyamulenge clash with Zaire's national army (FAZ)
	November. Banyamulenge attack Rwandan refugee camps; 700,000 refugees return to Rwanda, the rest move deeper into Zaire; UN decides not to intervene; formation of the Alliance of the Democratic Forces for the Liberation of Congo-Zaire (ADFL), headed by Kabila
1997	May. ADFL takes control of Zaire; Mobutu removed; Kabila becomes President; Zaire becomes the Democratic Republic of Congo (DRC)

RWANDA:

mid-nineteenth century	Expansion of King Rwabugiri's administration; large migration of Tutsi towards Mulenge (eastern Congo)
1907–16	German occupation
1910	International borders imposed. Rwanda loses North Kivu and Idjwi island to Congo
1916	Belgian occupation begins
1920s	Political unification. Rwanda's central court annexes the north-west and other peripheral regions
1928–29	Famine pushes 100,000 Rwandans into Uganda and Congo
1933	Belgium introduces identity (ID) cards that 'fix' ethnic identity
1947	Quasi-secularisation of divine (Tutsi) kingship completed
1959	Hutu social revolution
1959–61	150,000 Tutsi flee to Congo, Uganda and Burundi
1962	Independence from Belgium; southern Hutu rule (Kayibanda becomes president)

1963–64	Tutsi exiles invade Bugesera; pogroms follow and cause a further exodus of Tutsi to South Kivu
1973	Military coup by northern Hutu; Habyarimana becomes president
1981	France enhances aid to Rwanda to develop its north and north-west
1989	Severe economic crisis sets in
1990	October. Rwandese Patriotic Front (RPF) invades from Uganda; low-intensity warfare results
1992	November. Anti-Tutsi public speeches by Hutu Power politicians. Tutsi killed in Bugesera and other locations
1993	International report on human rights abuses; organisations warn of impending crisis
	August. Peace acccords signed in Arusha, Tanzania
1994	April. Habyarimana's assassination triggers a genocide in which 800,000 Tutsi and moderate Hutu perish. RPF relaunches its offensive
	July. RPF halts genocide and seizes power
1995	UN-led Operation Return peters out after initial successes; relations between Rwandan government and 'international community' deteriorate; Rwandan government dismantles camps for Internally Displaced Persons (IDPs); massacre in Kibeho (April) as last of the camps is closed
	August. The first post-genocide prime minister, Faustin Twagiramungu, resigns
1996	August to October. Rwandese Patriotic Army moves into eastern Zaire to assist the Banyamulenge uprising, destroy the refugee camps and lead the campaign to topple Zaire's President Mobutu Sese Seko; Rwanda denies being involved in Zaire
1997	July. Vice-President Paul Kagame explains Rwanda's military involvement and role in Zaire

Notes

INTRODUCTION

1. Workshop contribution by Mark Duffield, Oxford, 27 September 1995.
2. The *grosses légumes* (literally, fat vegetables) are the nation's *fat cats*, Zaire's corrupt politicians and administrators.
3. Lindsey Hilsum, *Times Literary Supplement*, 23 May 1997.
4. The linking of dominant international discourses with dominant or aspiring local ones has been highlighted also in recent debate on feminist scholarship. Although the initial intention of feminists may have been to celebrate 'our sisters in the struggle', authors like Chandra Mohanty (1994) and Anne-Marie Goetz (1991) have convincingly argued that early feminist scholarship was tainted by relations of power and inequality. They have shown, moreover, that 'Third World' women who represent 'Other' women are not above the influence of the forces that produce inequality and ethnocentricity.

CHAPTER 1

1. This process may have started in the mid-eighteenth century when Prince Ndabarasa, son of the Rwandan *mwami* Rujugira, occupied all of south Rwanda (Webster *et al.* 1992: 817).
2. Since 'r' and 'l' are interchangeable, I have mostly used 'r' but kept 'l' in quoted text. In the case of long vowels I have opted for simplified spellings, e.g. Tutsi (instead of 'Tuutsi') and Fulero (instead of 'Furiiru').
3. Prior to Belgian rule, German *Schutztruppe* had already brought some of the northern marshes into the fold of the *mwami*-ship (Louis 1963: 157).
4. For a detailed account of the consecration ritual, see Kalibwami 1991: 281–6.
5. Jean-Claude Willame, *Le Vif/L'Express*, 8 November 1996. The bravery of their forefathers was also recalled by some Banyamulenge in media interviews during the 1996 campaign (see Chapter 2). All translations from French and Dutch, quite numerous in this book, are my own work and responsibility.
6. The end of Kabila's maquis came in 1979 when his thoughts turned from socialism to ivory and gold (Cosma 1997: 99, 111), luxuries produced and traded according to strictly local regulations (Vwakyanakazi Mukohya 1991: 51–2). Kabila also struck lucrative deals with Zaire's corrupt-but-unpaid military (Cosma 1997: 108). After the maquis had lasted for over a decade, the injustices he inflicted on the population led to large-scale disenchantment and the dispersal of his followers. The political

death-knell was the witch hunt Kabila ordered, in which some 2,000 suspected witches were executed (1997: 111–12).

7. Willame 1997: 41, referring to Mafikiri Tsongo 1996: 3.

8. By the early 1990s, food grown in the marshlands, mainly sweet potatoes and sorghum, accounted for some 20 per cent of Rwanda's total agricultural output (van de Giesen and Andreini 1997: 115). As marshland is state property, it can only be cultivated with the approval, often tacit, of the local authorities. Having only weak use rights to the marshland they used to cultivate on a clan basis in the 1930s, farmers were now in danger of seeing allocated plots reclaimed by the authorities.

9. République Rwandaise (1989) *Compte-rendu de la Réunion tenue au Minagri en date du 02/05/1989 sur la Situation Alimentaire du Rwanda en Avril 1989*. Published by the Ministère de l'Agriculture, de l'Elevage et des Forêts, Kigali, 1989. The sum to be reimbursed was about £150,000.

10. For details, see Otunnu's excellent analysis (Otunnu 1999a).

11. Initially, the Political Bureau of the MPR had decided that the inhabitants of Masisi, North Kivu, should all be given Congolese citizenship provided they or their ancestors had arrived in Zaire before 1960. A new law resulted (no.71–002, 28 March 1971). Citizenship entailed voting rights and the right to stand in elections. Later that year, Bisengimana, the Bureau's director, was asked to clarify the status of the Rwandan refugees, mostly Tutsi, who had arrived in or after 1959. As they were political refugees, and not 'transplanted through the will of the colonial authority', Bisengimana argued that they were foreign and did not qualify for citizenship (quotation from *La législation de la République en matière de la Nationalité*, p. 25, reproduced in Reyntjens and Marysse 1996: 23). In an overreaction the law was amended to disqualify from citizenship any person of Rwandan (or Burundian) extraction who had arrived in the country after 1 January 1950.

12. This law (no. 73–021) made it possible to privately own lands previously categorised as 'vacant', which was a dubious term. Privatisation led to the emergence of a stratum of impoverished, landless youth who stood no chance of ever securing title-deeds.

13. Mayi-Mayi guerillas recruit from among Hunde and Nyanga communities in the zones of Masisi and Walikale; Bangilima recruit Hunde, Nyanga and Nande from Lubero and Rutshuru.

14. Dr Van der Wijck, *NRC Handelsblad*, 18 July 1994.

15. *Raleigh News & Observer*, 17 April 1994.

16. *Washington Post*, 17 April 1994. Alison Des Forges is a human rights worker with Human Rights Watch/Africa.

17. Filip Reyntjens in *Knack*, 20 July 1994; Tony Kabano interviewed by Els De Temmerman in *De Standaard Magazine*, 3 June 1994. Post-independence Rwanda was organised into some 150 *communes* spread over nine Prefectures. Parishes (*secteurs*) are a further sub-division.

18. *Le Figaro*, 17 June 1994.

19. *Libération*, 29 May 1994.

20. *The Independent*, 16 November 1996.

21. *The Independent*, 17 November 1996.

22. *The Guardian*, 17 May 1997.

23. *Newsweek*, 2 December 1996.

24. *The New Times Newspaper*, Kigali, 23–31 March 1998; quoted in Eltringham and Van Hoyweghen 2000: 225.
25. De Waal, African Rights, *NRC Handelsblad*, 23 July 1994.
26. *Le Nouvel Observateur*, 2 June 1994.
27. *La Dernière Heure*, 30–31 July 1994; emphasis added.
28. *Nouvel Observateur*, 2 June 1994.
29. *Times Literary Supplement*, 1 July 1994; *NRC Handelsblad*, 23 July 1994.
30. Reyntjens made the same point, but was more emphatic: 'One can say anything about Habyarimana, but not that he was a blood-thirsty dictator. The RPF has created that image with some success in order to legitimate its own war' (*Gazet van Antwerpen*, 31 July 1994).
31. *Le Figaro*, 14 June 1994.
32. Stephen Smith, *Libération*, 25 May 1994.
33. Stephen Smith, *Libération*, 27 May 1994.
34. See *The Times*, 29 April 1994.
35. De Waal, *Times Literary Supplement*, 1 July 1994; also *NRC Handelsblad*, 23 July 1994.
36. *The Guardian*, 29 January 1994.
37. Fax by Roméo Dallaire, 11 January 1994, subject: 'Request for protection of informant'. A copy of the fax has been reproduced in Adelman and Suhrke 1999: xxi–xxii.
38. *The Guardian*, 7 July 1994.
39. *The Guardian*, 19 July 1994. Those who believe that the timing of the RPF's invasion was determined in part by the reluctance of the international community to intervene in armed confict in Africa, maintain 'that Museveni knew from his close friend, Lynda Chalker (British Minister of Overseas Development), that Britain was relying on him to kick the French out of the Great Lakes region of Africa' (Otunnu 1999b: 11).
40. Hilsum, *The Guardian*, 11 July 1994.
41. Huband, *The Guardian*, 12 July 1994. Some journalists discovered how 'normal' aid practices had damaged Rwanda's ethnic relationships in the past. *The Guardian* referred to Lemarchand's 1982 study of the impact of a World Bank resettlement scheme – the Mutara Agriculture and Livestock Development Project – which had 'reduced the resource base of the Tutsis of the district, cutting down their herds and their grazing area. Lemarchand's warnings of the dangers involved [had been] ignored' (*The Guardian*, 20 July 1994).
42. McGreal, *The Guardian*, 15 July 1994.
43. Quotation from the *Rapport de la Commission d'information dépêchée à l'Est du Zaire, août-septembre 1994*, submitted to the Haut Conseil de la République.
44. *La Libre Belgique*, 15 May 1996. See also testimonies collected by Howard Adelman and Astri Suhrke (Adelman and Suhrke 1999: xviii–xix).
45. *Le Soir*, 14 September 1995.
46. New aggressors also appeared: local bandits willing 'to work' for the highest bidder, as well as sections of the FAZ (a more familiar appearance) which operated mostly alongside refugee militias. Awash with arms and unprecedented levels of international assistance, the region bred opportunistic banditry, a phenomenon both significant and mystifying (Willame 1997: 71). Banditry explained, for instance, the clashes between Nyanga and Hunde youngsters in early 1995.

47. In the 1960s, Mayi-Mayi fought alongside the 'Muleliste' rebels, reportedly under the command of Antoine Marandura. They took to the maquis in 1986, first building camps on the slopes of the Ruwenzori Mountains and later in the forests around Beni, in Nande territory. Brutal repression by the Zairean armed forces temporarily drove them underground (Willame 1997: 71–2).
48. See Amnesty International (1996) for details; also Pottier 1999a: 157.
49. *Le Soir*, 16 July 1996.
50. Based on a 1984 census which included Itombwe, Jean-Claude Willame proposed the number of (true) Banyamulenge be set at between 30,000 to 40,000. Using the same census, which showed that out of a total of 160,215 inhabitants in the zone of Fizi only 5,367 were registered as Banyarwanda or Barundi, Cosma also settled for a much smaller number (Cosma 1997: 26).
51. In the early 1990s, a new 'ethnic' group also emerged in south-western Uganda. To avoid being mistaken for Banyarwanda trouble-makers, the Kinyarwanda-speaking population of Bufumbira dropped the label Banyarwanda and took on Bafumbira (Otunnu 1999b: 47).
52. An observer on the ground, associated with the World Lutheran Federation, has remarked that nobody kept count and that the figure of 700,000, which US officials immediately accepted as dogma, is likely to have been well above the actual number of returnees (Lemarchand: personal communication). Suggesting that those left behind were all *interahamwe*, the inflated figure was intended to justify subsequent search and destroy operations in eastern Zaire.
53. Michela Wrong, *Financial Times*, 5 May 1997.
54. *De Standaard*, 14 September 1995. Twagiramungu is quoted in Chapter 4.
55. Unfamiliarity with the regions and cultures of Africa also marks the UN. In his most revealing article, Michael Barnett (1997) explains how unperturbed UN staff are by the lack of regional expertise. As an academic Middle East area specialist on secondment to the US Mission to the UN, Barnett initially covered Somalia. Then, after the US withdrew from Somalia in March 1994, and with Rwanda sliding into the abyss, his responsibilities shifted to Rwanda. Barnett knew 'little more about [Rwanda] than how to find it on a map', yet assumed primary responsibility for US peacekeeping operations there. He later reflected: 'As a political officer I was, by definition, an expert. Rwanda was my account; I was its owner and hence a Rwanda expert' (Barnett 1997: 554).
56. Adelman and Suhrke continue: 'These conclusions are drawn from interviews with some 4,000 Masisi who crossed into Rwanda on 13 April 1996, and another 4,000 who were waiting to cross. The conclusions were confirmed when another 2,000 prepared to cross on 29 April 1996. This does not mean that the local Hunde were not involved, but the instigators and main perpetrators were the extremist Hutus from Rwanda' (Adelman and Suhrke 1999: xviii–xix).

CHAPTER 2

1. Interviewed by Nik Gowing (see Gowing 1998: 4).
2. On 29 June 1998, the UN Secretary General's investigative team published its report on the post-Mugunga atrocities in eastern Zaire. The report confirmed that Rwanda's RPA had been directly involved in the killing of Hutu refugees, committing war

crimes and crimes against humanity – and possibly genocide (UN 1998: paragraphs 90–6).

3. *Washington Post*, 9 July 1997.

4. For a more sceptical view see François Ngolet (Ngolet 2000: 70).

5. Paul Kagame himself has been very clear on the extent of the international guilt. Referring to the international community in general, though more specifically to humanitarians, Kagame told Gourevitch that the 'insane policy' of protecting Hutu refugees had come about because confused Westerners needed '[to] fight off their guilt after the genocide'. He then added: 'There is a great amount of guilt' (Gourevitch 1998: 338).

6. See Alex de Waal's 'No Bloodless Miracle', *The Guardian*, 15 November 1996.

7. We should be aware, however, that Kagame continued, albeit with much greater sophistication, a way of dealing with truth that had already marked the Habyarimana regime. Institutionalised ways of dealing with truth and testimony have a long history in Rwanda (see Chapter 1).

8. *De Standaard*, 8 April 1994.

9. *De Standaard*, 9–10 April 1994.

10. Tony Kabano quoted in *Knack*, 1 June 1994.

11. *Knack*, 20 April 1994.

12. *De Standaard Magazine*, 3 June 1994.

13. This close relationship was exposed by John Ryle in *The Guardian*, 29 September 1995.

14. *Libération*, 22 May and 27 May 1994.

15. *Libération*, 18 May 1994.

16. On 20 August 1994, *The Economist* outlined both the 'school of racial determinism', favoured by many European colonists, and today's 'school of political correctness', which reduces ethnic complexities to a question of occupation and wealth. *The Economist*, however, was less successful in its attempt to define the middle-ground 'third school', which emphasises both the institutionalised social divisions of pre-colonial Rwanda and the racial politics of German and Belgian rule.

17. *NRC Handelsblad*, 23 July 1994; see also Chapter 8.

18. *De Standaard*, 23 July 1994.

19. *De Standaard*, 7 June 1994.

20. See Hilsum, *BBC Focus on Africa*, July–September 1994. De Temmerman, too, wrote about her traumas (De Temmerman 1994: 107).

21. In d'Hertefelt's overview of the clan system, all eighteen clans are said to be 'multi-class', i.e. made up of Hutu, Tutsi and Twa (d'Hertefelt 1971: 49).

22. See Julian Bedford, *The Independent*, 5 July 1994; Julian Nundy, *The Independent*, 6 July 1994.

23. For instance, Sam Kilcy on Kibeho, *The Times*, 24 April 1995; and on eastern Zaire, *The Times*, 8 November 1996.

24. *Raleigh News & Observer*, 17 April 1994.

25. *Washington Post*, 17 April 1994.

26. *The New York Review*, 20 October 1994.

27. Broadcast on 14 November 1996.

28. *International Herald Tribune*, 15 July 1994. Pfaff wrote his piece from Paris, but did not declare his sources of information.

29. *International Herald Tribune*, 15 July 1994.

30. *BBC Africa Report*, May/June 1994, p.15.

31. Hilsum exposed the inappropriateness of the idea of tribalism in a contribution to the popular Granta Books series (Hilsum 1995b).

32. *Le Soir*, 15 July 1994.

33. *De Standaard*, 18 July 1994.

34. *De Standaard*, 18 July 1994.

35. *NRC Handelsblad*, 18 July 1994.

36. *Financieel Ekonomische Tijd*, 25 July 1994.

37. *Gazet van Antwerpen*, 19 July 1994; *La Libre Belgique*, 19 July 1994. Ndahimana was right. The Arusha Peace Agreement established the principle that 'The National Army shall be at the disposal of the Government and shall be subordinated to its authority' (p. 75).

38. *Het Volk*, 22 July 1994.

39. *Le Monde*, 31 July 1994; also Jean-Pierre Langellier, *Le Monde*, 27 July 1994; *Gazet Van Antwerpen*, 25 July 1994.

40. De Temmerman questioned the attitude of an RPF medical doctor who provided care for refugees in need. 'It seems almost too good to be true: RPF soldiers who give medical care to returning refugees, who load returning refugees into trucks and drive them home, who say: "the citizens have been misled, we want them to return. There will be no revenge."' (*De Volkskrant*, 28 July 1994). De Temmerman suspected the care and concern were part of a sustained public relations campaign, something akin to what French troops were doing in the *Zone Turquoise*.

41. Bihozagara quoted in *Le Figaro*, 26 July 1994.

42. *Le Monde*, 23 July 1994.

43. *Le Soir*, 25 July 1994.

44. *De Morgen*, 25 July 1994.

45. *De Volkskrant*, 28 July 1994.

46. Personal interviews in north-western Rwanda, July to August 1994 (see Pottier 1994a).

47. *Libération*, 25 July 1994. Although it questioned RPA practices, *Libération* was also scathing about the French military presence in Rwanda, and condemned *Opération Turquoise* by highlighting disagreements among French officers serving in the zone (*Libération*, 21 July 1994).

48. *La Libre Belgique*, 26 July 1994.

49. *Le Soir*, 19 July 1994; compare with Kasfir, below. See also Otunnu 1999b.

50. See also *Le Courier de l'Escaut*, 29 July 1994.

51. *Le Figaro*, 26 July 1994.

52. *Het Volk*, 17 July 1994; *Gazet van Antwerpen*, 27 July 1994; *NRC Handelsblad*, 27 July 1994.

53. *De Volkskrant*, 27 July 1994.

54. The RPF's position had been defended by African Rights in *NRC Handelsblad*, 23 July 1994.

55. *De Volkskrant*, 27 July 1994.

56. *New York Times*, 25 July 1994; also 3 September 1994.

57. *International Herald Tribune*, 27 July 1994.

58. *Washington Post*, 27 July 1994.

59. *International Herald Tribune*, 1 August 1994.
60. *International Herald Tribune*, 1 August 1994.
61. In November 1992, the UN had sent troops into Somalia without properly assessing the inner workings of Somali society and politics. The intervention resulted in UN deaths, defeat and humiliation, and made the civil conflict more intractable (Lewis 1993: 1–3).
62. *International Herald Tribune* 25 July 1994.
63. *International Herald Tribune*, 25 July 1994.
64. *De Volkskrant*, 30 July 1994.
65. *International Herald Tribune*, 25 July 1994. The view expressed does not take into account how the make-up of the RPF troops had changed in the course of the war itself. Compare with *Independent on Sunday*, 24 July 1994, further down.
66. *New York Times*, 18 September 1994.
67. *The Independent*, 10 June 1994. The RPF's discipline and strong organisation are also stressed in Dowden's reflections on how he covered the genocide (Dowden 1995).
68. *The Guardian*, 21 June 1994.
69. *The Guardian*, 15 July 1994.
70. *Independent on Sunday*, 24 July 1994.
71. *Independent on Sunday*, 24 July 1994.
72. *The Times*, 15 July 1994.
73. John Ryle, *The Guardian*, 29 September 1995. The implication is that journalists have come to rely on relief workers whom they treat as experts on the region and its politics. Ryle notes a growing complicity because media exposure has become the lifeblood of agencies. Mark Duffield, too, has taken this up by arguing that 'agencies do not simply respond to media interest, they manipulate it. And they, in turn, may be manipulated by local political groups and the governments of donor countries. Such developments are connected to changes in the economy of television and newspaper reporting, to the rise of the globally mobile reporter-presenter and the decline of the regionally based area-specialist' (Duffield, workshop on 'The Fate of Information in the Disaster Zone', 27 September 1995, Oxford).
74. *Independent on Sunday*, 31 July 1994. Robert Moore was a foreign correspondent with ITN.
75. *The Guardian*, 7 November 1994.
76. *De Morgen*, 28 April 1995 (also Polman 1999); *The Sunday Times*, 23 April 1995.
77. Rik De Gendt in *De Standaard*, 24 April 1995. Randolph Kent, the UN Humanitarian Coordinator in Rwanda, would later refute the Government's claim that the strategy for Kibeho had followed an agreed plan. 'No agency or NGO,' Kent wrote, 'had ever agreed to the precipitous and unilateral action undertaken by the RPA. The RPA's initiative was totally unexpected, and for many it was a betrayal, a profound and fundamental sign of bad faith' (Kent 1996: 76 7).
78. *Le Courier de l'Escaut*, 24 April 1995.
79. For *De Standaard*, this was akin to admitting that a new genocide could be on its way.
80. *De Morgen*, 24 April 1995; *De Standaard*, 24 April 1995; *Gazet van Antwerpen*, 24 April 1995; *Le Courier de l'Escaut*, 24 April 1995.
81. *Le Vif/L'Express*, 28 April 1995.
82. *La Libre Belgique*, 24 April 1995.

83. Promised troops had not materialised either. In November 1994, Boutros Boutros-Ghali approved the dispatch to Goma of some 5,000 UN troops, but the UN Security Council subsequently delayed their deployment until 'some time' in 1995 (*Le Monde*, 2 December 1994). The troops never arrived in Goma.
84. *La Libre Belgique*, 24 April 1995.
85. *Le Soir*, 27 April 1995.
86. See *Le Peuple*, 24 April 1995; *Het Belang Van Limburg*, 24 April 1995; *De Volkskrant*, 24 April 1995.
87. *Le Soir*, 25 April 1995.
88. *La Libre Belgique*, 26 April 1995.
89. *De Volkskrant*, 29 April 1995.
90. *Libération*, 25 April 1995.
91. *NRC Handelsblad*, 22 November 1996.
92. *La Dernière Heure*, 12 May 1995.
93. *La Libre Belgique*, 12 May 1995.
94. *The Times*, 24 April 1995.
95. *The Times*, 24 April 1995.
96. The ambassador expressed concern about the grip of the RPA on the justice system: 'It is absolutely essential to limit the role of the army. This is an objective' (*La Libre Belgique*, 22 April 1995).
97. *The Guardian*, 24 April 1995.
98. *The Guardian*, 24 April 1995; emphasis added.
99. Coverage of the massacre in *The Irish Times* also mixed outcry and analysis, much in the manner Braeckman reacted, but the paper did not push the analysis as far as it could have done. Despite claiming to set Rwanda in context, reports followed the trend in British papers by lacking an appreciation of the rising tensions within government. See, for instance, the interview with Justin Kilcullen, director of the Irish agency Trocaire, and the analysis by Edward O'Loughlin (both in *Irish Times*, 25 April 1995). O'Loughlin's analysis, though, was a determined attempt to break free of the government/RPF's tightening hold on the flow of newsworthy information.
100. *International Herald Tribune*, 25 April 1995. Aid workers and some UN soldiers later accused Shaharyar Khan of 'deliberately playing down the death toll under pressure from an administration increasingly hostile to the UN presence in Rwanda' (*The Guardian*, 26 April 1995). Khan accepted the lower death toll because the initial count by the British Provost-Marshal, Colonel Cuthbert Brown, on the day of the massacre, had been conducted after nightfall. Cuthbert Brown returned to Kibeho the following day accompanied by General Tousignant, head of UNAMIR. Back in Kibeho, in Khan's own words, 'he went over the same ground . . . that was covered the night before and as a result of a carefully taken count, in broad daylight, he revised the estimate of the dead to "between 1500 and 2000". At night, the figure had seemed higher because the debris had included mangled clothes and abandoned sacks, pots and pans, which appeared in the dark like dead bodies. Moreover, many IDPs had obviously feigned death at night, but had later skulked away when the firing stopped. The provost-marshal and the Zambians [UN soldiers who had witnessed the massacre] agreed that the revised figure was nearest to reality and we issued it as our formal estimate and did not change it thereafter' (Khan 2000: 112).

101. *International Herald Tribune*, 27 April 1995.
102. For Lorch, Gashora qualified as a success story (*International Herald Tribune*, 28 April 1995).
103. *Le Vif/L'Express*, 8 November 1996.
104. See e.g. *New York Times*, 11 October 1996; *The Guardian*, 21 October 1996; *The Independent*, 25 October 1996.
105. *Financieel Ekonomische Tijd*, 16 November 1996. Reyntjens and Marysse (1996: 6) agree and estimate the figure to be between 20,000 and 50,000.
106. The figure of 400,000 was on the high side even when one takes account of the pockets of Banyamulenge in Uvira, Mwenga and the Fizi Baraka mountains (Nzongola-Ntalaja 1996; Ngolet 2000: 67).
107. See Kamanda wa Kamanda, Zaire's Home Affairs minister, quoted in *Financieel Ekonomische Tijd*, 12 November 1996.
108. *Le Vif/L'Express*, 8 November 1996.
109. *Financieel Ekonomische Tijd*, 12 November 1996.
110. *Le Nouvel Observateur*, 21–27 November 1996.
111. *Financieel Ekonomische Tijd*, 12 November 1996.
112. *New York Times*, 28 October 1996.
113. *New York Times*, 28 October 1996.
114. *New York Times*, 28 October 1996. In referring to the 'ancestral kingdoms', McKinley appears to have accepted President Bizimungu's argument about a pre-colonial Greater Rwanda. Details of Bizimungu's speech were reported on 29 October 1996.
115. *New York Times*, 22 October 1996.
116. *The Guardian*, 21 October 1996.
117. *The Guardian*, 27 October 1996.
118. For most of November 1996, journalists were banned from the battle zone around Goma. The restriction began early in the month and remained in force until well after the mass return home of some 700,000 refugees (*De Morgen*, 9–10 November 1996; *De Volkskrant*, 22 November 1996).
119. *The Independent*, 25 October 1996; also 23 October 1996.
120. *The Independent*, 3 November 1996.
121. Braeckman notes: 'In Gisenyi, across the border from Goma, credible sources testify having sighted black American soldiers alongside Rwandese Patriotic Army soldiers' (*Le Soir*, 13 November 1996).
122. *The Times*, 26 October 1996.
123. *Le Peuple*, 12 November 1996.
124. *Het Belang van Limburg*, 19 November 1996.
125. *Le Nouvel Observateur*, 14 November 1996.
126. *New York Times*, 3 November 1996.
127. *New York Times*, 15 November 1996.
128. *Libération*, 11 November 1996.
129. For major critiques of the international humanitarian aid effort, see Michela Wrong in *The Financial Times* (3 December 1996) and Sam Kiley in *The Times* (8 November 1996). For a contribution in the US press, see William Pfaff, *International Herald Tribune*, 18 November 1996.
130. Mark Bowden, SCF's Africa director, quoted in *The Financial Times*, 3 December 1996.

131. *International Herald Tribune*, 15 November 1996; emphasis added.
132. Journalists faced 'a lingering fear of being removed from the country if they openly challenged the US, and thereby the Rwandan government position. The fear was not unfounded' (Gowing 1998: 44).
133. *Le Soir*, 13 November 1996.
134. *Le Figaro*, 14 November 1996.
135. *New York Times*, 2 November 1996.
136. The story of this massacre, so close to the Banyamulenge/Mayi-Mayi joint operation against Mugunga (see Pottier 1999a), is somewhat surprising. If this massacre did take place, but no other journalists seem to have reported it, it may need to be explained in terms of the total unreliability of Mayi-Mayi or (more likely) in terms of the continuing clashes over land.
137. *The Times*, 13 November 1996.
138. *The Times*, 15 November 1996.
139. *The Times*, 13 November 1996; 21 November 1996.
140. *De Morgen*, 15 November 1996.
141. *The Guardian*, 15 November 1996.
142. *New York Times*, 27 November 1996.
143. *De Standaard*, 26 November 1996.
144. *The Independent*, 14 November 1996.
145. *The Independent*, 23 October 1996; 25 October 1996.
146. André Kisasse Ngandu led the Conseil de la Résistance pour la Démocratie (CRD), one of the four political parties regrouped within the ADFL.
147. *Het Belang van Limburg*, 25 November 1996.
148. *The Guardian*, 28 December 1996.
149. *The Independent*, 14 November 1996; *Le Vif/L'Express*, 8 November 1996.
150. Rwandan Tutsi exiles joined the 'Muleliste' rebellion on the principle of reciprocal assistance. Lemarchand specifies: 'There was a common awareness of the advantages that either party would draw from the realization of the other's objectives: if the Congolese ['rebels'] were to gain permanent control over the [eastern] border areas, the refugees would then enjoy the benefit of a 'privileged sanctuary' for organizing border raids into Rwanda; likewise, if Rwanda's republican [Hutu] regime should fall before the completion of their task, the Congolese could expect similar advantages for themselves' (Lemarchand 1970: 213). The principle explains why some thirty years later a Congolese rebellion could be launched from within a Tutsi-ruled Rwanda.
151. *Libération*, 8 January 1997.
152. *International Herald Tribune*, 16–17 November 1996.
153. *New York Times*, 18 February 1997.
154. *New York Times*, 21 February 1997.
155. *The Guardian*, 23 March 1997.
156. In his earlier profile of rebel leader Kabila (*New York Times*, 3 November 1996), McKinley had taken seriously the diplomats and aid officials who had said it was 'clear that the rebellion serves the interests of the Tutsi-led governments in Rwanda and Burundi'.
157. *New York Times*, 17 February 1997.
158. *The Times*, 11 March 1997.
159. *New York Times*, 6 March 1997.

160. *New York Times*, 6 March 1997.
161. *New York Times*, 10 March 1997.
162. *The Times*, 16 April 1997.
163. *The Times*, 5 May 1997.
164. *The Times*, 10 March 1996.
165. *The Times*, 5 May 1997.
166. *The Guardian*, 17 May 1997.
167. *Financial Times*, 22 March 1997. However, a subsequent editorial in the *Financial Times* (26 March 1997) would reconfirm that Kabila 'is no longer seen as the catspaw of neighbouring states which wish to dismember Zaire.'
168. *Financial Times*, 16 April 1997.
169. *Financial Times*, 26 April 1997.
170. *Financial Times*, 5 May 1997.
171. On 3 January 1997, *The New York Times* reported how ADFL rebels and Mayi-Mayi had fought a six-hour battle in Butembo, despite the recent partnership. The clash was said to have followed an unsuccessful attempt by Mayi-Mayi to assassinate Kisasse Ngandu, the ADFL leader who had ordered that Mayi-Mayi disarm and retrain.
172. *Het Nieuwsblad*, 25 November 1996.
173. *De Volkskrant*, 9 November 1996.
174. *Le Soir*, 23–24 November 1996.
175. *Libération*, 8 November 1996.
176. *Het Belang van Limburg*, 25 November 1996.
177. *La Libre Belgique*, 28 December 1996.
178. Dominique Le Guilledoux in *Le Monde*, 13 November 1996.
179. *Le Soir*, 29 November 1996.
180. *Le Soir*, 29 November 1996.
181. On a different occasion, another Mayi-Mayi leader confirmed to another journalist, Gert van Langendonck, that he too was unsure about the Banyamulenge agenda. '"We still do not know what [the Banyamulenge] want. We are waiting to be contacted by their leaders"' (*De Morgen*, 20 November 1996). Van Langendonck understood that Mayi-Mayi was a catch-all term for several loosely structured groups whose allegiance could be bought, but whose overriding goal was to remove from Kivu and Zaire everything 'Rwandan' and recover the ancestral lands. Van Langendonck did not portray the ADFL as homogenous.
182. *Le Soir*, 25 November 1996.
183. *Het Nieuwsblad*, 7 January 1997.
184. *Het Belang van Limburg*, 7 January 1997.
185. *Het Volk*, 7 January 1997.
186. *L'Autre Afrique*, 27 May–6 June 1998. Mayi-Mayi political activity continues today. In August 2000, the Mayi-Mayi Union des Forces Vives pour la Libération et la Démocratie (UFLD–Mayi Mayi) accused Rwanda, now in its second Congolese war, 'of trying to "fool" international and Congolese opinion by announcing that it would withdraw its troops 200 km from the frontlines' (IRIN-CEA update 992, 18 August 2000).
187. *Het Volk*, 18 March 1997.
188. *La Libre Belgique*, 16–17 November 1996.
189. *Libération*, 16 November 1996.

190. *Financial Times*, 17 January 1997.
191. *Financial Times*, 5 March 1997 and 22 March 1997.
192. *Financial Times*, 10 March 1997.
193. *The Observer*, 13 April 1997.
194. *The Guardian*, 21 May 1997.
195. *The Observer*, 30 August 1998.

CHAPTER 3

1. For details on the controversy, see *African Affairs*, October 1998, pp. 577–8, and *African Affairs*, January 1999, pp. 119–22.
2. For an overview and a reassessment, see Newbury 1988: 3–10; Vidal 1991: 34.
3. Maquet conducted his research in 1950–51, not in the 1930s.
4. Davidson was interviewed by Martin Sommers, *De Morgen*, 7 August 1994.
5. I use the term revisionism to refer to the systematic attempt to discredit and obliterate all post-independence research in order to reinstate Kagame-Maquet's functionalist account of pre-colonial Rwanda. My usage goes beyond the RPF's own use of the term, which denotes disagreement with the view that ethnicity is the 'creation of colonialism' (Goyvaerts 1998: 93).
6. In *Rwanda: Death, Despair and Defiance* (African Rights 1994b, September), following correspondence in *Anthropology Today* and in *The Times Literary Supplement* regarding earlier pieces by de Waal (1994a, 1994b), African Rights acknowledged that ethnicity was not 'created' by the European colonialists; instead, a 'crystallisation of the Hutu–Tutsi opposition occurred before . . . the colonialists arrived.' The process is now attributed to Rwabugiri, who 'preferred to rely solely on the Tutsi, helping to cement their dominance, and thereby making the Hutu–Tutsi ethnic boundary more rigid' (African Rights 1994b: 4).
7. *Times Literary Supplement*, 1 July 1994; *NRC Handelsblad* 23 July 1994.
8. *Guardian Education*, 1 November 1994.
9. See also the BBC documentary mentioned in Chapter 2.
10. Goyvaerts, too, wants to reinstate a history which does away with the pre-colonial roots of ethnicity and revives the Maquet/Kagame model, thus heaping all blame for contemporary ethnic strife on the European coloniser (Goyvaerts 1998).
11. Mudenge interviewed in *The Guardian*, 3 May 1994.
12. *Ottawa Citizen*, 17 March 1994.
13. *NCR Handelsblad*, 23 July 1994; *Times Literary Supplement*, 1 July 1994.
14. Robert Block's treatment of Nahimana, however, is fair. He writes about the Nahimana of the early 1990s – Nahimana the intellectual turned extremist and war criminal. Block mentions that the genocidal rhetoric of Hutu extremists found inspiration in Nahimana's work, but he does not as such attempt to assess Nahimana's scholarly output of the 1970s. The latter has proved valuable not only in terms of understanding the past in north-western Rwanda, but also that of North Kivu (see Fairhead 1990: 63–4).
15. Key papers by Nahimana at the time of his research (esp. Nahimana 1981) highlighted the loss of autonomy in the north-west as a result of a Belgo-Tutsi (royal court) military campaign in the 1920s. This was a time of drastic change *well-documented in colonial archives*, even though it was only in 1952 that Belgium officially admitted how it had created modern Rwanda's political boundaries. The

Colonial Council (*Conseil colonial*) reported: 'Rwanda's political unification (...)
has been achieved from the outside and from above. The state structure results
from an exterior force, which, in a mechanical sense, has regrouped under the same
authority – under the same [royal] drum –, populations and lands hitherto dispersed'
(*Bulletin officiel du Congo belge*, 1952, p. 1984, quoted in Reyntjens 1985: 98).

16. *Le Monde* 15 June 1995, quoted in Prunier 1997: 367.

17. Written in the national language and widely distributed, *Kinyamateka* was a vehicle
for social communication which prioritised political news. André Sibomana, who
became the newspaper's editor in 1988, recalled: 'For many Rwandans living in
the countryside, *Kinyamateka* was the only source of written information, the only
publication which would bring news in their lives every other week. People used
to wait for *Kinyamateka* in the villages and the hills. They read it out loud in the
evenings' (Sibomana 1999: 27).

18. It does not follow, however, that the pro-democracy crowds of 1959 always acted
clearly and refrained from injustices or atrocities. Kalibwami testifies that the
crowds unfairly attacked a number of moderate Tutsi chiefs and sub-chiefs, and
that they attacked both 'culprits' and responsible leaders. He much regrets the
confusion (Kalibwami 1991: 483).

19. Cross-ethnic solidarity, of a most heroic nature, also occurred in the face of death
during the genocide (African Rights 1994b; Jefremovas 1995).

20. Kanyarengwe lost his position as RPF president following 'a pause for reflection'
in February 1998. Major-General Paul Kagame, then Rwanda's vice-president,
decided to occupy the position himself (Reyntjens 1999b).

21. It is ironic that Mgr Classe should be condemned (and rightly so) for his racial fantasies, while Rudahigwa is praised for being 'a force of moderation'. Rudahigwa's
enthronement in 1946 embodied the 'consecration of Rwanda to Christ the King',
and was not so much a moderate political move as the realisation of Classe's grand
project and dream (Kalibwami 1991: 281–99). During the ceremony, presided over
by Classe himself, Rudahigwa addressed Christ: 'I recognise that You are the
Sovereign Master of Rwanda, the root from which springs all power and strength.
Lord Jesus, it is You who made our country' (cited in Kalibwami 1991: 284).

22. In March 1997, the new governor of South Kivu declared that several 'Banyamulenge' had taken advantage of the confusion of war to move into high-level positions.
He told them to step down and make room for 'autochthonous' Zaireans (*Het Volk*,
18 March 1997).

23. Interview conducted in the context of the Joint Evaluation of Emergency Assistance
to Rwanda, Kigali, 3 May 1995. Despite the priority, Rwanda's government is prudent to keep the teaching of Rwandan history within Rwanda 'mostly submerged'
(*The Guardian*, 19 December 2000).

24. *New Vision* via Africa News Online, 19 May 1998.

25. See Ian Stewart, Associated Press, 10 May 1998.

26. They are associated with the ultra-conservative wing of the Flemish CVP (Social
Christian Party) and certain Catholic NGOs. The following 'reflection' by Johan
Ketelers, Caritas International, made in the aftermath of the Kibeho massacre,
exemplifies the kind of scriptwriting Rutayisire has in mind:

Having recently toured the [Great Lakes] region on behalf of Caritas International, Johan
Ketelers says that the events in Kibeho invite reflection. 'When peasants prefer the security
but also squalor of a refugee camp over their own sweet-little homes, which often lie no

farther than some thirty kilometers, they must have sound reasons for doing so. In Rwanda, where the lack of agricultural land is acute, the Hutu peasant is strongly attached to whatever land he still possesses; when he abandons that land or refuses to return to it despite repeated pleas, then there is something seriously amiss. The peasant is a perfect barometer for reading Rwanda's political situation.' (*Het Belang Van Limburg*, 25 April 1995)

Ketelers has a tacit understanding with his readers that the 'sound reasons' refer to present-day injustices and not to farmers' involvement in the genocide. His argument does apply to many IDPs, not in the least to those who at a given moment had gone home only to return to the camps, but it loses credibility because of the *omission* of any reference to genocide. Ketelers, though, was likely to reach the hearts (and pockets) of many good catholic farmers who understood his kind of language.

In another interview, Ketelers spoke of Hutu refugees as having been mere spectators in the genocide! About the refugees he said to *Kerk en Leven*, a publication of the Flemish catholic church: 'Adults are frequently no longer able to forget the horrors they have seen' (*Kerk en Leven*, 5 April 1995). The phrasing, which implies passive involvement in the killings, reinforces the Hutu extremists' denial that they carried out genocide. Prunier (1995) has noted a similar tendency in faxes certain White Fathers sent from Rwanda during the genocide. These faxes described the violence 'as "happening" but the perpetrators [were] never identified' (Prunier 1995: 251).

CHAPTER 4

1. Fieldwork was carried out under the auspices of the Joint Evaluation of Emergency Assistance to Rwanda, a Steering Committee comprising 37 agencies: OECD countries, EU and UN agencies, international organisations, and NGO umbrella organisations. The main objective was to draw lessons relevant for responding to future complex emergencies, including their prevention. My chief task was to obtain refugee views on international assistance. Preliminary visits to the camps (Ngara, Goma, Bukavu) were undertaken from 24 April to 8 May 1995, while the research proper (Ngara, Goma) took place between 25 June and 25 July 1995.

2. A further aspect of this suspension is that the perpetrators of genocide almost invariably deny responsibility for their barbarous acts and blame the victims for the violence inflicted. In Burundi, the Tutsi extremists who killed the democratically elected President N'Dadaye and so sparked off the violence in which some 25,000 Tutsi were butchered by Hutu (who feared a repeat of the 1972 genocide) claimed *they had to kill* N'Dadaye because his Frodebu party was plotting to wipe out all Tutsi (Lemarchand 1997: xiv–xv). Similarly, Rwandan Hutu ideologues claimed that the 1994 massacres of Tutsi and moderate Hutu would not have taken place had the RPF not invaded. In both instances, the *interpretation* of ethnic violence, and the expectation of such violence, spawned acts of counter or so-called preventive genocide.

3. Although it was institutional responses that sealed the fate of the refugees in late 1996, many humanitarian workers were critical of UNHCR's tendency to stereotype the refugees. And there were critics within UNHCR itself. That the UN refugee agency is not neatly bounded became clear, for instance, in July 1994 when headquarters in

Geneva and field staff in Goma disagreed on whether, and how, refugees should be encouraged to return home (*New York Times*, 29 July 1994).

4. *The Observer*, 24 July 1994.
5. *De Morgen*, 25 July 1994.
6. *The Independent*, 21 March 1995.
7. For an example, see Sibomana in *NRC Handelsblad*, 11 November 1996.
8. *Le Soir*, 27 July 1995; emphasis added.
9. Disobedience was commonly triggered by excessive demands made upon the fostered child.
10. Interview, Lumasi camp, Tanzania, 28 June 1995.
11. Commune leaders had received their 'incentives' as camp assistants, not as commune administrators.
12. Interview, Lumasi camp, 28 July 1995.
13. It is well known that the killings in Butare, south Rwanda, started *two weeks* after Habyarimana's plane was shot down. They began when the northern presidential guard and *interahamwe* (MRND/CDR militias) came south 'to give the example' (see Chapter 1).
14. The NGO Collective was the counterpart to a Brussels-based consortium of NGOs (COOPIBO, SOS-Faim, Vredeseilanden).
15. Interview, Mugunga camp, 10 July 1995.
16. Claire Bourgeois, UNHCR medical coordinator in Goma, interviewed on 27 April 1995.
17. Regarding primary education, the input demanded of refugees was basic: 'Communities were asked to be responsible for the preparation of school sites and [the] erection of school shelters (tents and semi-permanent structures)' (Houtart 1995a: 3). In Ngara, primary education began by July 1995 with a three-shift system: 60,000 pupils were taught 3 hours a day, 5 days a week. Parents approved of the shift-system as it allowed children both to attend school and be involved in the daily struggle for survival.
18. *Het Belang van Limburg*, 10 February 1995.
19. *De Morgen*, 14 January 1995.
20. In an interview in July 1995, Butare's (new) prefect admitted that after one week in office his biggest concern was how to deal with the unlawful appropriation of temporarily abandoned homes and gardens.
21. Originally purchased by IFRC in anticipation of a refugee exodus from Burundi, the beans were donated to WFP when the expected exodus did not take place.
22. *Umuganda* was the communal labour system practised under Habyarimana.
23. Grogan and Sharp (1900: 118–19) refer to terracing, irrigation and an exceptional diversity of plants – including climbing beans.
24. *Le Figaro*, 18 February 1995.
25. *Le Figaro*, 18 February 1995.
26. In theory, the food basket consisted of 420g maize (or 350g maize meal), 120g beans, 25g oil, 50g CSB (corn soya blend) and 5g salt per person per day. This provided 2,343Kcal and 77.4g protein per day.
27. UNHCR Food Distribution Plan, 15 June 1995.
28. Interview, 12 July 1995.
29. *De Morgen*, 6 January 1995.
30. *De Standaard*, 14 September 1995.

31. Quoted in *Le Soir*, 25 July 1995.
32. *Le Soir*, 28 July 1995.
33. UNHCR dossier released in Kigali, quoted in *La Libre Belgique*, 22 September 1995.
34. *Gazet Van Antwerpen*, 1 August 1994.
35. US General Edwyn Smith, *De Standaard*, 21 November 1996.
36. *De Morgen*, 20 November 1996.
37. *International Herald Tribune*, 20 November 1996.
38. *Het Belang Van Limburg*, 21 November 1996.
39. *Het Volk*, 23–24 November 1996. Kagame was right that there were discrepancies, but no international donor went as low as a few tens of thousands. At the European summit in Ostend, Belgium, participating countries worked with the following numbers of 'missing' refugees: 800 to 900,000 (Belgium), 700,000 (France), about 500,000 (Germany) (*Le Monde*, 21 November 1996). UNHCR maintained the figure was around 600,000, but thought some 100,000 might be heading for Goma from Bukavu (*Le Figaro*, 21 November 1996).
40. *De Standaard*, 12 November 1996.
41. See 'No bloodless miracle', *The Guardian*, 15 November 1996.
42. *NRC Handelsblad*, 16 July 1994.
43. *Het Belang van Limburg*, 26 November 1996.
44. *Le Courier de l'Escaut*, 8 November 1996.
45. *De Morgen*, 8 November 1996.

CHAPTER 5

1. Michela Wrong, *The Financial Times*, 6 May 1997.
2. *Financial Times*, 27 February 1997.
3. *La Dernière Heure*, 9–11 November 1996.
4. *La Dernière Heure*, 12 November 1996.
5. *Le Figaro*, 12 November 1996.
6. *De Morgen*, 12 November 1996.
7. Canada offered the post-genocide Rwandan government substantial aid for its civil society projects ($ 3.3 million) and another $ 3 million for legal and judicial projects (Uvin 1998: 93).
8. Proof existed in bringing the banana bunches, found in Ferdinand's house, to the field from which they had disappeared. The stems fitted the cuts made on the plants.
9. *Le Monde*, 13 November 1996.
10. *Libération*, 27 May 1994.
11. The massacres allegedly committed by the RPF troops during Rwanda's civil war are now being investigated by Carla Del Ponte, the chief prosecutor of the International Criminal Tribunal for Rwanda (ICTR) in Arusha. Del Ponte, with whom President Paul Kagame has promised to cooperate, made the announcement in December 2000 (IRIN, 14 December 2000).
12. *Le Courier de l'Escaut*, 23–24 July 1994; *International Herald Tribune*, 28 July 1994.
13. *New York Times*, 23 July 1994; also *De Volkskrant*, 28 July 1994.
14. *Le Monde*, 23 July 1994.
15. See *De Morgen*, 28 July 1994.

16. *The Observer*, 24 July 1994; *Le Monde*, 24–25 July 1994.
17. *La Libre Belgique*, 18 July 1994.
18. *Le Monde*, 24–25 July 1994.
19. *NRC Handelsblad*, 18 July 1994.
20. *De Volkskrant*, 20 July 1994.
21. L. Chalker quoted in *The Guardian*, 27 July 1994. See also *New York Times*, 29 July 1994; *The Guardian*, 25 July 1994; *The Times*, 24 August 1994.
22. *Le Monde*, 23 July 1994.
23. *The Guardian*, 8 April 1995.
24. Personal interviews, Kigali, April–May 1995.
25. *Le Monde*, 29 April 1995.
26. The commission was set up promptly. On 27 April 1995, Rwanda's President, Pasteur Bizimungu, invited the US, Canada, Britain, France, The Netherlands, Belgium, Germany, the Organisation of African Unity (OAU) and the United Nations to participate, together with Rwanda, in the international inquiry. The commission was formally established in Kigali on 3 May 1995 and comprised the following members: Marc Brisset-Foucault, prosecutor (France); Bernard Dussault, diplomat (Canada); Koen de Feyter, professor of International Law (Belgium); Karl Flittner, diplomat (Germany); Ataul Karim, diplomat (United Nations organisations); Ashraf Khan, forensic pathologist (Great Britain); Maurice Nyberg, lawyer (US); Abdelaziz Skik, military expert (OAU); Christine Umutoni, lawyer (Rwanda); and Ernst Wesselius, prosecutor (The Netherlands). The Commission appointed Colonel-Major Abdelaziz Khik as its president, Bernard Dussault as its vice-president and Ernst Wesselius as its secretary and rapporteur.
27. *Le Courier de l'Escaut*, 28 April 1995.
28. *Le Monde*, 29 April 1995.
29. *Le Monde*, 29 April 1995. As one of only a handful of British soldiers serving in UNAMIR-2, Major Mark Cuthbert Brown later told David Orr: '[whoever investigates Kibeho] will find as many corpses as they want. The bodies are very widely distributed and there are individual graves all over the place. This is not the time to start digging them up' (*The Independent*, 28 April 1995). Cuthbert Brown was responsible for the UN's revised estimate of 2,000 dead (Khan 2000: 112; see also *The Times*, 26 April 1995).
30. *Le Monde*, 29 April 1995.
31. *Le Courier de l'Escaut*, 28 April 1995.
32. *Le Monde*, 29 April 1995.
33. *Le Monde*, 29 April 1995; *The Guardian*, 28 April 1995.
34. *Le Courier de l'Escaut*, 28 April 1995.
35. *Le Monde*, 29 April 1995.
36. *Le Soir*, 2 May 1995.
37. *De Standaard*, 25 April 1995.
38. *Le Soir*, 2 May 1995.
39. *Le Soir*, 2 May 1995.
40. *La Libre Belgique*, 11–12 March 1995. ARDHO workers denied that false accusations would be systematic, yet admitted that dealing with the military usually required several attempts before one could 'speak with the lions'. The RPA's continuous tussle with the civil structures for administration and justice meant that the protection of civilians was not guaranteed (see also Kent 1996: 75, 84). Events later

that year – Twagiramungu's 'resignation' (August) and Sendashonga's dismissal – resulted in ordinary Hutu losing important levers with which to exert pressure on their government (Prunier 1997: 369–71).

41. *De Morgen*, 25 April 1995.
42. *The Guardian*, 27 April 1995.
43. *Gazet Van Antwerpen*, 28 April 1995.
44. *The Times*, 25 April 1995; also reported in *De Standaard*, 25 April 1995, and *De Morgen*, 25 April 1995. *De Standaard* wrote: 'A dissident voice came from Great Britain, where Baroness Lynda Chalker, head of the Overseas Development Administration, accepted the Rwandan government explanation word for word.'
45. *The Times*, 25 April 1995.
46. *NRC Handelsblad*, 24 April 1995.
47. According to *NRC Handelsblad* (25 April 1995), Britain even offered to enlarge its direct aid to Rwanda.
48. *The Guardian*, 4 May 1995.
49. *La Libre Belgique*, 28 April 1995.
50. While not intended perhaps, SCF's advocacy reflected the post-Cold War funding climate with its expanded mandates for NGOs and the prospect of extra resources from home governments (see African Rights 1994c; Hulme and Edwards 1997).
51. *NRC Handelsblad*, 24 April 1995.
52. *Gazet Van Antwerpen*, 27 April 1995.
53. Stephen Smith, *Libération*, 21 May 1995.
54. *Libération*, 21 May 1995.
55. See ODA statement, *The Independent*, 21 March 1995.
56. *The Independent*, 21 March 1995; emphasis added.
57. *Libération*, 21 May 1995.
58. *La Libre Belgique*, 31 May 1995.
59. Amnesty International, News Service 91/95.
60. *La Libre Belgique*, 2 June 1995.
61. *The Times*, 29 April 1995.
62. *Le Vif/L'Express*, 8 November 1996.
63. See Willame 1997: 97 for details of this imagined polity.
64. *New York Times*, 29 October 1996; also *La Libre Belgique*, 30 October 1996.
65. *De Standaard*, 26 October 1996.
66. Willame 1997: 93–4, emphasis added. A copy of the speech, translated from Kinyarwanda into French, can be found in the Archives de l'Institut Africain-CEDAF, III-2985.
67. *The Times*, 9 November 1996.
68. *The Times*, 9 November 1996; also *Le Figaro*, 8 November 1996.
69. *The Guardian*, 15 November 1996. The same article quotes John Major: 'Literally hundreds upon hundreds of thousands of people . . . will undoubtedly face death in the next few weeks unless urgent action is taken. I believe, if Western governments have the capacity to help, that there is a strong moral obligation on us to help.'
70. *The Independent*, 20 November 1996.
71. *NRC Handelsblad*, 7 November 1996.
72. Burns argued that the US was impartial in the Kivu conflict: 'The reality is that we support neither Zaire nor Rwanda, and that our US ambassadors have tried hard to persuade these two countries they must halt hostilities. Moreover, the US has

strongly criticised the Rwandan government when it sent troops to the other side of the border. We do not help any side, neither militarily nor politically' (*Le Figaro*, 12 November 1996).

73. *The Guardian*, 15 November 1996.
74. *Le Figaro*, 14 November 1996.
75. *Le Courier de l'Escaut*, 14 November 1996.
76. Stromberg quoted in *De Volkskrant*, 11 November 1996.
77. It is possible, though, that the refugee pockets in question were made up of refugees who had fled from camps like Katale and Kahindo, attacked before the assault on Mugunga, and who never reached Mugunga. For a chronology of the fall of Mugunga, see Pottier 1999a: 150–1. UNHCR would later accept that some 500,000 refugees remained trapped in South Kivu. It was a figure the ADFL allegedly accepted, but Rwandan officials denied (*The Independent*, 20 November 1996).
78. See e.g. *The Guardian*, 5 November 1996; *The Independent on Sunday*, 10 November 1996.
79. *New York Times*, 22 November 1996.
80. *NRC Handelsblad*, 25 November 1996.
81. *NRC Handelsblad*, 22 November 1996.
82. In possession of the revised US figure, Seth Kamanzi, government adviser, challenged the UNHCR 'to show us where the refugees are located' (*NRC Handelsblad*, 22 November 1996). It was another opportunity to remind the world that aid agencies had a dirty habit of inflating their figures.
83. *The Times*, 18 November 1996.
84. *Libération*, 13 November 1996.
85. *Le Soir*, 14 November 1996.
86. *Financial Times*, 6 May 1997.
87. *The Guardian*, 20 November 1996.
88. *Libération*, 7 November 1996.

CHAPTER 6

1. It is somewhat ironic that the situation in the north-west is taken to be exemplary, given that the land sales in question robbed the poor of their entitlement and turned disillusioned youngsters into thugs prepared to kill for reward (see Chapter 1). André's observations on the north-west (André 1995) do not support an optimistic reading.
2. As all land in Rwanda belongs to the state, a person buying land in actual fact buys the right to use that land, not the land itself. Hence, when the authorities claim a piece of land for public use, they compensate only for the loss of buildings and crops (Gasasira 1995: 2). Compensation is often insufficient or simply not forthcoming (von Braun *et al.* 1991).
3. Articles published in 1959 in *Kinyamateka*, run from the Catholic mission at Kabgayi, regularly stressed 'that the abolition of *ubuhake* in 1954 could hardly be effective if people still depended on chiefs for tenure over their land'; *uburetwa was still a central issue* (Newbury 1981: 144).
4. The central court had its own internal tensions through the rivalry of its two clans – *Abanyiginya* and *Abeega* – which jockeyed for power throughout European rule (Newbury 1988: 57).

5. Some large projects, such as the OVAPAM project in Mutara, have been earmarked for privatisation (République Rwandaise 1998: 95).
6. Initial international comment on the impact of war on Rwanda's food production claimed there had been a near total loss of harvests and seeds. Farmers had eaten their seed supplies and Rwanda's devastated agricultural sector could not recover without outside technical intervention. With media assistance, and despite counter evidence, the disaster narrative continued right up to the end of 1994 (Pottier 1994a, 1996c). Facing much infrastructural damage and a huge debt burden left by the ousted government, and seeing much needed aid diverted to the refugee camps, the government of Rwanda did not object to this depiction of 'helpless Rwanda'. It was a strategy which might attract some desperately needed funds and introduce the notion of *drastic intervention*, a concept the government found convenient to accept in view of its own plans for villagisation.
7. *Knack*, 4 January 1995. A survey by the Ministry of Rehabilitation and Social Integration, December 1994, had identified state-controlled zones suitable for (re)settlement in Mutara (58,000 ha), Kibungo (64,550 ha), Bugesera (7,860 ha), Mayaga (245 ha) and Gisenyi (14,634 ha). These vacant lands included pasture lands in Gishwati forest (Gisenyi), the OVAPAM project in Mutara, and the presidential hunting domain in the north-east. It was envisaged, too, that the extensive marshlands along the Nyabarongo and its tributaries would be drained (*Le Nouvel Observateur*, 21–27 November 1996). Reclaiming the Nyabarongo was a project which originated in colonial times (Nezehose 1990: 44).
8. Quoted in *De Volkskrant*, 15 November 1996.
9. *Independent on Sunday*, 24 November 1996; *De Volkskrant*, 25 November 1996; *De Standaard*, 21 November 1996; *NRC Handelsblad*, 23 November 1996.
10. *De Standaard*, 19 November 1996.
11. See, for example, Braeckman's happy-to-be-home piece in *Le Soir*, 20 November 1996.
12. This is how Prime Minister Rwigema, Twagiramungu's successor, addressed the media in late 1996: 'When it comes to the recuperation of property, some basic rules exist *and it is up to the commune authorities to implement them.* For the past ten months we have put the final touches to the regulations regarding the return of property, so there really exists no legislative void today: *our people know exactly what they should do'* (*Le Soir*, 22 November 1996; emphasis added).
13. 'New caseload' refugees wanting to reclaim property were hampered also by the collective *stigma* they carried. This was confirmed by Pierre Sane, secretary-general of Amnesty International: 'The Rwandan refugees now returning home carry the stigma that they have had something to do with the genocide against Tutsi and moderate Hutu' (Sane quoted in *Het Volk*, 20 November 1996).
14. The relationship between commune and government is a fascinating topic for study, since the pursuit of commune-level autonomy, strong in Habyarimana's days, is likely to continue (see Seur, this chapter, p. 193).
15. Located in Rwanda's north-east, Mutara was sparsely populated at the time, with estimates ranging from 160,000 to 300,000 people, the majority of which were Tutsi repatriates. But many had returned with sizeable herds of cattle. While conditions for settlement were unfavourable (insufficient water for household consumption, irrigation and cattle watering), the area had been earmarked as suitable for resettlement.

16. The pre-registration exercise UNHCR conducted in June 1995 set the number of Muvumba refugees in Lumasi at 34,757. This compared with the commune's total population of 59,175 (1991 Census). But the total number of absentees could have been much higher than 60 per cent as not all refugees had ended up in Lumasi. A joint report by the World Food Programme and the Austrian Relief Programme (WFP/ARP 1994) suggested that of Muvumba's original population only 10.8 per cent remained.

17. Food cropping in Mutara may have been a marginal activity in terms of acreages cultivated (UNREO 1995), but it was crucial to the wider economy (Pottier 1994a) and vital to the successful resettlement of repatriates.

18. Fear also had a strong socio-cultural dimension, since farms with mature banana groves mostly had ancestors buried there. This gave returning 'new caseload' refugees a psychological advantage over repatriates fearful of ancestral revenge. Against the backdrop of genocide and post-genocide killings, the likelihood of ancestral revenge could not so easily be ignored. As Lestrade had noted in the early 1970s, no one ever contemplated starting a new banana grove, the homestead's pivotal point, on a deserted site for fear that the old occupants' ancestors would take revenge (Lestrade 1972: 229; also Pottier and Nkundabashaka 1992).

19. It would be interesting to research gacaca, the 'traditional' but lapsed neighbourhood-watch institution which the government has revitalised (République Rwandaise 1998), and find out whether or not gacaca controls the local discourse on public morality and exclusion. The development question is whether gacaca can stimulate change in the same way that cooperatives in the mid-1980s encouraged reflection on social equity and gender (see Pottier 1989b).

20. For details see Ndekezi 1984: 21.

21. The difficulties widows face are sometimes linked, too, to the stigma that accrues to their survival. The stigmatisation of survival received comment already in August 1994, for instance, when Venerande Nzambazamariya, former head of the Dutch volunteers in Rwanda (Stichting Nederlandse Vrijwilligers), said she had mixed feelings about returning, because 'it is not those who suffered most, who benefit from the victory.' Nzambazamariya was particularly concerned that Kigali's original Tutsi inhabitants, the kavukire, were being accused by repatriates of collaboration with the interahamwe (De Volkskrant, 24 August 1994).

22. Hajabakiga also refers to the creation of non-farm employment: 'We need to create other jobs but there's no way of doing that when people are scattered.' Details on how to create jobs are not given, but a sequence is insisted upon: villagisation first, off-farm jobs next. In a comment, IRIN specifies that the imidugudu policy 'has not been ratified in parliament and its legal status remains unclear' (IRIN, 13 October 1999).

23. The politics of imidugudu show up similarities with the Rango housing scheme I studied in Butare in 1985–86 (Pottier 1989a). Built as an SOS Hunger project, Rango contained many houses owned by local government employees who had speculated, correctly, that these houses were a good investment. Hilhorst and van Leeuwen found traces of a similar tendency (Hilhorst and van Leeuwen 1999: 33).

24. For the World Bank, the 'real' issue/assumption is that title deeds protect the richer farmers and encourage them to invest in land. Yet, as seen elsewhere in Africa, the absence of a cadastre is not necessarily problematic, while registering land titles may create more problems than it solves (Pottier 1999b: 60).

25. Patricia Hajabakiga (MINITERE) criticised the international community for its continued scepticism regarding *imidugudu*. She confirmed that the government is moving ahead with the relocation of every rural Rwandan (IRIN, 13 October 1999).

26. While the hand of Barrière's mentors seems apparent in his portrayal of 'customary law', we must not defend *ubukonde* as in any way superior to *isambu*. When we understand *ubukonde* historically, as an evolved and situated pratice, it is only too clear that the character and meaning of *ubukonde* has changed dramatically over time, especially following the 'encounter' with *isambu*. Although reinstated for Rwanda's north-west by an edict in 1961, the *umukonde* regime was not hailed in other parts of Rwanda. Not blind to its aberrations, Rwandans regularly canvassed to have *ubukonde* abolished, because the patron could at any moment take land back (Mbaguta 1968). Moreover, in the decades following independence, *ubukonde* in the north-west degenerated into such a skewed pattern of land-holdings that two-thirds of the population were excluded from agricultural projects (Godding 1987: 90–1). A survey in the late 1970s in Kanama, Gisenyi Prefecture, showed that household access to land varied from 0.02 acre to 2.4 hectares, with a mean of just under 0.5 acre per household (Godding 1980). The situation worsened in subsequent years (André 1995; André and Platteau 1996).

27. MINITERE = Ministry of Lands, Human Resettlement and Environmental Protection.

CONCLUSION

1. *The Guardian*, 29 September 1995.
2. The term mediascapes refer to 'the distribution of the electronic capabilities to produce and disseminate information . . . and to the images of the world created by these media' (Appadurai 1990: 7).
3. *De Standaard*, 22 November 1996.
4. Clear parallels exist with Ethiopian historiography, which, in the 1990s, became subjected to a third 'wave of revisionist writings, this time involving diaspora-politicians forced out by the Derg' (Triulzi, forthcoming).
5. This search must include a critique of that vast body of post-independence litera-ture on Rwandan history, but this will not be possible until the critics themselves become thoroughly familiar with the wealth of detail and argument these publi-cations contain. A respectful review demands in the first instance that the hasty, haphazard and uninformed approach, characteristic of the 'instant expert' of the past few years, be dropped.

Bibliography

Abu-Lughod, Lila (1986) *Veiled Sentiments*. Princeton: Princeton University Press.

Adelman, Howard (1999) 'Canadian Policy in Rwanda', in Howard Adelman and Astri Suhrke (eds.), *The Path of a Genocide: The Rwanda Crisis from Uganda to Zaire*. New Brunswick and London: Transaction Publishers, pp. 185–208.

Adelman, Howard and Astri Suhrke (1999) 'Preface', in Howard Adelman and Astri Suhrke (eds.), *The Path of a Genocide: The Rwanda Crisis from Uganda to Zaire*. New Brunswick and London: Transaction Publishers, pp. ix–xx.

Africa Direct (1997) The Great Genocide Debate. Conference Papers and Transcriptions. 27 July.

Africa Watch (1992) *Rwanda. Talking Peace and Waging War. Human Rights since the October 1990 Invasion*. Washington, DC: Africa Watch, 27 February.

African Rights (1994a) 'Rwanda: Who is killing; Who is dying; What is to be done?' *Discussion Paper* 2. London: African Rights, May.

African Rights (1994b) *Rwanda: Death, Despair and Defiance*. London: African Rights, September.

African Rights (1994c) 'Humanitarianism Unbound? Current Dilemmas Facing Multi-Mandate Relief Operations in Political Emergencies'. *Discussion Paper* 5. London: African Rights, November.

Allen, Tim and Hubert Morsink (1994) 'Introduction: When Refugees Go Home', in Tim Allen and Hubert Morsink (eds.), *When Refugees Go Home: African Experiences*. Geneva: UNRISD; London: James Currey; and Trenton: Africa World Press, pp. 1–13.

Amnesty International (1992) 'Rwanda: Persecution of Tutsi Minority and Repression of Government Critics'. London.

Amnesty International (1996) 'Zaire: Lawlessness and Insecurity in North and South Kivu'. London.

Amnesty International (1997) 'Deadly Alliances in Congo Forests'. London.

Anderson, Benedict (1991) *Imagined Communities: Reflections on the Origin and Spread of Nationalism*, revised edition. London: Verso.

André, Catherine (1995) 'Modes d'accès et d'occupation des terres: quelle justice sociale?', *Dialogue* 186: 83–94.

André, Catherine and Jean-Philippe Platteau (1996) 'Land Relations Under Unbearable Stress: Rwanda Caught in the Malthusian Trap'. Namur, Belgium: Centre de Recherche en Economie du Développement (CRED), Faculty of Economics, University of Namur. February.

Appadurai, Arjun (1990) 'Disjuncture and Difference in the Global Cultural Economy', *Public Culture* 2(2): 1–24.

Apter, David (1989) *Rethinking Development*. London: Sage.

Asad, Talal (1991) 'From the History of Colonial Anthropology to the Anthropology of Western Hegemony', in George Stocking (ed.), *Colonial Situations: Essays on the Contextualisation of Ethnographic Knowledge*. Madison, WI: University of Wisconsin Press, pp. 314–24.

AVEGA (1999) Field report by Mary Kaytezi Blewitt. November.

Banque Mondiale (1998) *La Pauvreté au Rwanda: Situation Actualisée*. Avec la collaboration du Ministère des Finances et de la Planification économique, le Ministère du genre, de la famille et des affaires sociales, le Ministère de l'agriculture et le Réseau des femmes. Kigali.

Barnett, Michael N. (1997) 'The UN Security Council, Indifference, and Genocide in Rwanda', *Cultural Anthropology* 12(4): 551–78.

Barrière, Olivier (1997) 'Réforme foncière au Rwanda: propositions de fonds en vue de l'élaboration d'une législation foncière cadre. Formulation de la stratégie de développement agricole Mission d'appui (PNUD/FAO)'. Unpublished paper, April.

Bose, Sugata (1997) 'Instruments and Idioms of Colonial and National Development: India's Historical Experience in Comparative Perspective', in Frederick Cooper and Randall Packard (eds.), *International Development and the Social Sciences: Essays on the History and Politics of Knowledge*. Berkeley: University of California Press, pp. 45–63.

Brisset-Foucault, Marc (1995) Report of the Independent International Commission of Inquiry on the Events at Kibeho, April 1995.

Bucyalimwe Mararo, S. (1996) 'Les enjeux de la guerre de Masisi', *Dialogue* 192: 87–92.

Byaruga, Emansueto Foster (1989) 'The Rwandese Refugees in Uganda', in Anders Hjort af Ornäs and M. A. Mohamed Salih (eds.), *Ecology and Politics: Environmental Stress and Security in Africa*. Uppsala, Sweden: Scandinavian Institute of African Studies, pp. 145–56.

Callamard, Agnès (1999) 'French Policy in Rwanda', in Howard Adelman and Astri Suhrke (eds.), *The Path of a Genocide: The Rwanda Crisis from Uganda to Zaire*. New Brunswick and London: Transaction Publishers, pp. 157–88.

Chossudovsky, Michel (1997) 'Economic Genocide in Rwanda', in Michel Chossudovsky, *The Globalisation of Poverty: Impacts of IMF and World Bank Reforms*. Penang, Malaysia: Third World Network, pp. 111–24.

Chrétien, Jean-Pierre (1985) 'Hutu et Tutsi au Rwanda et au Burundi', in J.-L. Amselle and E. M'Bokolo (eds.), *Au Coeur de l'Ethnie: Ethnies, Tribalisme et État en Afrique*. Paris: Editions La Découverte.

Chrétien, Jean-Pierre (1995) *Rwanda: Les Médias du Génocide*. Paris: Karthala.

Clay, Daniel, Fidele Byiringiro, Jaakko Kangasniemi, Thomas Reardon, Bosco Sibomana and Laurence Uwamariya (1995) 'Promoting Food Security in Rwanda through Sustainable Agricultural Productivity: Meeting the Challenges of Population Pressure, Land Degradation and Poverty'. Michigan State University, Department of Agricultural Economics. Unpublished paper, March.

Clifford, James (1986) 'Introduction: Partial Truths', in James Clifford and George E. Marcus (eds.), *Writing Culture: The Poetics and Politics of Culture*. Berkeley: University of California Press, pp. 1–26.

Clifford, James and George E. Marcus (eds.) (1986) *Writing Culture: The Poetics and Politics of Culture.* Berkeley: University of California Press.

Codere, Helen (1962) 'Power in Rwanda', *Anthropologia* 4(1): 45–85.

Connelly, Maureen (1997) 'Refugees or Hostages?' Paper presented at the conference 'Towards Understanding the Crisis in the Great Lakes Region'. Oxford, 1 February.

Cooper, Frederick (1997) 'Modernizing Bureaucrats, Backward Peasants, and the Development Concept', in Frederick Cooper and Randall Packard (eds.), *International Development and the Social Sciences: Essays on the History and Politics of Knowledge.* Berkeley: University of California Press, pp. 64–92.

Cornet, A. (1996) *Histoire d'une Famine: Rwanda 1927–30. Crise Alimentaire entre Tradition et Modernité.* Louvain-La-Neuve: Centre d'Histoire de l'Afrique, Université Catholique de Louvain.

Cornwall, Andrea and Nancy Lindisfarne (eds.), (1994) 'Dislocating Masculinity: Gender, Power and Anthropology', in Andrea Cornwall and Nancy Lindisfarne (eds.), *Dislocating Masculinity.* London: Routledge, pp. 11–47.

Cosma, Wilungula B. (1997) *Fizi 1967–1986. Le Maquis Kabila.* Brussels: Institut Africain – CEDAF; Paris: L'Harmattan.

Crapanzano, Vincent (1986) 'Hermes' Dilemma: The Masking of Subversion in Ethnographic Description', in James Clifford and George E. Marcus (eds.), *Writing Culture: The Poetics and Politics of Culture.* Berkeley: University of California Press, pp. 51–76.

Czekanowski, J. (1917) *Forschungen im Nil-Kongo Zwischengebiet.* Vol. 1: *Ethnographie.* Leipzig: Klinkhardt & Biermann.

Commission of the European Community (CEC) (1982) *Food Strategies: A New Form of Cooperation Between Europe and the Countries of the Third World.* Brussels: CEC, Publication DE40.

Davidson, Basil (1992) *The Black Man's Burden.* London: James Currey.

Depelchin, Jacques (1974) *From Pre-Capitalism to Imperialism: A History of Social and Economic Formations in Eastern Zaire.* Ph.D. dissertation, Stanford University.

Dowden, Richard (1995) 'Media Coverage. How I Reported the Genocide', in Obi Igwara (ed.), *Ethnic Hatred: Genocide in Rwanda.* London: Association for the Study of Ethnicity and Nationalism (ASEN) Publication, pp. 85–92.

d'Hertefelt, Marcel (1964) 'Mythes et idéologies dans le Rwanda ancien et contemporain', in J. Vansina, R. Mauny and L. Thomas (eds.), *The Historian in Tropical Africa.* London: Oxford University Press, pp. 219–38.

(1971) *Les Clans du Rwanda Ancien: Eléments d'Ethnosociologie et de l'Ethnohistoire.* Tervuren, Belgium: Musée Royale de l'Afrique Centrale.

de Dorlodot, Philippe (1996) *Les Réfugiés Rwandais à Bukavu au Zaïre: De Nouveaux Palestiniens.* Paris. L'Harmattan.

de Heusch, Luc (1966) *Le Rwanda et la Civilisation Interlacustre.* Brussels: Université de Bruxelles, Institut de Sociologie.

(1995) 'Rwanda: Responsibilities for a Genocide', *Anthropology Today* 11(4): 3–7. Translated from French. Original text: de Heusch, Luc (1995) 'Anthropology d'un génocide: le Rwanda', *Les Temps Modernes* 579 (49e année): 1–19.

de Lame, Danielle (1996) *Une Colline entre Mille ou Le Calme avant la Tempête: Transformations et blocages du Rwanda rural.* Tervuren, Belgium: Musée Royal de l'Afrique Centrale.

De Meire, G. (1928) 'Quelques considérations sur la nature de la propriété foncière au nord et au nord-ouest du Rwanda', *Carnets de l'AUCAM* (4e série) 1: 8–14.

De Temmerman, Els (1994) *De Doden Zijn Niet Dood: Rwanda, Een Ooggetuigenverslag.* Groot-Bijgaarden, Belgium: Globe.

de Waal, Alex (1994a) 'Genocide in Rwanda', *Anthropology Today* 10(3): 1–2.

(1994b) 'The Genocidal State: Hutu Extremism and the Origins of the "Final Solution" in Rwanda,' *The Times Literary Supplement*, July.

(1997) *Famine Crimes: Politics and the Disaster Relief Industry in Africa.* London: African Rights and the International African Institute.

Des Forges, Alison (1969) 'Kings Without Crowns: The White Fathers in Rwanda', in Daniel F. McCall, Norman R. Bennett and Jeffrey Butler (eds.), *Eastern African History.* New York: Praeger.

(1972) 'Defeat is the Only Bad News: Rwanda under Musiinga, 1896–1931'. Ph.D. Dissertation, Yale University.

(1999) *Leave None to Tell the Story: Genocide in Rwanda.* New York: Human Rights Watch; Paris: International Federation of Human Rights.

Department for International Development, UK (DFID) (1999) *Rwanda.* London: DFID, Country Strategy Paper.

Eboussa-Boulaga, F. (1977) *La Crise du Muntu.* Paris: Présence Africaine.

(1981) *Christianisme sans Fétiche. Révélation et Domination.* Paris: Présence Africaine.

Eltringham, Nigel and Saskia Van Hoyweghen (2000) 'Power and Identity in Post-Genocide Rwanda', in Ruddy Doom and Jan Gorus (eds.), *Politics of Identity and Economics of Conflict in the Great Lakes Region.* Brussels: Vrije Universiteit Brussel (VUB) Press, pp. 215–42.

Fairhead, James (1989a) *Food Security in North and South Kivu (Zaire), 1989.* Final consultancy report for Oxfam. Part 1, Section 1. London: Oxfam.

(1989b) *Food Security in North and South Kivu (Zaire), 1989.* Final consultancy report for Oxfam. Part 1, Section 2. London: Oxfam.

(1990) 'Fields of Struggle: Towards a Social History of Farming Knowledge and Practice in a Bwisha Community, Kivu, Zaire'. Ph.D. dissertation, School of Oriental and African Studies, University of London.

(1997) 'Demographic Issues in the Great Lakes Region', in Save the Children (ed.), *The Crisis of the Great Lakes: Some Proposed Solutions. Report of the Meeting on 'Practical Approaches to the Crises of the Great Lakes' held at Sundridge Park, Kent, on 24–26 March 1997.* London: Save the Children, pp. 55–62.

(2000) 'The Conflict Over Natural and Humanitarian Resources', in E. Wayne Nafziger, Frances Stewart and Raimo Väyrynen (eds.), *The Origins of Humanitarian Emergencies: War and Displacement in Developing Countries.* Oxford: Oxford University Press, pp. 147–78.

Fédération internationale des droits de l'homme (FIDH, Paris), Africa Watch (Washington), Union interafricaine des droits de l'homme et des peuples (Ouagadougou), Centre international des droits de la personne et du développement démocratique (Montréal) (1993) *Rapport de la Commission Internationale d'Enquête sur les Violations des Droits de l'Homme au Rwanda Depuis le 1er Octobre 1990.* Paris: FIDH, March.

Ferguson, James (1994) *The Anti-Politics Machine: 'Development', Depoliticization, and Bureaucratic Power in Lesotho.* Cambridge: Cambridge University Press.

Fisiy, Cyprian (1998) 'Of Journeys and Border Crossings: Return of Refugees, Identity, and Reconstruction in Rwanda', *African Studies Review* 41(1): 17–28.

Foucault, Michel (1980) *Power/Knowledge. Selected Interviews and Other Writings, 1972–77.* New York: Pantheon Books.

   (1982) *The Archaeology of Knowledge and the Discourse on Language.* New York: Pantheon Books.

Gahima, Gerald (1997) 'What is Understood by Justice in Rwanda today?' Paper presented at the Newick Park Initiative conference on 'The Role of the Churches in the Restoration of Justice in Rwanda'. Kigali, 19–21 August.

Gasasira, Ephrem (1995) 'Rwanda: la question foncière après la guerre'. Kigali: MINAGRI/UNDP, April.

Godding, J.-P. (1980) 'Les conseillers communaux, pour quoi faire?', *Dialogue* 83: 12–26.

   (1987) 'Les grands projets de développement rural et le développement des communes', in A. Nkundabashaka and J. Voss (eds.), *Les Projets de Développement Rural: Réussites, Échecs et Stratégies nouvelles.* Butare: Université National du Rwanda/International Centre for Tropical Agriculture, pp. 85–98.

   (1997) *Réfugiés Rwandais au Zaïre.* Paris: L'Harmattan.

Goetz, Anne-Marie (1991) 'Feminism and the Claim to Know: Contradictions in Feminist Approaches to Women and Development', in Rebecca Grant and Kathleen Newland (eds.), *Gender and International Relations.* Milton Keynes: Open University, pp. 133–57.

Gourevitch, Philip (1998) *We Wish To Inform You That Tomorrow We Will Be Killed With Our Families: Stories from Rwanda.* London: Picador.

Gowing, Nik (1997) *Media Coverage: Help or Hindrance in Conflict Prevention.* New York: Carnegie Commission on Preventing Deadly Conflict, Carnegie Corporation of New York. Prepublication draft, May.

   (1998) 'New Challenges and Problems for Information Management in Complex Emergencies. Ominous Lessons Learnt from the Great Lakes and Eastern Zaire'. Background paper to the 'Dispatches from Disaster Zones' Conference. Oxford, 28 May.

Goyvaerts, Didier (1998) 'Centraal-Afrika, de pers en de revisionisten', *Vlaams Marxistisch Tijdschrift* 3: 87–93.

Gravel, Pierre (1968) *Remera: A Community in Eastern Ruanda.* The Hague: Mouton.

Grogan, Ewart and Arthur Sharp (1900) *From the Cape to Cairo: The First Traverse of Africa from South to North.* London: Hurst and Blackett.

Groupe Milima (1996) 'Lettre de Müller Ruhimbika à la Commission des Nations-Unies des droits de l'homme'. Uvira, Zaire, 11 July 1996.

Hilhorst, Thea and Mathijs van Leeuwen (1999) *Villagisation in Rwanda.* Wageningen Disaster Studies No. 2. The Netherlands: University of Wageningen (Faculty of Social Sciences).

Hilsum, Lindsey (1994) 'Domesday', *BBC Focus on Africa*, July/September.

   (1995a) Reporting Rwanda: The Media and the Aid Agencies. Report prepared for Joint Evaluation of Emergency Assistance to Rwanda, Study III (1996, Vol. 3).

(1995b) 'Where is Kigali?', *Granta Books* 51: 145–79.

(1997) 'In the Land of the Lion King', *Times Literary Supplement*, 23 May.

Hintjens, Helen (1997) 'Genocide and Obedience in Rwanda'. Paper presented at the conference 'Conflict and Identity in Africa', University of Leeds, African Studies Unit, 15–17 September.

(1999) 'Explaining the 1994 Genocide in Rwanda', *Journal of Modern African Studies* 37(2): 241–86.

Hoben, Susan (1989) *School, Work and Equity: Educational Reform in Rwanda*. African Research Studies No. 16. Boston: African Studies Centre, Boston University.

Honke, Gudrun (1990) (ed.) *Au Plus Profond de l'Afrique: Le Rwanda et la Colonisation Allemande, 1885–1919*. Wuppertal: Peter Hammer Verlag.

Houtart, Myriam (1995a) 'Education in Emergency. A Right for the Young Generation, a Means for Stability and Survival, a Response to Psycho-social Needs. Kagera Region Experience'. Ngara, Tanzania: United Nations High Commissioner for Refugees (UNHCR). February.

(1995b) 'Community Services and Education. Ngara, Kagera Region, Tanzania'. Ngara: UNHCR, April.

Hulme, David and Michael Edwards (1997) (eds.) *NGOs, States and Donors: Too Close for Comfort?* London: Macmillan Press, in association with Save the Children.

Human Rights Watch/Africa (1996) 'Forced to Flee: Violence against the Tutsis in Zaire', July.

(1997a) 'What Kabila is Hiding: Civilian Killings and Impunity in Congo', October.

(1997b) 'Uncertain Course: Transition and Human Rights Violations in the Congo', December.

Human Rights Watch/Africa and Fédération Internationale des Ligues des Droits de l'Homme (FIDH) (1995) Communiqué, dated 24 April 1995.

Iliffe, John (1987) *The African Poor: A History*. Cambridge: Cambridge University Press.

Internationalist Group (1997) *From Mobutu to Kabila, Congo: Neo-Colonialism Made in USA*. New York: The Internationalist Group.

Jaspars, Susanne (1994) 'The Rwandan Refugee Crisis in Tanzania: Initial Successes and Failures in Food Assistance'. *Network Paper* 6. London: ODI Relief and Rehabilitation Network.

Jefremovas, Villia (1991a) 'Petty Commodity Production and Capitalist Enterprise: Brick and Roof Tile Making in Rwanda'. Ph.D. dissertation, University of Toronto.

(1991b) 'Loose Women, Virtuous Wives, and Timid Virgins: Gender and the Control of Resources in Rwanda', *Canadian Journal of African Studies* 25(3): 378–95.

(1995) 'Acts of Human Kindness: Hutu, Tutsi and The Genocide', *Issue: A Journal of Opinion* 23(2): 28–31.

(1997) 'Contested Identities: Power and the Fictions of Ethnicity, Ethnography and History in Rwanda', *Anthropologica* 23: 1–14.

Johansson, Peik (1995) 'International Press Coverage of the Rwanda Conflict'. Helsinki: Report prepared for the Joint Evaluation of Emergency Assistance to Rwanda (1996, Vol. 2).

Joint Evaluation of Emergency Assistance to Rwanda (1996a) *The International Response to Conflict and Genocide: Lessons from the Rwanda Experience*. Vol. 2: *Early Warning and Conflict Management*. Copenhagen: Steering Committee of the Joint Evaluation to Emergency Assistance to Rwanda, Ministry of Foreign Affairs.

(1996b) *The International Response to Conflict and Genocide: Lessons from the Rwanda Experience.* Vol. 3: *Humanitarian Aid and Effects.* Copenhagen: Steering Committee of the Joint Evaluation to Emergency Assistance to Rwanda, Ministry of Foreign Affairs.

(1996c) *The International Response to Conflict and Genocide: Lessons from the Rwanda Experience.* Vol. 4: *Rebuilding Rwanda.* Copenhagen: Steering Committee of the Joint Evaluation to Emergency Assistance to Rwanda, Ministry of Foreign Affairs.

Kagame, Alexis (1952) *Le Code des Institutions Politiques du Rwanda Précolonial.* Brussels: Institut Royal Colonial Belge (IRCB).

(1954) *Les Organisations Socio-Familales de l'Ancien Rwanda.* Brussels: Académie Royale des Sciences Coloniales.

(1956) *La Philosophie Bantu-Rwandaise de l'Etre.* Brussels: Académie Royale des Sciences Coloniales.

(1958) *L'Histoire du Rwanda.* Leverville: Bibliothèque de l'Etoile.

(1972) *Un Abrégé de l'Ethno-histoire du Rwanda Précolonial.* Classe des sciences morales et politiques. Mémoires XXXVIII, 3. Butare: Editions Universitaires du Rwanda.

(1975) *Un Abrégé de l'Histoire du Rwanda.* Butare: Editions Universitaires du Rwanda.

Kalibwami, Justin (1991) *Le Catholicisme et la Société Rwandaise, 1900–1962.* Paris/Dakar: Editions Présence Africaine.

Kamukama, Dixon (1997) *Rwanda Conflict: Its Roots and Regional Implications.* Kampala: Fountain Publishers.

Karake, Mweusi (1997) Kibungo Experiments and Experiences – Lessons for Africa. Published by Kibungo Prefecture, Rwanda.

Karnik, Niranjan S. (1998) 'The Photographer, His Editor, Her Audience, Their Humanitarians: How Rwanda's Pictures Travel Through the American psyche', *Association of Concerned Africa Scholars Bulletin* 50/51: 35–42.

Keane, Fergal (1996) *Season of Blood: A Rwandan Journey.* Harmondsworth: Penguin Books.

Kent, Randolph (1996) 'The Integrated Operation Centre in Rwanda: Coping with Complexity', in Jim Whiteman and David Pocock (eds.), *After Rwanda: The Coordination of United Nations Humanitarian Assistance.* London: Macmillan; New York: St Martin's Press, pp. 63–85.

Khan, Shaharyar M. (2000) *The Shallow Graves of Rwanda.* London: I. B. Tauris & Co.

Kimona Kicha, A. (1982) 'Evolution du système matrimonial Bembe'. MA dissertation, Université de Lumumbashi.

Larbi, W. Odame (1995) 'Land Reform Potential in Rwanda'. Report for Newick Park Initiative, Relationships Foundation, Cambridge. December.

Lemarchand, René (1968) 'Les relations de clientèle comme agent de contestation: le case du Rwanda', *Civilisations* 18(4): 553–72.

(1970) *Rwanda and Burundi.* New York: Praeger.

(1977) 'Rwanda', in R. Lemarchand (ed.), *African Kingships in Perspective.* London: Frank Cass, pp. 67–92.

(1982) *The World Bank in Rwanda. The Case of the Office de Valorisation Agricole et Pastorale du Mutara (OVAPAM).* Bloomington: Indiana University, African Studies Program.

(1996, 1997) *Burundi: Ethnic Conflict and Genocide.* Cambridge: Cambridge University Press (first published 1994).

(1998) 'Genocide in the Great Lakes: Which Genocide? Whose Genocide?', *African Studies Review* 41(1): 3–16.

Lestrade, A. (1972) 'Notes d'ethnographie du Rwanda', *Archief voor Antropologie* 17. Tervuren, Belgium: Koninklijk Museum voor Midden-Afrika.

Lewis, I. M. (1993) 'Misunderstanding the Somali Crisis', *Anthropology Today* 9(4): 1–3.

Linden, Ian (1977) *Church and Revolution in Rwanda.* Manchester: Manchester University Press.

(1998) 'The Role of INGOs in Rwanda, 1990–98'. Paper presented at the Regional Consultative Workshop on Comprehending and Mastering African Conflicts. Bamako, Mali, 19–21 November.

Livingston, Steven and Todd Eachus (1995) 'US Television Coverage of Rwanda'. Study prepared for the Joint Evaluation of Humanitarian Assistance to Rwanda, Study II (1996, Vol. 2).

(1999) 'Media Coverage and US Foreign Policy', in Howard Adelman and Astri Surhke (eds.), *The Path of a Genocide: The Rwanda Crisis from Uganda to Zaire.* Trenton, NJ: Transaction Books, pp. 209–28.

Longman, Timothy (1995) 'Genocide and Socio-Political Change: Massacres in Two Rwandan Villages', *Issue: A Journal of Opinion* 23(2): 18–21.

Louis, Roger (1963) *Ruanda-Urundi, 1884–1919.* Oxford: Clarendon Press.

Loveridge, Scott (1992) 'Sources of Household Revenue, Farm Exports and Their Impact on Food Availability among Agricultural Households in Rwanda. Agricultural Year 1990'. Publication DSA (Division des Statistiques Agricoles, MINAGRI) No. 24. Kigali: Ministry of Agriculture and Livestock, Division of Agricultural Statistics.

Ludden, David (1992) 'India's Development Regime', in Nicholas Dirks (ed.), *Colonialism and Culture.* Ann Arbor: University of Michigan Press, pp. 247–87.

Mackintosh, Anne (1996) 'International Aid and the Media', in Tim Allen, Kate Hudson and Jean Seaton (eds.), *War, Ethnicity and the Media.* London: South Bank University, School of Education, pp. 37–56.

Mafikiri, Tsongo (1996) 'Mouvements de la population, accès à la terre et question de la nationalité au Kivu', in Paul Mathieu, Pierre-Joseph Laurent and Jean-Claude Willame (eds.), *Démocratie, Enjeux Fonciers et Pratiques Locales en Afrique.* Brussels: Cahiers Africains/Afrika-Studies 23/24; Paris: L'Harmattan, pp. 180–201.

Malkki, Liisa (1992) 'National Geographic: The Rooting of Peoples and the Territorialization of National Identity Among Scholars and Refugees,' *Cultural Anthropology* 1: 24–44.

(1995) *Purity and Exile: Violence, Memory and National Cosmology among Hutu Refugees in Tanzania.* Chicago: University of Chicago Press.

(1996) 'Speechless Emissaries: Refugees, Humanitarianism, and Dehistoricization', *Cultural Anthropology* 11(3): 377–404.

Mamdani, Mahmood (1995) 'Indirect Rule, Civil Society and Ethnicity', in Preben Kaarsholm (ed.), *From Post-Traditional to Post-Modern?: Interpreting the Meaning of Modernity in Third World Urban Societies.* Roskilde University (Denmark): International Development Studies, pp. 220–27.

(1996) 'From Conquest to Consent as the Basis of State Formation: Reflections on Rwanda', *New Left Review* 216: 3–36.

Maquet, Jacques (1954) *Le Système des Relations Sociales dans le Ruanda Ancien.* Tervuren, Belgium: Musée Royal du Congo Belge.

(1961) *The Premise of Inequality.* London: Oxford University Press, for the International African Institute.

Marysse, Stefaan and Filip Reyntjens (eds.) (1997) *L'Afrique des Grands Lacs: Annuaire 1996–97.* Paris: L'Harmattan.

Mbaguta, J. M. (1968) 'Le système de l'économie terrienne de l'ubukonde', *Remarques Africaines* X (No. 309): 66–9.

McNulty, Mel (1999) 'Media Ethnicization and the International Response to War and Genocide in Rwanda', in Tim Allen and Jean Seaton (eds.), *The Media of Conflict: War Reporting and Representations of Ethnic Violence.* London: Zed Books, pp. 268–86.

Meschy, Lydia (1973) 'Kansegere: une colline au Rwanda de l'occupation pionnière au surpeuplement'. Thèse de doctorat de 3ème cycle Ecole Pratique de Hautes Etudes (VIe section), CNRS, Paris.

Meschy, Lydia (misspelled as Meschi) (1974) 'Évolution des structures foncières au Rwanda: le cas d'un lignage hutu,' *Cahiers d'Etudes Africaines* 14(1) 53: 39–51.

Mohanty, Chandra (1994) 'Under Western Eyes: Feminist Scholarship and Colonial Discourses', *Feminist Review* 30: 61–87. Reprinted in Patrick Williams and Laura Chrisman (eds.), *Colonial Discourse and Post-Colonial Theory: A Reader.* London: Harvester Wheatsheaf.

Moore, Henrietta and Megan Vaughan (1994) *Cutting Down Trees: Gender, Nutrition and Agricultural Change in the Northern Province of Zambia, 1890–1990.* Cambridge: Cambridge University Press.

Muchukiwa, Bosco (s.d.) Enjeux des conflits ethniques dans les hauts plateaux d'Itombwe (Zaïre). Note manuscrite, Archives de l'Institut Africain-CEDAF, III-2695.

Mudimbe, V. Y. (1985) 'African Gnosis, Philosophy and the Order of Knowledge: An Introduction', *African Studies Review* 28(2–3): 149–231.

Muhayeyezu, Albert (1996) 'Evolution de la Législation Foncière au Rwanda'. Paper presented at 'Séminaire National sur les Problèmes Fonciers au Rwanda'. Kigali, December.

Mullen, Joseph (1995) 'From Colony to Nation: The Implosion of Ethnic Tolerance in Rwanda', in Obi Igwara (ed.), *Ethnic Hatred: Genocide in Rwanda.* London: ASEN publication, pp. 21–34.

Nahimana, Ferdinand (1981) 'Les principautés hutu du Rwanda Septentrional', in *La Civilisation Ancienne des Peuples des Grands Lacs.* Paris: Karthala; Bujumbura: Le Centre de Civilisation Burundaise, pp. 115–37.

Ndekezi, Sylvestre (1984) *Rituel du Mariage Coutumier au Rwanda.* Kigali: Imprimerie de Kigali.

Newbury, David (1997) 'Guerillas in the Mist'. E-mail circular, 25 April 1997.

(1998) 'Understanding Genocide', *African Studies Review* 41(1): 73–97.

Newbury, M. C. (1974) 'Deux lignages au Kinyaga', *Cahiers d'Etudes Africaines* 14: 26–38.

(1978) 'Ethnicity in Rwanda: The Case of Kinyaga', *Africa* 48(1): 17–29.

Newbury, M. Catharine (1981) 'Ubureetwa and Thangata: Comparative Colonial Perspectives', in *La Civilisation Ancienne des Peuples des Grands Lacs*. Paris: Karthala; Bujumbura: Le Centre de Civilisation Burundaise, pp. 138–47.

(1988) *The Cohesion of Oppression: Clientship and Ethnicity in Rwanda, 1860–1960*. New York: Columbia University Press.

Newbury, Catharine and David Newbury (1994) 'Rwanda: The Politics of Turmoil', *Raleigh News & Observer*, 17 April.

Nezehose, Jean Bosco (1990) *Agriculture Rwandaise: Problématique et Perspectives*. Kigali: INADES – Formation – RWANDA.

Ngolet, François (2000) 'African and American Connivance in Congo-Zaire', *Africa Today* 47(1): 65–85.

Nkundabashaka, A. and J. Voss (eds.) (1987) *Les Projets de Développement Rural: Réussites, Échecs et Stratégies Nouvelles*. Butare: Université Nationale du Rwanda / International Centre for Tropical Agriculture.

Nzongola-Ntalaja, Georges (1996) 'Conflict in Eastern Zaire', *Zaire News*, 19 November.

O'Hanlon, Rosalind and David Washbrook (1992) 'After Orientalism: Culture, Criticism and Politics in the Third World', *Comparative Studies in Society and History* 34(1): 141–67.

Office of the Humanitarian Coordinator (1995) *Rwanda: Humanitarian Situation Report – April 1995*. Kigali: Office of the Humanitarian Coordinator (UN).

Otunnu, Ogenga (1999a) 'Rwandese Refugees and Immigrants in Uganda', in Howard Adelman and Astri Suhrke (eds.), *The Path of a Genocide: The Rwanda Crisis from Uganda to Zaire*. New Brunswick and London: Transaction Publishers, pp. 3–29.

Otunnu, Ogenga (1999b) 'An Historical Analysis of the Invasion by the Rwanda Patriotic Front', in Howard Adelman and Astri Suhrke (eds.), *The Path of a Genocide: The Rwanda Crisis from Uganda to Zaire*. New Brunswick and London: Transaction Publishers, pp. 31–49.

Pabanel, Jean-Pierre (1991) 'La question de la nationalité au Kivu', *Politique Africaine* 41: 32–40.

Palmer, Robin (2000) Report and Reflections on the Rwandan Draft National Policy Workshop. Kigali, 2–3 November 2000.

Pender, John (1997) 'Understanding Central Africa's Crisis,' in Africa Direct (ed.), *Rwanda: The Great Genocide Debate. Conference Papers and Transcriptions, 27 July 1997*. London: Africa Direct.

Philo, Greg (1998) (ed.) 'The Zaire Rebellion and the British Media. An analysis of the reporting of the Zaire crisis in November 1996 and 1997 by the Glasgow Media Group', background paper to 'Dispatches from the Disaster Zone' conference. London, 27–28 May.

Platteau, J.-P. (1992) *Land Reform and Structural Adjustment in Sub-Saharan Africa: Controversies and Guidelines*. FAO Economic and Social Development, 107. Rome: Food an Agriculture Organization (FAO).

Polman, Linda (1999) 'The Problem Outside', *Granta* 67: 217–40.

Pottier, Johan (1986) 'The Politics of Famine Prevention: Ecology, Regional Production and Food Complementarity in Western Rwanda', *African Affairs* 85 (No. 339): 207–37.

(1989a) 'Three is a Crowd: Knowledge, Ignorance and Power in the Context of Urban Agriculture in Rwanda', *Africa* 54(4): 461–77.

(1989b) 'Debating Styles in a Rwandan Cooperative: Reflections on Language, Policy and Gender', in Ralph Grillo (ed.), *Social Anthropology and the Politics of Language*. Sociological Review Monograph 34. London: Routledge, pp. 41–60.

(1993) 'Taking Stock: Food Marketing Reform in Rwanda, 1982–1989', *African Affairs* 92: 5–30.

(1994a) *Food Security and Agricultural Rehabilitation in Post-War Rwanda. August–September 1994*. Report for Save The Children Fund, with John Wilding. London: Save The Children Fund.

(1994b) 'Agricultural Discourses: Farmer Experimentation and Agricultural Extension in Rwanda', in Ian Scoones and John Thompson (eds.), *Beyond Farmer First*. London: Intermediate Technology Publications, pp. 83–8.

(1994c) 'Poor Men, Intra-household Bargaining and the Politics of Household Food Security', in Ingrid Yngström, Patricia Jeffery, Kenneth King and Camilla Toulmin (eds.) *Gender and Environment in Africa: Perspectives on the Politics of Environmental Sustainability*. Edinburgh: Centre of African Studies, University of Edinburgh, pp. 156–74.

(1995) 'Representations of Ethnicity in Post-Genocide Writings on Rwanda', in Obi Igwara (ed.), *Ethnic Hatred: Genocide in Rwanda*. London: ASEN Publication, pp. 29–53.

(1996a) 'Relief and Repatriation: Views by Rwandan Refugees; Lessons for Humanitarian Aid Workers', *African Affairs* 95(380): 403–29.

(1996b) 'Why Aid Agencies Need Better Understanding of the Communities They Assist: The Experience of Food Aid in Rwandan Refugee Camps', *Disasters* 20(4): 323–36.

(1996c) 'Agricultural Rehabilitation and Food Insecurity in Post-War Rwanda: Assessing Needs, Designing Solutions', *Institute of Development Studies Bulletin* 27(3): 56–76.

(1999a) 'The "Self" in Self-Repatriation: Closing Down Mugunga Camp, Eastern Zaire', in Richard Black and Khalid Koser (eds.), *The End of the Refugee Cycle? Refugee Repatriation and Reconstruction*. Oxford: Berghahn Books, pp. 142–70.

(1999b) *Anthropology of Food: The Social Dynamics of Food Security*. Cambridge: Polity Press.

(2000) 'Reporting the New Rwanda: The Rise and Cost of Political Correctness, with Reference to Kibeho', in Ruddy Doom and Jan Gorus (eds.), *Politics of Identity and Economics of Conflict in the Great Lakes Region*. Brussels: VUB University Press, pp. 121–47.

Pottier, Johan and James Fairhead (1991) 'Post-Famine Recovery in Highland Dwisha, Zaire: 1984 in Its Context', *Africa* 61(4): 537–70.

Pottier, Johan and Augustin Nkundabashaka (1992) 'Intolerable Environments: Towards a Cultural Reading of Agrarian Policy in Rwanda', in David Parkin and Elisabeth Croll (eds.), *Bush Base: Forest Farm*. London: Routledge, pp. 146–68.

Prioul, C. (1976) 'Pour une Problématique de l'Aménagement de l'Espace Rural au Rwanda', *L'Informateur* 9.

Prunier, Gérard (1995) *The Rwanda Crisis, 1959–1994: History of a Genocide*. London: Hurst.

(1997) *The Rwanda Crisis, 1959–1994: History of a Genocide*. London: Hurst. 1995 reprinted with additional chapter.

Ralibera, R. (1959) 'Théologien-prêtre africain et le développement de la culture africaine', *Présence Africaine* 27–28: 154–87.

Reisdorff (1952) 'Enquêtes Foncières au Ruanda'. Unpublished study.

République Rwandaise (1989) *Compte-rendu de la Réunion Tenue au Minagri en Date du 02/05/1989 sur la Situation Alimentaire du Rwanda en Avril 1989*. Kigali: Ministère de l'Agriculture, de l'Elevage et des Forêts.

République Rwandaise (1998) *Seminaire National sur la Formulation de la Stratégie Agricole: Rapport de Synthèse des Documents de Travail*. Kigali: Ministère de l'Agriculture, de l'Elevage, de l'Environnement et du Développement Rural. (Seminar held in Kigali on 21–23 October 1997.)

Reyntjens, Filip (1985) *Pouvoir et Droit au Rwanda. Droit Public et Evolution Politique, 1916–1973*. Tervuren, Belgium: Musée Royal de l'Afrique Centrale.

(1994) *L'Afrique des Grands Lacs en Crise. Rwanda, Burundi: 1988–1994*. Paris: Karthala.

(1999a) 'A Dubious Discourse on Rwanda', *African Affairs* 98(1): 119–22.

(1999b) *La Guerre des Grands Lacs: Alliances Mouvantes et Conflits Extraterritoriaux en Afrique Centrale*. Paris: L'Harmattan.

Reyntjens, Filip and Stefaan Marysse (eds.) (1996) *Conflits au Kivu: Antécédents et Enjeux*. Antwerp: Universiteit Antwerpen, Centre for the Study of the Great Lakes Region of Africa.

Richards, Paul (1996) *Fighting for the Rain Forest: War, Youth and Resources in Sierra Leone*. Oxford: James Currey; Portsmouth: Heineman.

Rieff, David (1995) *Slaughterhouse: Bosnia and the Failure of the West*. New York: Simon and Schuster.

Ruhashyankiko, Nicodème (1985) *Le Droit Foncier au Rwanda*. Butare: Université National de Rwanda.

Rwabukumba, Joseph and Vincent Mudandagizi (1974) 'Les formes historiques de la dépendance personnelle dans l'état rwandais', *Cahiers d'Etudes Africaines* 14(1) 53: 6–25.

Ryle, John (1998) 'Information in Disaster Zones: An Anatomy of Ignorance'. Paper presented at the 'Dispatches from Disaster Zones' conference. London, 27–28 May.

(2000) 'The Hazards of Reporting Complex Emergencies in Africa', *Transnational Law & Contemporary Problems* 10(1): 85–105.

Said, Edward (1993) '*From* Orientalism', in Patrick Williams and Laura Chrisman (eds.), *Colonial Discourse and Post-Colonial Theory: A Reader*. London: Harvester Wheatsheaf. Originally published 1978.

Sanders, E. R. (1969) 'The Hamitic Hypothesis: Its Origin and Functions in Time Perspective', *Journal of African History* 10(4): 521–32.

Saucier, Jean-François (1974) 'Patron–Client Relationship in Traditional and Contemporary Southern Rwanda'. Ph.D. dissertation Columbia University, New York.

Save The Children Fund (SCF) (1996) 'Zaire: Military Intervention Is Not The Answer'. News statement released on 6 November 1996.

Seur, Han (1999) 'Return to Normalcy? Emergency Aid and Development Projects in Rwanda after 1994'. Paper presented at the international workshop 'Evaluation of Humanitarian Assistance in Emergency Situations'. Wageningen Agricultural University, The Netherlands, 25–26 June.

Sibomana, André (1999) *Hope for Rwanda: Conversations with Laure Gilbert and Hervé Deguine.* Translated by Carina Tertsakian. London: Pluto Press.

Silvestre, V. (1974) 'Différenciations socio-économiques dans une société à vocation égalitaire: Masaka dans le paysannat d'Icyanya', *Cahiers d'Etudes Africaines* 14: 104–69.

Simmance, Alan, Trevor Page and Adama Guindo (1994) *Zaire: Reassessment Report.* Geneva: Department of Humanitarian Affairs, June.

Sirven, P., J. F. Gotanègre and G. Prioul (1975) *Géographie du Rwanda.* Brussels: A. De Bock.

Smets, G. (1960) 'L'ubukonde des Banyarwanda, une forme d'occupation du sol', in *Congrès International des Sciences Anthropologiques et Ethnologiques. Compte Rendu de la Troisième Session, Bruxelles 1948.* Tervuren, Belgium: Musée Royale de l'Afrique Centrale.

Stockton, Nicholas (1996) 'Rwanda: Rights and Racism'. Unpublished paper released in December 1996.

Triulzi, Alessandro (forthcoming) 'Battling with the Past: A Note on Ethiopian Historiography', in Wendy James, Donald Donham, Eisei Kurimoto and Alessandro Triulzi (eds.), *Remapping Ethiopia.* Oxford: James Currey.

Tshibanda Mbwabwe wa Tshibanda (1976) 'Rutshuru, une zone surpeuplée. Présentation d'un dossier des archives de la zone', *Likundoli*, Série C, No. 1.

Twagiramutara, Pancrace (1976) *Rapport à l'Espace, Rapport Social: Contribution à l'Étude de Leurs Liaisons à Partir du Cas du Rwanda.* Louvain: Université Catholique de Louvain.

United Nations Rwanda Emergency Office (UNREO) (1995) 'Natural Resource Utilization in the Mutara Region of Northeast Rwanda. A Review of Programming (draft, 6/6/95)'. Prepared by Katie Frohardt and Tim Meisburger. Kigali: UNREO.

United Nations (1998) Report on the Situation of Human Rights in the Democratic Republic of the Congo, submitted by the Special Rapporteur, Mr Roberto Garreton, pursuant to Economic and Social Council decision 1998/260 of 30 July 1998.

Uvin, Peter (1998) *Aiding Violence: The Development Enterprise in Rwanda.* West Hartford, CT: Kumarian Press.

USAID (1994) *Zaire: Assessment Report.* Kinshasa: USAID, Bureau for Humanitarian Response.

Vansina, Jan (1962) *L'évolution du Royaume Rwanda des Origines à 1900.* Brussels: Académie Royale des Sciences d'Outre-Mer.

—— (1963) 'Les régimes fonciers Ruanda et Kuba – une comparaison', in Daniel Biebuyck (ed.), *African Agrarian Systems.* London: Oxford University Press, pp. 348–63.

—— (1973) *Oral Tradition: A Study in Historical Methodology.* Harmondsworth: Penguin Books.

Vanwalle, Rita (1982) 'Aspecten van staatsvorming in West-Rwanda', *Afrika-Tervuren* 28: 64–78.

Van de Giesen, Nick and Marc S. Andreini (1997) 'Legal Quagmires: Wetland Use and Development in Rwanda and Zimbabwe', *Law & Anthropology. International Yearbook for Legal Anthropology* 9: 105–23.

Van Hoyweghen, Saskia (1999) 'The Urgency of Land and Agrarian Reform in Rwanda', *African Affairs* 98 (No. 392): 353–72.

Vassall-Adams, Guy (1994) *Rwanda: An Agenda for International Action.* Oxford: Oxfam.

Vaughan, Megan (1996) 'The Character of the Market: Social Identities in Colonial Economics', *Oxford Development Studies* 24(1): 61–77.

Vidal, Claudine (1969) 'Le Rwanda des anthropologues ou le fétichisme de la vache', *Cahiers d'Etudes Africaines* 9(3): 384–401.

—— (1973) 'Colonisation et décolonisation du Rwanda: la question Tutsi–Hutu', *Revue Française des Sciences Politiques et Africaines* (Paris) 91: 32–47.

—— (1974) 'Economie de la société féodale rwandaise', *Cahiers d'Etudes Africaines* 14(1): 52–74.

—— (1985) 'Situations ethniques au Rwanda', in Jean-Loup Amselle and Elikia M'Bokolo (eds.), *Au Coeur de l'Ethnie: Ethnies, Tribalisme et Etat en Afrique.* Paris: Editions la Découverte, pp.167–85.

—— (1991) *Sociologie des Passions: Côte d'Ivoire, Rwanda.* Paris: Editions Karthala.

Vis, H. L., C. Yourassowsky and H. Van Der Borght (1975) *A Nutritional Survey in the Republic of Rwanda.* Butare: Institut National de Recherche Scientifique.

Vlassenroot, Koen (1997) '"Des serpents déloyaux": de positie van de Banyarwanda in Oost-Zaire/DRC', *Noord-Zuid Cahier* 22(4): 45–58.

Vlassenroot, Koen (2000) 'Identity and Insecurity. The Building of Ethnic Agendas in South Kivu', in Ruddy Doom and Jan Gorus (eds.), *Politics of Identity and Economics of Conflict in the Great Lakes Region.* Brussels: VUB University Press, pp. 263–88.

von Braun, Joachim, Hartwig de Haen and Juergen Blanken (1991) *Commercialization of Agriculture under Population Pressure: Effects on Production, Consumption and Nutrition in Rwanda.* Research Report 85. Washington, DC: International Food Policy Research Institute.

Vwakyanakazi Mukohya (1991) 'Import and Export in the Second Economy in North Kivu', in Janet McGaffey (ed.), *The Real Economy of Zaire: The Contribution of Smuggling and Other Unofficial Activities to National Wealth.* London: James Currey, pp. 43–71.

Waller, David (1993). *Rwanda: Which Way Now?* Oxfam Country Profiles. Oxford: Oxfam Publications.

Webster, J. B., B. A. Ogot and J.-P. Chrétien (1992) 'The Great Lakes Region, 1500–1800,' in B. A. Ogot (ed.), *General History of Africa.* Vol. V: *Africa from the Sixteenth to the Eighteenth Century.* Paris: UNESCO, pp. 776–827.

Willame, Jean-Claude (1997) *Banyarwanda et Banyamulenge: Violences Ethniques et Gestion de l'Identitaire au Kivu.* Brussels: Institut Africain-CEDAF; Paris: L'Harmattan.

Woodward, David (1996) 'The IMF, the World Bank and Economic Policy in Rwanda: Economic, Social and Political Implications'. Unpublished report for Oxfam (UK and Ireland).

World Bank (1993) *Rwanda: Poverty Reduction and Sustainable Growth.* Washington, DC: World Bank, 23 November.

World Bank (1995) 'Evaluation du programme de rapatriement et de réinstallation des réfugiés rwandais'. Kigali, 3 April.

World Food Programme/Austrian Relief Programme (1994). 'Joint Assessment Mission. Muvumba and Ngarama Communes, Byumba Prefecture, 8–11 December 1994'. Prepared by Francesco del Re and Albertien van der Veen. Kigali.

Young, Crawford (1970) 'Rebellion and the Congo', in Robert Rotberg and Ali Mazrui (eds.), *Protest and Power in Black Africa.* New York: Oxford University Press, pp. 968–1011.

Zur, Judith (1994) 'The Psychological Impact of Impunity', *Anthropology Today* 10(3): 12–17.

Index

Adelman, Howard, 36, 153, 213–14
Africa Watch, 22
African Renaissance, 57
African Rights, 32, 62, 115, 125–6, 167–8,
    216, 222
Albright, Madeleine, 39
American Mineral Fields, 45, 98, 106, 152
Amnesty International, 38, 56, 168
André, Catherine, 192, 229
Angola, 57–8, 107
anthropology, 110–12, 114, 203–5
Arusha Accords, 68, 187–9, 196, 216

Barnett, Michael, 214
Barrière, Olivier, 188, 196–200, 232
Belgian colonial administration, 13, 15, 20, 25,
    35, 46, 114, 118, 120, 171, 183, 222
Belgium, 53, 59, 61, 71, 82, 165, 226–7
Bembe, 17–18, 42, 44, 51, 101, 127
Benaco, 64, 135
Bihozagara, Jacques, 69, 76–7, 79
Bisengimana, Barthélémy, 27–8, 100, 212
Bossema, Wim, 70–1, 100
Boutros-Ghali, Boutros, 153, 156, 174, 218
Braeckman, Colette, 60, 67, 69–70, 77–8, 80,
    83, 88, 100, 102–3, 108, 176, 218–19, 230
Braid, Mary, 87, 92–3
bridewealth, 16, 191–2
    see also land, widows
Britain (UK), 31, 39, 45, 53, 59, 62–3, 73, 107,
    149, 153, 165, 173, 175, 227–8
Brittain, Victoria, 94, 98, 100, 104
Brown, Mark Cuthbert, 160, 218, 227
Bugesera, 12, 22, 26, 195, 206
Burundi, 17–18, 26, 74, 153, 187
    genocide, 34, 50, 75, 224
    see also refugees
Buyse, Axel, 59, 62–3, 67–8, 108
Bwisha, 19, 24–6

Canada, 36, 153, 226–7
CARE, 136, 141–2

Central Intelligence Agency (CIA), 88
Ceppi, Jean-Philippe, 69, 78
Chalker, Lynda, 39, 165, 213, 228
Chrétien, Jean-Pierre, 5, 63
class, 9, 29, 37, 65–6, 97, 113–14, 118, 122,
    124–5, 200, 215
    and ethnic strife, 10, 22, 30, 33–4
Clinton, Bill, 4, 32, 45, 71, 73, 152, 157,
    173, 176
coffee, 21, 183
Colson, Marie-Laure, 101, 104, 108
Concern, 135–6, 141
Cosma, Wilungula, 18
Cuba, 94, 153

De Beers, 98, 152
De Heusch, Luc, 120
De Temmerman, Els, 61, 63, 69, 78, 80, 216
De Waal, Alex, 34–5, 117, 121, 126, 149, 167,
    215, 222
Des Forges, Alison, 30, 66, 156, 212
Davidson, Basil, 113–14
Department For International Development
    (DFID), viii
    see also Overseas Development
    Administration (ODA)
Depelchin, Jacques, 16–17, 19
Derycke, Erik, 63, 77, 164
d'Hertefelt, Marcel, 120, 215
diaspora, 47
Dowden, Richard, 73, 217
Duffield, Mark, 211, 217

Eritrea, 57
Ethiopia, 22, 57, 194
ethnicity, 116, 124–5, 223
    see also class, race
European Union/Commission, 165, 168,
    172

Fairhead, James, 19, 24, 153
famine, 11, 20, 189

Fédération internationale des droits de
    l'homme (FIDH), 22, 31, 38, 60,
    128, 163
food aid/security, 141, 143–4, 184–5
Food and Agriculture Organisation (FAO),
    188, 196–9
fostering, 134–5
France, 31, 36, 41, 44–5, 53, 59, 61–2, 71,
    88, 151, 153, 172–3, 226–7
French, Howard, 97
Fulero, 16, 51

Gahima, Gerald, 177
Gasana, Anastase, 127, 148, 161, 170, 173
Gasasira, Ephrem, 181, 188, 190, 196, 200
genocide (Rwanda), 30–37, 107, 109–10,
    112–14, 117–19, 128, 137, 139, 142–4,
    147, 151, 156, 158, 161, 164, 169, 172,
    176–7, 181, 190, 215, 231
  aftermath of genocide, 39–46
  against Zairean Tutsi, 171
  discourse of genocide, 130, 153
  and international indifference, 37–40
  international press coverage, 59–62
  threat of genocide, 104
  see also Burundi
Germany, 45, 99, 112, 118, 153, 171, 199,
    226–7
Gersony report, 156
Gesellschaft für Technische zusammenarbeit
    (GTZ), 137–8
Goma, 132–50
Gourevitch, Philip, 56–7, 168–9, 215
Gowing, Nik, 54–6, 153, 175
Guyvaerts, Didier, 109–10, 127, 222
Greater Rwanda, 24, 46–8, 170–1, 219
guilt, 150, 154–60
  see also morality

Hamitic hypothesis, 67, 120, 122
Hilhorst, Thea, 194–6, 231
Hilsum, Lindsey, 4, 55, 58, 61, 63, 67, 73,
    105, 216
Hintjens, Helen, 121, 123
Human Rights Watch (HRW), 41, 56,
    128, 163
Hunde, 20, 25–9, 40–1, 91–2, 102, 170, 214
Hutu Power, 7, 9, 22, 32, 34, 62, 69, 122,
    125, 137

Internally Displaced Persons (IDPs), 7, 29,
    40, 76–8, 156, 158–9, 161–2, 164, 167,
    218, 224
International Committee of the Red Cross
    (ICRC), 168

International Monetary Fund (IMF), 21, 33, 38
isambu, 183, 197–9, 232

Jefremovas, Villia, 112, 114, 192

Kagame, Alexis, 46–7, 110–12, 123–4, 203–4,
    207
Kalibwami, Justin, 123–5, 223
Kamali, Sylvestre, 69
Kamanzi, Seth, 174, 229
Kasfir, Nelson, 72–3, 216
Kayibanda, Grégoire, 35, 123
Keane, Fergal, 64–6, 121
Kent, Randolph, 217
Khan, Shaharyar, 80, 163, 218
Kibeho camp/massacre, 40, 53, 56, 59, 76–81,
    107, 140, 155, 160–70, 176, 217–18,
    223, 227
Kibumba, 132, 142
Kiley, Sam, 74, 79, 88, 91, 96–8, 215, 219
Kinshasa, 82, 87, 95–6, 98–9, 106, 108,
    152, 154
Kinyamateka, 123–4, 223, 229
Kisangani, 17, 97

land legislation/tenure, 21, 180–1, 196–7
  and Banya-Mulenge, 17
  disputes, 12, 26
  inheritance, 197
  privatisation, 180
  shortage, 10–11, 27
  women's rights, 190–3
  see also isambu, uburetwa
Lemarchand, René, 122, 131, 206, 213, 220
Linden, Ian, 121
Longman, Timothy, 33
Lugan, Bernard, 36
Lumasi, 135–6, 140–1, 190, 224, 231
Lumumba, Patrice, 3
Lumumbashi, 97, 105

Mackintosh, Anne, 38, 117
Malkki, Liisa, 50, 169
Mamdani, Mahmood, 122, 125, 134
Mandela, Nelson, 2–3, 152, 164
Maquet, Jacques, 17, 109–11, 113, 115, 117,
    121, 204, 207, 222
Marysse, Stefaan, 83, 219
Masisi, 12, 20, 25–7, 29, 40–1, 68, 86, 92, 102,
    172, 214
Mayi-Mayi, 29, 41, 49, 85, 90–4, 100, 102–4,
    212, 214, 220–1
Mbuji-Mayi, 96, 152
McGreal, Chris, 74, 79–80, 86–7, 91, 96, 105,
    106, 108

McKinley, James, 85–8, 90, 92, 95–7, 170,
    219–20
Médecins Sans Frontières (MSF), 29, 68, 133,
    142, 147, 157, 164, 168, 174
Melvern, Linda, 75
memory (and history), 10, 12, 34, 43, 50–1,
    93–4, 101–2, 108, 113, 115, 126, 169,
    182, 206
Meschy, Lydia, 122
Michigan State University, 179–81, 196
migration, 11–12, 16
    of Banya-Mulenge, 16–19
    planned/colonial, 20, 24
Ministry of Rehabilitation and Social
    Reintegration (MINIREISO), 159,
    189–90, 230
morality, 154–6, 191–3, 195–6, 200–1,
    207, 231
Mouvement Révolutionnaire National pour le
    Développement (MRND), 22, 68
Mudimbe, V. Y., 5–6, 203–4
Mugunga, 88–9, 92, 103, 137, 143, 153, 177,
    214, 220, 224, 229
Muleliste rebellion, 17, 27, 214, 220
Mullen, Joseph, 114–15, 120
Musuhura, 135–6

Nahimana, Ferdinand, 60, 121–2, 222
National Conference (Zaire 1992), 28, 45, 84
Nazism, 31–2, 62
N'Dadaye, Melchior, 34, 75, 224
Ndeze II, 20, 25–6
Netherlands (The), 53, 59, 61–2, 71, 227
Newbury, Catharine, 14, 30, 66, 119, 121, 199
Newbury, David, 3, 30, 66
Ngandu, André Kisasse, 93, 101, 103, 106,
    220–1
Ngara, 132–50
Ngolet, François, 106, 215
north–south divide (Rwanda), 15, 33, 35–7,
    61, 67, 131, 144–8
Norwegian People's Aid (NPA), 134–5, 146
Nsanzuwera, François-Xavier, 78
Nyanga, 12, 20, 27–9, 41, 102

off-farm employment, 180, 184–5, 200, 231
Ogata, Sadako, 149–50
Operation Return, 155
Opération Turquoise, 39, 61, 63, 66, 71
Orr, David, 87, 93
Overseas Development Administration
    (ODA), 132, 158
    see also Department For International
    Development (DFID)

Oxfam, 29, 38, 166, 174
    see also Stockton, Nicholas

Pan-Africanism (New), 57–8, 63, 80, 89, 97,
    101, 105, 152
Parmelee, Jennifer, 67
Pfaff, William, 66–7, 215, 219
population density, 19, 184, 198
Pronk, Jan, 77, 157–8, 164–5
Prunier, Gérard, 126, 156–7, 206, 224

race and racism, 14, 41, 87, 122
    racial fantasies, 64, 124–5, 215, 223
    racialising ethnicity, 15, 82, 112–14, 117,
        120–1
    and Zaire government, 88
refugees, 130–50
    1959-ers, 15, 23–4, 27
    from Burundi, 21, 34, 141
    youth, 135
repatriation, 137, 139, 146–8, 157, 187
Reyntjens, Filip, 83, 104, 122, 212–13, 219
Richards, Paul, 130
Richburg, Keith, 72
Rieff, David, 89
Rogeau, Olivier, 77, 83
Rudahigwa (mwami), 223
Rudasingwa, Théogène, 61
Ruhimbika, Müller, 43, 83
Rutayisere, Wilson, 128, 164, 167–8, 223
Rutshuru, 20, 25–7, 41
Rwabugiri (mwami), 11–16, 24, 65, 110,
    112, 116–18, 120, 197, 205, 222
Ryle, John, 49, 54, 215, 217

Said, Edward, 5, 6
Save The Children (UK), 48–50, 89, 165–6,
    228
Sendashonga, Seth, 160–1, 228
Sibomana, André, 223–4
Smith, Stephen, 31, 37, 61, 89, 94, 108
Social Revolution (1959), 15, 123–6, 223
Somalia, 36, 72, 74, 89, 151, 214, 217
South Africa, 57–8, 99
Stockton, Nicholas, 174–5
Suhrke, Astri, 153, 213–14

Tanzania, 13, 19, 65, 112, 115, 117, 205, 215
    see also Ngara
Tshisekedi, Etienne, 97, 102
Twa, 13, 19, 65, 112, 115, 117, 205, 215

ubuhake, 13, 65, 110–11, 114–17,
    183, 229

ubukonde, 14, 117, 123, 182, 197–8, 231
uburetwa, 13, 24, 110–11, 118, 183–4, 198–9, 229
Umutoni, Christine, 165, 168, 187, 227
United Nations Assistance Mission to Rwanda (UNAMIR, UNAMIR-II), 69–71, 76, 159, 162, 164, 227
United Nations Children's Fund (Unicef), 165
United Nations Development Programme (UNDP), 188, 196–8, 199
United Nations High Commissioner for Refugees (UNHCR), 26, 76, 89, 131–50, 155–7, 174, 194, 224–6, 229, 231
United States of America, 31, 39, 44–5, 53, 58–9, 62–3, 90, 99, 106, 126, 149, 152–3, 165, 227–8
Uwilingiyimana, Agathe, 30, 39, 60, 158

Vanderostyne, Mon, 92, 100, 103, 108
Vansina, Jan, 50
van Hoyweghen, Saskia, 195–6

van Leeuwen, Mathijs, 194–6, 231
Vassall-Adams, Guy, 111
Vidal, Claudine, 13, 83, 85, 122, 204
villagisation, 181–2, 185, 193–4, 197, 200, 230
Vlassenroot, Koen, 42
Vogel, Steve, 71–2

widows, 136, 143, 186, 190, 192–3, 200, 231
    see also land, bridewealth
Wilkinson, Ray, 69, 75, 132
Willame, Jean-Claude, 5, 18, 40, 83
World Bank, 22, 33, 38, 180, 196–7, 200, 231
World Food Programme (WFP), 137, 141, 143–4, 190, 225, 231
World Health Organisation (WHO), 138
Wrong, Michela, 89, 98–9, 104, 108, 219

Zambia, 6, 218
Zone Turquoise, 138, 216

Other books in the series

64 *Bankole-Bright and Politics in Colonial Sierra Leone: The Passing of the 'Krio Era', 1919–1958*   Akintola Wise

65 *Contemporary West African States*   Donal Cruise O'Brien, John Dunn and Richard Rathbone

66 *The Oromo of Ethiopia: A History, 1570–1860*   Mohammed Hassen

67 *Slavery and African Life: Occidental, Oriental and African Slave Trades* Patrick Manning

68 *Abraham Esau's War: A Black South African War in the Cape, 1899–1902* Bill Nasson

69 *The Politics of Harmony: Land Dispute Strategies in Swaziland*   Laurel Rose

70 *Zimbabwe's Guerrilla War: Peasant Voices*   Norma Kriger

71 *Ethiopia: Power and Protest: Peasant Revolts in the Twentieth Century* Gebru Tareke

72 *White Supremacy and Black Resistance in Pre-Industrial South Africa: The Making of the Colonial Order in the Eastern Cape, 1770–1865* Clifton C. Crais

73 *The Elusive Granary: Herder, Farmer, and State in Northern Kenya* Peter D. Little

74 *The Kanyok of Zaire: An Institutional and Ideological History to 1895* John C. Yoder

75 *Pragmatism in the Age of Jihad: The Precolonial State of Bundu* Michael A. Gomez

76 *Slow Death for Slavery: The Course of Abolition in Northern Nigeria, 1897–1936*   Paul E. Lovejoy and Jan S. Hogendorn

77 *West African Slavery and Atlantic Commerce: The Senegal River Valley, 1700–1860*   James Searing

78 *A South African Kingdom: The Pursuit of Security in Nineteenth-Century Lesotho*   Elizabeth A. Eldredge

79 *State and Society in Pre-Colonial Asante*   T. C. McCaskie

80 *Islamic Society and State Power in Senegal: Disciples and Citizens in Fatick*   Leonardo A. Villalon

81 *Ethnic Pride and Racial Prejudice in Victorian Cape Town: Group Identity and Social Practice*   Vivian Bickford-Smith

82 *The Eritrean Struggle for Independence: Domination, Resistance and Nationalism, 1933–1941*   Ruth Iyob

83 *Corruption and State Politics in Sierra Leone*   William Reno

84 *The Culture of Politics in Modern Kenya*   Angelique Haugerud

85 *Africans: The History of a Continent*   John Illiffe

86 *From Slave Trade to 'Legitimate' Commerce*   Robin Law

87 *Leisure and Society in Colonial Brazzaville*   Phyllis M. Martin

88 *Kingship and State: The Buganda Dynasty*   Christopher Wrigley

89 *Decolonization and African Life: The Labour Question in French and British Africa*   Frederick Cooper

90 *Misreading the Landscape: Society and Ecology in African Forest Savannah Mosaic*   James Fairhead and Melissa Leach

91 *Peasant Revolution in Ethiopia: The Tigray People's Liberation Front, 1975–1991*   John Young

92 *Senegambia and the Atlantic Slave Trade*   Boubacar Barry

93 *Commerce and Economic Change in West Africa: The Oil Trade in the Nineteenth Century*   Martin Lynn

94 *Slavery and French Colonial Rule in West Africa: Senegal, Guinea and Mali*   Martin Klein

95 *East African Doctors: A History of the Modern Profession*   John Iliffe

96 *Middleman of the Cameroons Rivers: The Duala and their Hinerland*   Ralph A. Austen and Jonathan Derrick

97 *Masters and Servants of the Cape Eastern Frontier, 1760–1803*   Susan Newton-King

98 *Status and Respectability in the Cape Colony, 1750–1870*   Robert Ross

99 *Slaves, Freedmen and Indentured Laborers in Colonial Mauritius*   Richard B. Allen

100 *Transformations in Slavery: A History of Slavery in Africa*   Paul E. Lovejoy

101 *The Peasant Cotton Revolution in West Africa: Côte d'Ivoire, 1880–1995*   Thomas J. Bassett